INSTRUCTOR'S MANUAL

to accompany

FUNDAMENTALS OF CORPORATE FINANCE

Second Edition

Stephen A. Ross
Randolph W. Westerfield
Bradford D. Jordan

Prepared by
Bradford D. Jordan
University of Missouri
Harold F. Thiewes
Mankato State University

IRWIN
Burr Ridge, Illinois
Boston, Massachusetts
Sydney, Australia

Printed in the United States of America.

ISBN 0-256-11116-2

5 6 7 8 9 0 EB 0 9 8 7 6 5 4

PREFACE
FROM THE AUTHORS

This Instructor's Manual is intended for use with the 2nd edition of *Fundamentals of Corporate Finance.* This preface describes the various features of this manual and provides some tips on using it. It also discusses the transparency package and videos that accompany this edition of the text.

QUICK SUMMARY OF THE INSTRUCTOR'S MANUAL

The Instructor's Manual (IM) has three main sections. The first section runs about 275 pages and contains chapter outlines and other lecture materials designed for use with the Annotated Instructor's Edition of the text. There is an annotated outline for each chapter in this section, and, included in the outlines, there are lecture tips, ethics notes, and suggested overhead transparencies. The second section of the IM contains approximately 100 pages of detailed solutions to all of the end of chapter problems. The third section contains selected transparency masters.

THE ANNOTATED INSTRUCTOR'S EDITION

The Annotated Instructor's Edition of the text contains extensive references to the IM regarding lecture tips, ethics notes, and the availability of transparencies. The lecture tips vary in content and purpose; they may provide an alternative perspective on a subject, suggest important points to be stressed, give further examples, or recommend other readings. The ethics notes present background on topics that can be used to motivate classroom discussion of *finance-related* ethical issues. The inside front cover of the Instructor's Edition contains further information.

THE TRANSPARENCY SET

The 2nd edition of *Fundamentals* features a much expanded transparency set. There are now approximately 350 different exhibits, figures, tables, and problems for classroom use. Our goal is to provide complete coverage of the text topics, thereby allowing the instructor to pick and choose among the various overheads and custom-tailor course offerings. For instructors who so desire, there are a sufficient number of transparencies for a full course without the need for supplemental materials.

Transparency Types

To provide for some variation in the overheads and to allow for differences in use among instructors, we created six different types:

1. **Chapter Outlines** For each chapter, the first transparency is simply a broad outline of the chapter contents. We use these to start a lecture and briefly overview the chapter subjects before plunging in. We also reuse them to summarize and reinforce the main elements of a subject before we move on.

2. **Important Figures and Tables** These transparencies are taken from the text and correspond to the most important chapter exhibits. They generally provide a convenient means of discussing and explaining the chapter materials. They are very useful for making certain that students understand what is being explained and why.

3. **Key Issues** The key issues transparencies provide a means of organizing discussion on various topics. They are intended to help frame questions and broad issues that students need to understand and be able to address.

4. **Supplemental Examples and Exhibits** For some subjects, examples and illustrations not found in the text are supplied as a way to expand on some subjects, reinforce chapter discussions, or provide additional examples of important calculations.

5. **Interactive Problems** Almost every chapter contains some interactive overheads. These usually involve important calculations or problems in which some numbers or comments are missing and replaced with blanks. Because the instructor can ask students for the needed information, these transparencies provide a good springboard for classroom participation, and they break up some of the monotony that can exist when overheads are used. They are also are a good way of making sure that students are paying attention and not just taking dictation. As a convenience for users, the third section of the IM contains completed transparency masters for this group of overheads. These masters make it clear what numbers need to be filled in and where they need to go.

6. **Solution Transparencies** For each chapter, we selected some representative end of chapter problems and created transparencies for classroom use. Like the interactive problem overheads, these usually contain a few blanks that can be filled in during a discussion of the problem as a means of motivating student attention and involvement. Complete solutions to these problems are found in the second part of the IM.

About the Ready Notes

The Ready Notes are intended to improve notetaking by students. All of the overheads in the transparency set have been reduced in size (to provide room to write) and then bound in an inexpensive supplement. Having these available frees students from the need to copy background information, tabular material, or figures. Instead, they can concentrate on what is being said and what is important about the material. We have found that students who use the Ready Notes pay much better attention and are much more willing to participate in classroom discussion, particularly in very large classes. The Ready Notes are perforated and three-hole punched so that they can be detached and combined in a loose-leaf notebook with other materials if that is desirable.

Tips for Transparency Use

Different instructors will prefer to present material and discuss topics in different ways. The sequencing and numbering of the overheads in the transparency set is simply a reflection of the page order in which material appears in the Annotated Instructor's Edition of the text. This sequencing is not necessarily optimal for presentation purposes, and the transparencies can be readily reordered. For example, on a few occasions, a discussion in the text will reference a table or figure that, for design reasons, appears on a previous or subsequent page. When this occurs, the transparencies may not be in the best order for classroom explanation and discussion. Similarly, the solution transparencies are placed at the end of each chapter, but instructors may wish to work problems on particular subjects immediately following a discussion to reinforce the important elements.

VIDEOS

We chose a total nine videos to accompany the 2nd edition of *Fundamentals*. These videos feature Paul Solman, the Emmy award-winning business and economics correspondent for the MacNeil/Lehrer NewsHour, on a variety of text-related topics. They each run about eight to ten minutes and are a useful (and fun) way of breaking up some of the material as well as illustrating real-world applicability and relevance. A brief description of the videos and some suggested uses follow.

Video #1: Exxon: Corporate Goals and Social Welfare

Should a corporation pursue social goals? With the Exxon Valdez supertanker oil spill as the backdrop, this video examines what many feel is a potential for conflict between the goal of the corporation and the goals of society. It goes well with Problem 3 at the end of Chapter 1, and it is a useful lead-in to a class discussion of social responsibility and ethics. It contains footage of Exxon's annual meeting following the spill, so students can get a feel for how contentious shareholder meetings can be. This material also goes well with the discussion of corporate governance in Chapter 12.

Video #2: Valuing the Stock Market

How does a company's book, or accounting, value relate to its value as a going concern? This video examines Gillette's market and book values and discusses how accounting information can be used to at least roughly value a firm. It goes well with Chapters 2 and 3 because it dwells on market versus book values and the uses of accounting information. It also goes well with a discussion of fundamental analysis in the context of semistrong market efficiency in Chapter 11.

Video #3: Bond Buccaneers

This video goes well with Chapter 6 because it discusses bond basics and bond trading. The bonds discussed are defaulted LDC obligations (the political equivalent of junk bonds), so the video adds an interesting and useful international flavor to the material.

Video #4: Financial Reality and the Entrepreneur

How do new products and their inventors get funded? This video spotlights high-tech inventor and entrepreneur Raymond Kurzweil's innovative electronics products and his tactics for acquiring the necessary financial backing to bring them to market. It goes with Chapters 8 and 9 on capital budgeting because it illustrates the origin of new ideas through entrepreneurship. It also shows how real-world capital budgeting decisions involve much more than simple number-crunching. The video also goes well with Chapter 13 on raising long-term financing.

Video #5: Test Your Insider I.Q.

When do diligent research and smart investing become illegal insider trading? This video discusses just what is and what is not insider trading, and it emphasizes that the distinction is sometimes a little murky. It goes well with a discussion of market efficiency and the value of private information (Chapter 11). It also provides a good springboard for a discussion of broader ethical issues concerning insider information.

Video #6: Junk Bonds

Are junk bonds really junk? This video discusses how junk bonds came to play such an important role in American corporate finance, and it dispels some of the misconceptions surrounding junk bond financing. It goes well with Chapter 12 on long-term debt. It also goes with Chapter 15 on capital structure and Chapter 21 on takeovers.

Video #7: Celtics IPO

Who would have bet against Larry Bird and his teammates in their heyday? And when the Boston Celtics decided to raise money with an initial public offering, or IPO, the stock looked like a sure winner, but were investors the victims of a winner's curse? This video discusses the Boston Celtic's IPO, and it goes extremely well with the IPO discussion in Chapter 13. It is very useful for illustrating the dangers of IPO investing.

Video #8: Leveraged Legacy

Leveraged buyouts, or LBO's, have received a lot of bad press. Using Duracell as an example, this video shows how LBO's, when properly done, can revitalize a company and help it just keep going and going and going . . . . This LBO discussion goes well with Chapter 15 on capital structure and Chapter 21 on acquisitions. It provides a good balance to a lot of the negative publicity surrounding junk bond financing by describing the successful Duracell LBO.

Video #9: Debt Swap

International investing creates unique opportunities for creative financing and financial engineering. This video discusses one such financial arrangement, a three-way international (in Mexico) debt and equity swap. It goes very well with discussions of international financing (in Chapter 22), financial engineering (Chapter 24), and long-term financing with unusual debt instruments (Chapter 12).

ACKNOWLEDGEMENTS

We would first like to thank two of our colleagues, Todd Milbourn of Indiana University and Robert B. Pierce of Central Missouri State University, for proofing and checking the end of chapter solutions found in the IM. This type of work is not a great deal of fun, and we appreciate their careful efforts. We also thank Paul Weise, a University of Missouri doctoral student, for proofing the entire IM.

Most of the ethics materials were contributed by Darryl E. J. Gurley of Northeastern University, to whom we are very grateful.

Lastly, Ellen Cleary, Joanne Dorf, and Ann Sass of Richard D. Irwin and Meg Turner of Burrston House did a great job of supervising the production of this IM. Of this select group, we owe special thanks to Ellen Cleary for her dedicated and painstaking efforts.

In closing, we always welcome comments, criticisms, and suggestions. It doesn't do us any good to develop these things if they aren't useful. Please contact us and let us know what you like and don't like.

H.F.T
S.A.R.
R.W.W.
B.D.J.

December, 1992

Alternative Course Formats

Fundamentals of Corporate Finance, 2nd ed., can be readily adapted to meet the individual preferences of course instructors and the differing backgrounds and needs of introductory finance students. Three course outlines are described below, but these are only possibilities and many other permutations exist. Chapters marked * may be assigned as outside reading if time is short. Chapters marked ** may be covered in part or omitted without loss of continuity if time is short.

Course Outline
A Broad Survey Course

Chapter	Topic
1	Introduction to Corporate Finance
2	Financial Statements, Taxes, and Cash Flow
3	Working with Financial Statements
4**	Long-Term Financial Planning and Corporate Growth
5	First Principles of Valuation: The Time Value of Money
6	Valuing Stocks and Bonds
7	Net Present Value and Other Investment Criteria
8	Making Capital Investment Decisions
9	Project Analysis and Evaluation
10	Some Lessons from Capital Market History
11	Return, Risk, and the Security Market Line
12*	Long-Term Financing: An Introduction
13*	Issuing Securities to the Public
14	Cost of Capital
15**	Financial Leverage and Capital Structure Policy
16	Dividends and Dividend Policy
17	Short-Term Finance and Planning

A Course Emphasizing Valuation and Current Issues

Chapter	Topic
1	Introduction to Corporate Finance
2	Financial Statements, Taxes, and Cash Flow
5	First Principles of Valuation: The Time Value of Money
6	Valuing Stocks and Bonds
7	Net Present Value and Other Investment Criteria
8	Making Capital Investment Decisions
10	Some Lessons from Capital Market History
11	Return, Risk, and the Security Market Line
12*	Long-Term Financing: An Introduction
13*	Issuing Securities to the Public
14	Cost of Capital
15	Financial Leverage and Capital Structure Policy
16	Dividends and Dividend Policy
20	Options and Corporate Securities
21	Mergers and Acquisitions
22	International Corporate Finance
21**	Leasing
24**	Risk Management

A Course Emphasizing Traditional Topics

Chapter	Topic
1	Introduction to Corporate Finance
2	Financial Statements, Taxes, and Cash Flow
3	Working with Financial Statements
4	Long-Term Financial Planning and Corporate Growth
5	First Principles of Valuation: The Time Value of Money
6	Valuing Stocks and Bonds
7	Net Present Value and Other Investment Criteria
8	Making Capital Investment Decisions
9**	Project Analysis and Evaluation
10	Some Lessons from Capital Market History
11	Return, Risk, and the Security Market Line
12*	Long-Term Financing: An Introduction
13*	Issuing Securities to the Public
14	Cost of Capital
17	Short-Term Finance and Planning
18	Cash and Liquidity Management
19	Credit Management
23*	Leasing

Table of Contents

Part I: Course and Lecture Materials

Part II: End of Chapter Solutions

Chapter **Page**

PART I

COURSE MATERIALS AND LECTURE NOTES

CHAPTER 1
INTRODUCTION TO CORPORATE FINANCE

TRANSPARENCIES

T1.1:	**Chapter Outline**
T1.2:	**A Simplified Organizational Chart**
T1.3:	**Forms of Organization and Goal of Financial Management**
T1.4:	**The Agency Problem and Financial Markets**
T1.5:	**Cash Flows between the Firm and Financial Markets**

CHAPTER ORGANIZATION

T1.1: Chapter Outline

1.1 CORPORATE FINANCE AND THE FINANCIAL MANAGER
- What Is Corporate Finance?
- The Financial Manager
- Financial Management Decisions

1.2 THE CORPORATE FORM OF BUSINESS ORGANIZATION
- Sole Proprietorship
- Partnership
- Corporation
- A Corporation by Another Name...

1.3 THE GOAL OF FINANCIAL MANAGEMENT
- Possible Goals
- The Goal of Financial Management
- A More General Goal

1.4 THE AGENCY PROBLEM AND CONTROL OF THE CORPORATION
- Agency Relationships
- Management Goals
- Do Managers Act in the Stockholders' Interests?

ANNOTATED CHAPTER OUTLINE

1.1 CORPORATE FINANCE AND THE FINANCIAL MANAGER

A. What Is Corporate Finance?

Corporate finance is the study of the answers to the following questions:

1. *What long-term investments should we make?*

2. *Where will we get the funds to pay for our investment?*

3. *How will we collect from customers and pay our bills?*

In other words, the answers to the capital budgeting question, the capital structure question, and the net working capital question are all part of corporate finance.

B. The Financial Manager

T1.2: A Simplified Organizational Chart

The *Chief Financial Officer, CFO.*

Controller—handles cost and financial accounting, tax payments and information systems.

Treasurer—handles cash management, financial planning, and capital expenditures.

Corporate finance is concerned with the issues faced by the treasurer.

C. Financial Management Decisions

The financial manager is concerned with three primary corporate financial decisions.

Capital budgeting—process of planning and managing a firm's investments in fixed assets. The key concerns are the *size*, *timing*, and *riskiness* of cash flows.

Capital structure—mix of debt and equity used by a firm. What are the least expensive sources of funds? Is there a best mix? When and where to raise funds?

Working capital management—managing short-term assets and liabilities. How much cash and inventory to keep around? What is our credit policy? Where will we obtain short-term loans?

1.2 THE CORPORATE FORM OF BUSINESS ORGANIZATION

T1.3: Forms of Organization and Goal of Financial Management

A. Sole Proprietorship

A business owned by one person. Simple, but involves *unlimited liability*. Its life is limited to the owner's, and the equity that can be raised is limited to the proprietor's wealth.

B. Partnership

A business in which there are multiple owners.

General partnership—all partners share in gains or losses; all have unlimited liability for all partnership debts.

Limited partnership—one or more *general partners* will run the business and have unlimited liability. A *limited partner's* liability is limited to her contribution to the partnership.

C. Corporation

A business created as a distinct legal entity composed of one or more individuals or entities.

Corporations are the most important form of business organization in the U.S. There are several advantages to the corporate form:

1. *Limited liability for stockholders.*

2. *Unlimited life for the business.*

3. *Ownership can be easily transferred.*

These characteristics make it easier for corporations to raise capital. The primary disadvantage to the corporate form is *double taxation.*

Lecture Tip, page 10: *The following example provides a brief case summary which may be used for a class discussion concerning the issues of possible corporate civil neglect and/or the extent to which corporate owners should be protected by limited liability.*

Dow Corning is a joint venture of Corning Corporation and Dow Chemical Corporation, with each owning 50 percent of Dow Corning's outstanding shares. In 1975, Dow Corning introduced a new use for silicone—breast implants. In 1990, a civil jury awarded a California woman $7.3 million on the claim that her leaking implants caused autoimmune disorder. Dow Corning announced it would appeal the judgment.

In January 1991, the New York Times *reported that Dow Corning had faced 250-300 similar cases over the implants' life but, until 1990, the victims agreed to suppression orders. These orders effectively kept the public uninformed regarding safety issues associated with silicon breast implants.*

Dow Corning established the Dow Information Center Hotline to provide information concerning the safety of implants. In June 1991, Newsweek reported that, for many years, internal Dow Corning documents had noted potential health risks associated with implants. The article charged that Dow Corning used the legal process to keep the internal studies from reaching the public. In February 1992, the Food and Drug Administration concluded the implants' safety had not been established and restricted their use to clinical studies. In response, Dow Corning closed its implant manufacturing facilities.

The instructor can present this situation to the class and inquire as to the ethics of using the legal system to limit adverse information and to what extent responsibility should be assumed by both Corning and Dow Chemical, given their limited liability as the owners of Dow Corning.

Lecture Tip, page 10: *Although the corporate form of organization has the advantage of limited liability, it has the disadvantage of double taxation. A small business of 35 or fewer stockholders is allowed by the Internal Revenue Service to form an S Corporation. The S Corporation organizational form provides limited liability but allows pretax corporate profits to be distributed on a pro rata basis to individual shareholders, who would be obligated to only pay personal taxes on the distributed income.*

D. A Corporation by Another Name...

Laws and regulations differ from country to country but the essential features of public ownership and limited liability remain.

1.3 THE GOAL OF FINANCIAL MANAGEMENT

A. Possible Goals

The possible goals are legion—some involve profit, some not.

B. The Goal of Financial Management

From the stockholders' perspective, the goal in buying a firm's stock is to gain financially.

The goal of financial management is to maximize the current value per share of the existing stock.

C. A More General Goal

A more general goal of financial management is to maximize the market value of the owners' equity.

1.4 THE AGENCY PROBLEM AND CONTROL OF THE CORPORATION

T1.4: The Agency Problem and Financial Markets

A. Agency Relationships

The relationship between stockholders and management is called an *agency relationship.* This occurs when one party (*principal*) pays another (*agent*) to represent them. The possibility of conflicts of interest between the parties is termed the *agency problem.*

B. Management Goals

Agency costs—two types: *direct* and *indirect.* Direct costs come about in compensation and perquisites for management. Indirect costs are the result of monitoring managers and of suboptimal decisions (from the owners' perspective) by management.

Ethics Note, page 14: *When shareholders elect a board of directors to oversee the corporation, the election serves as a control mechanism for management. The board of directors holds all legal responsibility for corporate actions. However, this responsibility is to the corporation itself and not necessarily to the stockholders. The following is an interesting springboard for a discussion of directors' and managers' duties:*

In 1986, Ronald Perelman engaged in an unsolicited takeover offer for Gillette. Gillette's management filed litigation against Perelman and subsequently entered into a standstill agreement with Perelman. This action eliminated the premium that Perelman offered shareholders for their stock in Gillette.

A group of shareholders filed litigation against the board of directors in response to its actions. It was pursuantly discovered that Gillette had entered into standstill agreements with ten additional companies. When questioned regarding the rejection of Perelman's offer, management responded that there were projects on line that could not be discussed (later revealed to be the sensor razor, which proved to be the most profitable new venture in Gillette's history). Thus, despite appearances, management's actions may have been in the best interests of the corporation, and this situation indicates that management may consider factors other than the bid alone when considering a tender offer.

Ethics Note, page 15: *The following situation can be presented to the class as an example of the magnitude of one type of agency expense, and one corporation's attempt to control perquisites and thereby reduce direct agency costs:*

On March 26, 1992, Digital Equipment Corporation moved to curb expense accounts and eliminate an estimated $30 million in annual abuses. An internal memo had stated that abuses were getting worse, noting $1,000 bar bills as an example of such abuses. The $30 million might appear trivial when compared to the estimated total expense costs of $6.5 billion. However, DEC was facing a $110 million loss for the first half of its fiscal year and desired to send a message to both employees and stockholders that it intended to control both costs and abuses. This warning came on the heels of a workforce cut of 10,500 employees between September 1989 and March 1992. These cuts were a result of poor forecasting of sales growth and a misestimation of the economic recession.

Lecture Tip, page 15: *Insight into the agency relationship can be provided with an example of the classroom environment. For example, the class must work end-of-chapter problems and submit them to you, the instructor, for grading. You find it necessary to institute a costly monitoring device which consumes much of your effort and time, parallel to a corporation's internal audit, to ensure that the students, as employees, act in a particular manner. More generally, if students could be trusted to simply learn the material, then costly exams and grading would be unecessary. Instead, costly monitoring must be performed.*

Examples of agency conflicts can also be found in various periodicals which can be considered for outside class readings. A few suggested examples are provided below:

1) *"Did the Time Decision Torpedo the Hostile Bid?" Mergers and Acquisitions, January/February 1990, by Jonathan J. Lerner. This article discusses the Time/Warner merger, which occurred despite Paramount's higher bid for Time. The article also discusses the 1989 Delaware Chancery Court ruling which allowed Time's and Warner's Boards of Directors to pursue the merger even though Time's shareholders might prefer the immediate gains offered by Paramount's cash bid.*

2) *"Who Owns This Company, Anyhow?," Fortune, July 29, 1991, by Rob Norton. This article discusses the rising ownership of stock by institutions and further discusses the closer attention institutions are directing to how companies are managed and how executives are compensated. It discusses the market for corporate control as a crude device for disciplining managers.*

3) *"The Shareholder As Second-Class Citizen," Accountancy, April, 1991, by Denis Keenan. This article discusses shareholder ownership in the UK. The article also makes reference to rising institutional ownership and suggests that some boards appear to run companies in complete disregard of smaller shareholders, paying themselves too much, not allowing a discussion of issues during the general meeting, and so on.*

C. Do Managers Act in the Stockholders' Interests?

Managerial compensation—firm performance and management compensation and prospects are linked.

Control of the Firm—management can be replaced by several methods which involve stockholders.

Stakeholders—someone other than a stockholder or creditor who potentially has a claim on a firm.

Lecture Tip, page 16: *California Public Employees' Retirement System (CalPERS) is the largest institutional shareholder in the United States, controlling $68 billion of pension funds. Traditionally, CalPERS acts as an activist shareholder, sponsoring proxy initiatives on topics ranging from corporate strategy to executive compensation. In the fall of 1991, CalPERS began meeting with corporate executives regarding their initiatives. During the winter of 1992, CalPERS offered 11 different initiatives for shareholder vote, regarding the composition of directors, executive pay, and corporate strategy.*

Ownership of common stock provides a right to sponsor initiatives for shareholder vote, but is CalPERS an ordinary shareholder? The instructor might ask the class if the voting rights should pass through to the stakeholders in CalPERS or should the investment managers of the fund determine the voting practices of the shares held?

Lecture Tip, page 16: *A periodical reference concerning the stakeholders' interest in the firm can be found in the following article:*

"Do Poison Pills Make You Strong?," The Economist, June 29, 1991. This article discusses the nature of the share contract and the stakeholder interest in the firm. The article also provides an insight into the economics of contracts between the firm and its stakeholders, and the residual risk stakeholders encounter.

1.5 FINANCIAL MARKETS AND THE CORPORATION

T1.5: Cash Flows between the Firm and Financial Markets

A. Cash Flows to and from the Firm

A firm issues securities to realize cash for investment in assets. The operating cash flows generated from the investment in assets allows for payment of taxes, reinvestment in new assets, and payment of interest and dividends to the investors in the firm's securities. The financial markets bring the buyers and sellers of debt and equity securities together.

B. Primary versus Secondary Markets

Primary market—refers to the original sale of securities. *Public offers, SEC registration,* and *underwriters* are part of this market.

Secondary market—refers to the resale of securities. *Stock exchanges (NYSE, AMEX)* and the *over-the-counter, OTC, market (NASDAQ)* are part of this market.

Listing—stocks that trade on an exchange are said to be *listed.*

1.6 OUTLINE OF THE TEXT

Part One:	Overview of Corporate Finance
Part Two:	Financial Statements and Long-Term Financial Planning
Part Three:	Valuation of Future Cash Flows
Part Four:	Capital Budgeting
Part Five:	Risk and Return
Part Six:	Long-Term Financing
Part Seven:	Cost of Capital and Long-Term Financial Policy
Part Eight:	Short-Term Financial Planning and Management
Part Nine:	Topics in Corporate Finance

1.7 SUMMARY AND CONCLUSIONS

CHAPTER 2
FINANCIAL STATEMENTS, TAXES, AND CASH FLOW

TRANSPARENCIES

CHAPTER ORGANIZATION

T2.1: Chapter Outline

2.1 THE BALANCE SHEET
- Assets: The Left-Hand Side
- Liabilities and Owners' Equity: The Right-Hand Side
- Net Working Capital
- Liquidity
- Debt versus Equity
- Market Value versus Book Value

2.2 THE INCOME STATEMENT
- GAAP and the Income Statement
- Non-cash Items
- Time and Costs

2.3 TAXES
Corporate and Personal Tax Rates
Average versus Marginal Tax Rates

2.4 CASH FLOW
Cash Flow from Assets
Cash Flow to Creditors and Stockholders

2.5 SUMMARY AND CONCLUSIONS

ANNOTATED CHAPTER OUTLINE

2.1 THE BALANCE SHEET

T2.2: The Balance Sheet

A. Assets: The Left-Hand Side

What the firm owns. Current versus Fixed. Tangible versus Intangible.

B. Liabilities and Owner's Equity: The Right-Hand Side

What the firm owes. Current versus Long-term. *Shareholders' equity* is total assets less liabilities.

C. Net Working Capital

The difference between a firm's current assets and its current liabilities.

D. Liquidity

The order of assets on the balance sheet reflects their liquidity. Liability order reflects time to maturity.

Liquidity as a continuum reflects an ability to convert an asset to cash with little or no loss of value.

Liquidity has an opportunity cost—the more liquid an asset is, the less profitable it usually is.

Lecture Tip, page 27: *Some students seem to get a little confused when they try to understand that excessive cash can be undesirable. For example, they sometimes leave an accounting principles class with the belief a large current ratio is always favorable.*

The instructor may wish to mention that a cash balance is a use of funds that has an opportunity cost. Students can be asked what a company could do with cash if it were not on deposit in a bank account. The best answer is that it could be paid out to stockholders. Other answers include paying off debt and investing in productive assets. In broader terms, students need to understand that the change in a firm's holding of cash is not the same as its cash flow. The (misnamed) accounting statement of cash flows tends to create this confusion. This statement is deferred to Chapter 3 to avoid any further reinforcement of this error.

E. Debt versus Equity

Precedence of debt over equity to firm's cash flows.

Gains or losses of the business may be magnified for stockholders by financial leverage.

F. Market Value versus Book Value

Irrelevance of book (historical cost) value and importance of market (exchange) value for decision making.

Some of the most important assets and liabilities do not appear on the balance sheet, e.g., talented managers and products that bring lawsuits. Especially true in service industries.

Lecture Tip, page 28: *It is noted in Chapter 2 that accounting, or historical, costs are not especially important to financial managers while market values are. Some students have difficulty recognizing that the passage of time and changing circumstances will almost always mean that the price an asset would fetch if sold today is quite different from its book, or historical, value. Sometimes an example or two of familiar instances is enough to make the point. For instance, the market values versus historical costs less depreciation of used cars (both ordinary and collectable) and houses (in, say, California versus Texas) may help.*

It may be that some students, while acknowledging the difference between historical cost and market value, ask why market value is considered the more important of the two. The simplest answer is market value represents the cash price people are willing and able to pay. After all, it is cash that must ultimately be paid or received for investments, interest, principal, dividends, and so forth.

Lecture Tip, page 28: *It may be beneficial for the instructor to discuss why book values are below market values in Example 2.2. The instructor can mention that favorable earnings expectations for Klingon Corp. cause a higher market valuation of the assets relative to their historical (book) costs, and the equity valuation benefits from the market's appraisal of this future earning power.*

2.2 THE INCOME STATEMENT

T2.3: GAAP versus Cash Flow Time Line

A. GAAP and the Income Statement

Accounting's "realization" principle for revenue, the "matching" principle for costs, and their incongruence with actual cash flow timing.

Ethics Note, page 30: *The instructor may wish to discuss Blockbuster Video's accounting practices and ask whether they were potentially deceptive. Some basic facts are presented here; for greater detail, see "Shorts, Lies, and Videotape" in* CFO Magazine *December, 1991.*

Blockbuster expanded from 100 video rental "superstores" to 700 between 1987 and 1989. Profits rose to $15.5 million in 1988 with sales of $137 million and the stock rose sevenfold over the same period. However, on May 8, 1989, Bear Stearns & Co. reported that Blockbuster's 100% rise in 1988 per-share profits was achieved with excessively aggressive accounting practices. When Blockbuster bought an existing video chain, it stretched out the accounting charge for the acquisition's goodwill over 40 years. This resulted in lower expenses over the short term. Although higher profits were realized in the short term, if growth slackened, the extended goodwill schedule would hurt later earnings.

Additionally, the acquisitions were financed with stock instead of cash, and this required Blockbuster to keep its share price high by maintaining high earnings' growth. Sales of franchises and videotapes to new franchisees were included in operating income. A franchisee paid Blockbuster a $9,000 opening fee, a $35,000 initial franchisee fee, and a $35,000 software licensing fee to use Blockbuster's computer system. Initial inventory was also purchased from the head office. In 1988, Blockbuster received 28 percent of its revenue from these payments.

If Blockbuster continued opening stores, this practice would be fine, but if franchise growth stopped, it would hurt earnings. Also, if the current amortization schedule was shortened to five years, Bear Stearns figured EPS would have changed from the reported $.58 to merely $.32. Blockbuster also depreciated its videotapes over long periods of time by industry standards, again increasing earnings.

B. Non-cash Items

For many firms, the most important non-cash item is depreciation.

C. Time and Costs

Long run versus short run: The key is variability of costs; all costs are virtually fixed for very small periods while nearly all costs are variable if enough time is allowed.

Variable and fixed costs, useful in analyzing cash flows and preparing budgets, are not the same as product and period costs identified by accountants.

Lecture Tip, page 31: *Distinguishing between fixed and variable costs can have important implications for estimating and budgeting cash flows. It is sometimes helpful to remind students that variable costs are those cash outflows which change with the level of output, while fixed costs are constant. Moreover, when discussing the long-run versus short-run, students don't always recall the economic concept of the short-run as the period when virtually all costs are fixed as opposed to the long-run when virtually all costs are variable. An important thing to note is that what are short-run and long-run time periods will vary for different types of businesses.*

2.3 TAXES

T2.4: Taxes
T2.5: Marginal versus Average Corporate Tax Rates

A. Corporate and Personal Tax Rates

As of December 1992, corporate tax rates are not strictly increasing; the marginal rates are 15%, 25%, 34%, 39%, and then 34% again.

B. Average versus Marginal Tax Rates

The average rate is below the marginal rate to $335,000, at which point the average tax rate is equal to the marginal rate of 34%; the "bubble" of 39% adds taxes which offset the initial lower brackets.

<u>Example: Average versus Marginal</u>

Taxable income		$150,000
.15 × $50,000	=	7,500
.25 × $25,000	=	6,250
.34 × $25,000	=	8,500
.39 × (150,000 – 100,000)	=	19,500
Total taxes	=	$ 41,750

Average tax rate = $41,750/150,000 = 27.8%; Marginal tax rate = 39%

Lecture Tip, page 33: *It is useful to stress the situations in which marginal tax rates are relevant and those in which average tax rates are relevant. For purposes of computing a company's total tax liability, the average tax rate is the correct rate to apply to before-tax profits. However, in evaluating the cash flows which would be generated from a new investment, the marginal tax rate would be correct since the new investment would* *generate profits that would be taxed above the company's existing profit figure. The student may wish to remember that the relevant tax rate to apply to capital investment decisions (Chapter 8) is the marginal tax rate. The student should also note that, for corporations with taxable income greater than $335,000, the marginal tax rate and the average tax rate are equal (there is effectively a flat-rate tax), but it is still important to note the distinction between marginal and average tax rates.*

2.4 CASH FLOW

T2.6: Cash Flow Example (2 pages)
T2.7: Cash Flow Summary

Based upon the balance sheet identity
Assets = Liabilities + Equity

The equivalent cash flow statement is
Cash Flow from Assets = Cash Flow to Creditors + Cash Flow to Owners

The words "creditors" and "bondholders" are used interchangeably as are "owners" and "stockholders."

A. Cash Flow from Assets

CF(A) = Operating Cash Flow ± Capital Spending
± Additions to Net Working Capital

Operating cash flow is:
Earnings before interest and taxes (EBIT)
+ Depreciation
– Current Taxes

(Net) Capital Spending is:
Ending fixed assets
– Beginning fixed assets
+ Depreciation

Additions to Net Working Capital (NWC) is:
Ending NWC – Beginning NWC

Negative Cash Flow from Assets is not unusual for growing firms.

B. Cash Flow to Creditors and Stockholders

Cash Flow to Bondholders (Creditors) is:
Interest paid
+ Principal paid
– New borrowing

Cash Flow to Stockholders (Owners) is:
Dividends paid
+ Stock repurchased
– New stock issued

2.5 REVIEW PROBLEM

This section is a review problem. An original example based upon Hermetic, Inc. is presented in the transparencies below.

T2.8: Hermetic, Inc., Balance Sheet
T2.9: Hermetic, Inc., Income Statement
T2.10: Hermetic, Inc., Cash Flow from Assets

2.6 SUMMARY AND CONCLUSIONS

T2.11: Solution to Problem 2.6
T2.12: Solution to Problem 2.11

CHAPTER 3
WORKING WITH FINANCIAL STATEMENTS

TRANSPARENCIES

T3.1: Chapter Outline
T3.2: Hermetic, Inc., Balance Sheet
T3.3: Hermetic, Inc., Income Statement
T3.4: Statement of Cash Flows
T3.5: Hermetic, Inc., Statement of Cash Flows
T3.6: Hermetic, Inc., Common-Size Balance Sheet (2 pages)
T3.7: Hermetic, Inc., Common-Size Income Statement
T3.8: Things to Consider: Financial Ratios
T3.9: Categories of Financial Ratios
T3.10: Common Financial Ratios
T3.11: The Du Pont Identity
T3.12: Ratio Comparison across Business Types
T3.13: A Brief Case History of Hermetic, Inc.
T3.14: Solution to Problem 3.4
T3.15: Solution to Problem 3.15
T3.14: Solution to Problem 3.23
T3.15: Solution to Problem 3.27

CHAPTER ORGANIZATION

T3.1: Chapter Outline

3.1 CASH FLOW AND FINANCIAL STATEMENTS: A CLOSER LOOK

Sources and Uses of Cash
The Statement of Cash Flows

3.2 STANDARDIZED FINANCIAL STATEMENTS

Common-Size Statements
Common-Base-Year Financial Statements: Trend Analysis

3.3 RATIO ANALYSIS

Short-Term Solvency Measures
Long-Term Solvency Measures
Asset Management or Turnover Measures
Profitability Measures
Market Value Measures

3.4 THE DU PONT IDENTITY

ROE = ROA × Equity multiplier

3.5 USING FINANCIAL STATEMENT INFORMATION

Why Evaluate Financial Statements?
Choosing a Benchmark
Problems with Financial Statement Analysis

3.6 SUMMARY AND CONCLUSIONS

ANNOTATED CHAPTER OUTLINE

3.1 CASH FLOW AND FINANCIAL STATEMENTS: A CLOSER LOOK

A. Sources and Uses of Cash

T3.2: Hermetic, Inc., Balance Sheet

1. Activities that bring in cash are sources.
   Firms raise cash by selling assets, borrowing money or selling securities.

2. Activities that involve cash outflows are uses.
   Firms use cash to buy assets or make payments to providers of capital.

3. Mechanical rules for determining Sources and Uses:

Uses
Increases in assets
Decreases in equity and liabilities

Sources
Decreases in assets
Increases in equity and liabilities

Lecture Tip, page 53: *Student often experience difficulty when conceptualizing an increase in the cash balance, an asset, as a use of cash (they typically think of an increase in cash as a source of cash). It may be helpful to stress that a cash increase (a use) on the balance sheet must be realized through a reduction in another asset account (a source) or through an increase in a liability or an equity account (a source). Put another way, building up bank balances is definitely a use of cash because that same cash could be used to pay dividends.*

B. The Statement of Cash Flows

Idea is to group cash flows into one of three categories

operating activities
investment activities
financing activities

T3.3: Hermetic, Inc., Income Statement

T3.4: Statement of Cash Flows

A General Statement of Cash Flows

Operating Activities

+ Net Income
+ Depreciation

+ Any decrease in current assets (except cash)
+ Any increase in current liabilities

– Any increase in current assets (except cash)
– Any decrease in current liabilities

Investment Activities

+ Ending net fixed assets
– Beginning net fixed assets
+ Depreciation

Financing Activities

± Change in notes payable
± Change in long-term debt
± Change in common stock
– Dividends

Putting it all together:

± Net cash flow from operating activities
± Fixed asset acquisition
± Net cash flow from financing activities

= Net increase (decrease) in cash

T3.5: Hermetic, Inc., Statement of Cash Flows

3.2 STANDARDIZED FINANCIAL STATEMENTS

A. Common-Size Statements

Useful in comparisons of unequal size firms

T3.6: Hermetic, Inc., Common-Size Balance Sheet (2 pages)
T3.7: Hermetic, Inc., Common-Size Income Statement

1. Common-Size Balance Sheet
   Express individual accounts as a percent of total assets

2. Common-Size Income Statement
   Express individual items as a percent of sales

B. Common-Base-Year Financial Statements: Trend Analysis

Select a base year, then express each item or account as a percentage of the base-year value of that item (useful for picking up trends).

1. Combined Common-Size and Base-Year Analysis
   Express each item in base year as a percent of either assets or sales. Then, compare each subsequent year's common-size percent to the base-year percent (abstracts from the growth in assets and sales).

3.3 RATIO ANALYSIS

T3.8: Things to Consider: Financial Ratios

Things to Consider Concerning Financial Ratios

What aspects of the firm are we attempting to analyze? Generally, the aspects of interest are "fuzzy" (e.g., liquidity or utilization) and often both abstract and relative.

What information goes into a particular ratio and how does that information relate to the aspect of the firm being analyzed?

What is the unit of measurement? (e.g., dollars? days? turns?)

What would a "good" ratio look like? A "bad" one?

T3.9: Categories of Financial Ratios

Categories of Financial Ratios

-Short-Term Solvency
Ability to pay bills in the short-run

-Long-Term Solvency
Ability to meet long-term obligations

-Asset Management
Intensity and efficiency of asset use

-Profitability
The bottom line

-Market Value
Going beyond financial statements

T3.10: Common Financial Ratios

A. Short-Term Solvency Measures (Liquidity Ratios)

1. Current Ratio
   Current assets/Current liabilities
   Hermetic $745/$435 = 1.71

2. Quick Ratio
   (Current assets − inventory)/Current liabilities
   Hermetic $(745 − 385)/$435 = .83

3. Other Liquidity Ratios
   Cash ratio
   Cash/Current liabilities
   Hermetic $50/$435 = .115 or about 12%

   NWC/Total assets
   Hermetic $(745 − 435)/$1845 = .17 or 17%

   Interval measure
   Current assets/Daily operating costs

Lecture Tip, page 62: *Students often think that a high current ratio is favorable for a company. The instructor might suggest that the class reconsider the statement of cash flows. All asset balances must be supported by funds sources which have a cost to the firm. If the ratio is higher than the norm for the industry, the company would be maintaining larger amounts of long-term debt or equity relative to current assets. If a company could operate with lower levels of current assets without negatively impacting operations (the big "if"), this situation would be preferred since it would lower financial costs. (The issue of a benchmark will later be discussed in Section 3.5.)*

Lecture Tip, page 63: *The instructor may want students to consider the interaction of ratios at this point in the text. The instructor could suggest a company scenario in which the current ratio exhibits no change over a two or three year trend. However, the quick ratio experiences a steady decline. This would indicate that the company is operating with lower levels of the more liquid assets relative to current liabilities. The instructor could alert the student to the possible dangers:*

1. The company is operating with lower levels of the more liquid assets, and this situation should be monitored. A problem could arise should a large amount of current liabilities be due for payment. However, this may not be a major concern if the company had access to available lines of credit at a bank.

2. This situation also indicates that larger levels of inventory, relative to current liabilities, have accumulated in the firm. The instructor could state that an examination of other ratios is required to further explore this situation. It would be helpful to examine the level of inventory relative to sales (a lead into the turnover section).

B. Long-Term Solvency Measures (Financial Leverage)

1. Total Debt Ratio
(Total assets – Total equity)/Total assets
Hermetic $(1,845 – 1,185)/$1,845 = .36 or 36%

Variations:
Debt/Equity = (Total assets – Total equity)/Total equity
Equity multiplier = Total assets/Total equity = 1 + Debt/Equity

2. Long-term Debt Ratio
Long-term debt/(Long-term debt + Total equity)
Hermetic $225/$(225 + 1,185) = .16 or 16%

3. Times Interest Earned (TIE)
EBIT/Interest
Hermetic $200/$20 = 10 times

4. Cash Coverage
(EBIT + Depreciation)/Interest
Hermetic $(200 + 30)/$20 = 11.5 times

The numerator, earnings before depreciation, interest and taxes (or EBDIT), is often used as a measure of cash flow to meet obligations. Amortization, if any, is also usually added to the numerator (resulting in EBDITA).

C. Asset Management Measures (Turnover Ratios)

1. Inventory Turnover

COGS/Inventory
Hermetic $480/$385 = 1.25 times

Days sales in inventory: 365/Inventory turnover
Hermetic 365/1.25 = 292 days

2. Receivables Turnover

Sales/Accounts receivable
Hermetic $710/$310 = 2.29 times

Days sales in receivables (days sales outstanding)
365/Receivables turnover
Hermetic 365/2.29 = 159 days

3. Asset Turnover Ratios (variations on a theme)

NWC turnover = Sales/NWC

Fixed asset turnover = Sales/Net fixed assets

Total assets turnover = Sales/Total assets
Hermetic $710/$1,845 = .385 times

Lecture Tip, page 67: *The instructor may wish to mention that there may be significant inconsistencies in the methods used to compute ratios by financial advisory firms (Example: Table 3.10, a page from Robert Morris Associates) due to the nature of the industry (in reference to footnote 4). When using ratios supplied by others, it is important to always be aware of the exact financial items which go into the ratio. A manufacturer would typically consider inventory at cost and thus relate inventory to cost of goods sold. However, a retailer might maintain its inventory level based on retail price. If the latter case is true, the inventory level should be related to sales in order to accurately compute the inventory turnover. The markup would cancel in the numerator and denominator and give an accurate indication of turnover based on cost.*

D. Profitability Measures (The Bottom Line)

These measures are based upon book values, not market values, and so may not convey much useful information.

1. Profit margin
   Net income/Sales
   Hermetic $126.55/$710 = 17.8%

2. Return on Assets
   Net income/Total assets
   Hermetic $126.55/$1,845 = 6.8%

3. Return on Equity
   Net income/Total equity
   Hermetic $126.55/$1,185 = 10.7%

Lecture Tip, page 70: *The instructor may wish to emphasize that, in most instances, return on equity is the most important accounting indication of management's success in accomplishing the shareholders' valuation objective. The significance of this ratio will be further explored in Section 3.4, "The Du Pont Identity."*

E. Market Value Measures (for publicly traded firms)

Price/Earnings ratio
Market-to-book ratio

Lecture Tip, page 71: *The instructor could ask students to consider how the market-to-book ratio could be interpreted if the student was considering the purchase of the company's stock. Some might feel a ratio less than one would be preferred since the stock is selling below the equity value on the books. One could use this point to comment that the market is evaluating the company's future earning power while the book value figures reflect the cost at which stock had previously been issued and the amount of the past retained earnings on the company's balance sheet. The students could then be asked to consider which is more important. The instructor could also mention that valuation techniques concerning a company's future earnings will be explored in Chapter 5 and later chapters. Additionally, the efficiency of the market's pricing will be examined, beginning with Chapter 10, "Capital Market History."*

3.4 THE DU PONT IDENTITY

T3.11: The Du Pont Identity

How does financial leverage transform return on assets into return on equity?

$$Return\ on\ Equity = \frac{Net\ Income}{Total\ equity} = \frac{Net\ Income}{Assets} \times \frac{Assets}{Equity}$$

That is, ROE = Return on assets × Equity multiplier

Decomposing ROA into profit margin and asset turnover gives

$$ROE = \frac{Net\ Income}{Sales} \times \frac{Sales}{Assets} \times \frac{Assets}{Equity}$$

That is,

Profit margin × Asset turnover × Equity multiplier
Operating efficiency × Asset use × Financial leverage
Hermetic = .178 × .385 × 1.56 = 10.7%

3.5 USING FINANCIAL STATEMENT INFORMATION

A. Why Evaluate Financial Statements?

1. Internal Uses:
   Evaluating performance, spotting trouble, generating projections

2. External Uses:
   Making credit decisions, evaluating competitors, assessing acquisitions

Lecture Tip, page 75: *Much of financial statement analysis is rooted in a manufacturing tradition with the large, industrial corporation at its center. That is, many of the notions about statement analysis grew out of a view of business in which more or less specialized plant and equipment is used to turn raw goods into finished goods which are sold on credit.*

This view was modified by the advent of the large, retail corporation, but the emphasis on balance sheet assets (receivables, inventories, plant and equipment) and the measures associated with them remain.

Because of this manufacturer/retailer tradition, much of the conventional wisdom about statement analysis is inappropriate to many of today's business situations. Take, for example, professional services firms such as those formed by lawyers, accountants, doctors, management consultants, computer programmers, and engineers. Or consider television networks, radio stations, colleges and universities. The most valuable assets of such firms are not on the balance sheet, their liquidity is not in a stock of current assets, and their liabilities are not all represented. Rather, their assets are human capital, licenses, viewership, and reputation; their liquidity lies in an ability to generate revenues; and their liabilities include negligence, malpractice, and malfeasance.

Thus, financial statement analysis as we know it is a product of our economic history. We can expect it to evolve to encompass new economic realities, but as it does it is important to understand its perspective and the limitations imposed by it.

B. Choosing a Benchmark

Example: Ratio Comparison Across Business Types—What's My Line?[1]

Identify the electric utility (B), retail jeweler (E), auto manufacturer (A), Japanese trading company (D), and supermarket chain (C) using their common-size statements and financial ratios

Key common-size accounts in the comparison:
Inventories, receivables, property and equipment, debt

Key ratios in the comparison:
Profit margin, inventory turnover, total asset turnover
The principle is essentially management by exception.

---

[1]The example is adapted from Fruhan, Kester, Mason, Piper, and Ruback, *Case Problems in Finance*, 10th ed. (Homewood, Illinois: Richard D. Irwin, Inc.), 1992, p. 20, with the permission of the publisher.

T3.12: Ratio Comparison across Business Types

1. Time-trend Analysis
   Significant changes to be looked into.

2. Peer Group Analysis
   Significant differences are to be examined.
   Industry group comparisons are common (SIC).

C. Problems with Financial Statement Analysis

-no underlying financial theory
-finding comparable firms
-what to do with conglomerates
-differences in accounting practices
-differences in fiscal year
-differences in capital structure
-seasonal variations
-one-time events

T3.13: A Brief Case History of Hermetic, Inc.

Lecture Tip, page 80: *The following example is useful in illustrating the kinds of problems that can come up in comparing financial statements:*

A "Spot the Potential Problems" Example

Hermetic is a wholesale firm with a January 1 to December 31 fiscal year. Several competitors use a July 1 to June 30 fiscal year. Most of Hermetic's sales are to small retailers on credit terms. Some competitors are cash-and-carry only. About 50% of Hermetic's annual sales occur in the last quarter, October to December.

Hermetic generally uses trade credit from manufacturers to finance its inventories. At the end of the year, however, Hermetic takes advantage of after-season clearance sales by manufacturers to stock up on inventory, financing the purchases with bank loans.

While Hermetic uses First-In-First-Out inventory accounting, many of its competitors use Last-In-First-Out. Furthermore, Hermetic owns its warehouses and equipment while some competitors lease theirs.

Implications:

The January to December fiscal year and year-end inventory build-up have given rise to relatively high (compared to other times of the year) levels of receivables, inventory, payables, and notes—producing the following ratios:

Inventory turnover: $480/$385 = 1.25 turns
Days sales in inventory: 365/1.25 = 292 days

Receivables turnover: $710/$310 = 2.29 turns
Days in receivables: 365/2.29 = 159 days

Total asset turnover: .385 turns
Total debt ratio: $(1,845 − 1,185)/$1845 = 36%

By averaging quarterly or semi-annual balance sheet values the January to December fiscal year and seasonal sales effect can be mitigated (problems with reporting services comparisons may persist).

The inventory accounting may lead to Hermetic showing a higher level of inventory (increasing price environment) or lower level (declining price environment) compared to competitors.

If competitors have not had to capitalize their leases, Hermetic will show substantially higher plant and equipment amounts, and possibly have a comparatively lower ROA and ROE as a result. Of course, lease payments are cash flows while depreciation is not, but the income statement doesn't make that distinction.

3.6 SUMMARY AND CONCLUSIONS

T3.14: Solution to Problem 3.4
T3.15: Solution to Problem 3.15
T3.14: Solution to Problem 3.23
T3.15: Solution to Problem 3.27

CHAPTER 4
LONG-TERM FINANCIAL PLANNING AND GROWTH

TRANSPARENCIES

CHAPTER ORGANIZATION

T4.1: Chapter Outline

4.1 WHAT IS FINANCIAL PLANNING?
- Growth as a Financial Management Goal
- Dimensions of Financial Planning
- What Can Planning Accomplish?

4.2 FINANCIAL PLANNING MODELS: A FIRST LOOK
- A Financial Planning Model: The Ingredients
- A Simple Financial Planning Model

4.3 THE PERCENTAGE OF SALES APPROACH
- An Illustration of the Percentage of Sales Approach

4.4 EXTERNAL FINANCING AND GROWTH
EFN and Growth
Financial Policy and Growth

4.5 SOME CAVEATS OF FINANCIAL PLANNING MODELS

4.6 SUMMARY AND CONCLUSIONS

ANNOTATED CHAPTER OUTLINE

4.1 WHAT IS FINANCIAL PLANNING?

A. Growth as a Financial Management Goal

Growth is a by-product of increasing value.

B. Dimensions of Financial Planning

Planning horizon (usually 2-5 years)

Aggregation (lumping accounts together)

C. What Can Planning Accomplish?

Interactions (between investments and financing)

Options (investment and financing)

Avoiding Surprises (contingency plans)

Feasibility and Internal Consistency

4.2 FINANCIAL PLANNING MODELS: A FIRST LOOK

T4.2: Financial Planning Model Ingredients

A. A Financial Planning Model: The Ingredients

Sales Forecast
-most other considerations depend upon it

Pro Forma Statements
-the output summarizing different projections

Asset Requirements
-investment needed to support sales growth

Financial Requirements
-debt and dividend policies

The "Plug"
-designated source(s) of external financing

Economic Assumptions
-state of economy, interest rates, inflation

T4.3: Example: A Simple Financial Planning Model

Lecture Tip, page 95: *Some students may complain that the effects of aggregation produce "unrealistic" results, as in aggregating depreciation and interest expense in costs, or pooling all sorts of assets to get the capital intensity ratio. While correct, this criticism is misdirected. The point of the method discussed is not to produce a detailed financial plan, but to highlight the relationships, especially between investments and financial policy, to be considered when planning for growth. The appendix presents a more detailed plan, while still finer and more sophisticated methods are in use.*

4.3 THE PERCENTAGE OF SALES APPROACH

The idea is that sales generate retained earnings. Retained earnings, plus any external funds raised, support an increase in assets. More assets lead to more sales, and the cycle starts over again.

A. An Illustration of the Percentage of Sales Approach

The Income Statement

Given forecasted sales and assuming a constant profit margin, what retained earnings can be expected?

Define:

S = previous period's sales
g = projected growth rate of sales

A = previous period's ending total assets
p = profit margin
b = retention or plowback ratio

Addition to retained earnings = p × S(1 + g) × b

The Balance Sheet

What assets are needed to support sales growth? If we assume 100% capacity utilization, a simplified approach is to use:

A × g = Increase in assets

Alternatively, we might use a *capital intensity ratio* (= Assets/Sales) to find the assets necessary to support $1 of sales. This can be different for different types of assets, e.g., a ratio of .5:1 for current assets and 1.5:1 for fixed assets.

However figured, if the increase in total assets exceeds the addition to retained earnings, the difference is *external financing needed,* EFN.

T4.4: The Percentage of Sales Approach
T4.5: Pro Forma Statements
T4.6: The Percentage of Sales Approach: A Financing Plan
T4.7: The Percentage of Sales Approach: An Alternative Scenario

Aside

If asset use is less than 100% of capacity, fixed assets will not necessarily need to increase by g. Sales supportable by full capacity = S ÷ % use.

Example: EFN

Sales, S,	= $9,362
Current assets	= $2,364.60
Net fixed assets	= $16,374.80
Profit margin, p,	= 14.34%
Plowback ratio, b,	= 50%
Payables	= 7% of assets

What external funds are needed for sales to increase 10%?

Addition to retained earnings:

$$= p \times S(1+g) \times b$$
$$= (.1434)(\$9{,}362.1)(1.1)(.5) = \$738.39$$

Increase in assets:

$$= A \times g \text{ (assuming 100\% capacity use)}$$
$$= (\$18{,}739.4)(.1) = \$1{,}873.9$$

Optional: suppose fixed assets are currently used at 90% of capacity. They will support sales of $10,402.3 (= $9,362.1/.9), so no new fixed assets would be needed. Current assets needed = (Current assets × g) = $236.5:

$$\text{EFN} = \$1{,}873.9 - 738.39 = \$1{,}135.51$$

Optional: Suppose payables increase with sales. The increase in spontaneous funds would be 7% × A × g = (.07)(18,739.4)(.1) = $131.2:

$$\text{EFN} = \$1{,}873.9 - 738.39 - 131.2 = \$1{,}004.31$$

Lecture Tip, page 100: *The instructor may wish to integrate the various issues presented in Chapters 2, 3 and 4 at this time. The company's plan for the sales increase must be supported by an investment in additional current and fixed assets (cash uses). On the liability side, current liabilities will increase (a source) due to the increase in the purchase of inventory. At this point, we have accounted for the investment in fixed assets and addition to net working capital (a net use).*

The balancing must come from some cash source: either from a retention of the current year's operating cash flow or through the issuance of new debt or new equity. These latter two items (new debt or new equity) represent the external financing needs or alternatives the company would consider for its cash sources.

Regression analysis is a commonly used technique to forecast financial requirements. The line of best fit relating sales to various individual asset categories will provide the analyst with a more accurate prediction of how a particular balance sheet account will change for varied levels of projected sales.

4.4 EXTERNAL FINANCING AND GROWTH

Other things the same, more growth means more external financing will be needed.

T4.8: Growth and External Financing
T4.9: Growth and Financing Needed for the Hoffman Company

A. EFN and Growth

Assuming no spontaneous sources of funds, EFN can be expressed as the increase in total assets less addition to retained earnings.

The increase in assets required is simply equal to the original assets multiplied by the growth rate. For low growth rates, a firm will run a surplus, resulting in a decline in the debt/equity ratio. As the growth rate increases, the surplus becomes a deficit as the requirement for new assets exceeds the addition to retained earnings.

B. Financial Policy and Growth

T4.10: Internal Growth Rate
T4.11: Sustainable Growth Rate

The internal growth rate is the growth rate that the firm can maintain with internal financing only.

Internal growth rate = (ROA × b) / (1 – ROA × b)

where b = plowback ratio

Sustainable growth rate is the maximum rate of growth a firm can maintain without increasing its financial leverage.

Sustainable growth rate = (ROE × b) / (1 – ROE × b)

where b = plowback ratio

Determinants of growth:

From the Du Pont identity, ROE can be viewed as the product of profit margin, assets turnover, and the equity multiplier. Anything that increases ROE will increase the sustainable growth rate by making the numerator larger and the denominator smaller.

So, sustainable growth depends on:

a. Operating efficiency, reflected in profit margin
b. Asset use efficiency, reflected in total asset turnover or capital intensity
c. Financial policy, reflected in debt/equity ratio
d. Dividend policy, reflected in retention or plowback ratio

Lecture Tip, page 109: *Wanting sales or revenues to grow by so much a year as a goal of the firm is properly understood as meaning: "Other things the same, we want sales to grow." The "other things the same" part is often not well understood. Here are some ideas to consider:*

-cutting margins might make sales "grow," but is it desirable? (can be related to demand elasticity)

-cutting the dividend might "pay" for growth, but is that desirable?

-increasing the proportion of borrowing might "pay" for growth, but is it desirable?

-employing more assets per dollar of sales might make sales "grow," but is it desirable?

4.5 SOME CAVEATS OF FINANCIAL PLANNING MODELS

The problem is that the models are really accounting statement generators rather than determinants of value. They ignore cash flows, timing, and risk.

Lecture Tip, page 110: *As presented here, growth "happens" as a consequence of financial policy and profitability. Of course, ultimately growth depends on selling more of something and some students may feel the chapter's treatment neglects relevant marketing aspects. Here, the point is to draw attention to the investment and financing implications of growth.*

Some may also be concerned that there is little management involvement when most of the investment and financing relationships are treated as given. While this is necessarily true to start with, potentially all aspects of profitability, asset investment, and financial policy are candidates for "management."

4.6 SUMMARY AND CONCLUSIONS

T4.12: Solution to Problem 4.8
T4.13: Solution to Problem 4.22

CHAPTER 5
FIRST PRINCIPLES OF VALUATION: THE TIME VALUE OF MONEY

TRANSPARENCIES

T5.1: Chapter Outline
T5.2: Future Value for a Lump Sum
T5.3: Interest on Interest Illustration
T5.4: Future Value of $100 at 10 Percent (Table 5.1)
T5.5 Present Value for a Lump Sum
T5.6: Present Value of $1 for Different Periods and Rates
T5.7: The Basic Present Value Equation
T5.8: An Example: A Penny Saved
T5.9: The Basic Present Value Equation—Revisited
T5.10: Future Value Calculated (Fig. 5.6 - 5.7)
T5.11: Present Value Calculated (Fig. 5.8 - 5.9)
T5.12: Annuities and Perpetuities (4 pages)
T5.13: A 0% Financing Example
T5.14: Future Value for Annuities—A Short Cut
T5.15: Effective Annual Rates and Compounding (3 pages)
T5.16: Cheap Financing versus Rebate
T5.17: Ripov Retailing: An Example
T5.18: Solution to Problem 5.7
T5.19: Solution to Problem 5.16
T5.20: Solution to Problem 5.36

T5A.1: Amortization Schedule: Fixed Principal
T5A.2: Amortization Schedule: Fixed Payments
T5A.3: A Mortgage Application

CHAPTER ORGANIZATION

T5.1: Chapter Outline

5.1 FUTURE VALUE AND COMPOUNDING
- Investing for a Single Period
- Investing for More than One Period
- A Note on Compound Growth

5.2 PRESENT VALUE AND DISCOUNTING
- The Single Period Case
- Present Values for Multiple Periods

5.3 MORE ON PRESENT AND FUTURE VALUES
- Present versus Future Value
- Determining the Discount Rate
- Finding the Number of Periods

5.4 PRESENT AND FUTURE VALUES OF MULTIPLE CASH FLOWS
- Future Value with Multiple Cash Flows
- Present Value with Multiple Cash Flows

5.5 VALUING LEVEL CASH FLOWS: ANNUITIES AND PERPETUITIES
- Present Value for Annuity Cash Flows
- Future Value for Annuities
- Perpetuities

5.6 COMPARING RATES: THE EFFECT OF COMPOUNDING PERIODS
- Effective Annual Rates and Compounding
- Calculating and Comparing Effective Annual Rates
- EARs and APRs
- Taking It to the Limit: A Note on Continuous Compounding

5.7 SUMMARY AND CONCLUSIONS

APPENDIX 5A—LOAN TYPES AND LOAN AMORTIZATION

- 5A.1 PURE DISCOUNT LOANS
- 5A.2 INTEREST-ONLY LOANS
- 5A.3 AMORTIZED LOANS

ANNOTATED CHAPTER OUTLINE

5.1 FUTURE VALUE AND COMPOUNDING

Lecture Tip, page 129: *Many students find the phrases "time value of money" and "a dollar today is worth more than a dollar later" to be somewhat cryptic. In some ways, it might be better to say "the money value of time" and to state that a dollar today doesn't trade for less than a dollar later.*

Indeed, many of the phrases and much of the terminology surrounding exchanges of money now for money later are confusing to students. For example, present value as the name for money paid or received earlier in time and future value as the name for money paid or received later in time are a constant source of confusion. How, students ask, can money to be paid next year be a "present" value; how can money received today be a "future" value? They must be made aware that we mean earlier money and later money (or leftmost and rightmost amounts on the time line).

Many students never fully comprehend that present value, future value, interest rates, and interest rate factors are simply a convenient means for communicating the terms of exchange for what are essentially different kinds of money. One way to emphasize both the exchange aspect of the time value of money and that present dollars and future dollars are different kinds of money is to compare them to U.S. dollars and Canadian dollars.

Both are called dollars, but they're not the same thing. And just as U.S dollars rarely trade 1 for 1 for Canadian dollars, neither do present dollars trade 1 for 1 for future dollars. Just as there are exchange rates for U.S. dollars into Canadian and vice-versa, present value and future value factors represent exchange rates between earlier money and later money. Also, the same reciprocity that exists between the foreign exchange rates exists between future value and present value interest factors.

A. Investing for a Single Period

T5.2: Future Value for a Lump Sum
T5.3: Interest on Interest Illustration
T5.4: Future Value of $100 at 10 Percent (Table 5.1)

Given r, the interest rate, every $1 today will produce (1 + r) of future value (FV). So, FV = $X(1 + r), where $X is principal.

Example:

$100 at 10% interest gives $100(1.1) = $110.

B. Investing for More than One Period

Reinvesting the interest—*compounding*—interest on interest

$$FV = \$X(1 + r)(1 + r) = \$X(1 + r)^2$$

Example:

$100 at 10% for 2 periods: $\$100(1.1)(1.1) = \$100(1.1)^2 = \$121$

In general, for t periods, $FV = \$X(1 + r)^t$ where $(1 + r)^t$ is the future value interest factor, FVIF(r,t).

Example:

$100 at 10% for 10 periods: $\$100(1.1)^{10} = \$259.37$

FVIF(r,t): Factor can be obtained in various ways
-factor tables such as A.1 of Appendix in text
-scientific calculator with y^x key
-financial calculator

Lecture Tip, page 130: *It may be helpful to emphasize this compounding example on the chalkboard. The instructor could demonstrate the compounding of $100 at 10 percent by showing the future value at the end of year one. The instructor could then separate the $110 into $100 principal and $10 interest. One could then demonstrate that the $100 principal will then earn another $10 over the second year and the $10 interest earned at the end of the first year will earn $1 interest over the second year, resulting in a $121 end-of-year-two value.*

Example:

Present		End Yr. 1 Value		End Yr. 2 Value
$100	------>	$100	Principal------>	$110
		$ 10	Interest ------->	$ 11
$100		$110		$121

By stressing this paragraph's example and the initial example in the text, the students' intuition of compounding or interest-on-interest may be enhanced. This example is extended over five periods in Table 5.1 in the text. A failure to understand this compounding impact will create trouble for some students throughout the course.

C. A Note on Compound Growth

Compound growth is not limited to money; it shows up in many things (e.g., populations).

5.2 PRESENT VALUE AND DISCOUNTING

A. The Single Period Case

Given r, what amount today (*Present Value or PV*) will produce a given future amount?

Since future amount = \$X(1 + r), PV = future amount/(1 + r).

Example:

\$110 in 1 period at 10% has a PV of \$110/(1.1) = \$100.

Discounting—the process of finding PV

Lecture Tip, page 137: *It may be helpful to utilize the example of \$100 compounded at 10 percent to emphasize the present value concept. One can emphasize the basic formula:* $PV \times (1 + r)^t = FV$; *therefore,* $PV = FV \times [1 / (1 + r)^t]$. *The student should recognize that the discount factor is the inverse of the compounding formula. The instructor could ask the class to determine the present value of \$110 and \$121 if the amounts are received in one year and two years respectively, and the interest rate is 10 percent. The instructor could then demonstrate the mechanics:*

$$\$100 = \$110 \times [1 / (1 + .10)^1] = \$110 \times .0909$$
$$\$100 = \$121 \times [1 / (1 + .10)^2] = \$121 \times .8264$$

The students will recognize that it was an initial investment of \$100 and an interest rate of 10 percent that created these two future values.

B. Present Values for Multiple Periods

PV of future amount in t periods at r is:

PV = future amount × $[1/(1 + r)^t]$, where $[1/(1 + r)^t]$ is the discount factor or Present Value Interest Factor, PVIF(r,t).

Example:

\$259.37 10 periods from now has a PV at 10% of \$259.37 × $[1/(1.1)^{10}]$ = \$100 (the PVIF is .3855).

DCF (Discounted Cash Flow)—the process of valuation by finding the present value.

Lecture Tip, page 140: *This paragraph, along with figure 5.3, should be stressed. Some students will have trouble understanding that a given future amount is worth less today as the interest rate increases. One may want to remain with the previous example and provide a very simple example of a future amount of \$110 to be received in one year. The student would recognize that if interest rates are at 10%, she would be willing to invest \$100 today. The instructor could then ask the students what they would be willing to pay* *for the \$110 in one year if the interest rate was 20 percent. They should realize that they would have to pay less than \$100 if they are to realize a 20 percent return on an amount invested today. One could then emphasize that as interest rates increase, the present value of a fixed future amount would decrease. Emphasize that this is the opposite of what would occur if we considered the effect of increasing interest rates on a given amount we would invest today.*

T5.5: Present Value for a Lump Sum
T5.6: Present Value of \$1 for Different Periods and Rates (Fig. 5.3)

5.3 MORE ON PRESENT AND FUTURE VALUES

A. Present versus Future Value

Present Value factors are reciprocals of Future Value factors:

$$PVIF(r,t) = 1/(1 + r)^t \text{ and}$$
$$FVIF(r,t) = (1 + r)^t$$

So PVIF(r,t) = 1/FVIF(r,t) and vice-versa.

Example:

$$FVIF(10\%,4) = (1.1)^4 = 1.464 \text{ and } PVIF(10\%,4) = 1/(1.1)^4 = .683$$

Basic present value equation:

$$PV = FV \times [1/(1 + r)^t]$$

B. Determining the Discount Rate

T5.7: The Basic Present Value Equation
T5.8: An Example: A Penny Saved

Finding r in basic present value equation

$PV = FV \times [1/(1 + r)^t]$ (or $FV = PV(1 + r)^t$)

-financial calculator (supply PV, FV, and t; compute r)

-[t^{th} root of FV/PV] – 1

-look up either PVIF (PV/FV) or FVIF (FV/PV) in appropriate table across from t periods

Example:

What interest rate makes a PV of $100 become a FV of $150 in 6 periods?

-FV/PV = $150/100 =1.5, the 6th root of 1.5 is 1.0699, making r = 7%

-FV/PV gives an FVIF of 1.5, look across 6 periods in Table A.1 of Appendix, r = 7%

-PV/FV gives a PVIF of .6666, look across 6 periods in Table A.2 of Appendix, r = 7%

Lecture Tip, page 142: *This paragraph should be strongly emphasized. With the examples used thus far, there have always been four parts to the equation, one of which has been unknown. In finding the* future value, *we must know the present value, the interest rate and the time of the investment. In finding the* present value, *we must know the future value, the interest rate and the time of the investment. Although it may seem obvious, the instructor could ask the class "what must be known if we are attempting to determine the discount rate of an investment?" (PV, FV and t). The instructor could then use the previous example and ask the class to determine the discount rate or return on an investment if they invested $100 today and received $121 in two years. The students should remember that 10 percent generated the identity. The instructor could then show the solution process using Table A.1 or A.2. One could then proceed to examples covering longer time spans and demonstrate the repetition of the solution.*

C. Finding the Number of Periods

T5.9: The Basic Present Value Equation—Revisited

Finding t in the basic present value equation

$PV = FV \times [1/(1 + r)^t]$ (or $FV = PV(1 + r)^t$)

-financial calculator (supply PV, FV, and r; compute t)

-using $FV = PV(1 + r)^t$, make $(FV/PV) = (1 + r)^t$, $\ln(FV/PV) = t[\ln(1 + r)]$, then $t = [\ln(FV/PV)/\ln(1 + r)]$

-using PVIF (= PV/FV) or FVIF (= FV/PV), look under r in appropriate table.

Example:

How many periods before \$100 today grows to be \$150 at 7%?

-FV/PV = 150/100 = 1.5; 1 + r = 1.07; ln(1.5) = .405465 and ln(1.07) = .067659, so ln(FV/PV)/ln(1 + r) = .405465/.067659 = 6 periods.

-FV/PV gives an FVIF of 1.5, look under 7% in Appendix A, Table A.1, t = 6 periods.

Rule of 72—the time to double your money, (FV/PV) = 2, is approximately (72/r%) periods. The rate needed to double your money is approximately (72/t)%.

Example:

To double your money at 10% takes approximately (72/10) = 7.2 periods.

Example:

To double your money in 6 years takes approximately (72/6) = 12%.

5.4 PRESENT AND FUTURE VALUES OF MULTIPLE CASH FLOWS

A. Future Value with Multiple Cash Flows

T5.10: Future Value Calculated (Fig. 5.6 - 5.7)

There are two ways to calculate future values of multiple cash flows:

Compound the accumulated balance forward one period at a time, or calculate the future value of each cash flow and add them up.

B. Present Value with Multiple Cash Flows

T5.11: Present Value Calculated (Fig. 5.8 - 5.9)

There are two ways to calculate present values of multiple cash flows:

Discount the last amount back one period and add them up as you go, or discount each amount to time 0 and then add them all up.

5.5 VALUING LEVEL CASH FLOWS: ANNUITIES AND PERPETUITIES

T5.12: Annuities and Perpetuities (4 pages)
T5.13: A 0% Financing Example

A. Present Value for Annuity Cash Flows

Ordinary Annuity—multiple, identical cash flows occurring at the end of each period for some fixed number of periods.

The present value of an annuity of \$C per period for t periods at r percent interest is:

$$\text{Annuity present value} = \$C \times (1 - \text{PVIF}(r,t))/r$$

or

$$\text{APV} = \$C \times (1 - [1/(1 + r)^t])/r$$

The second term on the righthand side is the present value interest factor for annuities, PVIFA(r,t).

Example:

If you are willing to make 36 monthly payments of \$100 at 1.5% per period, what size loan (APV) can you obtain? PVIFA(1.5%, 36) = 27.66, so \$C × PVIFA(r,t) = \$100 × 27.66 = \$2,766

Table A.3 in Appendix A gives PVIFA(r,t)

Finding the payment, C, given APV, r, t.

Since APV = C × PVIFA(r,t), C = APV/PVIFA(r,t)

Example:

If you borrow \$400, promising to repay in 4 monthly installments at 1% a month, how much are your payments?

$$\text{APV} = C \times \text{PVIFA}(r,t) \text{ gives } \$400 = C \times \{1 - [1/(1.01)^4]\}/r$$
$$\$400 = C \times 3.9, \text{ so } C = \$400/3.9 = \$102.56.$$

Finding the Number of Payments given APV, r, and C.

$$\text{APV} = C \times (1 - (1/(1 + r)^t))/r$$

so

$$1 - (\text{APV}/C \times r) = [1/(1 + r)^t]$$

The latter is the PVIF(r,t), so proceed as before with logs (take inverses of both sides first) or look in the table under r%.

Example:

How many $100 payments are required to pay off a $5,000 loan at 1% per period?

1 − (APV/C × r) = $[1/(1 + r)^t]$ gives 1 − [($5,000/$100)(.01)] = $[1/(1.01)^t]$ so that 0.5 = $1/(1.01)^t$. Taking reciprocals of both gives 2 = $(1.01)^t$, thus ln(2) = (t)ln(1.01) gives t = 69.66 periods.

Finding the rate, r, given APV, C, and t.

Need a financial calculator, tables, or patience for trial and error (no analytic solution).

Table method—since APV = C × PVIFA(r,t), APV/C = PVIFA(r,t). Look in Table A.3 across from t periods.

Example:

A finance company offers to loan you $1,000 today if you will make 48 "low" monthly payments of $32.60. What rate is implicit in the loan? APV = C × PVIFA(r,t) means $1,000 = $32.60 × PVIFA(r,48) so that APV/C = $1,000/$32.60 = 30.67 = PVIFA(r,48). A PV table gives 2% (per month) for r.

Lecture Tip, page 153: *The instructor should emphasize that the annuity factor approach is a short-cut approach in the process of calculating the present value of multiple cash flows; however, the cash flow stream is a level stream of payments. The instructor could demonstrate using the example provided in the text:*

$$\begin{aligned} PV &= \$500/(1.1)^1 + 500/(1.1)^2 + 500/(1.1)^3 \\ &= \$454.55 + \$413.22 + \$375.66 \\ &= \$1{,}243.43 \end{aligned}$$

$$\begin{aligned} PV &= \$500 \times \{1/(1.1)^1 + 1/(1.1)^2 + 1/(1.1)^3\} \\ &= \$500 \times \{[1 - (1/1.1)^3]/.1\} \\ &= \$500 \times 2.48685 \\ &= \$1{,}243.43 \end{aligned}$$

It may also be helpful to have the class examine the PVIF tables and recognize that a factor in the PVIFA table is simply an addition of the column in the PVIF table over the time period in which a level cash flow stream is realized.

Lecture Tip, page 157: *The instructor may wish to summarize the discussion with a reference to the tables. The process of solving for a discount rate, or the number of periods required to meet a future value, is the same process whether dealing with one known future value or a known annuity. We must solve for a factor by relating either the* *annuity or future value to the present value. This ratio is the factor we must find in the tables:*

1) *If we are concerned only with one future payment, we would utilize Table A.2.*
2) *If we are concerned with an annuity, we would utilize Table A.3.*
3) *If we are determining the return or interest rate, we would identify the period the future cash flow would be realized (or the period in which the last annuity payment is realized) and then search across that time period's row until we find the factor or ratio. The column in which we find the factor identifies the return.*
4) *If we are searching for the time period involved, we would identify the return we expect and search down that column until we find the factor we have calculated. We would then identify the period involved by identifying the row in which the factor is located.*

B. Future Value for Annuities

T5.14: Future Value for Annuities—A Short Cut

One way—first, discount payments, then find the future value. Annuity future value = Annuity present value × $(1 + r)^t$.

Another way—annuity future value factor is:
(Future value factor – 1)/r, that is, FVIFA(r,t) = $[(1 + r)^t - 1]/r$.

AFV = C × $((1 + r)^t - 1)/r$

Example:

If you make 20 payments of $1,000 at the end of each period at 10% per period, how much will your account grow to be? $[(1.10)^{20} - 1]/.10 = 57.275$ so AFV = $1,000 × 57.275 = $57,275.

Lecture Tip, page 158: *It should be emphasized that Table A.4 assumes the first payment is made one period from the present, with the final payment made at the end of the annuity's life. Example: $1 deposited over three years at 10 percent with the first payment deposited one year from today:*

FV in three years = $1 × 3.31
= $3.31.

However, if the first of three payments is deposited today, the value in three years would have the added benefit of compounding the initial payment over the three year period. We can solve for this problem with an adjustment to the table. If the annuity is over "t" years, we use a factor equal to (FVIFA,r,t + 1) – 1. In the case of the above example,

FV in three years = \$1 × [(FVIFA,.10,4) − 1]
= \$1 × (4.6410 − 1)
= \$1 × (3.6410)
= \$3.641

The difference between the two amounts is due to the three-year compounding effect of the \$1 deposit made at the beginning of the annuity's life instead of at the end:

$\$3.641 - \$3.31 = \$1 \times [(1.1)^3 - 1] = .331$

The student could then be asked to consider the interest savings a homeowner might realize if she would make an early payment on a mortgage which has a remaining life of 20 years. One could also use this as an introduction to the discussion of "the effect of compounding periods" section, since homeowners' mortgage payments are paid monthly.

C. Perpetuities

Perpetuity—series of level cash flows forever

Perpetuity present value = C/r, since PPV × r must give payment, C.

Preferred stock is an important example of a perpetuity.

5.6 COMPARING RATES: THE EFFECT OF COMPOUNDING PERIODS

T5.15: Effective Annual Rates and Compounding (3 pages)
T5.16: Cheap Financing and Rebate

A. Effective Annual Rates and Compounding

Stated or quoted interest rate—rate before considering any compounding effects, such as 10% compounded quarterly.

Effective annual interest rate—rate, on an annual basis, that reflects compounding effects, such as 10% compounded quarterly gives an effective rate of 10.38% (from $(1.025)^4 - 1$).

B. Calculating and Comparing Effective Annual Rates (EAR)

To get the effective rate, divide the quoted annual rate by # of periods in a year (semi-annual = 2, quarterly = 4, monthly = 12, etc.), add 1, raise to the # of periods power, then subtract 1. That is,

$$EAR = [1 + (\text{quoted rate})/m]^m - 1 \quad \text{where } m = \text{\# of periods per year}$$

Example:

18% compounded monthly is $[1 + (.18/12)]^{12} - 1 = 19.56\%$ effective rate.

Use either the effective rate with years or the periodic rate (quoted/m) and appropriate number of periods (years × m) when finding present or future values.

Example:

What is the present value of $100 in two years at 10% compounded quarterly? Use either an effective rate of $[(1.025)^4 - 1]$ for 2 years or 2.5% for 8 periods to get PVIF(10.38%,2) or PVIF(2.5%,8) = .8207 for PV = $82.07.

Lecture Tip, page 162: *The instructor might stir interest in this section by asking how many students have taken out a loan to pay for (finance) the car they are driving. One might then ask one of the students to reveal the **annual** interest rate she/he is paying on the loan. Students will typically quote the loan in terms of the APR. The instructor could mention that the student is actually paying more than the rate she/he had just quoted and demonstrate the calculation of the EAR.*

C. EARs and APRs

T5.17: Ripov Retailing: An Example

Annual Percentage Rate (APR)—simply the rate per period × # periods per year, making it a quoted or stated rate.

Ethics Note, page 164: *A class discussion concerning the ethical implications of a business practice attempting to circumvent usury laws and the calculation of the true EAR is provided below:*

You are interested in the purchase of a new car. Trust Me Used Car Sales *offers you a $25,000 new car for a $903.33 monthly payment over the next five years. Usury laws (interest rate limits established by the state for credit transactions) disallow rates greater than 21%.*

The instructor could begin by asking the class to determine, or provide, the EAR on the transaction (IRR = 24%). The instructor might then ask if this transaction is "fair." Many students will have difficulty in establishing what is meant by fair. Responses might range from "if this is the market price, then there is no problem" to "if this is illegal, then we should not do it."

The instructor could introduce a follow-up question by asking, "would this transaction be fair if the established usury limit is 50% as in Delaware?"

Use of this problem can lead to a meaningful class discussion as well as provide an example for understanding the rudiments of annuities. Additionally, Circuit Courts of Appeals often ignore usury limits due to the undo harm that such interest rate limits might cause a business.

D. Taking It to the Limit: A Note on Continuous Compounding

Let q stand for the quoted rate (in decimal form). What happens as m in $(1 + q/m)^m$ or $1/[(1 + q/m)^m]$ gets arbitrarily large? The limit as m gets large of $(1 + q/m)^m$ is e^q and the limit as m gets large of $1/[(1 + q/m)^m]$ is e^{-q}. These are the FVIF and PVIF for continuous compounding and discounting for 1 period.

$EAR = e^q - 1$ under continuous compounding

Example:

10% compounded continuously has an $EAR = e^{.10} - 1 = 10.52\%$.

5.7 SUMMARY AND CONCLUSIONS

T5.18: Solution to Problem 5.7
T5.19: Solution to Problem 5.16
T5.20: Solution to Problem 5.36

APPENDIX 5A—LOAN TYPES AND LOAN AMORTIZATION

5A.1 PURE DISCOUNT LOANS

Borrower pays a single lump sum (principal and interest) at maturity.

Example: A U.S. Treasury bill

5A.2 INTEREST-ONLY LOANS

Borrower pays interest only each period and entire principal at maturity.

Example: A typical corporate bond

5A.3 AMORTIZED LOANS

Borrower repays part or all of the principal over the life of the loan. Two methods are 1) fixed amount of principal to be repaid each period, which results in uneven payments, and 2) fixed payment, which results in uneven principal reduction.

CHAPTER 6
VALUING STOCKS AND BONDS

TRANSPARENCIES

T6.1: Chapter Outline
T6.2: Bond Features
T6.3: Bond Rates and Yields
T6.4: Valuing a Bond
T6.5: A Discount Bond
T6.6: A Premium Bond
T6.7: Bond Price Sensitivity to YTM
T6.8: General Expression for the Value of a Bond
T6.9: Interest Rate Risk and Time to Maturity (Fig. 6.2)
T6.10: Sample *Wall Street Journal* Bond Quotation (Fig. 6.3)
T6.11: Common Stock Cash Flows
T6.12: Dividend Growth Model
T6.13: Stock Price Sensitivity to Dividend Growth, g
T6.14: Stock Price Sensitivity to Required Return, r
T6.15: More on Dividend Growth (2 pages)
T6.16: Sample Stock Market Quotation from the *Wall Street Journal* (Fig 6.4)
T6.17: Solution to Problem 6.8
T6.18: Solution to Problem 6.16
T6.19: Solution to Problem 6.23

CHAPTER ORGANIZATION

T6.1: Chapter Outline

6.1 BONDS AND BOND VALUATION

Bond Features and Prices
Bond Values and Yields
Interest Rate Risk
Finding the Yield to Maturity: More Trial and Error
Bond Price Reporting

6.2 COMMON STOCK VALUATION

Common Stock Cash Flows
Common Stock Valuation: Some Special Cases
Components of the Required Return
Stock Market Reporting

6.3 SUMMARY AND CONCLUSIONS

ANNOTATED CHAPTER OUTLINE

6.1 BONDS AND BOND VALUATION

A. Bond Features and Prices

Bonds—long term IOU's, usually interest-only loans (interest is paid by the borrower every period, and the principal is repaid at the end of the loan).

Coupons—the regular interest payments (if fixed amount—*level coupon*)

Face or par value—amount repaid at the end of the loan

Coupon rate—annual coupon/face value

Maturity—number of years until face value is paid

T6.2: Bond Features
T6.3: Bond Rates and Yields
T6.4: Valuing a Bond

B. Bond Values and Yields

The cash flows from a bond are typically the coupons and face value. Finding the market price of a bond requires discounting the coupons and face value at the market rate.

Yield to maturity (YTM)—the required market rate or rate that makes the discounted cash flows from a bond equal to the bond's price.

Example:

Suppose Wilhite Co. were to issue $1,000 bonds with 20 years to maturity. The annual coupon is $110. Similar bonds have a yield to maturity of 11%.

Present value of face value = $\$1{,}000/(1.11)^{20} = \$124.03$

Annuity present value of coupons = $\$110 \times (1 - 1/(1.11)^{20})/.11$
= $\$110 \times 7.9633 = \$875.96$

Adding the discounted face value and coupons together
\$124.03 + \$875.96 = \$1,000

Since the YTM and coupon rate are the same, price = face value.

Discount bond—a bond that sells for less than its par or face value. This is the case when the YTM is greater than the coupon rate.

T6.5: A Discount Bond

Example: Discount bond

If the YTM on bonds similar to that of the Wilhite Co. (\$1,000 bond, \$110 coupon, 20 years to maturity) were 13%, instead of 11%, the bonds would sell for:

Present value of face value = $\$1{,}000/(1.13)^{20} = \$86.78$

Annuity present value of coupons = $\$110 \times (1 - 1/(1.13)^{20})/.13$
= $\$110 \times 7.0248 = \$772.72$

Adding the discounted face value and coupons together
\$86.78 + \$772.72 = \$859.50

The difference between this price, \$859.50, and the par price of \$1,000 is \$140.50. This is equal to the present value of the difference between YTM coupons and Wilhite's coupons: \$130 − \$110 = \$20 per year for 20 years at 13% = \$20 × PVIFA(13%,20) = \$20 × 7.0248 = \$140.50.

Premium bond—a bond that sells for more than its par or face value. This is the case when the YTM is less than the coupon rate.

Lecture Tip, page 187: *The instructor should stress the issue that the coupon interest rate and par value are fixed by contract when the bond is issued. Therefore, the components in the numerator will never change over the life of the bond. However, after issuance, as the bond approaches maturity, the time remaining and the yield to maturity will change, causing the bond's value to either increase or decrease.*

Lecture Tip, page 188: *The instructor may wish to further explore the loss in value of \$115 (\$1,000 – \$885) which the bond experienced due to the rise in interest rates. The instructor should remind the class that when the 8% coupon bond was issued, bonds of similar risk and maturity were yielding \$80 per year.*

One year later, the ten-year bond has nine years remaining to maturity. However, bonds of similar risk are now issued to yield 10% (\$100 per year) over a nine-year period. The bond which we are examining yields only \$80 per year or \$20 less than a new bond which sells for \$1,000. The instructor should emphasize this point and the issue of the preceding paragraphs—the old bond must sell for less than \$1,000 based on present value mathematics:

Discount = (\$80 – \$100) × (PVIFA,10%,9)
= –\$20 × 5.7590
= –\$115.18
= Value of old 8% bond – Value of new 10% bond
= \$884.82 – \$1,000
= –\$115.18.

T6.6: A Premium Bond

Example: Premium bond

If the YTM on bonds similar to that of the Wilhite Co. (\$1,000 bond, \$110 coupon, 20 years to maturity) were 9% instead of 11% the bonds would sell for:

Present value of face value = $\$1,000/(1.09)^{20}$ = \$178.43

Annuity present value of coupons = $\$110 \times (1 - 1/(1.09)^{20})/.09$
= \$110 × 9.1285 = \$1,004.14

Adding the discounted face value and coupons together

\$178.43 + \$1,004.14 = \$1,182.57

The difference between this price, \$1,182.57 and the par price of \$1,000, \$182.57, is equal to the present value of the difference between Wilhite's coupons and YTM coupons, i.e., \$110 – \$90, or \$20 per year for 20 years at 9% = \$20 × PVIFA(9%,20) = \$20 × 9.1285 = \$182.57.

General expression for the value of a bond:

Bond value = Present value of the coupons + Present value of the face amount

Bond value = $[\ C \times (1 - 1/(1 + YTM)^t)/YTM\ ] + [\ F \times 1/(1 + YTM)^t]$

semiannual coupons—halve the annual coupon amount, halve the *quoted* annual YTM, and double the number of years.

T6.7: Bond Price Sensitivity to YTM
T6.8: General Expression for the Value of a Bond

Example:
A $1,000 bond with an 8% coupon rate maturing in 10 years will have what price if the market quoted YTM is 10%?

Present value of face value = $\$1{,}000/(1.05)^{20} = \$376.89$

Annuity present value of coupons $= \$40 \times (1 - 1/(1.05)^{20})/.05$
$= \$40 \times 12.4622 = \$498.49$

Adding the discounted face value and coupons together
$376.89 + $498.49 = $875.38

C. Interest Rate Risk

T6.9: Interest Rate Risk and Time to Maturity

Interest rate risk—refers to changes in bond prices arising from fluctuating interest rates (varying YTMs).

Ceteris paribus, the longer the time to maturity, the greater the interest rate risk.
Ceteris paribus, the lower the coupon rate, the greater the interest rate risk.

D. Finding the Yield to Maturity: More Trial and Error

It is usually a trial and error process to find the YTM via the general formula above. Knowing if the bond sells for a premium (YTM must be below coupon rate) or discount (YTM must be above coupon rate) is a help, but using a financial calculator is (by far) the quickest, easiest, and most accurate method.

Lecture Tip, page 192: *The class should be informed that finding the yield to maturity can be a tedious process of trial and error. It may help to pose a hypothetical situation in which a 10-year, 10% bond sells for $1,050. The instructor could ask the students whether paying a higher price than $1,000 would yield an investor more or less than 10%. Hopefully, the students will recognize that if they pay $1,000 for $100 per year, the bond would yield 10% but if they paid more than $1,000, the bond would be yielding less than 10%. Thus, a starting point to determine the yield would be the 9% factors (not 11%). However, if that same bond happened to be selling for $1,200, one might want to try 8% as a starting point, since we would be paying a higher price than par and realizing a lower yield.*

E. Bond Price Reporting

T6.10: Sample *Wall Street Journal* Bond Quotation

6.2 COMMON STOCK VALUATION

Stock valuation is more difficult than bond valuation because the cash flows are not explicit, the life is forever, and the market rate is not easily observed.

A. Common Stock Cash Flows

T6.11: Common Stock Cash Flows

The cash flow to holders of common stock consists of dividends plus a future sale price. By recursively substituting the next dividend plus end-of-period price for the future cash flows, the current price of a stock can be written

$$P_0 = \frac{D_1}{(1+r)^1} + \frac{D_2}{(1+r)^2} + \frac{D_3}{(1+r)^3} + \frac{D_4}{(1+r)^4} + \ldots$$

B. Common Stock Valuation: Some Special Cases

T6.12: Dividend Growth Model

Zero growth—implies $D_1 = D_2 = D_3 = D$, a constant

Since the cash flow is always the same, the present value is that for a perpetuity, C/r, or:

$$P_0 = D/r$$

<u>Example:</u>

At a 10% market rate, a stock expected to pay a \$2 dividend forever would be worth \$2/.10 = \$20.

Constant growth—$D_1 = D_0 \times (1 + g)$; $D_2 = D_1 \times (1 + g)$; in general $D_t = D_0 \times (1 + g)^t$

Example:

If the current dividend is \$2 and the expected growth rate is 5%, what is the value of D_5?

$$D_0 \times (1.05)^5 = \$2 \times 1.276 = \$2.55$$

An amount that grows at a constant rate forever is called a *growing perpetuity*. In this case the expression for the value of a stock now becomes:

$$P_0 = \frac{D_0(1+g)^1}{(1+r)^1} + \frac{D_0(1+g)^2}{(1+r)^2} + \frac{D_0(1+g)^3}{(1+r)^3} + \ldots$$

As long as g < r, the present value at the rate r of dividends growing at the rate g is:

$$P_0 = \frac{D_0(1+g)}{r-g} = \frac{D_1}{r-g}$$

In general, the price at any time t is written:

$$P_t = \frac{D_t\,(1+g)}{r-g} = \frac{D_{t+1}}{r-g}$$

Example:

It is 4 years since the dividend was \$2 as in the example above. What price do we expect to see?

$P_4 = D_5/(r - g) = \$2.55/.05 = \$51$

T6.13: Stock Price Sensitivity to Dividend Growth, g
T6.14: Stock Price Sensitivity to Required Return, r
T6.15: More on Dividend Growth (2 pages)

General Formula for a *Growing Perpetuity*

Present value of a growing perpetuity = $C_0(1 + g)/(r - g)$

Non-constant growth—usually a mix of "supernormal" growth early on and then a constant, "normal" growth rate later. In this case, we discount the individual "high" growth dividends and discount the dividend growth model stock value at the future, constant growth date.

Example:

The next three dividends for Fudgit Co. are expected to be \$0.50, \$1.00, and \$1.50. Then the dividends are expected to grow at a constant 5% forever. If the required return on Fudgit is 10%, what is P_0?

$$P_0 = \frac{D_1}{(1+r)^1} + \frac{D_2}{(1+r)^2} + \frac{D_3}{(1+r)^3} + \frac{P_3}{(1+r)^3}$$

where $P_3 = [D_3 \times (1 + g)]/(r - g)$ = \$1.5(1.05)/(.10 – .05) = \$1.575/.05 = \$31.50

$$P_0 = \frac{.50}{(1.1)^1} + \frac{1.00}{(1.1)^2} + \frac{1.50}{(1.1)^3} + \frac{31.50}{(1.1)^3}$$

= \$0.454 + \$0.826 + \$1.127 + \$23.67 = \$26.07

Lecture Tip, page 199: *In his book,* A Random Walk Down Wall Street, *pp. 82-89, (1985, W.W. Norton & Company, New York), Burton Malkiel does not discuss the constant growth formula, but rather gives four "fundamental" rules of stock prices. Loosely paraphrased the rules state:*

Other things the same:

1. *Investors pay a higher price per share the larger the growth rate of dividends*

2. *Investors pay a higher price per share the larger the proportion of earnings paid out in cash dividends*

3. *Investors pay a higher price per share the less risky the company's stock*

4. *Investors pay a higher price per share the lower interest rates are*

If the required return, r, is looked at as a riskless rate of interest, r_f, plus a risk premium, r_p, (so that $r = r_f + r_p$), it is easily shown that Malkiel's rules have counterparts in the dividend growth model that exert just these effects on stock price.

Of course, the tricky part is estimating the growth rate and required return. So, while the model is precise, its predictions may be substantially different from observed stock prices depending upon the values used .

Lecture Tip, page 203: *In this example $P_3 = D_4 / (.10 - .05)$. Some students have the tendency to incorrectly discount P_3 by $(1 + r)^4$, not $(1 + r)^3$. This is probably influenced because D_4 is used to determine P_3. It should be stressed that we are always bringing the next dividend back one period. The timing of P_3 determines the time period selected for the factor we use.*

C. Components of the Required Return

Rearrange $P_0 = D_1/(r - g)$ to give $r = D_1/P_0 + g$

Dividend yield—D_1/P_0

Capital gains yield—g (price appreciation)

r = dividend yield + capital gains yield

D. Stock Market Reporting

Lecture Tip, page 206: *It may stimulate the class interest to require the students to purchase a recent* Wall Street Journal *and have them examine the financial section. The instructor could pick out a familiar stock's name and have the class perform some of the calculations presented in the text. One could also have the student examine the dividend column for various stocks and point out the number of nondividend paying stocks in the financial section. This could reinforce the text discussion of how the market values the expected, future dividend stream.*

T6.16: Sample Stock Quotation from the *Wall Street Journal* (Fig. 6.4)

6.3 SUMMARY AND CONCLUSIONS

T6.17: Solution to Problem 6.8
T6.18: Solution to Problem 6.16
T6.19: Solution to Problem 6.23

CHAPTER 7
NET PRESENT VALUE AND OTHER INVESTMENT CRITERIA

TRANSPARENCIES

T7.1: Chapter Outline
T7.2: NPV Illustrated
T7.3: Payback Rule Illustrated
T7.4: Ordinary and Discounted Payback (Table 7.3)
T7.5: Discounted Payback Illustrated
T7.6: Average Accounting Return Illustrated
T7.7: Internal Rate of Return Illustrated
T7.8: Net Present Value Profile
T7.9: Multiple Rate of Return
T7.10: NPV Profile: Multiple IRR Problem
T7.11: IRR, NPV, and Mutually Exclusive Projects
T7.12: Percentage of Responding Firms Using Capital Budgeting Methods
T7.13: Solution to Problem 7.3
T7.14: Solution to Problem 7.5
T7.15: Solution to Problem 7.12 (2 pages)

CHAPTER ORGANIZATION

T7.1: Chapter Outline

7.1 NET PRESENT VALUE
- The Basic Idea
- Estimating Net Present Value

7.2 THE PAYBACK RULE
- Defining the Rule
- Analyzing the Payback Period Rule
- Redeeming Qualities
- Summary of the Payback Rule

7.3 THE DISCOUNTED PAYBACK RULE

7.4 THE AVERAGE ACCOUNTING RETURN

Analyzing the Average Accounting Return Method

7.5 THE INTERNAL RATE OF RETURN

Problems with the IRR
Redeeming Qualities of the IRR

7.6 THE PROFITABILITY INDEX

7.7 THE PRACTICE OF CAPITAL BUDGETING

7.8 SUMMARY AND CONCLUSIONS

ANNOTATED CHAPTER OUTLINE

"What Assets Should We Buy?" - The Capital Budgeting Decision

7.1 NET PRESENT VALUE

A. The Basic Idea

Net present value—a measure of the difference between the market value of an investment and its cost. While cost is often relatively straight forward, finding the market value of assets or their benefits can be tricky. The principle is to find the market price of comparables or substitutes.

Lecture Tip, page 220: *Although this point may seem rather obvious, it could be helpful to stress the issue of "net" in NPV. Some students may later carelessly calculate the PV of the inflows and fail to subtract out the cost of a capital asset. The PV of inflows is not NPV; rather NPV is the amount remaining after offsetting the PV of the inflows with the PV of the outflows. The NPV amount determines the additional value created by the firm undertaking the investment.*

B. Estimating Net Present Value

Discounted cash flow (DCF) valuation—finding the market value of assets or their benefits by taking the present value of future cash flows, i.e., by estimating what the future cash flows would trade for in today's dollars.

Net present value rule—an investment should be accepted if the net present value is positive and rejected if it is negative.

T7.2: NPV Illustrated

In other words, if the market value of the benefits is larger than the cost, an investment will increase value.

Lecture Tip, page 222: *The instructor may wish to give the student a perspective on the meaning of NPV. In terms of the present, if we accept a negative NPV project of -$2,422, the student might view this as an equivalent to the company investing $2,422 today with nothing received in return. Therefore, the total value of the firm would decrease by $2,422. This, of course, assumes that the various components (cash flows estimated, discount factor, etc.) used in the computation are correct.*

7.2 THE PAYBACK RULE

Ethics Note, page 224: *The American Association of Colleges and Universities estimates that 10 percent of all college students cheat at some time during their postsecondary education careers. The instructor might pose the ethical question of whether it would be proper for a publishing company to offer a new book* How to Cheat: A User's Guide. *The publishing company has a cost of capital of 8% and estimates it could sell 10,000 volumes by the end of year one and 5,000 volumes in each of the following two years. The immediate printing costs for the 20,000 volumes would be $20,000. The book would sell for $7.50 per copy and net the company a profit of $6.00 per copy after royalties (which would, of course, be quite small!), marketing costs, and taxes. Year one net would be $60,000.*

The instructor could ask if the investment is worth buying the publication rights and what is the payback of the investment? (Payback = $20,000/$60,000 = .33 years). Students should recognize that the quick payback results in a pure profit of $6.00 per book following the investment's recovery. However, the instructor might ask the class if the publishing of this book would encourage cheating and if the publishing company would want to be associated with this text and its message. Some students may feel that one should accept these profitable investment opportunities while others might prefer that the publication of this profitable text be rejected due to the behavior it could encourage.

A. Defining the Rule

Payback period—length of time until the accumulated cash flows equal or exceed the original investment.

Payback period rule—investment is acceptable if its calculated payback is less than some prespecified number of years.

Lecture Tip, page 224: *The payback period is computed by summing the cash inflows, beginning with period one, and stopping at the time period in which the accumulation of the cash inflows equals the initial cash outflow (as discussed in section 7.2). The* *instructor could mention that, in the case of an annuity, the payback can be quickly solved by forming the ratio of initial outflow to annuity payment. However, one should mention that this only applies in the case of an annuity. Problems 7.1 and 7.5 represent an annuity in which the short cut approach could be used while problem 7.2 presents a non-constant payment stream.*

T7.3: Payback Rule Illustrated

B. Analyzing the Payback Period Rule

No discounting involved

Doesn't consider risk differences

How to determine the cutoff point

Bias for short-term investments

C. Redeeming Qualities

Simple to use (mostly by ignoring long-term)

Bias for short-term promotes liquidity

Can be adjusted for risk in some sense (altering the cutoff)

D. Summary of the Payback Rule

<u>Advantages</u>

Easy to understand
Adjusts for uncertainty of later cash flow
Biased toward liquidity

<u>Disadvantages</u>

Ignores time value of money
Ignores cash flow beyond payback period
Biased against long-term projects

<u>Lecture Tip, page 227:</u> *The payback period can be interpreted as a naive form of discounting if we consider the class of investments with level cash flows over arbitrarily long lives. Since the present value of a perpetuity is the payment divided by the discount rate, a payback period cut-off can be seen to imply a certain discount rate. That is,*

Cost/annual cash flow = payback period cut-off
Cost = annual cash flow × payback period cut-off.

Now, if we consider the PV of a perpetuity to be:

$$PV = \text{annual cash flow} \times (1/r),$$

the correspondence between the discount rate, r, and the payback period cut-off is obvious. The longer the payback period, the lower the implied value of r, and vice versa.

7.3 THE DISCOUNTED PAYBACK RULE

T7.4: Ordinary and Discounted Payback (Table 7.3)
T7.5: Discounted Payback Illustrated

Discounted payback period—length of time until accumulated discounted cash flows equal or exceed the initial investment.

This technique entails all the work of NPV and yet it is arbitrary. A redeeming feature is that if the project ever pays back on a discounted basis, then it must have a positive NPV.

Why bother? You need cash flow estimates and a discount rate to compute the discounted payback. You might as well go ahead and figure out the NPV and know what you're getting.

Lecture Tip, page 228: *The instructor could mention that "the discounted payback is the time it takes to break even in an economic or financial sense." This indicates that if a project has a negative NPV, we would never break even in an economic sense and, therefore, the discounted payback period would not exist for the project. However, a negative NPV project could easily have a short ordinary payback period. Problem 7.5 provides an example of this point.*

7.4 THE AVERAGE ACCOUNTING RETURN

T7.6: Average Accounting Return Illustrated

Average accounting return (AAR)—in general:

Some measure of accounting profit/Some measure of average accounting value

In other words, it is a rather strained benefit/cost analysis that produces a pseudo rate of return. Because of all the accounting conventions involved and the lack of cash figures, it isn't clear what is being calculated.

The text gives the following specific definition:

Average net income/Average book value

Average accounting return rule—project is acceptable if its average accounting return exceeds a target return.

A. Analyzing the Average Accounting Return Method

Since it involves accounting figures rather than cash, it is not comparable to returns in capital markets;

It treats money in all periods as having the same value;

There is no objective way to find the cut-off rate.

7.5 THE INTERNAL RATE OF RETURN

Ethics Notes, page 233: *To comply with the Air Quality Control Act of 1989, a company must install three smoke stack scrubber units to its ventilation stacks at an installed cost of $355,000* ***per unit****. An estimated $100,000* ***per unit*** *could be saved each year over the five-year life of the ventilation stacks. The cost of capital is 14% for the firm. The analysis of the investment results in a NPV of –$11,692.*

Despite the financial assessment dictating rejection of the investment, public policy might suggest acceptance of the project. By fiat, certain types of pollution controls are required, but should the firm exceed the minimum legal limits and be responsible for the environment, even if this responsibility leads to a wealth reduction for the firm? The instructor could also pose the question, "Is environmental damage merely a cost of doing business?" Also, "could the investment in a healthier working environment result in lower long-term costs in the form of lower future health costs? If so, might this decision result in an increase in shareholder wealth?" Notice that if the answer to this second question is yes, then all this means is that our original analysis omitted some side benefits to the project. This point is discussed in Chapter 8 in greater detail.

Internal rate of return (IRR)—rate that makes the present value of the future cash flows equal to the initial cost or investment. In other words, the discount rate that gives a project a $0 NPV.

IRR rule—investment is acceptable if the required return is less than the IRR. Otherwise, it should be rejected.

T7.7: Internal Rate of Return Illustrated

Net present value profile—plot of an investment's NPV at various discount rates.

T7.8: Net Present Value Profile

NPV and IRR comparison: If a project's cash flows are conventional (costs are paid early and benefits are received over the life), and if the project is independent (meaning the decision to take it does not affect any other project), then NPV and IRR will give the same accept or reject signal.

Lecture Tip, page 236: *It may be helpful to provide an example of a decision involving dependent cash flows. The instructor could mention a capital budgeting decision in which a plot of land is purchased for the intent of building a factory which could produce a product that the marketing department estimates would have an expected future life of three years. However, the project can only be justified if, in three years at the end of the product's life cycle, the factory would undergo an expensive modification (cash outflow) and produce a second product, which would generate a cash inflow beginning one year after the factory modification. Such a project would have to be justified based on the cash flows of both projects and would generate more than one IRR. One could also use this example to consider the issue of "multiple discount rates," if desired.*

A. Problems with the IRR

Unconventional cash flows—if the cash flows are of loan type, meaning money in at first and cash out later, the IRR is really a borrowing rate and lower is better. The IRR is sometimes called the IBR (internal borrowing rate) in this case.

Multiple rates of return—if cash flows alternate back and forth between positive and negative (in and out), more than one IRR is possible. NPV rule still works just fine.

T7.9: Multiple Rate of Return
T7.10: NPV Profile: Multiple IRR Problem

Mutually exclusive investment decisions—if taking one project means another is not taken, the projects are mutually exclusive. The one with the highest IRR may not be the one with the highest NPV.

T7.11: IRR, NPV, and Mutually Exclusive Projects

Crossover rate—the discount rate that makes the NPV of two projects the same (assuming, of course, their NPV profiles cross). Find the crossover rate using the NPV profile or by taking the difference in the projects' cash flows and calculate the IRR.

Example:

If project A has a cost of $500 and cash flows of $325 for two periods, while project B has a cost of $400 and cash flows of $325 and $200 respectively, the incremental flows are:

Period	A	B	Incremental
0	-$500	-$400	-$100
1	325	325	0
2	325	200	125
IRR (%)	19.43	22.17	11.80

So the crossover is 11.8%. At this rate, NPV_A = $50.71 and NPV_B also = $50.71.

B. Redeeming Qualities of the IRR

People seem to prefer talking about rates of return to dollars of value.

Unlike NPV, which requires a market discount rate, IRR relies only on the project cash flows, which, if the IRR is high enough, may be all that is needed to accept or reject as a practical matter.

7.6 THE PROFITABILITY INDEX

Profitability index (PI) (or benefit/cost ratio)—present value of the future cash flows divided by the initial investment.

If a project has a positive NPV, then the PI will be greater than 1.

This method has ranking problems similar to the IRR when dealing with mutually exclusive projects, i.e., we're not necessarily looking for the biggest return per dollar, but the project that adds the greatest value.

7.7 THE PRACTICE OF CAPITAL BUDGETING

It is common practice among large firms to employ some discounted cash flow technique such as IRR or NPV along with payback period or average accounting return. It is suggested that this is one way to resolve the considerable uncertainty over future events that surrounds estimating the NPV.

T7.12: Percentage of Responding Firms using Capital Budgeting Methods

Lecture Tip, page 244: *While the resolution of uncertainty is one reason multiple criteria may be used to judge projects, another is the judging of managers. When managers are judged and rewarded on the basis of periodic accounting figures (quarterly profits, annual earnings, etc.), there is an incentive to evaluate projects with methods such as payback or average accounting return that make these numbers look good.*

7.8 SUMMARY AND CONCLUSIONS

T7.13: Solution to Problem 7.3
T7.14: Solution to Problem 7.5
T7.15: Solution to Problem 7.12 (2 pages)

CHAPTER 8
MAKING CAPITAL INVESTMENT DECISIONS

TRANSPARENCIES

T8.1: Chapter Outline
T8.2: Relevant Cash Flows
T8.3: Capital Budgeting: *Pro Formas*
T8.4: Capital Budgeting: The DCF valuation
T8.5: A Closer Look: NWC Spending
T8.6: Modified ACRS Property Classes and MACRS Depreciation Allowances
T8.7: MACRS Depreciation: An Example
T8.8: Fairways Equipment and Operating Costs
T8.9: Fairways Revenues, Depreciation, and Other Costs
T8.10: Fairways Pro Forma Income Statement
T8.11: Fairways Cash Flows
T8.12: Alternative Definitions of OCF
T8.13: Sample Problems (2 pages)
T8.14: A Cost-Cutting Proposal
T8.15: Sample Problem
T8.16: Setting the Bid Price (4 pages)
T8.17: Equivalent Annual Cost (3 pages)
T8.18: Solution to Problem 8.3
T8.19: Solution to Problem 8.5
T8.20: Solution to Problem 8.7
T8.21: Solution to Problem 8.10
T8.22: Solution to Problem 8.15
T8.23: Solution to Problem 8.21

CHAPTER ORGANIZATION

T8.1: Chapter Outline

8.1 PROJECT CASH FLOWS: A FIRST LOOK

Relevant Cash Flows
The Stand-Alone Principle

ANNOTATED CHAPTER OUTLINE

8.1 PROJECT CASH FLOWS: A FIRST LOOK

T8.2: Relevant Cash Flows

A. Relevant Cash Flows

Relevant cash flows—cash flows that come into or out of being because a project is undertaken, thus we are interested in incremental cash flows.

Incremental cash flows—any and all changes in the firm's future cash flows that are a direct consequence of taking the project.

Lecture Tip, page 256: *It should be strongly emphasized that the identification of a project's cash flows represents changes occurring in the financial statements as a result of accepting a project. The instructor may wish to provide a few examples of possible projects which would cause the student to consider the nature of an incremental item.*

Examples:

a) The development of a plant on land currently owned by the company versus the same development, but the land must be purchased. This example would also allow the instructor to discuss the concept of opportunity cost as in the text.

b) Tax shelter provided by depreciation: The relevant depreciation effect if we replace an old machine with a three-year remaining life and $5,000 per year depreciation. The instructor could state that a new machine would cost $45,000 and be depreciated over a five-year life ($9,000 per year depreciation assuming straight-line). The students should be aware that the incremental tax shelter is t × ($9,000 − $5,000) for years one through three. The instructor might also ask the students to consider the incremental tax shelter in years four through five [t × ($9,000 − 0)].

B. The Stand-Alone Principle

Viewing projects as "mini-firms" with their own assets, revenues, and costs allows us to evaluate the investments separately from the other activities of the firm.

8.2 INCREMENTAL CASH FLOWS

A. Sunk Costs

Sunk cost—a cash flow already paid or already promised to be paid. Obviously, these costs should not be included in the incremental flows of a project.

Example:

A firm has a policy of paying the tuition bills for any of its newly hired managers who attend an accredited MBA program on their own time. Two managers already taking MBA classes are assigned to develop a new product. Should their tuition costs be included in the project's cash flows?

Lecture Tip, page 257: *Personal examples of sunk costs may be helpful for the student's understanding of this issue. The instructor might ask the student to consider a hypothetical situation in which a college student had purchased a typewriter for $300 while in high school. A computer is now available with an elaborate word processing package for $400. Although the student may be reluctant to purchase the new computer because of the previous decision to purchase the typewriter, the student should question* *the factors that would be relevant in the decision. The current cost (computer cost less any cash from the possible sale of typewriter) relative to the future benefits (time saved on retyping errors, completing many homework assignments sooner, etc.).*

B. Opportunity Costs

Opportunity costs—any cash flows lost or foregone by taking one course of action rather than another. These apply to any asset or resource that has value if sold rather than used.

Example:

Would land, already owned by a firm but not being used, be "free" when considering the investment outlay for a plant to be built on it?

C. Side Effects

With multi-line firms, projects often affect one another—sometimes helping, sometimes hurting. The point is to be aware of such effects in calculating the incremental cash flows.

Erosion—revenues gained by a new project at the expense of the firm's existing products or services.

Example:

Every time Kellogg's brings out a new oat cereal, it probably causes some erosion of existing product sales.

D. Net Working Capital

New projects often require incremental investments in cash, inventories, and receivables that need to be included in cash flows if they are not offset by changes in payables. Later, as projects end, this investment is often recovered.

E. Financing Costs

Do not include any interest or principal on debt, dividends, or other financing costs in computing cash flows. Financing costs represent part of the division of cash flows from a project to providers of capital.

F. Other Issues

Use cash flow, not accounting numbers.
Use aftertax cash flows, not pretax (the tax bill is a cash outlay even though it is based on accounting numbers).

8.3 PRO FORMA FINANCIAL STATEMENTS AND PROJECT CASH FLOWS

A. Getting Started: Pro Forma Financial Statements

T8.3: Capital Budgeting: *Pro Formas*

Treat the project as a mini-firm:

1. Start with pro forma income statement (don't include interest) and balance sheet.

2. Determine the sales projection, variable costs, fixed costs, and capital requirements.

Lecture Tip, page 260: *Some students may question why we are ignoring interest since it is clearly a cash outflow. It should be emphasized that we do not ignore interest expense; rather, we are only evaluating the asset-related cash flow. It should be stressed that interest expense is a financing cost, not an operating cost. It is chiefly a reflection of how we choose to finance a project, and, ignoring some of the finer points of capital structure, it is usually not an important factor in determining the value of the project. Another way to see this is to think of the project as a mini-firm with its own balance sheet. In capital budgeting, we are trying to determine the value of the lefthand (asset) side of the balance sheet. How a project is financed only affects the composition of the righthand side of the mini-firm's balance sheet. The impact of debt is considered in deriving the required return figure (cost of capital, which will be discussed in a later chapter).*

B. Project Cash Flows

T8.4: Capital Budgeting: The DCF Valuation

From the pro forma statements, compute:

Cash flow from assets = + operating cash flow
− capital spending
− additions to net working capital

Operating cash flow = + earnings before interest and taxes (EBIT)
+ depreciation
− taxes

C. Project Total Cash Flow and Value

Tabulate total cash flows and determine NPV, IRR, and any other measure desired.

8.4 MORE ON PROJECT CASH FLOWS

A. A Closer Look at Net Working Capital

T8.5: A Closer Look: NWC Spending

How would one reconcile accounting conventions for sales and costs with the need for cash flow information? Include additions to net working capital.

Example:

Sales for the period are \$100 and costs \$75. With the following balance sheet information what is net cash flow?

	19X1	19X2
Receivables	\$20	\$25
Inventory	30	25
Payables	15	20
Net working capital	\$35	\$30

The decline in inventory indicates a \$5 cash inflow, the increase in payables indicates another \$5 cash inflow, while the \$5 increase in receivables means \$5 of sales were not collected. Adjusting for these,

$$\$100 - 75 + 5 + 5 - 5 = \$30 \text{ cash flow}$$

The same result is seen by noting that net working capital declined by \$5. Thus, (sales – costs – change in net working capital) = \$100 – 75 – (–5) = \$30.

Lecture Tip, page 265: *The NWC discussion is very important and should not be overlooked by the students. It may be helpful to reemphasize the point of NWC and operating cash flow through accounting entries.*

Example:

Consider the accounting entries for two separate sales at the end of the year-one for cash and the other on credit.

Cash	*\$10,000*	*Revenue*	*\$10,000*
Acc. Rec.	*\$ 5,000*	*Revenue*	*\$ 5,000*

The instructor should ask the students to consider the income statement and balance sheet impact from these two transactions at the end of the year. Assuming finished goods inventory = 80% of sales, the instructor should emphasize that cost of goods sold represents a cost that has already been paid out by the firm for these sales:

CofGS = $12,000 = ($10,000 + $5,000) × .8

Ignoring taxes, the students can see that, under accrual accounting, Revenue − Cost = $15,000 − $12,000 = +$3,000, but the company actually only received $10,000 cash and had cash expenses of $12,000. The students should easily recognize that operating cash flow = $10,000 − $12,000 = ***−$2,000****. The instructor could then demonstrate the cash flow relationship:*

Total cash flow	*= Oper. Cash Flow −*	*Additions to NWC − . . .*
−$2,000	*= $3,000 −*	*$5,000*

B. Depreciation

When computing depreciation, economic life and future market value are ignored.

Modified Accelerated Cost Recovery System (MACRS)—current depreciation rules governing asset lives and allowable depreciation deductions.

T8.6: Modified ACRS Property Classes and MACRS Depreciation Allowances
T8.7: MACRS Depreciation: An Example

Book value versus market value—if an asset's value when sold (i.e., salvage value) is larger than its book value, the excess depreciation is to be recaptured. That is, taxes are due on the amount received over book value. Be careful to include such taxes in calculating aftertax cash flows.

Lecture Tip, page 268: *The instructor may wish to question the students as to why a company might prefer accelerated depreciation, such as the ACRS tables, over straight-line depreciation. The students could consider the purchase of a five-year, $50,000 machine by a company with a 34% marginal tax rate.*

The instructor could mention that under both ACRS and straight-line depreciation, year-one depreciation is .2 × $50,000 = $10,000. However, under the ACRS rules, year-two depreciation is .32 × $50,000 = $16,000 versus the $10,000 under straight line.

Cash flow effect: .34 × $16,000 = $5,440 versus .34 × $10,000 = $3,400. The realization of the higher cash flow in the early years of a project's life, relative to later years, will result in a higher NPV for the project.

C. An Example: The Majestic Mulch and Compost Company (MMCC)

Another Example: Fairways Driving Range

Two friends are considering opening a driving range for golfers. Because of the growing popularity of golf, they estimate such a range could generate rentals of 20,000 buckets at $3 a bucket the first year, and that rentals will grow at 750 buckets a year thereafter. The price will remain a $3 per bucket.

Equipment requirements include:

ball dispensing machine	$2,000
ball pick-up vehicle	$8,000
tractor and accessories	$8,000

All the equipment is 5-year ACRS property, and is expected to have a salvage value of 10% of cost after 6 years.

Stocking a small shop selling tees, visors, gloves, towels, sun-block, etc., plus a checking account for the business make net working capital needs $3,000 to start. This amount is expected to grow at 5% per year.

Annual fixed operating costs are expected as follows:

Land lease	$12,000
Water	1,500
Electricity	3,000
Labor	30,000
Seed & Fertilizer	2,000
Gasoline	1,500
Equipment maintenance	1,000
Insurance	1,000
Other	1,000
Total	$53,000

T8.8: Fairways Equipment and Operating Costs

Expenditures for balls and baskets, initially $3,000, are expected to grow at 5% per year. The relevant tax rate is 15% and the required return is also 15%. The project is to be evaluated over a six year life.

Should the friends proceed?

Projected revenues, Fairways Driving Range:

Year	Buckets	Revenues
1	20,000	$60,000
2	20,750	62,250
3	21,500	64,500
4	22,250	66,750
5	23,000	69,000
6	23,750	71,250

Projected cost of balls and buckets:

Year	Balls & Buckets
1	$3,000
2	3,150
3	3,308
4	3,473
5	3,647
6	3,829

Depreciation on $18,000 of 5-year equipment:

Year	ACRS %	Depreciation	Book value
1	20.00%	$3,600	$14,400
2	32.00	5,760	8,640
3	19.20	3,456	5,184
4	11.52	2,074	3,110
5	11.52	2,074	1,036
6	05.76	1,036	0
		$18,000	

T8.9: Fairways Revenues, Depreciation, and Other Costs

Pro forma income statement, Fairways Driving Range:

Year	1	2	3	4	5	6
Revenues	$60,000	62,250	64,500	66,750	69,000	71,250
Variable costs	3,000	3,150	3,308	3,473	3,647	3,829
Fixed costs	53,000	53,000	53,000	53,000	53,000	53,000
Depreciation	3,600	5,760	3,456	2,074	2,074	1,036
EBIT	$400	$340	$4,736	$8,203	$10,279	$13,385
Taxes	60	51	710	1,230	1,542	2,008
Net income	$340	$289	$4,026	$6,973	$8,737	$11,377

Projected increases in net working capital

Year	Net working capital	Increase in NWC
0	$3,000	$3,000
1	3,150	150
2	3,308	158
3	3,473	165
4	3,647	174
5	3,829	182
6	4,020	–4,020

T8.10: Fairways *Pro Forma* Income Statement

Projected cash flows:

Year	EBIT	+ Depreciation	– Taxes	= Operating cash flow
0	$0	$0	$0	$0
1	400	3,600	60	3,940
2	340	5,760	51	6,049
3	4,736	3,456	710	7,482
4	8,203	2,074	1,230	9,047
5	10,279	2,074	1,542	10,811
6	13,385	1,036	2,008	12,413

Year	+ Operating cash flow	– Increase in NWC	– Capital spending	= Total cash flow
0	$ 0	$3,000	$18,000	–$ 21,000
1	3,940	150	0	3,790
2	6,049	158	0	5,891
3	7,482	165	0	7,317
4	9,047	174	0	8,873
5	10,812	182	0	10,630
6	12,413	–4,020	–1,530	17,963

Fairways Driving Range: NPV = $9,685; IRR = 27%

T8.11: Fairways Cash Flows

8.5 ALTERNATIVE DEFINITIONS OF OPERATING CASH FLOWS

Or, exercises in manipulating operating cash flows.

Let

OCF = operating cash flow
S = sales
C = operating costs
D = depreciation
T_c = corporate tax rate

Suppose S = $1,000, C = $600, D = $200, and T_c = 34%

EBIT = S – C – D = $1,000 – 600 – 200 = $200

Taxes = EBIT × T_c = (S – C – D) × T_c = $200 × .34 = $68

Operating cash flow (OCF) = EBIT + D – Taxes = $200 + 200 – 68 = $332

T8.12: Alternative Definitions of OCF

A. The Bottom-Up Approach

$$\begin{aligned} \text{OCF} &= \text{EBIT} + \text{D} - (\text{EBIT} \times \text{T}_c) \\ &= (\text{S} - \text{C} - \text{D}) + \text{D} - (\text{S} - \text{C} - \text{D}) \times \text{T}_c \\ &= [(\text{S} - \text{C} - \text{D}) \times (1 - \text{T}_c)] + \text{D} \\ &= \text{Net income} + \text{depreciation} \\ &= [(\$1{,}000 - 600 - 200) \times .66] + \$200 = \$332 \end{aligned}$$

This approach takes after tax income (bottom line with no interest expense) and adds back non-cash items.

B. The Top-Down Approach

$$\begin{aligned} \text{OCF} &= (\text{S} - \text{C} - \text{D}) + \text{D} - (\text{S} - \text{C} - \text{D}) \times \text{T}_c \\ &= (\text{S} - \text{C}) - (\text{S} - \text{C} - \text{D}) \times \text{T}_c \\ &= \text{Sales} - \text{Costs} - \text{Taxes} \\ &= \$1{,}000 - 600 - 68 = \$332 \end{aligned}$$

This approach simply leaves out non-cash items.

C. The Tax-Shield Approach

$$\begin{aligned} \text{OCF} &= (\text{S} - \text{C} - \text{D}) + \text{D} - (\text{S} - \text{C} - \text{D}) \times \text{T}_c \\ &= [(\text{S} - \text{C}) \times (1 - \text{T}_c)] + (\text{D} \times \text{T}_c) \\ &= [(\$1{,}000 - 600) \times .66] + (\$200 \times .34) \\ &= \$264 + 68 = \$332 \end{aligned}$$

Depreciation tax shield—the second part of the expression, $(\text{D} \times \text{T}_c)$.

T8.13: Sample Problems (2 pages)

8.6 SOME SPECIAL CASES OF DISCOUNTED CASH FLOW ANALYSIS

The following are illustrated by example.

A. Evaluating Cost-Cutting Proposals

T8.14: A Cost-Cutting Proposal Illustrated
T8.15: Sample Problem

Consider a $10,000 machine that will reduce operating costs (pre-tax) by $3,000 per year over a 5-year period. Assume no changes in net working capital and a scrap value of $1,000 at the end of the period. For simplicity, assume straight-line depreciation. The tax rate is 34% and the discount rate is 10%.

Using the tax-shield approach to find OCF,

$$\begin{aligned} \text{OCF} &= [(S - C) \times (1 - T_c)] + (D \times T_c) \\ &= [\$(0 - (-3{,}000)) \times .66] + (\$2{,}000 \times .34) \\ &= \$1{,}980 + 680 = \$2{,}660 \end{aligned}$$

The first part reflects the after-tax cost savings, while the second part gives the depreciation tax-shield.

The after-tax salvage value is:

Market value – (Market value – Book value) × T_c = $1,000 – $1000 × .34 = $660

The relevant cash flows are:

Year	OCF	Capital spending	Total
0	$0	–$10,000	–$10,000
1	2,660	0	2,660
2	2,660	0	2,660
3	2,660	0	2,660
4	2,660	0	2,660
5	2,660	+660	3,320

At 10% the NPV is $493.30 and the IRR is 11.86%.

B. Setting the Bid Price

The lowest price to bid is one that makes NPV = 0.

T8.16: Setting the Bid Price (4 pages)

The Army is asking for bids on multiple-use digitizing devices (MUDDs). The contract calls for 4 units to be delivered each year for the next 3 years. Labor and material costs are estimated to be $10,000 per MUDD. Production space can be leased for $12,000 per year. The project will require $50,000 in new equipment which is expected to have a salvage value of $10,000 at the end of the project. Making MUDDs will mean a $10,000 increase in net working capital. The tax rate is 34% and the required return is 15%. Assume straight-line depreciation.

Year	OCF	Additions to NWC	Capital spending	Total cash flow
0	0	−10,000	−50,000	−60,000
1	OCF	0	0	OCF
2	OCF	0	0	OCF
3	OCF	+10,000	+6,600	16,600 + OCF

Taking the present value of $16,600 in period 3 and subtracting this figure from the initial outlay of $60,000 gives:

Year	0	1	2	3
Cash flow	−49,085	OCF	OCF	OCF

Operating cash flow (OCF) is now an unknown ordinary annuity payment. The 3-year present value factor for an ordinary annuity at 15% is 2.283, so:

NPV = 0 = −$49,085 + (OCF × 2.283) implies
OCF = $49,085/2.283 = $21,500

Using the bottom-up approach to operating cash flow and depreciation of $50,000/3 = $16,667,

Operating cash flows = Net income + depreciation
$21,500 = Net income + $16,667
Net income = $4,833

Next, noting annual costs are $40,000 + $12,000,

Net income = $(S - C - D) \times (1 - T_c)$
$4,833 = (S × .66) − [$(52,000 + 16,667) × .66]
$50,153 = (S × .66)
Sales = $50,153/.66 = $75,989.73

Hence sales need be $76,000 per year or $19,000 per MUDD to get the required 15% return on investment.

C. Evaluating Equipment with Different Lives

T8.17: Equivalent Annual Cost (3 pages)

The following example presumes replacement chains are appropriate, assumes straight-line depreciation, a 34% tax rate, and a 15% required return.

Two types of batteries are being considered for use in electric golf carts by the City Country Club. Burnout batteries cost $36 each, have a life of 3 years, cost $100 per year to keep charged, and have a salvage value of $5. Longlasting batteries cost $60 each, have a life of 5 years, cost $88 per year to keep charged, and have a salvage value of $5.

Using the tax-shield approach, cash flows for Burnout are:

$$\begin{aligned} OCF &= [(S - C) \times (1 - T_c)] + (D \times T_c) \\ &= [\$(0 - 100) \times .66] + (\$12 \times .34) = -\$66 + 4 = -\$62 \end{aligned}$$

	Year					
	0	1	2	3	4	5
OCF	$0	–$62	–$62	–$62		
Capital spending	–36	0	0	3.3		
Total	–$36	–$62	–$62	–$58.7		

For Longlasting, the relevant cash flows are:

$$\begin{aligned} OCF &= [(S - C) \times (1 - T_c)] + (D \times T_c) \\ &= [\$(0 - 88) \times .66] + (\$12 \times .34) = -\$58 + 4 = -\$54 \end{aligned}$$

	Year					
	0	1	2	3	4	5
OCF	$0	–$54	–$54	–$54	–$54	–$54
Capital spending	–60	0	0	0	0	3.3
Total	–$60	–$54	–$54	–$54	–$54	–$50.7

We now need to calculate a cost per year for the two alternatives so as to make them comparable.

Equivalent annual cost (EAC)—an annuity that has the same present value as the actual costs (cash flows). To find the EAC, find the present value of costs (cash flows) and use this as the present value for an annuity with a like life.

The present value of costs for Burnout and Longlasting at the 15% required return are:
Burnout PV(cash flows) = \$175.4
Longlasting PV(cash flows) = \$239.4

The annuity factors for 3 and 5 periods at 15% are 2.283 and 3.352 respectively, so finding the annuity with the same present value gives:

Burnout: \$175.4 = EAC × 2.283 gives EAC = \$76.83
Longlasting: \$239.4 = EAC × 3.352 gives EAC = \$71.42

Longlasting is cheaper, so we choose it.

Lecture Tip, page 285: *The instructor could also ask the students to consider two alternative machines: machine A with a three-year life and machine B with a six-year life. If machine A is accepted, it must be replaced in three years with a new machine A. An alternative to EAC would be to calculate the PV of the costs of machine A over the six-year period and compare it to the PV of the cost of machine B over the same six-year period. This process would result in the same decision as under the EAC method.*

8.7 SUMMARY AND CONCLUSIONS

T8.18: Solution to Problem 8.3
T8.19: Solution to Problem 8.5
T8.20: Solution to Problem 8.7
T8.21: Solution to Problem 8.10
T8.22: Solution to Problem 8.15
T8.23: Solution to Problem 8.21

CHAPTER 9
PROJECT ANALYSIS AND EVALUATION

TRANSPARENCIES

T9.1: Chapter Outline
T9.2: Evaluating NPV Estimates
T9.3: Fairways Driving Range
T9.4: Fairways Scenario Analysis
T9.5: Fairways Sensitivity Analysis
T9.6: Fairways: Rentals versus NPV
T9.7: Fairways Total Cost
T9.8: Fairways Break-Even Analysis
T9.9: Fairways Accounting Break-Even
T9.10: More on Break-Even Analysis
T9.11: Fairways DOL (2 pages)
T9.12: Solution to Problem 9.1
T9.13: Solution to Problem 9.6
T9.14: Solution to Problem 9.12
T9.15: Solution to Problem 9.19

CHAPTER ORGANIZATION

T9.1: Chapter Outline

9.1 EVALUATING NPV ESTIMATES
- The Basic Problem
- Projected versus Actual Cash Flows
- Forecasting Risk
- Sources of Value

9.2 SCENARIO AND OTHER "WHAT IF" ANALYSES
- Getting Started
- Scenario Analysis
- Sensitivity Analysis
- Simulation Analysis

ANNOTATED CHAPTER OUTLINE

9.1 EVALUATING NPV ESTIMATES

T9.2: Evaluating NPV Estimates

To find an NPV is to put a market value on uncertain future cash flows. Projecting the future always involves error and potential error. Among the sources of error are biases and omissions.

A. The Basic Problem

Two reasons for positive NPV: 1) a good project, or 2) a bad job of estimating NPV.

Similarly, a negative NPV may be a bad project or a bad job of estimating NPV.

B. Projected versus Actual Cash Flows

Estimated cash flows are expectations or averages of possible cash flows, not exact figures (although, of course, if an exact figure were available you'd use it).

C. Forecasting Risk

Forecasting risk—the danger of making a bad (money losing) decision because of errors in projected cash flows. This risk is reduced if we systematically investigate common problem areas.

D. Sources of Value

The first and best guard against forecasting risk is to keep in mind that positive NPVs are considered economic rarities. For a project to have a positive NPV, it must have some competitive edge—be first, be best, be the only. Keep in mind the economic axiom that in a competitive market excess profits (the source of positive NPV) are zero.

Lecture Tip, page 297: *Perhaps the single largest source of positive NPVs are monopoly rents—profits above those necessary to keep resources employed in an endeavor that accrue as the result of being the only one able or allowed to do something. Often associated with patent rights and technological edges, such rents quickly dissipate in a competitive market.*

9.2 SCENARIO AND OTHER "WHAT IF" ANALYSES

"And time yet for a hundred indecisions,
And for a hundred visions and revisions,
Before the taking of a toast and tea."

- T.S. Eliot

What things are likely to be wrong and what will be their effect if they are?

A. Getting Started

Start with a base case—the expected cash flows—then ask "what if . . .?"

Lecture Tip, page 298: *Transparencies T9.3 through T9.11 are based on the financial information for Fairways Driving Range.*

T9.3: Fairways Driving Range

Example: Simplified Fairways Driving Range

Consider the following revised example of Fairways Driving Range. Rentals are expected to be 20,000 buckets a year at $3 per bucket. Equipment costs are $20,000, depreciated using straight-line over 5 years and have a zero salvage value. Variable costs are 10% of rentals and fixed costs are $45,000 per year. Assume no increase in working capital nor any additional capital outlays. The required return is 15% and the tax rate is 15%.

Revenues	$60,000
Variable costs	6,000
Fixed costs	45,000
Depreciation	4,000
EBIT	$5,000
Taxes (15%)	750
Net income	$4,250

Thus, cash flow is $5,000 + 4,000 – 750 = $8,250. At 15%, the five-year annuity factor is 3.352, so NPV based upon expected cash flows is:

Base-case NPV = –$20,000 + ($8,250 x 3.352) = $7,654

The following are different versions of "what if . . .."

B. Scenario Analysis

1. Worst-case/Best-case scenarios: putting lower and upper bounds on cash flows. Common exercises include poor revenues with high costs, and high revenues with low costs.

If, under most circumstances, the discounted projected cash flows are sufficient to cover the outlay, we can have a high level of confidence that the NPV is positive. Beyond that, it is difficult to interpret the meaning of the scenarios.

Lecture Tip, page 299: *A major misconception about a project's NPV at this point is that it depends upon how the cash flows actually turn out. This thinking misses the point that NPV is an ex ante valuation of the uncertain future. The distinction between the valuation of what is expected versus the ex post value of what transpired is often difficult for students to appreciate.*

An analogy useful in getting this point across is the market value of a new car. The potential to be a "lemon" is in every car, as is the possibility of it being a "cream puff." The greater or lesser the potential for a car to turn out to be troublesome or troublefree (expectations about the future) obviously influences its market value. The point, however, is that a new car doesn't have many different market values right now—one for each conceivable repair record. Rather, there is one market value embodying the different potential outcomes and their expected value. So it is with NPV—the potential for good and bad cash flows is reflected in a single market value.

T9.4: Fairways Scenario Analysis

Lecture Tip, page 299: *The instructor may wish to integrate this discussion of risk into the topics which will be discussed in Chapters 10 and 11. The variability between best and worst case in this chapter has to do with forecasting risk. Our chief concern is that our estimate of NPV (as opposed to the true, but unobservable, NPV) is wrong because we incorrectly identify the expected cash flows. In later discussion, we examine the economic risks that cause the actual cash flows to differ from the expected cash flows. It helps to point out that these risks are embodied in our required return.*

Also, the cases examined here aren't literally the best and worst cases. The true worst case is something absurdly unlikely, such as an earthquake that swallows our production facilities. Instead, the worst case represents the use of pessimistic forecasts in developing the expected cash flows.

<u>Example: Fairways Scenario Analysis</u>

Base-case scenario: rentals are 20,000 buckets, variable costs are 10% of revenue, fixed costs are $45,000 and depreciation is $4,000 per year.

Worst-case scenario: rentals are only 15,000 buckets, while variable costs are 12% of revenue, fixed costs remain the same.

Best-case scenario: rentals are 25,000 buckets, variable costs are 8% of revenue.

Scenario	Net income	Cash flow	%Return
Base case	$ 4,250	$ 8,250	30.2
Worst case	–9,400	–5,400	na
Best case	17,000	21,000	101.9

C. Sensitivity Analysis

To conduct a sensitivity analysis, hold all projections constant except one, alter that one, and see how sensitive cash flow is to that one when it changes—the point is to get a fix on where forecasting risk may be especially severe. You may want to use the worst case-best case idea for the item being varied. Common exercises include varying sales, variable costs, and fixed costs.

T9.5: Fairways Sensitivity Analysis
T9.6: Fairways: Rentals versus NPV

Example: Fairways Sensitivity Analysis

Base case: rentals are 20,000 buckets, variable costs are 10% of revenue, fixed costs are $45,000 and depreciation is $4,000 per year.

Worst-case sales: rentals are only 15,000 buckets.

Best-case sales: rentals are 25,000 buckets.

Scenario	Revenue	Cash flow	%Return
Base case	$60,000	$ 8,250	30.2
Worst case	45,000	–4,500	na
Best case	75,000	19,725	95.1

D. Simulation Analysis

Using computers, the interactions of different inputs and likely scenarios may be realized through simulating the different possible cash flows that result. Going back to the new car analogy, simulation is a way to see the different potential outcomes that are to be valued.

9.3 BREAK-EVEN ANALYSIS

Break-even analysis is a widely used technique for analyzing sales volume and profitability. More to the point, it determines the sales volume necessary to cover costs and implicitly asks "Are things likely to go that well?"

Ethics Note, page 302: *The following case might be used to discuss the nature of break-even analysis and a possible ethical quandary involved with this analysis.*

Researchers associated with South Miami Hospital (SMH) developed a new experimental laser treatment for heart patients. It is considered by its development team and the physicians who use the laser to be a lifesaving advance. It should be noted that the physicians who are touting the laser hold a significant stake in the company that produces the laser.

To offer a substitute for a balloon angioplasty to treat heart blockages, the experimental laser was developed at a cost of $250,000. SMH estimates that it will cost $20,000 to install the laser. The procedure requires a nurse at $50 per hour, a technician at $30 per hour and a physician who is paid $750 per hour. Patients are billed $3,000 for the procedure compared to $1,500 for the traditional balloon treatment.

The instructor could ask the students to determine the break-even for the new procedure. Answer:

Fixed cost = \$250,000 + \$20,000 = \$270,000
Variable cost = \$50 + \$30 + \$750 = \$830

Cash B.E. = \$250,000 / (\$3,000 − \$830) = 115.2 hours,

or approximately 116 patients (assuming a one hour procedure per patient)

The instructor could next mention that this procedure is considered experimental and, as such, would not be covered by most insurers. The experimental nature of this procedure means that part of the development costs are being paid by the patient.

The instructor could ask the class the following two questions:

1. *Is it ethical for the patient to pay for R&D costs prior to the introduction of the final product?*

2. *Is it proper for physicians to recommend this procedure when they have a vested interest in its usage?*

A. Fixed and Variable Costs

Variable costs (VC)—costs that change as the volume of sales changes (direct labor and materials, for example).

A simplifying assumption is to make variable costs a constant amount per unit of output, i.e.,

variable costs = quantity × cost per unit
VC = Q × v

When this is assumed, v is also the *marginal cost.*

Fixed costs (FC)—costs that are constant over a period regardless of the level of sales.

1. *Total costs, (TC)*—sum of fixed costs (FC) and variable costs (VC)

$$TC = FC + VC$$
$$TC = FC + (Q \times v)$$

T9.7: Fairways Total Cost

Example: Fairways Total Cost

Buckets	Variable cost	Fixed cost	Total cost
0	$ 0	$45,000	$45,000
15,000	4,500	45,000	49,500
20,000	6,000	45,000	51,000
25,000	7,500	45,000	52,500

2. *Average cost versus marginal cost*—total cost divided by output gives average cost. Average cost will exceed marginal cost in all cases except where fixed costs are $0. But since fixed costs are a type of sunk cost (in the current period at least) the relevant cost in considering additional production is variable or marginal cost.

Lecture Tip, page 304: *The student should recognize that as quantity increases, total fixed costs remain constant, but, on a per unit basis, they decrease with increasing volume. On a per unit basis, as quantity increases, total cost per unit approaches variable cost per unit. If a company expects a high sales volume, the company may desire to exploit the possible economies of scale by investing more in fixed costs in an effort to lower variable cost per unit. However, this could create future financial problems if sales expectations fail to materialize. The instructor might mention that this sensitivity to earnings declines will be examined later in this chapter through the discussion of the degree of operating leverage.*

If the instructor desires to expand on this issue, he or she could introduce two alternative cost structures and have the students consider what minimum quantity of sales would be required to favor one project over another. Example:

$$FC_{(Proj.\ A)} + VC_{(Proj.\ A)} \times Q = FC_{(Proj.\ B)} + VC_{(Proj.\ B)} \times Q$$
$$\$10,000 + \$6 \times Q = \$25,000 + \$3 \times Q$$
$$Q^{*} = 5,000 \text{ units}$$

The instructor could then mention that a company would have to expect beyond 5,000 units of sales to justify accepting the increased fixed costs or operating risk of project B. Additionally, the forecasting risk is much greater with project B. The instructor may wish to integrate this example with the discussion on operating leverage. Note the comment on page 315 in the "implications of operating leverage" section: "The higher the degree of operating leverage, the greater is the potential danger from forecasting risk."

B. Accounting Break-Even

The sales volume at which net income = $0

C. Accounting Break-Even: A Closer Look

What sales level gives $0 net income (assuming things are the same year to year)? This happens when sales equals total costs.

P = price per unit
v = (variable) cost per unit
Q = units or quantity
FC = fixed costs
D = depreciation
t = tax rate

Net income is sales less total costs less taxes,

Net income = $[(Q \times P) - (FC + (Q \times v) + D)] \times (1 - t)$

At break-even, net income = 0, so,

$\$0 = [(Q \times P) - (FC + (Q \times v) + D)] \times (1 - t)$

Dividing both sides by $(1 - t)$ and rearranging gives sales equals total costs,

$Q \times P = FC + (Q \times v) + D$

Further rearranging gives: $Q = (FC + D) / (P - v)$

That is, net income is zero at the quantity Q = fixed costs plus depreciation divided by the contribution margin (price less variable cost).

T9.8: Fairways Break-Even Analysis
T9.9: Fairways Accounting Break-Even

9.4 OPERATING CASH FLOW, SALES, VOLUME, AND BREAK-EVEN

A. Accounting Break-Even and Cash Flow

Ignoring taxes for simplification:

1. First calculate Q necessary for accounting break-even. Using the simplified Fairways example:

$Q = (FC + D) / (P - v)$
$Q = \$(45{,}000 + 4{,}000) / \$(3 - .30) = 18{,}148$ buckets

Since operating cash flow = net income + depreciation,

at Q = 18,148: operating cash flow = \$0 + \$4,000 = \$4,000.

2. At (accounting) break-even Q, the sum of the (undiscounted) cash flows is just equal to the depreciable investment and the project's payback period is exactly equal to its life.

3. A project that just breaks even on an accounting basis will have a negative NPV at any positive discount rate.

B. Sales Volume and Operating Cash Flow

Again, ignoring taxes for simplification:

OCF = net income + depreciation
$OCF = [((P - v) \times Q) - FC - D] + D$
$OCF = (P - v) \times Q - FC$

This is a linear relation with slope (P – v) and intercept FC.

C. Cash Flow, Accounting, and Financial Break-Even Points

T9.10: More on Break-Even Analysis

(Illustrated with simplified Fairways and no taxes)

Rearranging $OCF = (P - v) \times Q - FC$ and solving for Q:

$$Q = (FC + OCF) / (P - v)$$

1. Accounting Break-Even Revisited—Q at which net income is \$0. To get the accounting break-even let OCF = D and solve for $Q = (FC + D) / (P - v)$.

2. Cash Break-Even—Q at which cash flow is \$0. Let OCF = \$0, then the cash break-even point (ignoring taxes) is $Q = FC / (P - v)$:

$$Q = \$45{,}000 / (3 - .30) = 16{,}667$$

3. Financial Break-Even—Q at which NPV = \$0.

What OCF has a present value equal to the initial investment?

$20,000 = OCF × 3.352 (15%, 5-year annuity factor)
OCF = $20,000 / 3.352 = $5,967

What Q gives an OCF of $5,967?

Q = $(45,000 + 5,967) / $(3 – .30) = 18,877 buckets

9.5 OPERATING LEVERAGE

There is almost always some flexibility in production in deciding between fixed and variable costs. Fixed costs, however, generally magnify forecasting errors.

A. The Basic Idea

operating leverage – The degree to which a project or firm uses fixed costs in production. Plant and equipment (capital intensive), and noncancellable rentals are typical sources of fixed costs.

B. Implications of Operating Leverage

Since fixed costs do not change with sales, they make good situations better and bad situations worse, i.e., they "lever" results.

C. Measuring Operating Leverage

Degree of operating leverage (DOL)—degree to which a percentage change in Q (quantity) affects operating cash flow.

Percentage change in OCF = DOL × percentage change in Q

DOL = 1 + FC / OCF

DOL depends upon the Q you start with in determining OCF above.

T9.11: Fairways DOL (2 pages)

Example: Fairways DOL

At Q = 20,000 buckets (and ignoring taxes), OCF for Fairways is $9,000 and fixed costs are $45,000.

DOL = 1 + ($45,000 / $9,000) = 6

If the number of buckets should increase by 5%, OCF should change by (6 × 5%) = 30%. At 21,000 buckets OCF = –$45,000 + ($2.70 × 21,000) = $11,700 which is a 30% increase.

Lecture Tip, page 316: *An alternative calculation could also be presented to the class. With Q = 50 boats, (P – v) = $20, FC = $500, we have:*

(P – v) × Q	$1,000
– FC	– 500
OCF	$ 500

DOL	= (P – v) × Q / OCF = 1 + FC / OCF
$1,000 / $500	= 1 + $500 / $500.

The student could recognize that it is only FC which causes (P – v) × Q to differ from OCF and, if FC = 0, then DOL = 1, and sales revenue and OCF would experience the same rate of change.

D. Operating Leverage and Break-Even

In general, the lower the fixed costs and the degree of operating leverage, the lower is the break-even point (however you measure it). If a project can be started with low fixed costs and later switched to high fixed costs if it turns out well, this is a valuable option.

9.6 ADDITIONAL CONSIDERATIONS IN CAPITAL BUDGETING

A. Managerial Options and Capital Budgeting

Managerial options—the opportunity to change something, which is valuable.

1. *Contingency planning* involves determining what will be done if this or that actually happens. This can be explored with "what if" analysis.

a. *Option to expand*—ignoring the option to expand can result in underestimating NPV.

b. *Option to abandon*—ignoring the option to abandon can result in underestimating NPV because the right to quit a loser is valuable.

c. *Option to wait*—waiting for favorable conditions or simply for some uncertainty to be resolved, is a valuable option.

2. *Strategic options* refer to possible future investments that may result from an investment under consideration.

B. Capital Rationing

Most notions of what is being pursued by capital budgeting rules are void when *soft* or *hard* rationing goes on. *Soft rationing* is self-imposed, often for administrative reasons that have little or nothing to do with value maximization. *Hard rationing*, the lack of funds at any rate, is often associated with financial distress.

9.7 SUMMARY AND CONCLUSIONS

T9.12: Solution to Problem 9.1
T9.13: Solution to Problem 9.6
T9.14: Solution to Problem 9.12
T9.15: Solution to Problem 9.19

CHAPTER 10
SOME LESSONS FROM CAPITAL MARKET HISTORY

TRANSPARENCIES

T10.1: Chapter Outline
T10.2: Percentage Returns (Fig. 10.2)
T10.3: Inflation and Returns (2 pages)
T10.4: Value of a $1 Investment (2 pages)
T10.5: S&P 500 Risk Premiums
T10.6: Small Stock Risk Premiums
T10.7: S&P 500 versus Small Stocks
T10.8: A $1 Investment in Different Types of Portfolios (Fig. 10.4)
T10.9: Year-to-Year Total Returns on Common Stocks
T10.10: Year-to-Year Total Returns on Small-Company Stocks
T10.11: Average Returns and Volatility
T10.12: Year-to-Year Total Returns on Bonds and Bills (Fig. 10.7)
T10.13: Year-to-Year Inflation (Fig. 10.8)
T10.14: Using Capital Market History
T10.15: Average Annual Returns: 1926-1990 (Table 10.2)
T10.16: Frequency Distribution of Returns on Stocks: 1926-1990 (Fig 10.9)
T10.17: Historical Returns, Standard Deviations, and Distributions (Fig. 10.10)
T10.18: The Normal Distribution (Fig. 10.11)
T10.19: Reaction of Stock Prices to New Information
T10.20: Solution to Problem 10.3
T10.21: Solution to Problem 10.13

CHAPTER ORGANIZATION

T10.1: Chapter Outline

10.1 RETURNS
- Dollar Returns
- Percentage Returns

ANNOTATED CHAPTER OUTLINE

Historically, there has been a reward for bearing risk, and, the more risk taken, the larger have been the rewards.

10.1 RETURNS

A. Dollar Returns

Income component—direct cash payments such as dividends or interest

Price change—loosely, capital gain or loss

Total dollar return = dividend income + capital gain (or loss)

The return calculation is unaffected by the decision to cash out or hold securities.

Lecture Tip, page 336: *The issues discussed on pages 335 and 336 need to be stressed. Many students will feel that if you don't sell the security, you won't have to consider the capital gain or loss involved. The instructor may wish to mention that this is true for tax purposes—only realized income must be reported. However, in measuring a security's pretax performance, whether some investor chooses to liquidate his or her position is immaterial. Also, if we did not annualize total returns, we would have a very difficult task comparing and evaluating the various securities available in the market.*

T10.2: Percentage Returns

B. Percentage Returns

Refers to the rate of return per dollar invested.

Percentage Return = Dividend Yield + Capital Gains Yield

Dividend Yield = D_{t+1} / P_t *Capital Gains Yield* = $(P_{t+1} - P_t)/P_t$

10.2 INFLATION AND RETURNS

T10.3: Inflation and Returns (2 pages)

A. Real versus Nominal Returns

Nominal returns—returns <u>not</u> adjusted for inflation; percentage change in nominal dollars.

Real returns—returns that have been adjusted for inflation; percentage change in purchasing power.

Lecture Tip, page 339: *The instructor may wish to introduce the impact of taxes on real purchasing power. The instructor could mention that the real return on risk-free Treasury bills was slightly below 1% over the period 1929 to 1990. If the inflation rate averaged 5%, our nominal return would have been be about 6%. If we are in a 28% marginal federal tax bracket (and we ignore state taxes) and these rates continue, a \$100 investment would realize \$6 before tax, but, on an aftertax basis, we would realize \$4.32—below the inflation rate of 5%. This return would not afford us the ability to purchase an item in the future that we could purchase today for \$100 (assuming the product experienced the same inflation rate as the average product in the inflation index).*

B. The Fisher Effect

1. The Fisher effect is a theoretical relationship between nominal returns, real returns, and the expected inflation rate. Let R be the nominal rate, r be the real rate, and h be the expected inflation rate,

$$(1 + R) = (1 + r) \times (1 + h)$$

hence $R = r + h + (r \times h)$. Since $(r \times h)$ is usually small, the nominal rate is often simply thought of as the real rate plus the expected inflation rate.

2. A definition whereby the real rate can be found by deflating the nominal rate by the inflation rate: $r = (1 + R)/(1 + h) - 1$.

10.3 THE HISTORICAL RECORD

The following are the basis for the nominal, pretax rates of return as reported by Ibbotson and Sinquefield:

-**Common stocks**: 500 largest U.S. companies (the S&P 500 index)
-**Small stocks**: smallest 20% of U.S. firms listed on the NYSE
-**Long-term corporate bonds**: high-quality, 20 years to maturity
-**Long-term government bonds**: U.S. government bonds, 20 years to maturity
-**T-bills**, 3 months to maturity
-also annual rates of inflation measured by the CPI

Lecture Tip, page 341: *Many students may not recall their statistics, and a brief review may be in order.*

Security returns are examples of random variables*—categories of numbers for which in any particular instance more things can happen than will happen—and the things that can happen have an associated probability of occurrence.*

Random variables are typically characterized by their probability distributions (i.e., a graph, table, or function that relates the potential values of the random variable to its associated probabilities) along with measures of its central tendency and dispersion (the deviation from that central tendency). The normal distribution is a common probability distribution; mean, median, and mode measure central tendency, while variance and standard deviation are common measures of dispersion.

A. A First Look

T10.4: Value of a $1 Investment (2 pages)

Lecture Tip, page 342: *An expansion on the relationship of various securities' returns could be accomplished through examination of security return data over the period 1970 through 1990 (Table 10.1). The lowest return realized by T-bills was 3.8% in 1972 while the largest return realized by T-bills was 14.7% in 1981. However, the total return of stocks ranged from a low of −26% in 1974 to a high of 37% in 1975 (the second highest returns were 32% in 1980 and 1985). T-bills, reflecting the Fisher effect, experienced their highest returns over the 1970 decade in 1974 (8%), the year in which the S&P 500 realized its lowest return. Additionally, in 1975, when T-bill rates (and inflation) fell back to return 5.8% for the year, the S&P returned 37% (its highest return of the period reported). One could use this data to indicate the degree to which inflation negatively affects stock returns while increasing the nominal return on short-term investments.*

Lecture Tip, page 343: *The set of transparencies, T 10.4, T 10.5, T 10.6 and T 10.7, are provided if the instructor wishes to further explore the historical return behavior relative to the January effect extensively discussed in the literature. The transparencies show both the historical returns with the month of January excluded and monthly risk premiums of the S&P 500 and small stocks. The instructor may wish to present this information following the examination of Figure 10.4 (Transparency 10.8). This information may also be appropriate for the discussion of Section 10.4, which investigates risk premiums on securities.*

The instructor might present some plausible reasons for the existence of the January effect. Some plausible reasons cited by financial theorists are: 1) Tax loss selling—small firms are more subject to year-end tax loss selling because of their higher volatilities; 2) Information releases—January is a month containing many important corporate news releases, or 3) Problems in measurement for small firms attributed to the bid/ask spread. For a more detailed discussion of the January effect, one could refer to the article, "Size-Related Anomalies and Stock Return Seasonality" by Donald B. Keim, published in the June, 1983 edition of the Journal of Financial Economics.

T10.5: S&P 500 Risk Premiums
T10.6: Small Stock Risk Premiums
T10.7: S&P 500 versus Small Stocks
T10.8: A $1 Investment in Different Types of Portfolios (Fig. 10.4)

B. A Closer Look

T10.9: Year-to-Year Total Returns on Common Stocks (Fig. 10.4)
T10.10: Year-to-Year Total Returns on Small-Company Stocks (Fig. 10.5)

10.4 AVERAGE RETURNS: THE FIRST LESSON

T10.11: Average Returns and Volatility
T10.12: Year-to-Year Total Returns on Bonds and Bills (Fig. 10.7)
T10.13: Year-to-Year Inflation (Fig. 10.8)

A. Calculating Average Returns

$$\sum_{i=1}^{T} \frac{R_i}{T} \quad \text{add them up, divide by T}$$

B. Average Returns: The Historical Record

Average historical returns, 1926-1990

Investment	Average return %
Common stocks	12.1
Small stocks	17.8
Long-term corporate bonds	5.5
Long-term government bonds	4.9
U.S. Treasury bills	3.7
Inflation	3.2

C. Risk Premiums

T10.14: Using Capital Market History

Using the T-bill rate as the risk-free return and common stocks as an average risk, define the *excess return* as the difference between an average risk return and returns on T-bills.

Risk premium—reward for bearing risk, the difference between a risky investment return and the risk-free rate.

Lecture Tip, page 347: *The instructor should mention that this analysis of risk and return is based on annual data. If our investment horizon is extended over a longer period, common stocks, as evidenced by history, may be less of a risk that would be suggested by annual data. Although there is a fair probability than we could experience* *a negative return during a particular year, it is highly unlikely that we would experience a return from common stocks below that realized by T-bills if we would consider a five-year holding period. Based on historical returns, if we extended a holding period to ten years, the probability would be extremely small that common stocks would underperform T-bills. The instructor could suggest to the student that if one is saving for retirement in an I.R.A., defined contribution pension plan, or some similar vehicle, it would only be logical for the student, who will soon be an employee confronted with this decision, to place 100% of the invested funds into common stock and not worry about short-term value fluctuations. History indicates the student will be significantly ahead when ready to retire in the Bahamas.*

T10.15: Average Annual Returns: 1926-1990 (Table 10.2)

D. The First Lesson

Risky investments earn a risk premium. For common stocks the average risk premium has been 8.4% (historically).

10.5 THE VARIABILITY OF RETURNS: THE SECOND LESSON

A. Frequency Distributions and Variability

T10.16: Distribution of Returns on Common Stocks, 1926-1990 (Fig. 10.9)

B. The Historical Variance and Standard Deviation

Historical returns constitute a sample, so sample statistics are in order.

Variance—the average squared deviation between actual returns and their mean

$$VAR(R) \equiv \sigma^2 = \frac{\sum_{i=1}^{T}\left(R_i - E(R)\right)^2}{T - 1}$$

Example: Variance of common stock returns, 1985-1988

Year	Actual return	Average return	Deviation	Square deviatic
1985	.3216	.1817	.1399	.01957
1986	.1847	.1817	.0030	.00000
1987	.0523	.1817	–.1294	.01674
1988	.1681	.1817	–.0136	.00018
Totals	.7267		0.00	.03651

So, VAR(R) = .03651/(4 – 1) = .01217 and standard deviation = .1103.

C. The Historical Record

T10.17: Historical Returns, Standard Deviations, and Distributions (Fig. 10.10)

D. Normal Distribution

T10.18: The Normal Distribution and Common Stock Returns

Historical returns on securities have probability distributions that are approximately normal. The normal distribution is completely described by its mean and variance. Common stock returns have a mean of 12.1% and standard deviation of about 21%. An observation on a normally distributed random variable has a 66% chance of being within plus or minus one standard deviation of the mean, and a 95% chance of being within plus or minus two standard deviations.

E. The Second Lesson

Based upon the means and variances of securities' historical returns, the second lesson is:

The greater the potential reward, the greater is the risk.

F. Using Capital Market History

Based upon the historical risk premium to common stocks, an investment of "average risk" should return about 8.4% above the T-bill rate.

Lecture Tip, page 356: *It is often difficult to get students to appreciate the risk involved in investing in common stocks. They see the average return and largely ignore the variance. A simple exercise illustrating the risk of the different securities can be performed using Table 10.1. Each student (or the entire class) is given some endowment "points" to invest. They are then allowed to pick a security class. Using a random number table and the last two digits of the year, the security's distribution is randomly sampled. The endowment points are then adjusted by the draw outcome. The exercise is most telling when the number of draws is limited to between 1 and 5.*

10.6 CAPITAL MARKET EFFICIENCY

Efficient capital market—market in which current market prices fully reflect available information. That is, one in which costless trading rules do not consistently beat the market.

A. Price Behavior in an Efficient Market

T10.19: Reaction of Stock Prices to New Information

B. The Efficient Market Hypothesis

Efficient market hypothesis (EMH)—asserts that modern U.S. stock markets are, as a practical matter, efficient.

The important implication of the EMH is securities represent *zero NPV* investments—meaning that they are expected to return just exactly their risk-adjusted rate.

Competition among investors and traders makes a market efficient.

Lecture Tip, page 359: *Although a full discussion of efficient markets goes beyond the scope of introductory corporate finance courses, the instructor may wish to ask the students if they have ever heard of a "hot investment buy." Most students probably have heard a friend claim to have such a tip, or the students have heard someone mention that a broker recommended the purchase of a particular company. The instructor could then question the students concerning the value of this information. "If this company was undervalued, why wouldn't the investing community, with all its high-paid security analysts, be purchasing stock since they would have access to this information prior to when we receive it from a stockbroker?"*

Some students may also have the feeling that since some companies, such as Phillip Morris or Wal Mart, have realized extremely large returns over their recent history, there may be some easy money to be made. One could simply mention that the past earnings history is what has driven its price to the current lofty levels but the current price has already factored in (discounted) the market's belief of these companies' future earnings potential.

C. Some Common Misconceptions about the EMH

1. Market efficiency does not mean that it doesn't make a difference how you invest, since the risk/return trade-off still applies, but rather that you can't expect to consistently "beat the market" on a risk-adjusted basis using costless trading strategies.

2. Stock price fluctuations are evidence that the market is efficient since new information is constantly arriving—prices that don't change are evidence of inefficiency.

3. The EMH doesn't say prices are random. Instead, the previously unknown information that causes price *changes* arrives in random fashion. As a result, price changes can't be predicted before they happen.

Ethics Note, page 360: *Program trading is simply automated trading generated by computer algorithms designed to react to changes in the market. Program trading enables traders to quickly respond to up or down market movements. Thus, program trading occurs more quickly than traditional floor trading. It has been argued that it is unethical for investment banking houses to operate automated trading programs for their own accounts. One reason is that the bank, with its high speed, automated response, may be trading ahead of its customers. If this trading affects prices, then the bank is not acting in the best interests of its customers.*

There has been a great deal of discussion about the impact of program trading on market volatility, and there doesn't seem to be a real consensus. In any case, it is clear that program trading can impact the market. For example, a large, erroneously executed sell order (which was literally a clerical mistake) on March 25, 1992 resulted in a 12 point loss in the DJIA (a .31% drop in the DJIA's value). This trade occurred during the final minute of trading, 3:58 - 3:59 p.m. Had the error occurred earlier in the trading day, this action could have caused a greater drop in market value.

D. The Forms of Market Efficiency

1. *Weak form efficiency*—A form of the theory that suggests you can't beat the market by knowing past prices.

2. *Semi-strong efficiency*—Perhaps the most controversial form of the theory, it suggests you can't consistently beat the market using publicly available information. That is, you can't win knowing what everyone else knows.

3. *Strong form efficiency*—The form of the theory that states no information of any kind can be used to beat the market. Evidence shows this form does not hold.

Capital market history and the EMH:

1. Prices respond very rapidly to new information.
2. Future prices are difficult to predict.
3. Mispriced stocks (those whose future price level can be predicted accurately) are difficult to identify and exploit.

Ethics Note, page 361: *Insider trading is illegal, but determination of what constitutes insider trading is difficult. Rule 10B-5 of the Security and Exchange Act of 1934 states: "It shall be unlawful for any person, directly or indirectly, by use of any means or instrumentality of interstate commerce, or of the mails, or of any facility on a national securities exchange, (1) to employ any device, scheme, or artifice to defraud, (2) to make any untrue statement of a material fact or omit to state a material fact necessary in order to make the statements made, in light of the circumstances under which they were made, not misleading, (3) to engage in any act, practice, or course of business which operates or would operate as a fraud or deceit upon any person, in connection with the purchase or sale of any security."*

While from this rule any act that would materially manipulate the market would be illegal, several court cases have more clearly defined insider trading. For insider trading to exist, there must be a fiduciary relationship between the parties. Actions of the inside trader do not have to meet the legal requirements of being a fraud; they merely have to have the appearance of acting as a fraud or deceit. Accidental discovery does not constitute a fiduciary relationship.

The court decided in Chiarella v. United States *that an employee of a printing firm, who was requested to proofread proxies which contained unannounced tender offers (and unnamed targets) was not guilty of insider trading because the employee determined the identity of the target through his own expertise.*

However, a member of a company's board of directors, who has knowledge of the company's future prospects, may not individually trade on this information prior to public disclosure. See SEC v. Texas Gulf Sulfur, 401 F.2d 833 (2d Cir. 1968).

10.7 SUMMARY AND CONCLUSIONS

T10.20: Solution to Problem 10.3
T10.21: Solution to Problem 10.13

CHAPTER 11
RETURN, RISK, AND THE SECURITY MARKET LINE

TRANSPARENCIES

T11.1: Chapter Outline
T11.2: Calculating the Expected Return
T11.3: Calculating the Variance
T11.4: Calculation of the Expected Return (Table 11.3)
T11.5: Expected Returns and Variances
T11.6: Portfolio Expected Returns
T11.7: Portfolio Variance
T11.8: Portfolio Expected Returns and Variances
T11.9: Announcements, Surprises, and Expected Returns
T11.10: Standard Deviations of Annual Portfolio Returns
T11.11: Portfolio Diversification (Fig. 11.1)
T11.12: Beta Coefficients for Selected Stocks
T11.13: Portfolio Betas
T11.14: Portfolio Expected Return and Beta
T11.15: Return, Risk, and Equilibrium
T11.16: The Capital Asset Pricing Model
T11.17: The Security Market Line (SML) (Fig. 11.4)
T11.18: Solution to Problem 11.7
T11.19: Solution to Problem 11.15

CHAPTER ORGANIZATION

T11.1: Chapter Outline

11.1 EXPECTED RETURNS AND VARIANCES
- Expected Return
- Calculating the Variance

11.2 PORTFOLIOS
- Portfolio Weights
- Portfolio Expected Returns
- Portfolio Variance

11.3 ANNOUNCEMENTS, SURPRISES, AND EXPECTED RETURNS
Expected and Unexpected Returns
Announcements and News

11.4 RISK: SYSTEMATIC AND UNSYSTEMATIC
Systematic and Unsystematic Risk
Systematic and Unsystematic Components of Return

11.5 DIVERSIFICATION AND PORTFOLIO RISK
The Effect of Diversification: Another Lesson from Market History
The Principle of Diversification
Diversification and Unsystematic Risk
Diversification and Systematic Risk

11.6 SYSTEMATIC RISK AND BETA
The Systematic Risk Principle
Measuring Systematic Risk
Portfolio Betas

11.7 THE SECURITY MARKET LINE
Beta and the Risk Premium
The Security Market Line

11.8 THE SML AND THE COST OF CAPITAL: A PREVIEW
The Basic Idea
The Cost of Capital

11.9 SUMMARY AND CONCLUSIONS

ANNOTATED CHAPTER OUTLINE

11.1 EXPECTED RETURNS AND VARIANCES

In this section, we are concerned with finding central tendency and dispersion measures when given probabilities of *future* events.

A. Expected Return

T11.2: Calculating the Expected Return

Let S denote the total number of states of the world, R_i the return in state i, and p_i the probability of state i. Then the expected return is given by:

$$E(R) = \sum_{i=1}^{S}\left(p_i \times R_i \right)$$

Example:

(1) State of economy	(2) Probability of state	(3) Return if state occurs	Product (2)×(3)
+1% change in GNP	.25	−.05	−.0125
+2% change in GNP	.50	.15	.0750
+3% change in GNP	.25	.35	.0875
	1.00		$E(R)$ = .15

Projected or expected risk premium—the expected return − risk-free rate = $E(R) - R_f$

B. Calculating the Variance

T11.3: Calculating the Variance
T11.4: Calculation of Expected Return
T11.5: Expected Returns and Variances

$$Var(R) \equiv \sigma^2 = \sum_{i=1}^{S}\left[p_i \times \left(R_i - E(R) \right)^2 \right]$$

Example:

(1) State of Economy	(2) Probability of state	(3) Return if state occurs	(4) Squared deviation	Product (2)×(4)
+1% change in GNP	.25	−.05	.04	.01
+2% change in GNP	.50	.15	0	.00
+3% change in GNP	.25	.35	.04	.01
	1.00	$E(R)$ = .15		σ^2 = .02

Lecture Tip, page 370: *Some students experience confusion in understanding the mathematics of the variance calculation (Equation 10.6) on page 353 and the variance calculation on page 370. Some may have the feeling they should divide the variance of an expected return by (n − 1). The instructor should state that the probabilities account for this division.*

The instructor may wish to have the students think of "n" as the number of possible states we are considering and this could correspond to a particular year.

Example:

Year	*State*	*Stock's Return*
1990	*Boom Year*	*+30%*
1991	*Poor Year*	*−10%*
1992	*Average Year*	*+15%*

Average Return $= (.30 + -.10 + .15) / 3$
$= (1/3) \times .3 + (1/3) \times -.10 + (1/3) \times .15$
$= .1167$

If we feel these events are equally likely in 1993, the variance calculation for the 1993 expected return is identical to dividing by "n."

Variance $= [(.3 - .1167)^2 + (-.10 - .1667)^2 + (.15 - .1667)^2] / 3$
$= 1/3 \times (.3 - .1167)^2 + 1/3 \times (-.10 - .1667)^2 + 1/3 \times (.15 - 1667)^2$

In this situation (1/n) represents the probability of the particular state's occurrence in 1993. This issue is mentioned on page 370 but the concept in this paragraph should be stressed.

11.2 PORTFOLIOS

A portfolio is a collection of securities, such as stocks and bonds, held by an investor.

A. Portfolio Weights

Portfolios can be described by the percentages of the portfolio's total value invested in each security, i.e., by the *portfolio weights.*

Example:

If two securities in a portfolio have a combined value of $10,000 and $6,000 is invested in IBM and $4,000 in GM then

weight IBM	=	$6,000/$10,000	= .60 or 60%
weight GM	=	$4,000/$10,000	= .40 or 40%

B. Portfolio Expected Returns

T11.6: Portfolio Expected Returns

The expected return on a portfolio is the sum of the product of the individual security's expected returns and their portfolio weights. Let x_i denote a security's portfolio weight, then

$$E(R_p) = \sum_{i=1}^{N} \left(x_i \times E(R_i) \right)$$

<u>Example:</u>

If the expected return on IBM stock is 15% and that of GM is 10%, and $6,000 is invested in IBM stock while $4,000 is invested in GM stock, the portfolio expected return is:

$$E(R_p) = \left[x_{IBM} \times E(R_{IBM})\right] + \left[x_{GM} \times E(R_{GM})\right] = [.60 \times .15] + [.40 \times .10] = .13$$

C. Portfolio Variance

T11.7: Portfolio Variance
T11.8: Portfolio Expected Returns and Variances

Unlike expected return, the variance of a portfolio is *not* the weighted sum of the individual security variances. Combining securities into portfolios can reduce the variability of returns.

Example:

Consider a portfolio with equal amounts invested in three stocks:

State of economy	Probability of state	Return to stock A	Return to stock B	Return to stock C	Return on portfolio
+1% change in GNP	.25	−.05	.00	.20	.050
+2% change in GNP	.50	.15	.10	.10	.117
+3% change in GNP	.25	.35	.20	.00	.183
Expected return		.15	.10	.10	.117

The variances of the stock returns and the portfolio return are:

$\sigma_A^2 = .25 \times (-.05 - .15)^2 + .50 \times (.15 - .15)^2 + .25 \times (.35 - .15)^2 = .02$

$\sigma_B^2 = .25 \times (.00 - .10)^2 + .50 \times (.10 - .10)^2 + .25 \times (.20 - .10)^2 = .005$

$\sigma_C^2 = .25 \times (.20 - .10)^2 + .50 \times (.10 - .10)^2 + .25 \times (.00 - .10)^2 = .005$

$\sigma_P^2 = .25 \times (.05 - .117)^2 + .50 \times (.117 - .117)^2 + .25 \times (.183 - .117)^2 = .00221$

The calculations show that the portfolio variance is less than that for the individual securities in the portfolio.

Lecture Tip, page 375: *At this point, the student has experienced a large number of mathematical formulas—probability weights, portfolio weights, and so on. It may be helpful to review all of the calculations, beginning with the process of using the probability weights to calculate an individual stock's variance and ending with the process of using the portfolio weights to calculate a portfolio's variance.*

11.3 ANNOUNCEMENTS, SURPRISES, AND EXPECTED RETURNS

T11.9: Announcements, Surprises, and Expected Returns

A. Expected and Unexpected Returns

Total return = Expected return + Unexpected return

$R = E(R) + U$

The total return, R, differs from the expected return, $E(R)$, because of surprises giving rise to unexpected return, U.

B. Announcements and News

Announcement—the release of information not previously available in its entirety.

Announcements have two parts: *Expected part and surprise part.*

The *expected part* is "discounted" information used by the market to formulate $E(R)$ early on, while the surprise is news that influences U.

"Discounted" information—information that has already been factored into the expected return (price) of a security.

The tie-in to efficient markets is obvious. The assumption here is that markets are semi-strong efficient; that is, public information is incorporated into prices.

Lecture Tip, page 376: *It may be helpful to select a recent news item from the* Wall Street Journal (WSJ) *to support the "Announcement and News" section. As an example, a January 30, 1992, article on page C1 was headlined "Greenspan Sends Prices Into Tailspin—Dow Plunges 47.18, Bonds Fall on Hint of Inaction at Fed." A sentence from the article reads "If investors become convinced that the Fed isn't going to help the economy, a full-blown correction could materialize, some analysts suggested." Such news items could allow the instructor to question the students as to whether such stock price corrections indicate market inefficiency or the market adjusting to new information.*

11.4 RISK: SYSTEMATIC AND UNSYSTEMATIC

A. Systematic and Unsystematic Risk

Risk consists of surprises—unanticipated events. Surprises are of two kinds:

Systematic risk—a surprise that affects a large number of assets, each to a greater or lesser extent—sometimes called *market risk.*

Unsystematic risk—a risk or surprise that affects at most a small number of assets—sometimes called *unique risk.*

Example:

Changes in GNP, interest rates, and inflation are examples of *market risks,* affecting all firms more or less.

A strike, a plant accident, a takeover, and a CEO's resignation are examples of *unique risks.*

Lecture Tip, page 378: *The difference between systematic and unsystematic risk could be expanded using the strike example. The students could be asked to read the paragraph on the oil strike. All should agree this would be a unique or unsystematic effect for one company. However, one might ask the students to consider a strike by the UAW against the auto industry and whether this action could have a carry-over impact on other industries and possibly the entire economy. The students should recognize that it is not the event but rather the impact of the event which determines whether it is a systematic or unsystematic effect.*

B. Systematic and Unsystematic Components of Return

Total return = Expected return + Unexpected return

$R = E(R) + U$

$R = E(R) + \textit{Systematic portion} + \textit{Unsystematic portion}$

Let m denote the *market* or *systematic portion* and ε represent the *unique* or *unsystematic portion* of risk. Then,

$R = E(R) + m + \varepsilon$

11.5 DIVERSIFICATION AND PORTFOLIO RISK

A. The Effect of Diversification: Another Lesson from Market History

Portfolio variability can be quite different from the variability of individual securities (see prior example on portfolio variance).

T11.10: Standard Deviations of Annual Portfolio Returns

A typical single stock on NYSE has a standard deviation of annual returns of 49.24%, while the typical 100 or more stock portfolio of NYSE stocks has a standard deviation of annual returns just under 20%.

B. The Principle of Diversification

T11.11: Portfolio Diversification

Principle of diversification—principle stating that combining imperfectly related assets can produce a portfolio with less variability than the typical individual asset.

The portion of variability present in a typical single security that is not present in a portfolio of securities is termed *diversifiable risk.* The level of variance that is present in collections of assets is termed *undiversifiable risk.*

C. Diversification and Unsystematic Risk

When securities are combined into portfolios, their *unique or unsystematic* risks tend to cancel each other out, leaving only the variability that affects all securities to a greater or lesser degree. Thus, *diversifiable risk* is interchangeable with *unsystematic risk.*

Large portfolios have little or no unsystematic risk.

D. Diversification and Systematic Risk

Systematic risk cannot be eliminated by diversification since it represents the variability due to influences that affect all securities to a greater or lesser extent.

For obvious reasons, *systematic risk* and *undiversifiable risk* apply to the same variability.

Total risk = systematic risk + unsystematic risk

Total risk = undiversifiable risk + diversifiable risk

11.6 SYSTEMATIC RISK AND BETA

A. The Systematic Risk Principle

<u>The principle:</u>
The reward for bearing risk depends only upon the systematic or undiversifiable risk of an investment (since unsystematic risk can be diversified away).

<u>The implication:</u>
The expected return on an asset depends only upon that asset's systematic risk.

A corollary:
No matter how much total risk an asset has, its expected return depends only upon its systematic or undiversifiable risk.

B. Measuring Systematic Risk

Beta coefficient (β)—a measure of how much systematic risk an asset has relative to an average risk asset.

T11.12: Beta Coefficients for Selected Companies

Lecture Tip, page 384: *This point, "the market does not reward risks that are born unnecessarily," should be strongly emphasized, possibly with a reference back to Figure 11.1. Many investment companies offer investors a choice between income-oriented mutual funds, consisting of bonds and stocks in more established companies with higher dividend payouts, and growth-oriented funds which are typically composed of stocks of smaller companies which retain a higher percentage of earnings to reinvest back into the company. Investors desiring growth-oriented funds typically assume a much greater degree of systematic risk and would expect a higher return. However, both funds eliminate the unsystematic element of risk through the diversification these funds provide.*

C. Portfolio Betas

T11.13: Portfolio Betas

While portfolio variance is not equal to a simple weighted sum of individual security variances, portfolio betas are equal to the weighted sum of individual security betas.

Example:

Using betas from Table 11.8 of the text:

(1) Stock	(2) Amount invested	(3) Portfolio weight	(4) Beta coefficient	Product (3)×(4)
IBM	$6,000	50%	.95	.475
General Motors	$4,000	33%	1.05	.350
Wal-Mart	$2,000	17%	1.25	.208
Portfolio	$12,000	100%		1.033

11.7 THE SECURITY MARKET LINE

A. Beta and the Risk Premium

A riskless asset has a beta of 0. When a risky asset ($\beta \neq 0$) is combined with a riskless one, the resulting expected return is the portfolio weighted sum of their expected returns and the portfolio beta is the portfolio weighted sum of their betas. By varying the amount invested in each type of asset, we can get an idea of the relation between portfolio expected return and portfolio beta.

Example:

Let a portfolio be comprised of an investment in Stock A with a beta of 1.2 and expected return of 18%, and a T-bill with a 7% return. Using what has already been said about portfolio returns and betas, some possible portfolio results are:

Proportion invested in Stock A	Proportion invested in R_f	Portfolio expected return	Portfolio beta
0%	100%	7%	0
25%	75%	9.75%	.30
50%	50%	12.50%	.60
75%	25%	15.25%	.90
100%	0%	18%	1.20
125%	–25%	20.75%	1.56

A greater than 100% investment in the risky asset and negative weight on T-bills represent money borrowed at the riskless rate.

The portfolio expected return/beta combinations lie on a straight line with slope

$$\frac{Rise}{Run} = \frac{E(R_A) - R_f}{\beta_A} = \frac{.18 - .07}{1.2} = .092 = 9.2\%$$

1. *The Reward-to-Risk Ratio*: What is the expected return per "unit" of systematic risk? That is, what is the ratio of risk premium to amount of systematic risk? For Stock A in the above example, the ratio is (.18 – .07)/1.2 = .092 or 9.2%, the same as the slope of the Stock A/risk-free asset portfolio line.

2. *The Basic Argument*: Since systematic risk is all that matters in determining expected return, the reward-to-risk ratio, i.e., the risk premium per unit of systematic risk, must be the same for all assets. If it were not, people would buy up the asset offering the higher reward-to-risk ratio and ignore the asset with the lower ratio.

3. *The Fundamental Result*: In an active, competitive market in which only systematic risk affects expected return, *the reward-to-risk ratio must be the same for all assets in the market.* That is,

$$\frac{E(R_A) - R_f}{\beta_A} = \frac{E(R_B) - R_f}{\beta_B}$$

In other words, the expected returns and betas of all assets must plot on the same straight line.

Lecture Tip, page 386: *The instructor may wish to mention that a great number of investors, both individual and institutional, commonly borrow money from their broker to purchase stocks. The interest rate paid on margin accounts is known as the call loan rate, and is slightly above the Treasury bill rate. The intent of such loans is obvious—a higher return for the investor. However, higher potential returns imply higher risks and portfolio betas.*

T11.14: Portfolio Expected Return and Beta
T11.15: Return, Risk, and Equilibrium

Lecture Tip, page 390: *This issue of asset market equilibrium should be strongly emphasized in the class lecture. Rational investors, operating in the same market, would quickly exploit any disequilibrium in which one asset is expected to offer a higher risk-adjusted return than another.*

B. The Security Market Line

The line which gives the expected return/systematic risk combinations of assets in a well functioning, active financial market is called the **security market line.**

T11.16: The Capital Asset Pricing Model
T11.17: The Security Market Line (SML) (Fig. 11.4)

Lecture Tip, page 392: *Although the realized market risk premium has on average been about 8.4%, the historical average should not be confused with a current expectation. There is abundant evidence that the realized market return has varied about significantly through time. The historical average value should be treated accordingly. On the other hand, there is currently no really accepted means of coming up with a good* ex ante *estimate of the market risk premium, so the historical average might be as good a guess as any.*

1. *Market Portfolios*: Suppose we have a portfolio of all the assets in the market, and call it the *market portfolio*. This portfolio by definition has "average" systematic risk, i.e., it has a beta of 1. Since all assets must lie on the security market line when appropriately priced, so must the market portfolio. Denote the expected return on the market portfolio $E(R_M)$. Then,

$$\frac{E(R_M) - R_f}{\beta_M} = \frac{E(R_M) - R_f}{1} = E(R_M) - R_f = SML\ slope$$

The slope of the **SML**, $E(R_M) - R_f$, is called the *market risk premium.*

2. *The Capital Asset Pricing Model*: Since the expected return to any asset i, $E(R_i)$, must satisfy the same reward-to-risk ratio as the market portfolio,

$$\frac{E(R_i) - R_f}{\beta_i} = E(R_M) - R_f$$

Rearranging terms gives the *Capital Asset Pricing Model* (*CAPM*) equation

$$E(R_i) = R_f + [\ E(R_M) - R_f\ ] \times \beta_i$$

The CAPM states that the expected return on asset depends upon:

1. *The time value of money,* as measured by R_f.

2. *The reward per unit of systematic risk,* $E(R_M) - R_f$.

3. *The asset's systematic risk,* as measured by β.

Example:

Suppose an asset has twice the systematic risk as an average risk asset. That is, suppose a stock has a beta of 2. If the risk-free rate as measured by T-bills is 7%, and the expected risk premium on the market portfolio is 5%, what is the stock's expected return according to the SML?

$E(R_i) = .07 + (.05)(2) = .07 + .10 = .17$ or 17%

11.8 THE SML AND THE COST OF CAPITAL: A PREVIEW

A. The Basic Idea

To determine the appropriate discount rate for use in evaluating an investment's worth we need to ascertain the investment's riskiness and determine the expected return on alternative investments of similar risk. That is:

1. Determine an investment's amount of systematic risk, β.
2. Find the expected return in the financial market for that β.

Lecture Tip, page 395: *Students will remember that, under efficient markets, an investment in a publicly-traded company will result in an NPV of $0. The instructor may wish to mention that the efficient markets hypothesis does not imply that a company's investments in new projects would have an NPV of $0. Companies always attempt to invest in projects with a positive NPV. Companies that have consistently been successful in this endeavor will trade at higher prices, reflecting the market's belief that they will probably continue to do so in the future (a high P/E ratio). This success has driven the company's stock price up to the level where the NPV will be 0 for an investor who purchases this company's stock. Conversely, if a company has a history of realizing a negative NPV on its projects, the stock price will fall reflecting this expectation of poor performance, but the investment in this poorer-performing company will still be expected to return an NPV of $0; i.e., return is a function of the beta risk.*

B. The Cost of Capital

Cost of capital—the minimum expected return an investment must offer to be attractive. Sometimes referred to as the *required return.*

The cost of capital, when taken as the market rate on a financial asset of equal systematic risk, is an *opportunity cost.*

11.9 SUMMARY AND CONCLUSIONS

T11.18: Solution to Problem 11.7
T11.19: Solution to Problem 11.15

CHAPTER 12
LONG-TERM FINANCING: AN INTRODUCTION

TRANSPARENCIES

T12.1: Chapter Outline
T12.2: Features of a Hypothetical bond
T12.3: The Bond Indenture
T12.4: Bond Ratings
T12.5: Preferred Stock
T12.6: Common Stock
T12.7: Effects of a Stock Sale
T12.8: Patterns of Corporate Financing (Table 12.2, 2 pages)
T12.9: Bankruptcy Liquidation
T12.10: Absolute Priority Rule
T12.11: The Long-Term Financial Deficit (Fig. 12.2)
T12.12: Bankruptcy Reorganization
T12.13: Solution to Problem 12.2
T12.14: Solution to Problem 12.9
T12.15: Solution to Problem 12.10

CHAPTER ORGANIZATION

T12.1: Chapter Outline

12.1 CORPORATE LONG-TERM DEBT
Is It Debt or Equity?
Long-Term Debt: The Basics
The Indenture

12.2 BOND RATINGS

12.3 SOME DIFFERENT TYPES OF BONDS
Zero Coupon Bonds
Floating-Rate Bonds
Other Types of Bonds

12.4 PREFERRED STOCK
Stated Value
Cumulative and Noncumulative Dividends
Is Preferred Stock Really Debt?
The Preferred Stock Puzzle

12.5 COMMON STOCK
Par and No Par Stock
Authorized versus Issued Common Stock
Capital in Excess of Par Value
Retained Earnings
Market Values versus Book Values
Shareholders' Rights
Dividends
Classes of Stock

12.6 PATTERNS OF LONG-TERM FINANCING

12.7 LONG-TERM FINANCING UNDER FINANCIAL DISTRESS AND BANKRUPTCY
Liquidation and Reorganization
Agreements to Avoid Bankruptcy

12.8 SUMMARY AND CONCLUSIONS

ANNOTATED CHAPTER OUTLINE

12.1 CORPORATE LONG-TERM DEBT

-Creditors generally have no voting rights.
-Payment of interest on debt is a tax deductible business expense.
-Unpaid debt is a liability, which if not paid may cause bankruptcy.

A. Is it Debt or Equity?

B. Long-Term Debt: The Basics

Major forms are *public issue* and *private placement.*

T12.2: Features of a Hypothetical Bond

Long-term debt—loosely, bonds with a maturity of one year or more

Short-term debt—less than a year to maturity, also called *unfunded debt*

Bond—strictly speaking, secured debt; but used to describe all long-term debt

C. The Indenture

T12.3: The Bond Indenture and Bond Types

Indenture—written agreement between the firm and the creditors detailing the terms of borrowing. Also known as *deed of trust*. Generally, the indenture includes the following provisions:

1. Terms of the bonds
2. The total face amount of bonds issued
3. A description of any property used as security
4. The repayment arrangements
5. Any call provisions
6. Any protective covenants

1. Terms of a bond—face value, par value, and form

   Registered form—ownership is recorded, payment made directly to owner
   Bearer form—payment is made to holder (bearer) of bond

2. Security—debt classified by collateral and mortgage

   Collateral—strictly, pledged securities
   Mortgage securities—secured by a mortgage on real property—*blanket mortgage* pledges all real property

   Debenture—an unsecured debt with 10 or more years to maturity
   Note—a debenture with 10 years or less to maturity

3. Seniority—order of precedence of claims

   Subordinated debenture—of lower priority than senior debt

4. Repayment—early repayment in some form is typical

   Sinking fund—an account managed by the bond trustee for early redemption

5. Call provision—allows company to "call" or repurchase part or all of issue

   Call premium—amount by which the call price exceeds the par value
   Deferred call—firm can't call bonds for some designated time
   Call protected—what a bond is during the period it can't be called

6. Protective covenants—indenture conditions that limit the actions of firms

   Negative covenant—"thou shalt not" sell major assets, merge, pay dividends in excess of $X, and so on

   Positive covenant—"thou shall" keep working capital at or above $X, provide audited financial statements, keep property insured and in good condition, and so on

Lecture Tip, page 411: *The instructor might note that bearer bonds will become obsolete in the near future. Since bearer bonds are not registered with the corporation, the bondholders could simply not report the interest income received on their tax return. In an attempt to eliminate this potential for tax evasion, all bonds issued after July 1983 must be in registered form.*

Lecture Tip, page 411: *The instructor may wish to have the class consider the difference in a secured bond's yield versus a debenture's yield. Since a secured bond offers additional protection in the event of bankruptcy, investors would have a preference for this type of security and, accordingly, be willing to accept a lower yield-to-maturity or return. The added security for the bondholder comes at a cost—a lower yield. This same principle holds in the case of senior debt versus subordinated debt. However, in the case of a bond issued by a financially strong company, such as Phillip Morris, this added protection may be irrelevant and result in an insignificant impact on yield.*

12.2 BOND RATINGS

T12.4: Bond Ratings

12.3 SOME DIFFERENT TYPES OF BONDS

A. Zero Coupon Bonds

Zero coupon bonds are bonds offered at deep discounts because there are no coupons. Although no interest is actually paid, firms deduct the implicit interest amount while holders must report it as income. The interest is equal to the period-to-period change in the amortized value of the bond.

Lecture Tip, page 414: *Most students are familiar with Series EE savings bonds. The instructor could mention that these are essentially zero coupon bonds. The investor pays one-half of the face value and must hold the bond for a given number of years before the face value of the savings bond is realized. An attractive feature of the savings bond is that, unlike nongovernment zero coupon bonds, the investor would not have to pay taxes on the savings bond until the bond is redeemed by the investor. The instructor could also mention that government bonds are not taxed by state governments, although federal taxes would apply. However, the disadvantage of a savings bond is a lower yield since it has no default risk.*

B. Floating-Rate Bonds

Floating-rate bonds (floaters)—coupon payments adjust periodically according to an index such as the T-bill rate or the rate on other Treasury issues. Other common features:

1. *put* provision—holder can sell back to issuer at par
2. coupon rate has a floor and a ceiling

Lecture Tip, page 416: *The instructor may wish to mention that the floating-rate bond concept is also involved with the variable rate mortgage many students may select when purchasing their future homes. Such rates are often tied to rates on marketable securities and the mortgage interest cost will be adjusted, typically on an annual basis, to reflect changes in the interest rate environment. From the bank's perspective the homeowner has signed (issued) a "floating-rate bond" which the bank holds as its investment. Additionally, many variable rate mortgages involve caps.*

A detailed summary of the factors that affect interest rate changes is provided on a daily basis in the "Credit Markets" section of The Wall Street Journal.

C. Other Types of Bonds

Income bonds—coupon is paid if income is sufficient
Convertible bond—can be traded for a fixed number of shares of stock
Put bond—allows holder to redeem for par (opposite of call)

12.4 PREFERRED STOCK

Preferred stock has precedence over common stock in the payment of dividends and in case of liquidation. Its dividend is usually fixed, and the stock is often without voting rights.

T12.5: Preferred Stock

A. Stated Value

The value to be paid to preferred holders in the event of liquidation.

B. Cumulative and Noncumulative Dividends

A firm's directors can vote to omit the preferred dividend.

Cumulative dividends—current preferred dividend plus all arrearages (unpaid back dividends) to be paid before common stock dividends can be paid.

C. Is Preferred Stock Really Debt?

Why issue or hold preferred? As "stock," 70% of the dividends from preferred are tax exempt for corporate holders (most preferred is held by corporations). So, although the issuer doesn't get any tax break, the yields (and dividends) on preferred are often quite low.

D. The Preferred Stock Puzzle

A substantial amount of preferred stock is issued by regulated utilities who can pass the cost along to customers.

While having some features of debt, preferred can't put the firm in bankruptcy. Also, the tax disadvantage only applies if the firm is expected to pay taxes. Finally, preferred sometimes doesn't come with voting rights.

12.5 COMMON STOCK

Common stock—a claim against the earnings and assets of the firm with lowest precedence, but often with voting rights.

T12.6: Common Stock

A. Par and No Par Stock

Par—some value assigned to stock for no particular reason
Dedicated capital—total par value of shares outstanding
No par—no particular value assigned

B. Authorized versus Issued Common Stock

All shares to be sold must be *authorized* by the articles of incorporation.

Limits to authorized shares
-Some states impose taxes based on authorized shares.
-Current shareholders may not want a large number authorized.

C. Capital in Excess of Par Value

This is also known as *capital surplus* or *additional paid-in capital.*

D. Retained Earnings

T12.7: Effects of a Stock Sale

Retained earnings are earnings not paid out as dividends.

Book value—the sum of par value, capital in excess of par and accumulated retained earnings.

E. Market Values versus Book Values

Market value—what the stock actually trades for.

Treasury stock—stock issued and then later repurchased by the firm.

F. Shareholder Rights

Basically, they get to elect the directors.

1. *Cumulative voting*—when the directors are all elected at once. Total votes that each shareholder may cast are usually equal to the number of shares × the number of directors to be elected. In general, if N directors are to be elected, it takes 1/(N + 1) percent of the stock + 1 share to assure a deciding vote for one directorship. Good for getting minority shareholder representation on the board.

2. *Straight (majority) voting*—the directors are elected one at a time, and every share gets one vote. Good for freezing out minority shareholders.

> *Staggered elections*—directors' terms are rotated so that they aren't elected at the same time. This makes it more difficult for a minority to elect a director, and makes takeovers harder.

3. *Proxy voting*—grant of authority by a shareholder to someone else to vote his or her shares. *Proxy fight*—struggle between management and outsiders for control of the board, waged by getting shareholders' proxies.

Other rights usually include:

1. sharing proportionately in dividends paid
2. sharing proportionately in any liquidation value
3. voting on matters of importance (e.g., mergers)

Sometimes shareholder rights include:

1. the right to purchase any new stock sold—the *preemptive right*

Lecture Tip, page 423: *The instructor may wish to add that, even though corporate democracy rules, political democracy does have its place at the annual stockholders' meeting. All shareholders are invited and welcome, even if an individual shareholder owns only one share of a company's stock. Although the meeting's agenda might dictate otherwise, any individual shareholder would normally have the right to question management regarding the company's operations.*

G. Dividends

Dividends—a return on capital directly or indirectly contributed to the corporation by the shareholders.

1. Payment of dividends is at the discretion of the board of directors. A firm cannot default on an undeclared dividend, nor be made bankrupt because of nonpayment of dividends.

2. Dividends are not tax deductible for the paying firm.

3. Dividends received by individuals are usually considered ordinary income. Corporations may exclude at least 70% of dividends received from other firms from taxable income.

H. Classes of Stock

Many firms have more than one class of stock, one purpose of which may be to create unequal voting power.

12.6 PATTERNS OF LONG-TERM FINANCING

Lecture Tip, page 427: *The instructor may wish to add that changes in the tax codes may influence the corporate world's willingness to issue greater quantities of debt. Tax reforms enacted over the 1980's lowered the top marginal tax rate of individuals below the top corporate tax rate. This change may have encouraged corporations to issue greater quantities of debt and retire equity, since the corporation could better use the interest deduction to shelter operating income from taxation.*

T12.8: Patterns of Corporate Financing (Table 12.2, 2 pages)

Several features of long-term financing:

1. Internally generated funds have been the dominant source.
2. The primary use of such funds has been capital spending.
3. Corporations have been net issuers of securities.

12.7 LONG-TERM FINANCING UNDER FINANCIAL DISTRESS AND BANKRUPTCY

Financial distress:
1. *Business failure*—business terminates with a loss to creditors
2. *Legal bankruptcy*—bankruptcy is a legal proceeding for liquidating or reorganizing
3. *Technical insolvency*—when a firm defaults on a legal obligation
4. *Accounting insolvency*—happens when total book liabilities exceed total book assets

Bankruptcy—here, the transfer of some or all the firm's assets to creditors.

A. Liquidation and Reorganization

Liquidation—termination of the business, selling off all assets.

Reorganization—keeping the business going, often issuing new securities to replace the old.

T12.9: Bankruptcy Liquidation

1. *Bankruptcy liquidation* (*Chapter 7* or *straight liquidation*)—involves the following typical sequence of events:

   1. A petition is filed in federal court (voluntary or involuntary).
   2. A trustee-in-bankruptcy is elected by creditors to liquidate assets.
   3. After bankruptcy administration costs are paid, liquidation proceeds are distributed to creditors.
   4. If anything remains, shareholders get it.

T12.10: Absolute Priority Rule
T12.11: The Long-Term Financial Deficit (Fig. 12.2)

Absolute Priority Rule (APR)—rule giving the distribution of proceeds from liquidation. The following is a summary of the priorities:

1. Expenses associated with the bankruptcy
2. Other expenses arising after filing but before appointment of a trustee
3. Wages, salaries, commissions
4. Contributions to employee benefit plans
5. Consumer claims
6. Government tax claims
7. Unsecured creditors
8. Preferred stockholders
9. Common stockholders

Two qualifications to the APR:

1. Secured creditors get the proceeds from the sale of the security.
2. Courts have seen fit to reorder the priorities.

T12.12: Bankruptcy Reorganization

2. *Bankruptcy Reorganization* (*Chapter 11*)—involves the following typical sequence of events:

1. Voluntary or involuntary petition is filed.
2. A judge approves or disapproves the petition and a time for filing claims is set.
3. The firm continues to run the business.
4. The firm submits a reorganization plan.
5. Creditors and shareholders are divided into classes. A class accepts the plan if a dollar-amount majority agrees.
6. If accepted by creditors, the plan is confirmed by court.
7. Payments in cash, property, and securities made; new securities may be issued.

B. Agreements to Avoid Bankruptcy

Voluntary arrangements to restructure debt are often made. *Extension* postpones the date of payment, while *composition* involves a reduced payment.

12.8 SUMMARY AND CONCLUSIONS

T12.13: Solution to Problem 12.2
T12.14: Solution to Problem 12.9
T12.15: Solution to Problem 12.10

CHAPTER 13
ISSUING SECURITIES TO THE PUBLIC

TRANSPARENCIES

T13.1: Chapter Outline
T13.2: The Basic Procedure for a New Issue
T13.3: A Red Herring
T13.4: A Tombstone Ad
T13.5: Alternative Issue Methods
T13.6: Initial Public Offerings Categorized by Gross Proceeds (Table 13.2)
T13.7: Top 10 U.S. Underwriters for 1990 (Table 13.3, 2 pages)
T13.8: Average Initial Returns by Month for SEC-Registered IPOs (Fig. 13.2)
T13.9: Number of Offerings by Month for SEC-Registered IPOs (Fig. 13.3)
T13.10: Costs of Going Public (Table 13.7)
T13.11: Five Conclusions on Flotation Costs
T13.12: Rights Offerings: Basics
T13.13: Rights Offerings: Value of a Right
T13.14: Rights Offerings: Issues
T13.15: New Issues and Dilution
T13.16: Solution to Problem 13.2
T13.17: Solution to Problem 13.8
T13.18: Solution to Problem 13.9

CHAPTER ORGANIZATION

T13.1 Chapter Outline

13.1 THE PUBLIC ISSUE

The Basic Procedure for a New Issue

13.2 ALTERNATIVE ISSUE METHODS

13.3 THE CASH OFFER
- Choosing an Underwriter
- Types of Underwriting
- The Aftermarket
- The Green Shoe Provision
- The Underwriters
- The Offering Price and Underpricing

13.4 NEW EQUITY SALES AND THE VALUE OF THE FIRM

13.5 THE COSTS OF ISSUING SECURITIES

13.6 RIGHTS
- The Mechanics of a Rights Offering
- Number of Rights Needed to Purchase a Share
- The Value of a Right
- Ex Rights
- The Underwriting Arrangements
- Rights Offers: The Case of Time Warner
- Effects on Shareholders
- The New Issues Puzzle

13.7 DILUTION
- Dilution of Proportionate Ownership
- Dilution of Value: Book versus Market Values

13.8 ISSUING LONG-TERM DEBT

13.9 SHELF REGISTRATION

13.10 SUMMARY AND CONCLUSIONS

ANNOTATED CHAPTER OUTLINE

13.1 THE PUBLIC ISSUE

A. The Basic Procedure for a New Issue

T13.2: The Basic Procedure for a New Issue

1. Obtain approval from Board of Directors.
2. File *registration statement* with the SEC. (Regulation A exempts issues of less than $1.5 million from most registration requirements.)
3. SEC requires a minimum 20-day waiting period; firm distributes *preliminary prospectus (red herring).*
4. On effective date price is set and selling begins.

Lecture Tip, page 444: *The instructor may wish to add that the registration statement requirements imposed on corporations by the SEC results in corporations rarely issuing commercial paper in maturities longer than nine months.*

T13.3: A Red Herring

Lecture Tip, page 445: *The instructor could ask the class why the SEC would not require a corporation to list an offering price. The class should remember the volatility that can occur in the market and the impact of systematic risk on security prices. Should market conditions improve between the date of the preliminary prospectus issuance and the date of actual sale, one might expect the securities would be valued at a higher price. The opposite could occur should market conditions deteriorate.*

T13.4: A Tombstone Ad

13.2 ALTERNATIVE ISSUE METHODS

T13.5: Alternative Issue Methods

Public Offer

General cash offer—offered to public
Rights offer—new stock offered to current shareholders
IPO (Initial public offering)—unseasoned new issue
Seasoned new issue—offered by firm with shares in circulation

13.3 THE CASH OFFER

Underwriters—investment firms that act as intermediaries between the issuing firm and the public. Some services they provide include:

1. advice on type of security and offer method
2. advice on price
3. selling

Syndicate—a group of underwriters, formed to share the underwriting risk.

Spread—the difference between the underwriter's buying price and the offering price; it is the underwriter's main source of compensation.

A. Choosing an Underwriter

Competitive offer basis—taking the underwriter that bids the most for the securities.
Negotiated offer basis—the more common (and expensive) method.

Lecture Tip, page 447: *The underwriter's spread is defined as the difference between offering price and the price at which the underwriter purchases the securities from the issuing corporation. In a study of utility stock issues by Bhagat and Frost, published in the* Journal of Financial Economics *in 1986, average spreads were found to be lower for competitive issues (3.1%) than for negotiated issues (3.9%). However, as the textbook states, "there is evidence that competitive underwriting is cheaper" but "the dominance of negotiated underwriting...[is] the subject of ongoing debate."*

Additionally, if a company's stock is particularly risky, the spread demanded by the underwriter would tend to be larger. This would be caused by the underwriter bidding less for the shares, relative to a given offering price.

B. Types of Underwriting

1. *Firm commitment underwriting*—the most prevalent form for seasoned new issues. The underwriter buys the entire issue of securities at an agreed upon price from the issuer, and assumes responsibility for reselling them.

2. *Best efforts underwriting*—common with IPOs, the underwriter promises to sell as much as possible at the offer price, but unsold securities are returned to the issuer.

T13.6: Initial Public Offerings Categorized by Gross Proceeds (Table 13.2)

C. The Aftermarket

The period during which the syndicate agrees to sell only for the offer price. The principal underwriter may *buy* shares below the market price to "stabilize" (a euphemism for "take the brunt of the punishment for mispricing") the market.

D. The Green Shoe Provision

Sometimes called an *overallotment option, the Green Shoe provision* gives members of the syndicate the right to buy additional shares (beyond those originally set to be sold) from the issuer at the original offer price. Since it is only invoked if the issue is selling above the offer price, it is a cost to issuers and a benefit to the underwriters.

E. The Underwriters

T13.7: Top 10 U.S. Underwriters for 1991 (Table 13.3, 2 pages)

F. The Offering Price and Underpricing

The underpricing of new issues, especially IPOs, appears to be common.

1. Evidence on underpricing

2. Why does underpricing exist?
Smaller, more speculative issues account for much of the underpricing.

It is argued that because "underpriced" IPOs are oversubscribed while "overpriced" issues are avoided, underpricing is necessary to allow the average (read, uninformed) investor to make a normal return across all issues.

Underpricing is a kind of insurance for underwriters against legal suits by angry stock buyers if issues were overpriced. Underwriters must balance this against the potential loss of firms' business for underpricing.

Lecture Tip, page 449: The Wall Street Journal *reports numerous examples of IPOs. As an example, a February 27, 1992 article, page C6, was titled "Index Rises 1.77% as Volume Climbs; Synopsys Leaps 75% in Initial Trading." The instructor could use this as another example of the underpricing of IPOs. The stock rose 13 1/2 points to 31 1/2 from its offering price of 18. However, the instructor may wish to add that demand was so strong that the stock opened at 28 1/2, 10 1/2 above the offering price.*

A study by Ibbotson, Sindelar, and Ritter (Journal of Applied Corporate Finance, *1988) found that the difference between offering price and market price at the end of the first day was 16.37% for a sample of over 8,000 IPOs issued over 1960 through 1987. More detailed results from this study are provided in the text. However, a later study by Ritter in* The Journal of Finance, *1991, titled "The Long-Run Performance of Initial*

Public Offerings," found IPOs tend to underperform the market over the three-year period following issuance. Ritter's sample of over 1,500 IPOs for the period 1975 through 1984 realized a holding period return of 34.47% over the three-year period. The return was measured from the opening day's closing price. However, a control sample, matched by industry and market value, realized a holding period return of 61.86% over the same period.

Lecture Tip, page 453: *The instructor may wish to mention the general comments of a recent* Wall Street Journal *article, "IPOs Are Flooding Into Strong Stock Market," January 21, 1992, page C1. According to the article, the strong stock market in late '91 and early '92 was causing many companies that took on large debt in leveraged buy-outs (LBOs) during the mid-1980s to take these former LBO companies public. For information concerning the details of a particular company's IPO, the instructor may refer to the article.*

T13.8: Average Initial Returns by Month for SEC-Registered IPOs (Fig. 13.2)
T13.9: Number of Offerings by Month for SEC-Registered IPOs (Fig. 13.3)

Lecture Tip, page 457: *The lecture tip on page 449, describing the Synopsys IPO, could also be used at this point to provide the class with an example of the excessively high demand for certain IPOs. The instructor could then discuss the underwriter's allocation responsibility.*

13.4 NEW EQUITY SALES AND THE VALUE OF THE FIRM

Stock prices tend to decline following the announcement of a new equity issue, and rise on news of a debt offering. Some suggested reasons for this include:

1. Managerial information. The thinking is that stock is issued when managers know the firm's stock is overpriced. At least, the market thinks the managers think the stock is overpriced, and reacts accordingly.

2. Debt usage. Issuing new equity may signal that the firm has too much debt.

3. Issue costs. There are substantial costs involved in issuing securities and these are typically higher for equity.

13.5 THE COSTS OF ISSUING SECURITIES

Issuing securities involves *flotation costs*. These may be classified as

1. the spread
2. other direct expenses (legal and accounting fees, registration and printing costs)
3. indirect expenses
4. abnormal returns
5. underpricing
6. the Green Shoe provision

T13.10: Costs of Going Public (Table 13.7)

The total cost of going public, 1977-1982, averaged 21.22% for firm commitment underwritings, and 31.87% for best efforts underwritings.

T13.11: Five Conclusions on Flotation Costs

Five conclusions on underwriting costs:

1. There are substantial economies of scale in issuing securities.
2. Best efforts offers cost more.
3. For smaller issues, the cost of underpricing may exceed direct issue costs.
4. Underpricing is more severe for best efforts offers than for firm commitments.
5. It costs more to float an IPO than a seasoned offering.

13.6 RIGHTS

Privileged subscription—an issue of common stock offered to existing stockholders. The terms of the offer are evidenced by share warrants or *rights*. Rights are often traded on exchanges or over the counter.

A. The Mechanics of a Rights Offering

T13.12: Rights Offerings: Basics

Early stages are the same as for general cash offer, i.e., obtain approval from directors, file a registration statement, etc. Difference is in the sale of the securities. Current shareholders get rights to buy new shares. They can (1) subscribe (buy) the entitled shares, (2) sell their rights, or (3) do nothing.

B. Number of Rights Needed to Purchase a Share

$$\textit{Number of new shares} = \frac{\textit{Funds to be raised}}{\textit{Subscription price}}$$

Shareholders get one right for each share already owned. The number of rights needed to buy a new share is:

$$\textit{Number of rights needed to buy a share} = \frac{\textit{\# Old shares}}{\textit{\# New shares}}$$

<u>Example:</u>

Suppose a firm with 200,000 shares outstanding wants to raise $1,000,000 through a rights offering. Each current shareholder gets one right per share held. The following table illustrates how the subscription price, number of new shares to be issued, and the number of rights needed to buy a share are related, ignoring flotation costs.

Subscription price	Number of new shares	Number of rights needed to buy a share
$25	40,000	5
$20	50,000	4
$10	100,000	2
$ 5	200,000	1

Lecture Tip, page 464: *The student should be aware that with each subscription price, the firm would raise the needed $5,000,000. The instructor could ask the class why a subscription price of $25 per share (200,000 new shares) was not presented in the table. Many students should recognize that if the subscription price is $25 when the market price is $20, no present stockholder would exercise the rights since they could purchase the stock at a lower price on the market. The instructor could mention that if the rights offer is to work and the company realize its needed $5,000,000, the subscription price must be below the market price. The final paragraph in the "Effects on Shareholders" subsection (Section 13.6) discusses the arbitrary nature of the subscription price, provided it is below the market price of the company's stock. A further problem could arise if the market price falls below the subscription price. Damage from this problem may be avoided through a standby agreement with an underwriter. Such an arrangement requires the underwriter to purchase the unsubscribed shares (A further comment on this standby agreement is offered in "The New Issues Puzzle" subsection of Section 13.6).*

C. The Value of a Right

T13.13: Rights Offerings: Value of a Right

A right has value if the subscription price is below the share price. How much a right is worth depends on how many rights it takes to buy a share, and the difference between the stock price and the subscription price.

If it takes N rights to buy 1 share, value = $\dfrac{\textit{initial stock price} - \textit{subscription price}}{N + 1}$

D. Ex Rights

When a *privileged subscription* is used, the firm sets a *holder-of-record* date. The stock sells rights-on, or cum rights, until four business days before the holder-of-record date. After that the stock sells *ex rights.*

The ex rights price = $1/(N + 1) \times (N \times$ initial stock price + subscription price)

Example:

Suppose the firm mentioned above decides upon a subscription price of $20, with 50,000 shares to be issued. Assume the 200,000 shares outstanding currently trade for $35. Using the formula for the value of a right, where $N = 4$, a right is worth ($35 – $20)/(4 + 1) = $15/5 = $3. The ex rights price is expected to be 1/5 × (4 × $35 + $20) = $160/5 = $32.

Lecture Tip, page 466: *The instructor may wish to link the stock behavior of ex rights with ex dividends. The instructor could mention that the time line presented in Figure 13.4 applies to stocks trading ex rights as well as stocks trading ex dividend. Both dividend and rights declarations involve setting an ex date, which is four business days before to the record date. In both situations, the share price reacts on the ex date to reflect the value of the right or dividend which would not be received if the shares were purchased after the ex date.*

E. The Underwriting Arrangements

Standby underwriting—firm makes a rights offering and the underwriter makes a commitment to "take up" (purchase) any unsubscribed shares. In return, the underwriter receives a *standby fee.* In addition, shareholders are usually given *oversubscription privileges*, the right to purchase unsubscribed shares at the subscription price.

F. Rights Offers: The Case of Time Warner

T13.14: Rights Offerings: Issues

Time Warner's rights offering was somewhat unusual. As originally proposed, the subscription price would vary, dependent upon the percentage of the issue actually sold. This feature was later dropped. As is typical of most rights offerings, only 2 percent of the rights were neither exercised nor sold. However, oversubscription rights were used to absorb the unsold stock.

The underwriters's basic compensation was approximately 3 percent of the issue for management services, standby commitments, and other services.

G. Effects on Shareholders

As long as shareholders either exercise or sell their rights, they will be no better or worse off. It doesn't matter what subscription price the firm sets as long as it is below the market price.

H. The New Issues Puzzle

Although there is evidence that rights offers are cheaper than general cash offers, they are relatively infrequent in the U.S. Arguments for underwritten cash offerings:

1. Underwriters get higher prices (dubious given underpricing).
2. Underwriters insure against a failed offering (dubious value, for which they charge).
3. Other: proceeds of offering are available sooner, advice from underwriters is valuable (questionable).

13.7 DILUTION

Types:

1. Dilution of percentage ownership
2. Dilution of market value
3. Dilution of book value and EPS

A. Dilution of Proportionate Ownership

This occurs when the firm sells stock through a general cash offer and new stock is sold to persons who previously weren't shareholders. For many large, publicly held firms this simply isn't an issue, the shareholders being many and varied to begin with. For some firms with a few large shareholders it may be of concern.

B. Dilution of Value: Book versus Market Values

A stock's market value will fall if the NPV of the financed project is negative, and will rise if the NPV is positive. Whenever a stock's book value is greater than its market value, selling new stock will dilute the *book value.*

The example in the text involves selling $2 million of stock for $1 million of market value versus selling $2 million of stock for $3 million of market value. In both cases the book value falls, but in the latter case the market value per share rises.

T13.15: New Issues and Dilution

13.8 ISSUING LONG-TERM DEBT

A public issue of debt involves pretty much the same process as a stock issue, except that the registration statement must indicate an indenture.

More than 50% of all long-term debt is privately placed. *Term loans* are direct business loans with maturities of one to five years, usually amortized over the life of the loan. *Private placements* are long-term loans with bond-like features made by a single lender or a small group of investors.

<u>Differences between direct private placement and public issue of debt:</u>

1. No SEC registration for private placement.
2. Direct placements often have more restrictive covenants.
3. It is easier to renegotiate a private placement in the event of default.
4. A private placement costs less than a public issue (although the interest rates on private placements are generally higher, reflecting their lower cost and flexibility).

Overall, the costs of issuing debt are substantially less than those for issuing equity.

13.9 SHELF REGISTRATION

Shelf registration—SEC Rule 415 allows companies to register all the securities they expect to issue within the next two years at the same time and sell the issues whenever they want during those two years. Both debt and equity issues can be registered.

Qualifications for shelf registration:

1. Securities must be investment grade.
2. No debt defaults in past three years.
3. Aggregate value of outstanding stock > $150 million.
4. No violations of Securities Act of 1934 in past three years.

A 1985 study in the *Journal of Finance* found shelf registration to be cheaper than conventional underwriting. Still, few eligible firms have used the procedure.

13.10 SUMMARY AND CONCLUSIONS

T13.16: Solution to Problem 13.2
T13.17: Solution to Problem 13.8
T13.18: Solution to Problem 13.9

CHAPTER 14
COST OF CAPITAL

TRANSPARENCIES

T14.1:	**Chapter Outline**
T14.2:	**Cost of Capital**
T14.3:	**Dividend Growth Approach**
T14.4:	**Estimating the Dividend Growth Rate**
T14.5:	**SML Approach**
T14.6:	**Costs of Debt and Preferred**
T14.7:	**The Weighted Average Cost of Capital (WACC)**
T14.8:	**Example: Water's Beginning WACC**
T14.9:	**Divisional and Project Costs of Capital**
T14.10:	**The Security Market Line and the Weighted Average Cost of Capital**
T14.11:	**The Security Market Line and the Subjective Approach (Fig. 14.2)**
T14.12:	**Example: Penultimate Paralegal**
T14.13:	**Solution to Problem 14.3**
T14.14:	**Solution to Problem 14.10 (2 pages)**
T14.15:	**Solution to Problem 14.13**
T14.16:	**Solution to Problem 14.15**

CHAPTER ORGANIZATION

T14.1: Chapter Outline

14.1 THE COST OF CAPITAL: SOME PRELIMINARIES
- Required Return versus Cost of Capital
- Financial Policy and Cost of Capital

14.2 THE COST OF EQUITY
- The Dividend Growth Model Approach
- The SML Approach

14.3 THE COSTS OF DEBT AND PREFERRED STOCK
- The Cost of Debt
- The Cost of Preferred Stock

ANNOTATED CHAPTER OUTLINE

14.1 THE COST OF CAPITAL: SOME PRELIMINARIES

T14.2: Cost of Capital

A. Required Return versus Cost of Capital

Cost of capital, required return, appropriate discount rate—denote the same opportunity cost of using capital in one way as opposed to an alternative investment in the financial market having the same systematic risk.

required return is from an investor's point of view
cost of capital is the same return from the firm's point of view
appropriate discount rate is the same return yet again to be used in a PV calculation

B. Financial Policy and Cost of Capital

Capital structure—the firm's combination of debt and equity which is taken as given for now. Choosing a capital structure is discussed in chapter 15.

A firm's cost of capital will reflect the average riskiness of all its securities, which individually may be less risky (bonds) or more risky (common stock).

14.2 THE COST OF EQUITY

A. The Dividend Growth Model Approach

T14.3: Dividend Growth Approach

Estimating the cost of equity capital using the constant growth model:

$$P_0 = \frac{D_0 \times (1 + g)}{R_E - g} = \frac{D_1}{R_E - g}$$

Rearranging terms and solving for the cost of equity gives:

$$R_E = \frac{D_1}{P_0} + g$$

which is, of course, the dividend yield plus growth rate (capital gains).

1. Implementing the Approach

Price and latest dividend are directly observed—g must be estimated.

Estimating g—Typically use historical growth rates or analysts' forecasts.

T14.4: Estimating the Dividend Growth Rate

One simple way is to average annual dividend changes over the last 4 or 5 years:

Example:

Year	Dividend	Dollar change	Percentage change
1986	$4.00	-	-
1987	4.40	$.40	10.00
1988	4.75	.35	7.95
1989	5.25	.50	10.53
1990	5.65	.40	7.62

Average growth rate = (10 + 7.95 + 10.53 + 7.62)/4 = 9.025%

2. Advantages and Disadvantages of the Approach

-Approach only works for dividend paying firms.
-R_E is very sensitive to the estimate of g.
-History may not be a reliable predictor of the future.
-Risk is only indirectly accounted for by the use of price.

Lecture Tip, page 490: *The text mentions that there are other ways to compute* g. *Rather than use the arithmetic mean as in the example, the geometric mean (giving the average compound growth rate) could be used. OLS regression with the log of dividends as the dependent variable and time (1,2,3 etc.) as the independent variable has also been suggested.*

Lecture Tip, page 491: *Some students may question how one would value a non-dividend paying firm since, as the text states in the following paragraph, "the dividend growth model is obviously only applicable to companies that pay dividends." In anticipation of this question, the instructor might mention that, in the case of growth-oriented, non-dividend-paying firms, analysts might look at the trend in earnings or use similar firms to project the future date of the first expected dividend and its future growth rate. However, such processes are subject to much greater "estimation error" and when companies fail to meet (or even exceed) analysts' estimations, the stock price can experience a high degree of variability.*

Lecture Tip, page 491: *There are numerous examples of earnings disappointments provided in* The Wall Street Journal. *The class could find it interesting to hear of a recent earnings' disappointment and consider the percentage stock price change which a failure to meet growth expectations would cause. Examples are routinely found in the* Journal. *One such is provided in the April 1, 1992 "Abreast of the Market" section on page C2: "Bristol-Myers Squibb tumbled 2 to 76 1/4. Several analysts downgraded their ratings on the stock after the company said first-quarter sales growth was below expectations."*

B. The SML Approach

T14.5: SML Approach

R_E depends upon:

1. The risk-free rate, R_f
2. The expected market risk premium, $E(R_M) - R_f$
3. The amount of systematic risk as measured by β

So that we may write:

$$R_E = R_f + \beta_E \times \left[E(R_M) - R_f\right]$$

1. Implementing the Approach

Betas are widely available from various sources. T-bill rates are often used for R_f. The sticky point is the market risk premium, i.e., the market price of a unit of systematic risk. Either the historical average, 8.4%, or an average of analysts' forecasts may be used.

2. Advantages and Disadvantages of the Approach

-Consistent with capital market history, the approach adjusts for risk.
-It's applicable to virtually all publicly traded stocks, not just those paying stable dividends.
-The past may not predict the future for market risk premium and beta.

14.3 THE COSTS OF DEBT AND PREFERRED STOCK

A. The Cost of Debt

T14.6: Costs of Debt and Preferred

Usually there is no need to estimate beta or market risk premium.

Cost of debt (R_D)—the interest rate on new debt can easily be estimated using the yield-to-maturity on outstanding debt or by knowing the debt's bond rating and looking up the rate on new issues of that rating.

Example:

If Pohl Corp. issued a 10-year bond 5 years ago with a coupon rate of 13% that currently sells for $1,075, what is Pohl's cost of debt?

Assuming annual interest, the yield-to-maturity that makes an annuity of $130 per period for 5 periods plus $1,000 face value in 5 periods have a present value of $1,075 is 10.97 or approximately 11%.

Lecture Tip, page 494: *It may be beneficial to re-emphasize the distinction between coupon rate and yield-to-maturity (cost of debt) to the class. The instructor could ask the class to reconsider the material discussed in Chapter 6, "Valuing Stocks and Bonds." Otherwise, some students will have a tendency to simply select the coupon rate as the cost of debt.*

B. The Cost of Preferred Stock

To determine the cost of preferred stock, use the formula

$$R_P = D_P/P_0$$

14.4 THE WEIGHTED AVERAGE COST OF CAPITAL

A. The Unadjusted Weighted Average Cost of Capital

T14.7: The Weighted Average Cost of Capital (WACC)

E—the *market* value of the firm's equity (#shares common × price per share)

D—the *market* value of the firm's debt (#bonds × price per bond)

V—the combined *market* value of the firm's equity and debt, $V = E + D$

Capital structure weights—*E/V* and *D/V*

Unadjusted *weighted average cost of capital* is given by:

$$WACC\ (unadjusted) = \left(\frac{E}{V}\right) \times R_E + \left(\frac{D}{V}\right) \times R_D$$

Lecture Tip, page 496: *It may be helpful to mention and differentiate between the three types of weightings in the capital structure equation: book, market, and target. End-of-chapter problem 8 allows the student the opportunity to practice the calculation of both book and market value weights. It may also be helpful to mention that the total market value of equity (the number of common shares outstanding times the current market price of a company's common share) measures the value of the three equity accounts (common stock, capital in excess of par value, and retained earnings) from the balance sheet.*

B. Taxes and the WACC

Aftertax cash flows require an aftertax discount rate. Letting T_C stand for the firm's marginal tax rate:

$$WACC = \left(\frac{E}{V}\right) \times R_E + \left(\frac{D}{V}\right) \times R_D \times (1 - T_C)$$

WACC—overall return the firm must earn on its assets to maintain the value of its stock.

T14.8: Example: Water's Beginning WACC

Example:

Water's Beginning has 1 million shares of common stock outstanding with a market price of $12 per share. The firm's outstanding bonds have ten years to maturity, a face value of $5 million, a coupon rate of 10%, and are priced at $985. The risk-free rate is 7%, and analysts' expected return for the market is 14%. Water's Beginning stock has a beta of 1.2 and is in the 34% marginal tax bracket.

Capital structure weights:

market value of equity = 1,000,000 × $12 = $12,000,000
market value of debt = $5,000,000 × .985 = $4,925,000

V = $12,000,000 + $4,925,000 = $16,925,000
D/V = $4,925,000/$16,925,000 = .29 or 29%
E/V = 1 – D/V = .71 or 71%

Cost of equity:

Using the SML approach:

$$R_E = R_f + \beta_E \times \left[E(R_M) - R_f\right]$$

so,

$$R_E = 7\% + 1.2 \times (14\% - 7\%) = 7\% + 8.4\% = 15.4\%$$

Cost of debt:

The yield-to-maturity on the debt is 10.25% before taxes.

Weighted average cost of capital:

$$WACC = \left(\frac{E}{V}\right) \times R_E + \left(\frac{D}{V}\right) \times R_D \times \left(1 - T_C\right)$$

$$WACC = .71 \times 15.4\% + .29 \times 10.25\% \times \left(1 - .34\right) = 12.9\%$$

C. Solving the Warehouse Problem and Similar Capital Budgeting Problems

The WACC for a project that is identical to the rest of the firm is the same as that for the firm.

14.5 DIVISIONAL AND PROJECT COSTS OF CAPITAL

T14.9: Divisional and Project Costs of Capital

A. The SML and the WACC

The WACC is the appropriate discount rate only if the proposed investment is similar to the overall existing business and only if it will be financed with the same capital structure weights.

Lecture Tip, page 502: *The instructor might have the class consider a situation in which a company maintains a large portfolio of marketable securities on its balance sheet. The instructor could ask the class to further consider the impact this large security balance would have on a company's current and acid-test ratios and how this might impact the company's ability to meet short-term obligations. The students should easily remember that a larger liquidity ratio implies less risk (and less potential profit). Although the revenue realized from the marketable securities would be less than the interest expense on the company's comparable debt issues, these holdings would result in a lowering of the firm's beta and WACC. This example allows the student to recognize that the expected return and beta of an investment in marketable securities would be below the company's WACC, and justification for such investments must be considered relative to a benchmark other than the company's overall WACC.*

T14.10: The Security Market Line and the Weighted Average Cost of Capital

B. Divisional Cost of Capital

When a firm has different operating divisions with different risks, its WACC is an average of the divisional required returns. In such cases the cost of capital for different risks within the same firm needs to be established.

Lecture Tip, page 502: *It may help students to distinguish between the average cost of capital to the firm and the required return on a given investment if the idea is turned around from the firm's point of view to one of an investor's. That is, consider an investor holding a portfolio of T-bills, corporate bonds and common stocks. Suppose there is an equal amount invested in each and further suppose that the securities have on average returned 5%, 10%, and 15% respectively. The average portfolio return will have been 10%. Now ask students if the investor should use the portfolio's average return of 10% to evaluate new security acquisitions, say T-bills offering 7% and common stocks expected to return 13%.*

C. The Pure Play Approach

Pure play—a company that has a single line of business.

The idea is to find the required return on a near substitute investment.

Lecture Tip, page 502: *The instructor could add that although company betas can be easily found from such publications as* Value Line *or* Merrill Lynch's *"beta book," such publications do not provide betas of individual company divisions. A quick method to identify divisional betas might be to identify publicly-traded companies which are in similar lines of business or* pure plays *as the text discusses. The analyst could then average these betas and apply it to the division or new project to determine a risk-adjusted cost of capital. However, as the text discusses, firms often rely on "The Subjective Approach" because of the difficulty in objectively establishing discount rates for individual projects.*

D. The Subjective Approach

T14.11: The Security Market Line and the Subjective Approach (Fig. 14.2)

Assign investments to "risk" categories that have higher and higher risk premiums.

Lecture Tip, page 503: *What an individual firm considers a risky investment and what the financial market considers a risky investment may not be the same. Recall that the market is concerned with systematic or undiversifiable risk. If a firm is considering an investment's total risk in assigning it to a risk category, the risk categories may not line up with the SML.*

For example, consider a firm with high systematic risk in its usual business that is considering adding a new product line with low systematic risk. A conventional subjective scheme might assign a higher discount rate to the new product line and a lower one to any expansion of existing business, just the opposite of the financial market's evaluation.

14.6 FLOTATION COSTS AND THE WEIGHTED AVERAGE COST OF CAPITAL

A. The Basic Approach

Weighted average flotation cost (f_A)—the sum over all securities of the flotation costs as a percent of the amount of security issued, multiplied by the target capital structure weight for that type of security:

The multiplier $1/(1 - f_A)$ is used to determine the gross amount of capital to be raised so that the after-flotation cost amount is sufficient to fund the investment.

B. Flotation Costs and NPV

If a project nominally requires an investment of amount I before flotation costs, the suggested procedure is to compute the gross capital requirement as $I \times 1/(1 - f_A)$, and to use this figure as the investment cost in calculating the NPV.

T14.12: Example: Penultimate Paralegal

Example:

Suppose Penultimate Paraprofessionals, Inc. is considering opening another accounting office. The expansion will cost \$50,000 and is expected to generate aftertax cash flows of \$10,000 per year in perpetuity. The firm has a target debt/equity ratio of .5. New equity has a flotation cost of 10% and a required return of 15%, while new debt costs 5% to issue and has a required return of 10%.

Cost of capital:

$$WACC = \left(\frac{E}{V}\right) \times R_E + \left(\frac{D}{V}\right) \times R_D \times \left(1 - T_C\right)$$

$$WACC = \frac{2}{3} \times 15\% + \frac{1}{3} \times 10\% \times \left(1 - .34\right) = 12.2\%$$

Flotation costs:

$$f_A = \frac{E}{V} \times f_E + \frac{D}{V} \times f_D$$

$$f_A = \frac{2}{3} \times 10\% + \frac{1}{3} \times 5\%$$

$$f_A = 8.33\%$$

NPV:

Investment – \$50,000/(1 – .083)	= \$54,526
PV of cash flow – \$10,000/.122	= \$81,967
NPV = –\$54,526 + \$81,967	= \$27,441

Lecture Tip, page 508: *Some students might recognize that while debt and new common stock issuance would be subject to flotation costs, the retained earnings component of equity would not involve flotation costs to the firm. It is reasonable to assume that companies, such as growth-oriented companies, which plan for high levels of investments, would tend to retain a significant amount of earnings to finance their future investments. The retention of these earnings does have a cost, but it would be lower than the cost of issuing new equity. The key point to make is that whenever external financing is used, there is a cost associated with that financing, and that cost is a relevant cash flow for capital budgeting purposes.*

14.7 SUMMARY AND CONCLUSIONS

T14.13: Solution to Problem 14.3
T14.14: Solution to Problem 14.10 (2 pages)
T14.15: Solution to Problem 14.13
T14.16: Solution to Problem 14.15

CHAPTER 15
FINANCIAL LEVERAGE AND CAPITAL STRUCTURE POLICY

TRANSPARENCIES

CHAPTER ORGANIZATION

T15.1: Chapter Outline

15.1 THE CAPITAL STRUCTURE QUESTION
Firm Value and Stock Value: An Example
Capital Structure and the Cost of Capital

15.2 THE EFFECT OF FINANCIAL LEVERAGE
The Impact of Financial Leverage
Corporate Borrowing and Homemade Leverage

ANNOTATED CHAPTER OUTLINE

15.1 THE CAPITAL STRUCTURE QUESTION

T15.2: Financial Leverage and Capital Structure Policy

A. Firm Value and Stock Value: An Example

Using the firm value identity, the value of the firm equals the market value of debt plus the market value of equity ($V = D + E$). When the market value of debt is given and constant, any change in the value of the firm results in an identical change in the value of equity (stock). The key to this reasoning lies in the fixed payment nature of debt and the derivative value nature of stock.

Maximizing the value of the firm is the goal of managing capital structure.

Lecture Tip, page 517: *The instructor might want to stress our lack of overall understanding when it comes to the optimal capital structure for a particular business. Stewart Myers, President of the American Finance Association in 1983, published his essay, "The Capital Structure Puzzle," in the July 1984* Journal of Finance. *Myers summarizes the various issues concerning capital structure, specifically the pecking order theory and what we know about corporate financing behavior. The instructor can refer to this article for further information regarding corporate financing behavior. It's a good article for students to read as well.*

It may be interesting to read Myers' own words from the opening paragraph of this article: "'How do firms choose their capital structure?' Again, the answer is, 'We don't know.'" Myers goes on to state that ". . . we know very little about capital structure. We do not know how firms choose the debt, equity or hybrid securities they issue . . . [T]here has been little if any research testing whether the relationship between financial leverage and investors' required return is as the pure MM theory predicts."

The instructor should stress that the work of Miller and Modigliani was an attempt to understand corporate behavior in this area. The instructor could add that Miller received the Nobel Prize in Economics in recognition of his contribution to this area. (Modigliani won earlier and his work on capital structure was cited at that time.)

B. Capital Structure and the Cost of Capital

Optimal capital structure—the debt/equity ratio that minimizes the WACC. (More precisely, it is the D/E ratio that minimizes WACC holding the firm's assets, and, therefore, its expected cash flows, constant.)

Lecture Tip, page 518: *The existence of an optimal or target capital structure makes intuitive sense to most students because it results in the lowest WACC and highest firm value. However, empirical evidence suggests that actual debt ratios vary widely across similar firms. As suggested in the previous lecture note, it is quite plausible that these target capital structures depend on factors which are yet to be understood.*

15.2 THE EFFECT OF FINANCIAL LEVERAGE

A. The Impact of Financial Leverage

T15.3: Financial Leverage, EPS, and ROE: An Example

Financial Leverage, EPS, and ROE: An Example

A proposed change in financial leverage:

	Current	Proposed
Assets	$5,000,000	$5,000,000
Debt	$0	$2,500,000
Equity	$5,000,000	$2,500,000
Debt/equity ratio	0	1
Share price*	$10	$10
Shares outstanding	500,000	250,000
Interest rate	na	10%

* *Assumes, for now, restructuring has no influence on share price. Alert students will recognize that whether any influence exists is what we're investigating. Also, we ignore taxes for now.*

Scenario analysis of current and proposed capital structures:

Current capital structure: No debt

	Recession	Expected	Expansion
EBIT	$300,000	$650,000	$800,000
Interest	0	0	0
Net income	$300,000	$650,000	$800,000
ROE	6%	13%	16%
EPS	$0.60	$1.30	$1.60

Proposed capital structure: D/E = 1; interest rate = 10%

	Recession	Expected	Expansion
EBIT	$300,000	$650,000	$800,000
Interest	250,000	250,000	250,000
Net income	$ 50,000	$400,000	$550,000
ROE	2%	16%	22%
EPS	$0.20	$1.60	$2.20

Lecture Tip, page 520: *The instructor may wish to provide the following example to better solidify the students' understanding of the variability in ROE due to leverage. At various sales levels, the instructor could ask the class to consider the difference between ROA and ROE for a firm with no debt in its capital structure. One could easily demonstrate that the two would be identical at all sales levels since assets = equity. The substitution of debt for equity results in ROE equalling ROA at only one level of sales (or, one level of EBIT in Figure 15.1). The fixed interest expense and lower number of common shares outstanding resulting from this substitution would cause ROE to change to a larger degree than the change in ROA, given any change in sales volume. The greater slope of the "with-debt" line in Figure 15.1 reflects this sensitivity.*

T15.4: Break-Even EBIT: A Quick Note
T15.5: Financial Leverage, EPS, and EBIT

We may conclude from T15.3 - T15.5 that:

1. The effect of financial leverage depends upon EBIT.

2. When EBIT is high, financial leverage raises EPS and ROE.

3. The variability of EPS and ROE is increased with financial leverage.

Lecture Tip, page 522: *Many students will feel that if a company expects to achieve the break-even EBIT, it should issue the debt. The instructor should emphasize that this is a break-even point relative to EBIT and EPS. Beyond this break-even point, EPS will be larger under the debt alternative but the student should also recognize that with additional debt, the firm will have additional financial risk which would increase the required return of its common stock. Required return increases might offset the increase in the EPS under leverage, resulting in a lower firm value, despite the higher EPS realized by the levered firm. The instructor could state that the MM models which are soon to follow will offer the class some insight on this relationship.*

B. Corporate Borrowing and Homemade Leverage

Homemade leverage—there's nothing special about corporate borrowing.

T15.6: Homemade Leverage: An Example

Example: Homemade leverage

Suppose the firm in the previous example does not change its capital structure. An investor can replicate the returns of the proposed borrowing on personal account by making her own D/E ratio equal 1 for the investment. That is, suppose an investor buys a total of 100 shares, 50 shares with her own money and 50 shares by borrowing $500 at 10% interest. The payoffs are:

	Recession	Expected	Expansion
EPS of unlevered firm	$0.60	$1.30	$1.60
Earnings for 100 shares	$60.00	$130.00	$160.00
Less interest on $500 at 10%	50.00	50.00	50.00
Net earnings	$10.00	$80.00	$110.00
Return on investment (net earnings /$500)	2%	16%	22%

Individual investors can also "unlever" the firm's borrowing by lending to the firm. Consider the investor who invests $250 in the stock of the levered firm and who also invests $250 in bonds paying 10%:

	Recession	Expected	Expansion
EPS for levered firm	$0.20	$1.60	$2.20
Earnings for 25 shares	$5.00	$40.00	$55.00
Plus interest on $250 at 10%	$25.00	$25.00	$25.00
Net earnings	$30.00	$65.00	$80.00
Return on investment (net earnings/$500)	6%	13%	16%

Thus, investors can do or undo any pattern of financing for themselves. And what they can do for themselves, they don't need, nor will they pay, the firm to do.

Example:

Consider two firms, U and L, with identical assets and identical EBIT under all circumstances. Firm U is all equity financed while Firm L uses debt and equity. We ignore taxes for simplicity:

$$V_U = E_U \qquad \text{and} \qquad V_L = E_L + D_L$$

If an investor buys 2% of E_U, she gets (2% × EBIT) in payoffs. Now, if this investor were to buy 2% of E_L and 2% of D_L (i.e., 2% of V_L) she gets (2% × (EBIT – interest)) in stock payoffs plus (2% × interest) in debt payoffs. Of course, (2% × (EBIT – interest)) + (2% × interest) = 2% × (EBIT – interest + interest) = (2% × EBIT).

Since both investments have the same payoff, they must have the same market price, i.e., 2% of E_U must be worth the same as 2% of $E_L + D_L$. Finally, this implies 2% of V_U must be worth the same as 2% of V_L, and ultimately that V_U must be equal to V_L.

15.3 CAPITAL STRUCTURE AND THE COST OF EQUITY CAPITAL

A. M&M Proposition I: The Pie Model

T15.7: M&M Propositions

M&M Proposition I—with no taxes and individuals are able to borrow at the same rate as firms, the firm cannot affect its value by altering its capital structure.

B. The Cost of Equity and Financial Leverage: M&M Proposition II

T15.8: M&M Proposition II

M&M Proposition II—a firm's cost of equity capital is a positive linear function of its capital structure:

$$\text{WACC} = R_A = E/V \times R_E + D/V \times R_D$$

Rearranging:

$$R_E = R_A + (R_A - R_D) \times (D/E)$$

That is, as more debt is used, the return on equity rises and the WACC remains the same.

Lecture Tip, page 524: *Many students will wonder why we are even considering a situation in which taxes do not exist. The instructor should emphasize that there is much uncertainty concerning the exact amount of debt to use to attain a value-maximizing capital structure. Endeavors to understand this "puzzle" focus on which risk-return trade-off is most favorable for the company's stockholders. A proper understanding of capital structure policy requires the student to view the capital structure issue in stages. The first stage will examine the risk-return trade-off in a world without taxes. Once we understand this trade-off, the class will proceed to an examination of the trade-off involving taxes and the impact this environment has on firm value.*

C. Business and Financial Risk

T15.9: More on Business and Financial Risk

The instructor may wish to skip over the asset beta/equity beta distinction. It only comes up in the text in Challenge Questions at the end of the chapter. The key point is that MM Proposition II shows that the firm's return on equity depends on its business and financial risk:

Business risk -the risk inherent in a firm's operations
-depends on systematic risk of firm's assets
-determines the first component of the required return on equity, R_A.

Financial risk -extra risk from using debt financing.
-determines the second component, $(R_A - R_D) \times D/E$

15.4 M&M PROPOSITIONS I AND II WITH CORPORATE TAXES

A. The Interest Tax Shield

The tax saving arising from the deductibility of interest.

B. Taxes and M&M Proposition I

T15.10: Debt, Taxes, and Bankruptcy

Value of the interest tax shield = $T_C \times D$. M&M Proposition I with taxes is thus:

$$V_L = V_U + T_C \times D$$

Lecture Tip, page 529: *The instructor may wish to have the class consider the impact a change in the corporate tax rate would have on a corporation's desire to issue debt, assuming the non-corporate tax environment experiences no changes in tax rates. It is important to state this assumption and recognize the trade-off between personal and corporate tax rates under the Miller '77 paper. However, a discussion of this issue is somewhat advanced knowledge for an introductory finance course. The final conclusion will be that higher tax rates create an environment in which corporations will have a greater incentive to shelter income.*

T15.11: Debt, Taxes, and WACC

C. Taxes, the WACC, and Proposition II

T15.12: Taxes, the WACC, and Proposition II

Let R_U represent the *unlevered cost of capital.*

M&M Proposition II with corporate taxes states:

$$R_E = R_U + (R_U - R_D) \times (D/E) \times (1 - T_C)$$

and

$$\text{WACC} = E/V \times R_E + D/V \times R_D \times (1 - T_C)$$

15.5 BANKRUPTCY COSTS

One limit to the use of debt is *bankruptcy costs.*

A. Direct Bankruptcy Costs

Legal and administrative expenses directly associated with bankruptcy.

B. Indirect Bankruptcy Costs

Financial distress costs—the direct and indirect costs of avoiding bankruptcy.

15.6 OPTIMAL CAPITAL STRUCTURE

-Firms borrow because tax shields are valuable.
-Borrowing is constrained by the costs of financial distress.

A. The Static Theory of Capital Structure

T15.13: The Optimal Capital Structure and the Value of the Firm

B. Optimal Capital Structure and the Cost of Capital

T15.14: The Optimal Capital Structure and the Cost of Capital

C. Optimal Capital Structure: A Recap

D. Capital Structure: Some Managerial Recommendations

1. *Taxes*—the higher the firm's tax rate, the more important are tax shields.

2. *Financial distress*—the lower is risk of financial distress, the more likely is borrowing.

15.7 THE PIE AGAIN

A. The Extended Pie Model

T15.15: The Extended Pie Model

Cash Flow (CF) = + Payments to stockholders (E)
+ Payments to bondholders (D)
+ Payments to governments (G)
+ Bankruptcy costs (B)
+ Other claims

B. Marketed Claims versus Nonmarketed Claims

The claims against cash flow that can be bought and sold are *marketed claims*, while those that cannot be are *nonmarketed claims.*

V_M—the value of marketed claims; V_N—the value of nonmarketed claims

V_T—the value of all claims against cash flow = $V_M + V_N$

$V_T = E + D + G + B + \ldots$

Given the firm's cash flows, the optimal capital structure is one that maximizes V_M, or equivalently, minimizes the value of V_N.

15.8 OBSERVED CAPITAL STRUCTURES

On average, U.S. nonfinancial companies borrow $1 for every $3 of equity.

Different industries typically have different debt/equity ratios, depending on income variability and the nature of their assets.

15.9 SUMMARY AND CONCLUSIONS

T15.16: Solution to Problem 15.2
T15.17: Solution to Problem 15.10
T15.18: Solution to Problem 15.14

CHAPTER 16
DIVIDENDS AND DIVIDEND POLICY

TRANSPARENCIES

T16.1: Chapter Outline
T16.2: Dividend Types (3 pages)
T16.3: Example of Procedure for Dividend Payment
T16.4: Does Dividend Policy Matter?
T16.5: Homemade Dividends
T16.6: Dividends and the Real World
T16.7: Establishing a Dividend Policy
T16.8: A Compromise Dividend Policy
T16.9: Cash Dividend versus Repurchase (2 pages)
T16.10: Solution to Problem 16.9
T16.11: Solution to Problem 16.11
T16.12: Solution to Problem 16.15

CHAPTER ORGANIZATION

T16.1: Chapter Outline

16.1 CASH DIVIDENDS AND DIVIDEND PAYMENT
- Cash Dividends
- Standard Method of Cash Dividend Payment
- Dividend Payment: A Chronology
- More on the Ex-Dividend Date

16.2 DOES DIVIDEND POLICY MATTER?
- An Illustration of the Irrelevance of Dividend Policy

16.3 REAL-WORLD FACTORS FAVORING A LOW PAYOUT
- Taxes
- Flotation Costs
- Dividend Restrictions

ANNOTATED CHAPTER OUTLINE

16.1 CASH DIVIDENDS AND DIVIDEND PAYMENT

T16.2: Dividend Types (3 pages)

A. Cash Dividends

Regular cash dividend—dividends paid in the usual course of business.

Extra cash dividend—may or may not be repeated.

Special and *liquidating dividends*—one time dividend that won't be repeated.

Lecture Tip, page 554: *Students may find it interesting to examine the various types of dividend policies companies have utilized by examining the stock quotations presented in* The Wall Street Journal. *The instructor could ask the students to bring a copy of the* Journal *and examine the* Explanatory Notes *box provided with the stock quotations. The instructor could then explain the presentation with a few examples such as the following from the April 9, 1992* Journal, *NYSE Composite Transactions:*

Stock Sym	**Div**	
AIR	.48	Normal dividend—previous quarter's dividend multiplied by 4: .12 × 4.
AEGON	3.72r	Cash dividend declared or paid in previous twelve months, plus a stock dividend.
AOF	.80e	Extra dividend—sum of the last four quarter's dividends.
x AHR	.75c	Stock went ex-dividend plus paid a liquidating dividend.

B. Standard Method of Cash Dividend Payment

C. Dividend Payment: A Chronology

T16.3: Example of Procedure for Dividend Payment

1. *Declaration date*—date the board resolves to pay a dividend.

2. *Ex-dividend date*—four business days before the record date; people who buy the stock on or after this date won't get the dividend.

3. *Record date*—firm prepares the list of shareholders to receive dividends.

4. *Payment date*—the check is in the mail.

D. More on the Ex-Dividend Date

The price per share is expected to decline by approximately the amount of the dividend on the ex-dividend date.

Lecture Tip, page 555: *The instructor may wish to have the class consider whether it would be advantageous to buy a stock on the day before the ex-dividend date. One could use the example in figure 16.2. If one bought the stock prior to the ex-dividend date, one would pay $10 per share. This would entitle the owner to receive the $1 dividend, which will be mailed to the holder of the stock on the payment date. The instructor could then ask the student to consider the value of the dividend plus the stock following the ex-dividend date. The students could then recognize that the owner would have a $1 dividend plus stock value of $9, or a combined value of $10. This would result in no arbitrage opportunity. However, the instructor could mention that those individuals who purchase prior to the ex-dividend date would have to pay taxes on the dividend received. In a* *sense, if the stock falls by the amount of the dividend, purchasing a stock prior to the ex-dividend date results in an after-tax value of:*

(Ex-Dividend Stock Price + Dividend − Tax on Dividend) < $10.

*Thus, if the marginal investor is in a positive tax bracket, there exists an incentive to avoid purchasing stock prior to the ex-dividend date, should the stock fall by the value of the dividend. If the instructor wishes to elaborate on this issue, one might mention that a study by Avner Kalay (*Journal of Finance, *1982) found that the actual average stock price decline on the ex-dividend date was less than the amount of the dividend; he found that (cum-dividend price − ex-dividend price) / dividend = .734. As the text states, one argument for this behavior is tax liability for which investors wish to be compensated. This issue is further explored in a later section of this chapter.*

16.2 DOES DIVIDEND POLICY MATTER?

A. An Illustration of the Irrelevance of Dividend Policy

Lecture Tip, page 556: *The proposition that dividend policy (as opposed to dividends) is irrelevant is a difficult one for many students. Intuitively, they know that* other things the same *higher dividends will make a firm more valuable. Of course, the difficult part is in understanding the qualification "other things the same." Of course, if the number of shares, cash flow, future investment, and borrowing could all be the same and current dividends increased, investors would pay more for the stock. But where would the money for such an increase come from? The point here is that something has to give (future dividends) if current dividends are to be increased.*

T16.4: Does Dividend Policy Matter?

As long as a firm's investments (assets) and consequently its cash flows, are held constant, any increase in earlier dividends can only come at the cost of a decrease in later dividends and vice-versa. That is, similarly to the irrelevance of capital structure, once the size of the pie is fixed, it doesn't matter how you cut it.

T16.5: Homemade Dividends

Homemade dividends—If investors want to change the cash payout pattern from their investment, they can do so by buying and selling shares. That is, they can create *homemade dividends*. And what they can do for themselves they don't pay extra for.

16.3 REAL-WORLD FACTORS FAVORING A LOW PAYOUT

A. Taxes

T16.6: Dividends and the Real World

When the marginal tax rate for individuals exceeds that for businesses, investors may prefer businesses to retain earnings rather than pay them out as dividends as a strategy to reduce taxes.

Expected return, dividends, and personal taxes—when dividends are taxed at higher rates than capital gains for individuals, there is an argument that the higher a firm's dividends, the higher its cost of capital (and lower its stock value) to make the after-tax returns equal between firms of the same risk. However, if investors self-select into *clienteles* on the basis of their tax rates, and the clienteles are satisfied, it isn't clear that dividend policy affects expected returns.

Lecture Tip, page 560: *Because many politicians, including (former) President Bush, favor a capital gains tax cut, the instructor may wish to have the class consider the impact this tax law change would have on a stockholder's preference for higher or lower dividend payments. The instructor could mention that, in the year prior to 1986, any gain on stock held for over one year was given preferential tax treatment—only 40 percent of that gain was subject to individual income taxes. (The instructor might also mention that the time period and amount exempted from federal taxes has varied over time, depending upon tax laws enacted by the United States Congress.) The instructor could ask the class if they would have had a greater or lesser preference for dividends after the removal or reduction of the capital gains tax.*

B. Flotation Costs

Firms that pay high dividends and simultaneously sell stock to fund growth will have higher total flotation costs than comparable firms with low payouts.

C. Dividend Restrictions

Most bond indentures and some state laws limit the dividends a firm can pay.

Lecture Tip, page 561: *The instructor may wish to have the students reflect on the agency relationship discussed in Chapter 1. Although the discussion there mainly focused on the conflict of interest between stockholders and management, a conflict also exists between stockholders and bondholders. As a result, bond indenture agreements contain restrictive covenants (discussed in Chapter 12). Dividend restrictions are one of the most common type of restrictive covenants. Such covenants might state that dividends cannot be paid if net working capital falls below a stated amount or future common stock dividends can only be paid from profits generated after the signing of the loan agreement.*

16.4 REAL-WORLD FACTORS FAVORING A HIGH PAYOUT

A. Desire for Current Income

Transaction costs may hamper homemade dividends. But the desire for high current income is not universal. Again, if investors self-select into *clienteles* according to income desires, and the clienteles are satisfied, it isn't clear that a firm can gain by paying higher dividends.

B. Uncertainty Resolution

Selling stock now also creates a *"bird-in-the-hand"* just as a dividend payment does. Once again, we are back to "other things the same," can paying a higher dividend make a stock more valuable? If a firm must sell more stock or borrow more money to pay a higher dividend now, it must necessarily return less to stockholders in the future. Finally, the uncertainty over future income—i.e., the firm's business risk—isn't changed by its dividend policy.

C. Tax and Legal Benefits from High Dividends

1. Corporate investors—there is a 70% - 80% *exclusion* from taxable income of dividends received by one corporation from another.

2. Tax-exempt Investors—pension funds, trust funds, and endowment funds are tax-exempt. Furthermore, some of these investors are prohibited from spending any "principal."

16.5 A RESOLUTION OF REAL-WORLD FACTORS?

A. Information Content of Dividends

Changes in the future amount of dividends (as opposed to simply a rearrangement over time) may be signaled by a change in dividends. The reaction to information conveyed by an increase or decrease in dividends is called the *information content effect.*

Lecture Tip, page 564: *Some students may question why a company's stock price would react favorably to announcements of a dividend increase since capital gains might be preferred over the tax consequences of the higher dividend. Should a student ask this question, the instructor could emphasize that the signalling value of the dividend increase would be positive. This positive value would be traded off against the tax loss associated with the dividend increase, resulting in a stock price increase. The instructor might also mention that false dividend signals could prove costly to a company should dividend increases not be supported by future higher earnings. Weak future earnings may result in the company being forced to later secure expensive external funds sources.*

B. The Clientele Effect

As already discussed, the clientele effect holds that investors self-select the dividend policy best for themselves. If the existing clienteles are satisfied, changes in dividend policy by firms are pointless.

Lecture Tip, page 565: *To put the clientele argument in a different light, consider the case of opening a new restaurant. Even though a lot of people like to eat hamburgers and french fries, if that clientele is already satisfied by a McDonalds you won't make a fortune opening a Burger King.*

16.6 ESTABLISHING A DIVIDEND POLICY

A. Residual Dividend Approach

T16.7: Establishing a Dividend Policy

Dividends are paid out of whatever earnings are left after all positive net present value investments have been funded and the desired debt/equity ratio is obtained. One result of such an approach is that quickly-expanding firms will pay little or no dividends while slower-growing firms will pay out relatively high proportions of earnings.

B. Dividend Stability

Dividends are generally more stable than earnings, and most managers feel that a stable dividend is good for the firm and stockholders.

C. A Compromise Dividend Policy

T16.8: A Compromise Dividend Policy

Ranked in order of importance, the objectives of dividend policy are:

1. Avoid rejecting positive NPV projects to pay a dividend.
2. Avoid cutting dividends.
3. Avoid issuing new equity.
4. Maintain a target debt/equity ratio.
5. Maintain a target dividend payout ratio.

Most firms appear to have a *target payout ratio*, a long-run proportion of earnings that is to be paid out in dividends.

Lecture Tip, page 573: *To illustrate the importance of not cutting dividends, consider the case of Unisys (the computer firm created by the 1986 merger of Burroughs and Sperry corporations). In the last week of September, 1990, Unisys announced it was suspending payment of its regular quarterly dividend (which had been 25¢ a share). The pre-merger companies had a record of over 100 years of regular dividend payments. On the day of the announcement the stock fell by 23% to a 52 week low, the largest decline of any Big-Board traded issue that day.*

16.7 STOCK REPURCHASE: AN ALTERNATIVE TO CASH DIVIDENDS

T16.9: Cash Dividend versus Repurchase (2 pages)

A. Cash Dividends versus Repurchase

Instead of paying out a cash dividend, a firm may buy back its shares. Ignoring taxes and other imperfections, the cash distributed and value of outstanding shares afterward remains the same.

Example:

Consider a firm with 50,000 shares outstanding and the following balance sheet:

Market Value Balance Sheet

Cash	$ 100,000	$ 0	Debt
Other Assets	900,000	1,000,000	Equity
Total	$1,000,000	$1,000,000	Total

Price per share is $20, Net income is $100,000, EPS is $2.00, and the P/E ratio is 10.

Assuming no taxes, commissions, or other imperfections, the firm is considering:

a) Paying a $1 cash dividend, or
b) Repurchasing 2,500 shares @ $20

1. Choose the cash dividend

Market Value Balance Sheet

Cash	$ 50,000	$ 0	Debt
Other Assets	900,000	950,000	Equity
Total	$ 950,000	$ 950,000	Total

Price per share is now $19 ($950,000/50,000). Net Income is still $100,000, so EPS still = $2.00, but the P/E ratio is now 9.5.

The total value to a stockholder of a share is still $20, $19 of stock + $1 in cash.

2. Choose the repurchase

Market Value Balance Sheet

Cash	$ 50,000	$ 0	Debt
Other Assets	900,000	950,000	Equity
Total	$ 950,000	$ 950,000	Total

Price per share remains $20 ($950,000/47,500). Net income is still $100,000, so EPS is now $2.10, but the P/E ratio is 9.5, the same as under the cash dividend.

The total value to a stockholder of a share is still $20.

B. Real-World Considerations in a Repurchase

The most important difference between a cash dividend and a repurchases is the tax treatment. The entire cash dividend is taxable, while only the *gain* (price – basis) on the repurchase is taxable.

C. Share Repurchase and EPS

While EPS does go up with a repurchase (there are, after all, fewer shares), the market value of those earnings, as reflected by the P/E ratio, is the same as that under a cash dividend.

16.8 STOCK DIVIDENDS AND STOCK SPLITS

Stock dividend—dividend paid in shares of stock rather than cash. Commonly expressed as a percentage, e.g., a 25% stock dividend (1 new share for every four old shares). As with a cash dividend, the stock price declines proportionally.

Stock split—again, new stock to stockholders, only this time a ratio (e.g., 2-for-1 split). Again the price drops proportionally.

> ***Lecture Tip, page 576:*** *The instructor may wish to introduce this topic by asking the students if they had ever heard someone state that Company X's stock would be a good stock to purchase because it is rumored the company will soon have a stock split. One could solicit a few feelings concerning this issue prior to demonstrating the accounting treatment of dividends and splits on the following page. One could conclude by mentioning that even though the ex-dividend is known, since it follows the declaration date, unusual stock price behavior has been documented surrounding the ex-dividend date of non-taxable stock dividends and splits. Grinblatt, Masulis and Titman (*Journal of Financial Economics, *1984) documented a five-day average abnormal return of two percent surrounding the ex-date. Although the rationale is not fully understood for this anomaly, the instructor might mention that, unlike the ex-dividend impact for cash dividends, this behavior cannot be argued away due to a tax impact. Results of this study might be a lead into the "Value of Stock Splits and Stock Dividends" subsection.*

A. Some Details on Stock Splits and Stock Dividends

Stock dividend—retained earnings are transferred to the par value and capital in excess of par.

Stock split—the par value per share is adjusted to reflect the split (no effect on retained earnings).

B. Value of Stock Splits and Stock Dividends

Benchmark case—no change in shareholder wealth.

Popular trading range—an argument in favor of splits that says investors don't like "high" prices because they make *round lots* (100 shares) harder to buy.

C. Reverse Splits

<u>Three popular reasons given:</u>

1. reduced trading transactions costs
2. "popular trading range" again (this time arguing prices can be too low)
3. respectability (don't want the "penny" stock label).

<u>Two technical reasons</u>:

1. stock exchanges have minimum price requirements
2. it's a way to force out small shareholders.

Lecture Tip, page 579: *The instructor may wish to read the sentence in the text ending with "so the stock dividend doesn't really have any economic effect." The instructor could then mention that empirical research has documented large stock price gains at the announcement of a company's decision to have a stock dividend. A plausible argument for this has to do with the signaling issue. The student should recognize that the value of the stock dividend is transferred from retained earnings into the common stock and capital in excess of par accounts. The instructor could remind the student that many bond covenants restrict cash dividend payments when retained earnings fall below a minimum level. Only those companies confident of future earnings would be willing to reduce retained earnings through a stock dividend.*

16.9 SUMMARY AND CONCLUSIONS

T16.10: Solution to Problem 16.9
T16.11: Solution to Problem 16.11
T16.12: Solution to Problem 16.15

CHAPTER 17
SHORT-TERM FINANCE AND PLANNING

TRANSPARENCIES

T17.1: Chapter Outline
T17.2: Operating and Cash Cycles Illustrated
T17.3: Hermetic, Inc., Operating Cycles
T17.4: Hermetic, Inc., Cash Cycles
T17.5: The Size of the Firm's Investment in Current Assets
T17.6: Carrying Costs and Shortage Costs
T17.7: Financing Policy for an "Ideal" Economy
T17.8: Alternative Asset Financing Policies
T17.9: A Compromise Financing Policy
T17.10: A Cash Budget for Ajax Co. (2 pages)
T17.11: Short-Term Borrowing
T17.12: Solution to Problem 17.7 (2 pages)
T17.13: Solution to Problem 17.9
T17.14: Solution to Problem 17.11

CHAPTER ORGANIZATION

T17.1: Chapter Outline

17.1 TRACING CASH AND NET WORKING CAPITAL

17.2 THE OPERATING CYCLE AND THE CASH CYCLE
- Defining the Operating and Cash Cycles
- The Operating Cycle and the Firm's Organizational Chart
- Calculating the Operating and Cash Cycles
- Interpreting the Cash Cycle

17.3 SOME ASPECTS OF SHORT-TERM FINANCIAL POLICY
- The Size of the Firm's Investment in Current Assets
- Alternative Financing Policies for Current Assets
- Which is Best?
- Current Assets and Liabilities in Practice

17.4 THE CASH BUDGET
Sales and Cash Collections
Cash Outflows
The Cash Balance

17.5 SHORT-TERM BORROWING
Unsecured Loans
Secured Loans
Other Sources

17.6 A SHORT-TERM FINANCIAL PLAN

17.7 SUMMARY AND CONCLUSIONS

ANNOTATED CHAPTER OUTLINE

17.1 TRACING CASH AND NET WORKING CAPITAL

A. Defining Cash in Terms of Other Elements

Net working capital + Fixed assets = Long-term debt + Equity
Net working capital = (Cash + Other current assets) − Current liabilities

Substituting for NWC in the balance sheet identity and rearranging gives

Cash = Long-term debt + Equity + Current liabilities − Current assets (other than cash) − Fixed assets

Using this equation,

Activities that Increase Cash:

- Increasing long-term debt
- Increasing equity
- Increasing current liabilities
- Decreasing current assets (other than cash)
- Decreasing fixed assets

Activities that Decrease Cash:

- Decreasing long-term debt
- Decreasing equity
- Decreasing current liabilities
- Increasing current assets (other than cash)
- Increasing fixed assets

Lecture Tip, page 592: *Concept question 17.1b asks the students to consider whether net working capital always increases when cash increases. It may be helpful to have the students consider the net working capital identity in a situation where a firm acquires cash via a long-term versus short-term source. As an example, the students should recognize that cash will increase when a firm borrows either long-term or short-term debt. If long-term debt is issued, the cash account (debit entry) would increase without any corresponding increase (credit entry) in the current liabilities. Thus, net working capital increases. However, if short-term debt is issued, the increase in cash would be offset by an increase in a current liability, resulting in no change in net working capital.*

17.2 THE OPERATING CYCLE AND THE CASH CYCLE

A. Defining the Operating and Cash Cycles

1. *Operating cycle*—the average time required to acquire inventory, sell it, and collect for it. Its two components are:

   a) *Inventory period*—time to acquire and sell inventory
   b) *Accounts receivable period*—time to collect on sale

2. *Cash cycle*—the average time between "cash out" for inventory and "cash in" from collections:

   Cash cycle = Operating cycle − Accounts payable period

where *accounts payable period* is time between receipt of inventory and payment for it

Lecture Tip, page 595: *Students should easily recognize that a company would prefer to take as long as possible before paying bills. The instructor could mention that some people view an account payable as free credit since no cash is initially paid. However, a supplying firm may add in the cost of this so-called free credit into the selling price of its product. The instructor may wish to add that the operating cycle begins when inventory is purchased (a debit entry to inventory is matched with a credit entry to accounts payable). The cash cycle begins with the payment of the accounts payable which was created when the inventory was initially purchased (a debit entry to accounts payable matched with a credit entry to cash).*

T17.2: Operating and Cash Cycles Illustrated

B. The Operating Cycle and the Firm's Organization Chart

Short-term financial management in a large firm involves coordination between the credit manager, marketing manager, and controller. Potential for conflict may exist if particular managers concentrate on individual objectives as opposed to overall firm objective.

C. Calculating the Operating and Cash Cycles

T17.3: Hermetic, Inc., Operating Cycles
T17.4: Hermetic, Inc., Cash Cycles

Example:

Using Hermetic, Inc., financial statements (see Chapter 2), calculate the operating and cash cycles.

The Operating Cycle

1. Finding the Inventory period:

Inventory turnover = COGS/Avg inventory = $480/$352.5 = 1.362 turns

Inventory period = 365/Inventory turnover = 365/1.362 = 268 days

2. Finding the accounts receivable period:

Receivables Turnover = Credit sales/Avg receivables = $710/$285 = 2.491 turns

Receivables period = 365/Receivables turnover = 365/2.491 = 146.527 or 147 days

3. Finding the operating cycle:

Operating cycle = Inventory period + Receivables period = 268 + 147 = 415 days

The Cash Cycle

1. Finding the payables turnover:

Payables turnover = COGS/Avg payables = $480/$235 = 2.043

Payables period = 365/payables turnover = 365/2.043 = 178.659 or 179 days

2. Finding the cash cycle:

Cash cycle = Operating cycle − Payables period = 415 − 179 = 236 days

D. Interpreting the Cash Cycle

The cash cycle increases as the inventory and receivables periods lengthen and it decreases as the payables period lengthens. The longer the cash cycle, the larger the financing requirement.

17.3 SOME ASPECTS OF SHORT-TERM FINANCIAL POLICY

If receipts could be perfectly timed to match outlays and if we knew when every inflow and outflow would be, there wouldn't be any need for cash balances and net working capital could be zero. It is the mismatch between money in and money out plus the uncertainty about future events which motivates businesses to keep net working capital positive.

Flexible (conservative) policy—high levels of current assets relative to sales, and relatively more long-term debt.

Restrictive (aggressive) policy—low levels of current assets relative to sales, and relatively more short-term debt.

> ***Lecture Tip, page 600:*** *The following section, "Interpreting the Cash Cycle," presents some general conclusions on the cash cycle. It may be beneficial to have the students consider the cash cycle of Slowpay. The students could reconsider the issues of a high versus a low turnover, discussed in Chapter 3. Many may feel the main demand on funds for Slowpay is attributed to the high inventory period of 73 days. However, the students should consider the implications of attempts to speed up the inventory turnover through reduced inventory purchases or attempts to accelerate sales. Such efforts may result in expanded credit terms and a slower receivables turnover. The instructor could also mention that optimal levels of working capital will be discussed in the following section.*

T17.5: The Size of the Firm's Investment in Current Assets

A. The Size of the Firm's Investment in Current Assets

Flexible policy actions include:

1. Keeping large cash and securities balances.
2. Keeping large amounts of inventory.
3. Granting liberal credit terms, resulting in large receivables.

Restrictive policy actions include:

1. Keeping low cash and securities balances.
2. Keeping small amounts of inventory.
3. Allowing few or no credit sales and minimizing receivables.

T17.6: Carrying Costs and Shortage Costs

There are costs and benefits to both flexible and restrictive policies. The different policies represent trade-offs between costs that rise with investment and costs that fall with investment.

Carrying costs—costs that rise with increases in the level of investment in current assets.

In general, liquid assets have low yields. There are substantial *opportunity costs* involved with relatively high levels of current assets.

Shortage costs—costs that fall with increases in the level of investment in current assets.

There are two kinds of shortage costs:

1. *Trading or order costs*—commissions, set-up, paperwork, etc...

2. *Costs related to safety reserves*—lost sales, business disruptions, lost customer goodwill.

Lecture Tip, page 602: *The students have probably heard the policy of just-in-time inventory discussed in another business class. The instructor might ask the students to consider the risks of such a policy and what cost the company is attempting to minimize (carrying cost) and what cost may be increased (shortage cost).*

B. Alternative Financing Policies for Current Assets

1. An Ideal Case: always finance short-term assets with short-term liabilities, long-term assets with long-term liabilities.

T17.7: Financing Policy for an "Ideal" Economy

2. Different Policies in Financing Current Assets

T17.8: Alternative Asset Financing Policies

Lecture Tip, page 605: *Some students may tend to think of permanent asset levels as fixed assets. The instructor may wish to emphasize that permanent assets entail both long-term assets and a component of current assets. Some students may not readily see a component of short-term assets as permanent assets and may be confused with figure 17.3, representing an "ideal economy" in which current assets = short-term debt. The instructor may wish to provide a very simplified example as presented below:*

	January	*February*	*March*	*April*
Current Assets	*$20,000*	*$30,000*	*$20,000*	*$20,000*
Fixed Assets	*$50,000*	*$50,000*	*$50,000*	*$50,000*
Short-term Debt	?	?	?	?
Long-term Debt	?	?	?	?

The instructor could then ask the student to consider the alternative financing policies presented in Figure 17.5. Policy F (flexible) would entail long-term debt of $80,000. The instructor could note that in March, the company would have excess cash of $10,000 which could be invested in marketable securities. This policy would result in a lower interest revenue relative to the interest expense it would be paying on the $10,000 of long-term debt. Under Policy R (restrictive), the company would borrow $70,000 of long-term debt since total assets never fall below $70,000 (permanent level). In February, when total assets are at $80,000, the additional $10,000 asset level would be supported by $10,000 of short-term debt, which would be paid off in March, when the asset level falls back to $70,000.

C. Which is Best?

T17.9: A Compromise Financing Policy

Things to be considered:

1. *Cash reserves*—safety versus profitability.

2. *Maturity hedging*—short-to-short, long-to-long, and ne'er the twain shall meet.

3. *Relative interest rates*—short-term rates are generally lower, but also more volatile.

D. Current Assets and Liabilities in Practice

17.4 THE CASH BUDGET

Cash budget—a schedule of projected cash receipts and disbursements.

A. Sales and Cash Collections

A cash budget begins with a *sales forecast* (daily, weekly, monthly, or quarterly). This forecast is then used to generate estimates of cash inflows and cash outflows.

Are any sales on credit and, if so, what is the *average accounts receivable period*? That is, how long after a sale will the firm collect?

B. Cash Outflows

Accounts payable—are any purchases on credit, and if so what is the average accounts payable period? That is, how long after a purchase before the firm pays?

Wages, taxes, and other expenses—usually given as a percent of sales.

Capital expenditures—from the capital budget.

Long-term financing expenses—interest, sinking funds, dividends.

Short-term borrowing—used as a "plug" later.

C. The Cash Balance

T17.10: A Cash Budget for Ajax Co. (2 pages)

Example: A Cash Budget

Monthly cash budget: First quarter for the Ajax Company.

-All sales on credit. The sales forecast is:

JAN	$55,000
FEB	$65,000
MAR	$65,000
APR	$60,000

-November sales were $80,000; December sales were $95,000; the average accounts receivable period is 45 days; December 31st receivables were $135,000.

-Wages, taxes, and other expenses are 30% of sales.

-All raw materials are purchased on credit with an average accounts payable period of 30 days. Raw materials are ordered two months in advance of forecasted sales, and are 50% of sales.

-An annual cash dividend of $100,000 is expected to be paid in March.

-No capital expenditures are planned for the first three months.

-The beginning cash balance is $41,000. The minimum cash balance is $25,000.

Cash collections for Ajax (all figures rounded to the nearest dollar)

	JAN	FEB	MAR
Beginning receivables	$135,000	$102,500	$ 92,500
Sales	55,000	65,000	65,000
Cash collections*	87,500	75,000	60,000
Ending receivables	102,500	92,500	97,500

*Cash collections—assuming level sales throughout the month, a 45-day collection period implies 1/2 of a month's sales are collected in the subsequent month and 1/2 in the second month after a sale. January collections are thus 1/2 of November sales plus 1/2 of December sales.

Cash disbursements for Ajax

	JAN	FEB	MAR
Payment of accounts (50% of next month's sales)	$ 32,500	$ 32,500	$ 30,000
Wages, taxes, and other expenses	16,500	19,500	19,500
Capital expenditures	0	0	0
Long-term financing expenses	0	0	100,000
Total	$49,000	$52,000	$149,500

Net cash inflow for Ajax

	JAN	FEB	MAR
Total cash collections	$ 87,500	$ 75,000	$ 60,000
Total cash disbursements	49,000	52,000	149,500
Net cash inflow	$ 38,500	$ 23,000	–$ 89,500

Cash balance for Ajax

	JAN	FEB	MAR
Beginning cash balance	$ 41,000	$ 79,500	$102,500
Net cash inflow	38,500	23,000	–$ 89,500
Ending cash balance	$ 79,500	$102,500	$ 13,000
Minimum cash balance	– 25,000	– 25,000	– 25,000
Cumulative surplus (deficit)	$ 54,500	$ 77,500	–$ 12,000

17.5 SHORT-TERM BORROWING

A. Unsecured Loans

T17.11: Short-Term Borrowing

Line of credit—a formal (*committed*) or informal (*uncommitted*) prearranged, short-term bank loan. Often on prime plus floating rate terms.

Commitment fee—a charge to secure a committed line of credit.

Compensating balances—deposits with a bank in a low- or non-interest bearing account as part of a loan agreement.

Cost of a compensating balance—if the compensating balance requirement is on the *used* portion, less money is actually available than is borrowed. If it is on the *unused* portion, the requirement becomes a commitment fee.

Example:

Consider a $50,000 line of credit with a 5% compensating balance requirement. The quoted rate on the line is prime + 6%, and the prime stands at 11%. Suppose the firm wants to borrow $28,500. How much do they have to borrow? What is the effective annual rate?

How much to borrow: $28,500 = (1 – .05) × Amount; Amount = $28,500/.95 = $30,000

What is the effective rate? At 17% per annum, the interest on $30,000 is $5,100. Interest rate = interest paid/amount available = $5,100/$28,500 = .17895 or 17.895%

Lecture Tip, page 612: *The instructor may wish to use the credit card example to emphasize the meaning of a line of credit. One could state that with credit cards, the consumer can utilize the line of credit to purchase goods. The line of credit remains active until we abuse the privilege (e.g., late payments, exceeding credit limit). However, there is a cost for this line, much as the compensating balance issue next discussed. Many students may have access to more than one credit card but hopefully have applied for only one. The instructor could mention that each credit card increases the total line of credit available but each card has an annual fee. It would not pay for students to secure the maximum number of credit cards since they would not need the combined lines of credit and would not wish to pay the annual fees associated with each card. In the same manner, companies do not want to secure excessive lines of credit since they would be burdened with fees for credit limits they would not use.*

B. Secured Loans

1. *Accounts receivable financing*

Assigning receivables—receivables are security for a loan, but the borrower remains responsible if a receivable can't be collected.

Factoring receivables—the receivable is sold at a discount to the factor.

Example:

Consider a firm with an average receivables period of 33 days. The firm can factor the receivables at a 2% discount. That is, the firm gets $0.98 for every $1.00 of receivables, i.e., in effect pays 2¢ to get 98¢ 33 days early. The interest rate for the 33 day collection period is .02/.98 = .0204 = 2.04% per period. Since there are approximately 11 33-day periods in a year, the APR = 11 × 2.04% = 22.44%. The effective annual rate is higher still, $(1.0204)^{11} - 1 = .24875$ or 24.875%.

2. *Inventory Loans*

Types of inventory loans:

Blanket inventory liens—the lender gets a lien against all the borrower's inventories.

Trust receipt—the lender buys the inventory which is held in "trust" by the borrower who gives a trust receipt acknowledging the arrangement.

Field warehouse financing—an independent company establishes a warehouse area on the borrower's premises and only releases goods from it upon the instructions of the lender.

C. Other Sources

Commercial paper—short-term IOUs issued by large, especially creditworthy firms.

Trade credit—borrowing from suppliers by purchasing goods on account.

17.6 A SHORT-TERM FINANCIAL PLAN

Based on the projected cash budget, the firm must consider how it will raise funds for cash deficit periods and what to do with surplus cash in other periods. For temporary imbalances, short-term borrowing and marketable securities would seem in order. For permanent short-falls or surpluses, a long-term solution is in order: a bond or equity issue for deficits, and dividends or a repurchase for surpluses.

17.7 SUMMARY AND CONCLUSIONS

T17.12: Solution to Problem 17.7 (2 pages)
T17.13: Solution to Problem 17.9
T17.14: Solution to Problem 17.11

CHAPTER 18
CASH AND LIQUIDITY MANAGEMENT

TRANSPARENCIES

CHAPTER ORGANIZATION

T18.1: Chapter Outline

18.1 REASONS FOR HOLDING CASH
- Speculative and Precautionary Motives
- The Transaction Motive
- Compensating Balances
- Costs of Holding Cash

18.2 UNDERSTANDING FLOAT
- Disbursement Float
- Collection Float and Net Float
- Float Management

18.3 CASH COLLECTION AND CONCENTRATION
- Components of Collection Time
- Cash Collection
- Lockboxes
- Cash Concentration
- Accelerating Collections: An Example

ANNOTATED CHAPTER OUTLINE

18.1 REASONS FOR HOLDING CASH

A. Speculative and Precautionary Motives

Speculative motive—to take advantage of unexpected opportunities (marketable securities and credit lines also satisfy this motive).

Precautionary motive—in contrast to the unexpected opportunity, the occasional unexpected outlay. (Again, credit and securities can also satisfy this motive.)

Lecture Tip, page 629: *What is needed to satisfy the speculative and precautionary motives is an ability to pay quickly—a need that is met with liquidity. Although cash is the most liquid asset, other assets, such as marketable securities, are near substitutes for cash. Furthermore, an ability to borrow quickly is also a close substitute for cash.*

B. The Transaction Motive

Since cash inflows and outflows are not perfectly synchronized, the cash balance serves as a buffer between collections and disbursements.

C. Compensating Balances

Sometimes required by banks in connection with loans, these may set a lower limit on cash balances.

D. Costs of Holding Cash

On the one hand, there is an opportunity cost to holding cash balances—the returns that could be earned if the funds were invested in some other asset(s). On the other hand, converting other assets into cash or borrowing have their costs. The target cash balance must take both of these into account.

Lecture Tip, page 630: *It may be helpful to have the students consider their personal cash balances. Some may deposit their weekly paycheck or student loan in a non-interest-paying checking account and use it throughout the quarter. The instructor could demonstrate that these students are foregoing interest they might receive on a savings account, even though the student's balance might approach a low level by the end of the term. On the other hand, if a student wants to maximize the interest he/she could receive on the savings account, he/she would have to be careful in monitoring the cash balance in the checking account to ensure the account maintains a minimum amount to cover checks written. The instructor could mention that a happy balance (no pun intended) exists between having too much idle cash in the student's checking account and too little cash which would require the student to constantly monitor the balance and give needless worry to possibly bouncing a check.*

The instructor could demonstrate this situation in terms of an equilibrium for a company—the marginal benefit of the liquidity that a large cash balance provides versus the marginal value of the interest received on Treasury bills; i.e., the investment of cash balances into Treasury bills is a zero net present value investment.

18.2 UNDERSTANDING FLOAT

T18.2: Cash and Liquidity Management

A. Disbursement Float

Book or *ledger balance*—what the firm's records show its cash balance to be.

Available or *collected balance*—what the bank says the cash balance is.

Float = available balance − book balance

Disbursement float—what happens when the firm writes checks that don't clear immediately.

B. Collection Float and Net Float

Collection float—what happens when the firm deposits checks that aren't cleared immediately.

Net float = disbursement float + collection float

Lecture Tip, page 632: *It may help to personalize the issue of float for the students. The instructor could ask the students if any of the students have written a check on the day or two prior to receiving their weekly payroll check, even though, on the day on which the check was mailed, their checking balance was not sufficient to cover the checks they had written. The students could view the payroll check received as a collection which they deposit prior to the mailed checks being returned for payment to the students' bank. When a student deposits the payroll check, the bank's record of the checking account balance would be larger than the amount recorded in the student's personal checking account records (book balance). On the day of payroll deposit, as the text states, "the bank thinks the firm [in our example, the student] has more cash than it really does."*

C. Float Management

The three components of float are:

1. *Mail float*—the time the check is in the mail

2. *Processing float*—handling time between receipt and deposit

3. *Availability float*—time to clear the banking system

Float management means speeding up collections (reducing collection float) and slowing disbursements (increasing disbursement float).

1. Measuring Float

There are two distinct cases:
a) periodic collections
b) continuous or *steady-state* collections.

For periodic collections, the average daily float is given by (check amount × days delay)/(# days in period).

Example: Periodic collections

Suppose a $10,000 check is mailed to Priam, Inc. every two weeks. It spends 2 days in the mail, a day and a half at Priam offices, and is credited to Priam's bank account 2 days after deposit. The total delay is 5½ days. Since there are 14 days in a fortnight, the float is $10,000 for 5.5 days, and $0 for 8.5 days (then the cycle starts over). The *average daily float* is (5.5 × $10,000 + 8.5 × 0)/14 or simply (5.5 × $10,000)/14 = $3,928.57.

Example: Continuous collections

Suppose average daily checks arriving at Hector Company amount to $2,000, and suppose further that they take an average of 3 days to arrive in the mail, 1 day to process, and 2 days to be credited to Hector's bank account. The total collection delay is 3 + 1 + 2 = 6 days, and average daily float is 6 × $2,000 = $12,000 (i.e., on any given day the amount paid but uncollected is $12,000). Eliminating all delays would free up $12,000, eliminating 1 day's delay frees up $2,000.

2. Cost of the (collection) float

The benefit of reducing collection delays is directly reflected in the change in the average daily float. Every dollar reduction in the average daily float is in effect a dollar freed up for use in perpetuity. And the change in the average daily float that any scheme to hasten collections might make is also the *most* the firm would be willing to pay for faster collections.

Example: Periodic collections

What is the most Priam would pay to speed up its collections by a half day? If the collections delay were reduced from 5.5 days to 5 days, the average daily float would go from (5.5 × $10,000)/14 to (5 × $10,000)/14. i.e., from $3,928.57 to $3,571.43. So the benefit of collecting a half day faster is $357.14, and this is the most they would pay.

Example: Continuous collections

How much would Hector Company save if they could reduce their collection delay from 6 days to 3 days? At 3 days, average daily float is 3 × $2,000 = $6,000 and the change in average daily float is $12,000 − $6,000 = $6,000.

Lecture Tip, page 634: *It may be helpful to reinforce the concept of net float through an example emphasizing the balance sheet change resulting from an increase in collection float and a decrease in disbursement float. One could begin by having the class consider a company that has credit sales of $100,000 per day. Inventory of $80,000 per day is purchased on credit. The company collects its average receivable in 30 days and takes an average of 20 days to pay its accounts payable. The balance sheet would appear as:*

Acc. Rec.	*$3,000,000*	*/ Acc. Pay.*	*$1,600,000*

This situation requires external funds sources (see Chapter 4) of $1,400,000. Checks, whether received or sent, will require three days for mail delivery. A negative net float of −$60,000 (−$100,000 × 3 + $80,000 × 3) exists. If the company could speed up its receivables collection by one day, only 29 days sales' would be in receivables. If the company could also delay its disbursements by one day, it would be taking 21 days to pay its payables. Net float would become a positive $120,000 (−$100,000 × 2 + $80,000 × 4). The balance sheet would initially change to:

Add. Cash	*$ 180,000*	*/ Acc. Pay. $1,680,000*
Acc. Rec.	*$2,900,000*	

The accounts receivable debit balance is reduced by $100,000, resulting in a source of funds. Additionally, the accounts payable credit balance is increased by $80,000, resulting in an additional source of funds. The net source equals this change in float of $180,000. The additional cash can be used to reduce the external funds required ($2,900,000 – $1,680,000) to $1,220,000.

Ethics Note, page 636: *For a lengthy discussion of legal and ethical questions and issues surrounding cash management, see* Institutional Investor, *September 1985, "Cash management: Where do you draw the line", by Barbara Donnelly, pp. 69-79. The story focuses on the E.F. Hutton check kiting scandal.*

18.3 CASH COLLECTION AND CONCENTRATION

T18.3: Check Clearing Illustrated

A. Components of Collection Time

The three basic parts of cash collection:
-mail delay, processing delay, clearing delay.

B. Cash Collection

Cash collection policies often depend on the nature of the business. The firm might select to have checks mailed to one location, numerous locations to reduce mailing time, or arrange for preauthorized payments.

C. Lockboxes

T18.4: Overview of Lockbox Processing (Fig. 18.3)

Lockboxes—special post office boxes, tended by banks on behalf of clients, to which checks are sent in an effort to reduce mail, processing, and clearing delays.

D. Cash Concentration

Concentration banking—sending surplus funds from remote, smaller banks to larger, centralized banks.

T18.5: Lockboxes and Concentration Banks (Fig. 18.4)

Wire transfers—an electronic transfer of funds between banks that eliminates mailing and check-clearing delays.

E. Accelerating Collections: An Example

18.4 MANAGING CASH DISBURSEMENTS

T18.6: Cash Disbursement (Fig. 18.6)

A. Increasing Disbursement Float

Increasing Disbursement Float

-Write check on distant bank.
-Call to verify statement.
-Play around with mail and postmarks. However, business mostly use the receipt date, not the postmark date, in determining whether or not a payment is on time; also, the post office does not allow postmarking without mailing)

B. Controlling Disbursements

18.7: Zero-Balance Accounts (Fig. 18.6)

Zero-balance account—rather than keep cash balances in several accounts to pay checks, funds are concentrated in a central account and funds are transferred from this account to *ZBA* accounts as checks are presented. The balance in the concentration account is typically lower than maintaining balances in several accounts.

Drafts—drafts differ from checks in that they are payable by the issuer rather than banks. Drafts are presented to the issuer by banks who act as agents. Only then do funds need to be deposited to cover them.

18.5 INVESTING IDLE CASH

A. Temporary Cash Surpluses

1. Seasonal or cyclical activities
2. Planned or possible expenditures—cash for capital expenditures, dividends, debt retirement, legal contingencies, acquisitions.

B. Characteristics of Short-Term Securities

C. Some Different Types of Money Market Securities

T18.8: Some Money Market Securities

MONEY MARKET INSTRUMENT	ISSUER	MATURITY	RISK, MARKETABILITY, DENOMINATION
U.S. Treasury Bills	U.S. Government	at issue; 90, 180, 270, 360 days	no default risk good secondary market $10,000 minimum
Short-term municipal securities	State & local governments	1 week to 1 year	some default risk good secondary market $5,000 and up
Commercial Paper	Finance companies Large companies Banks	few weeks to 270 days	backed with credit lines no secondary market $100,000 and up
Negotiable Certificates of Deposit (jumbo CDs)	Banks	at issue 30, 60, 90, 180, 270, & 360 days	no deposit insurance good secondary market $100,000 minimum
Repurchase Agreements (repos)	U.S. securities dealers, banks	overnight to several weeks	securities are collateral $1 million and up

Lecture Tip, page 648: *The instructor may wish to mention that the current money market rates are presented daily in* The Wall Street Journal. *Various money market instruments and their current rates can be found on the* Credit Markets *page in Section C, under the title* "Money Rates." *The instructor might remind the student that these rates change on a daily basis, as a function of market conditions.*

18.6 SUMMARY AND CONCLUSIONS

T18.11: Solution to Problem 18.4
T18.12: Solution to Problem 18.10

APPENDIX 18A—DETERMINING THE TARGET CASH BALANCE

Target cash balance—the desired cash balance as determined by the tradeoff between carrying costs and shortage costs.

Adjustment costs—costs associated with holding low levels of cash; shortage costs.

With a flexible working capital policy, the tradeoff is between the opportunity cost of cash balances and the adjustment costs of buying, selling, and managing securities.

A. The Basic Idea

T18.9: Costs of Holding Cash

B. The BAT (Baumol-Allais-Tobin) Model

Define:

C = optimal cash transfer amount (amount of securities to sell)
F = the fixed cost of selling securities to replenish cash
T = the cash needed for transactions over the planning period
R = opportunity cost of cash—the interest rate on marketable securities

Assume cash is paid out at a constant rate through time.

1. *The opportunity costs*—average cash balance × interest rate = $(C/2) \times R$

2. *The trading costs*—number of transactions × cost per transfer = $(T/C) \times F$

3. *The total cost*—opportunity costs + trading costs = $(C/2) \times R + (T/C) \times F$

4. *The solution*—the minimum occurs where opportunity costs = trading costs:

$$C/2 \times R = (T/C) \times F$$

Rearranging:

$$C^2 = (2T \times F)/R$$

Solving for C:

$$C = \sqrt{(2T \times F)/R}$$

This can also be found by differentiating total cost with respect to C:

$$TC = (C/2) \times R + (T/C) \times F$$

$$\frac{\partial TC}{\partial C} = R/2 - \frac{T \times F}{C^2}$$

Setting this to zero and solving for C yields:

$$C = \sqrt{(2T \times F)/R}$$

<u>Example:</u>

Hermes Co. has cash outflows of $500 a day, the interest rate is 10% and the cost of a transfer to cash is $25.

$T = 365 \times \$500 = \$182{,}500$ $F = \$25$ $R = .10$

$$C = \sqrt{(2T \times F)/R}$$

$$= \sqrt{2 \times \$182{,}500 \times \$25/.10}$$

$$= \sqrt{91{,}250{,}000}$$

$$= \$9{,}552.49$$

C. The Miller-Orr Model: A More General Approach

The Miller-Orr model offers a general approach to handling uncertain (random) cash flows.

T18.10: The Miller-Orr Model

1. The Basic Idea

Define

U^* = upper limit on cash balance
L = lower limit on cash balance
C^* = target cash balance

When the cash balance, a random variable, reaches U^*, the firm transfers $U^* - C^*$ dollars from cash to securities. If the cash balance falls below L, the firm sells $C^* - L$ worth of securities to add to cash.

2. Using the Model

Need the variance of cash flow per period, σ^2, and the interest rate per period (Note: Here cash flow refers to both the amounts that go into and come out of the cash balance). The period may be anything (day, week, month) as long as these two are consistent. Given L, the target balance and upper limit are given by:

$$C^* = L + (3/4 \times F \times \sigma^2/R)^{1/3} \quad \text{and} \quad U^* = 3 \times C^* - 2 \times L$$

Example:

Suppose F = \$25, R = 1% per month, and the variance of monthly cash flows is \$25,000,000 (i.e., a standard deviation of \$5,000 per month). Assume a minimum cash balance of \$10,000.

$$C^* = \$10{,}000 + (3/4 \times \$25 \times \$25{,}000{,}000/.01)^{1/3}$$
$$= \$10{,}000 + \$3{,}605.62 = \$13{,}605.62$$

$$U^* = 3 \times \$13{,}605{,}62 - 2 \times \$10{,}000$$
$$= \$40{,}816.86 - \$20{,}000 = \$20{,}816.86$$

D. Implications of the BAT and Miller-Orr Models

From both:

-The higher the interest rate (opportunity cost), the *lower* the target balance.
-The higher the transaction cost, the higher the target balance.

From Miller-Orr:

-The greater the variability of cash flows, the higher the target balance.

E. Other Factors Influencing the Target Cash Balance

-Flexible versus restrictive short-term financing policy.

-Compensating balance requirements.

-The number and complexity of checking accounts

CHAPTER 19
CREDIT AND INVENTORY MANAGEMENT

TRANSPARENCIES

T19.1: Chapter Outline
T19.2: Credit and Inventory Management
T19.3: The Cash Flows from Granting Credit
T19.4: Length of the Credit Period
T19.5: Credit Policy Effects
T19.6: Evaluating a Proposed Credit Policy
T19.7: The Costs of Granting Credit
T19.8: The Five C's of Credit
T19.9: ABC Inventory Analysis (Fig. 19.2)
T19.10: Costs of Holding Inventory (Fig. 19.4)
T19.11: Inventory Holdings for the Eyssell Corporation (Fig. 19.5)
T19.12: Solution to Problem 19.13
T19.13: Solution to Problem 19.20
T19.14: Solution to Problem 19.22

CHAPTER ORGANIZATION

T19.1: Chapter Outline

19.1 CREDIT AND RECEIVABLES
- Components of Credit Policy
- The Cash Flows from Granting Credit
- The Investment in Receivables

19.2 TERMS OF THE SALE
- The Basic Form
- The Credit Period
- Cash Discounts
- Credit Instruments

ANNOTATED CHAPTER OUTLINE

19.1 CREDIT AND RECEIVABLES

T19.2: Credit and Inventory Management

When credit is granted to other firms, it's called *trade credit*. When granted to consumers, it's called *consumer credit*.

A. Components of Credit Policy

1. *Terms of sale*—credit period, discounts and discount period, credit instrument

2. *Credit analysis*—who gets credit (and how much), and who doesn't

3. *Collection policy*—how to get borrowers to pay

B. The Cash Flows from Granting Credit

T19.3: The Cash Flows from Granting Credit

C. The Investment in Receivables

The investment in receivables depends upon the *average collection period* (a.k.a., days' sales in receivables, receivables period) and the *average daily credit sales.*

(Investment in)
Accounts receivable = Average daily sales × average collection period

Lecture Tip, page 667: *Some students might question why the amount of investment in accounts receivable is the daily sales times ACP. They may recognize that sales contain cost plus profit, and the investment required would be the cost of the receivables, not the profit margin in the receivables account. Should this question arise, the instructor could mention that this investment analysis refers to the funds committed to this balance. If the receivables balance could be reduced by 10 days, these 10 days receivables would be immediately freed up. Thus, the investment in receivables should be viewed in terms of the funds which are tied up for the company.*

19.2 TERMS OF THE SALE

1. The credit period
2. Cash discounts and discount period
3. The credit instrument

A. The Basic Form

a/*b*, net *c*—e.g., 1/10, net 30
In other words, (take this discount off the invoice price)/(if you pay in this many days), (else pay the full invoice amount in this many days).

B. The Credit Period

Credit period—the length of time before the borrower is supposed to pay.

Two components: *net credit period* and *cash discount period*

Invoice—bill for goods or services provided by the seller to the buyer.

1. *Invoice date*—begins the credit period, usually the shipping or billing date.

   Variations:

   ROG—receipt of goods
   EOM—end-of-month (The invoice date is the end of the month for all sales.)
   Seasonal dating—invoice date corresponds to "season" of goods

2. *Length of the credit period* depends upon:

   -Buyer's inventory and operating cycle
   -Perishability and collateral value
   -Consumer demand
   -Cost, profitability and standardization
   -Credit risk
   -The size of the account
   -Competition
   -Customer type

T19.4: Length of the Credit Period

C. Cash Discounts

1. *Cost of credit*—i.e., the cost of not taking discounts

periodic rate = (discount %)/(100 – discount %)
APR = periodic rate × 365/(net period – discount period)
EAR = $(1 + \text{periodic rate}/100)^{365/(\text{net period} - \text{discount period})} - 1$

Example: Cost of Foregone Discounts

On terms of 1/15, net 45 the cost of foregone discounts (assuming payment in 45 days) is:

periodic rate = 1/(100 – 1) = 1.01%
APR = 1.01% × 365/(45 – 15) = 1.01% × 12.167 = 12.29%
EAR = $(1 + .0101)^{12.167} - 1 = 1.130 - 1 = .130$ or 13%

2. *Trade discounts*—unlike true discounts, these are not an inducement to early payment, but are the regular terms.

3. *The cash discount and the ACP*—offering discounts generally reduces the ACP. Whether or not receivables are also reduced depends upon the effect of the discount on the amount of credit sales as well as the ACP.

Lecture Tip, page 670: *The instructor may have to stress that when a company does not take advantage of discount terms such as sales terms of 2/10, net 30, the company is effectively borrowing the invoice cost for 20 days at a 2 percent cost. Some students might suspect that since the company does not have to pay its bill for 30 days, the company secures the use of the funds for 30 days. The instructor should emphasize that it is the marginal time period for funds usage, not the total time period allowed before payment, that is relevant in determining the effective annual rate. Although this is heavily emphasized under* ***Cost of the Credit****, an added classroom comment may be helpful.*

D. Credit Instruments—the evidence of indebtedness

Open account—transaction evidenced by invoice and recorded on the books.

Promissory note—an IOU used when some trouble in collecting is expected.

Commercial draft—*sight draft* (due on presentation), *time draft* (due at some date), *trade acceptance* (buyer "accepts" draft, i.e., promises to pay at a later date), *banker's acceptance* (bank accepts draft, i.e., promises to pay at a later date).

19.3 ANALYZING CREDIT POLICY

A. Credit Policy Effects

T19.5: Credit Policy Effects

1. *Revenue effects*—payment is received later, but price and quantity sold may be increased.

2. *Cost effects*—the cost of running a credit scheme and collecting receivables.

3. *The cost of debt*—firm must finance receivables.

4. *The probability of nonpayment*—always get paid if you sell for cash.

5. *The cash discount*—affects payment patterns and amounts.

B. Evaluating a Proposed Credit Policy

T19.6: Evaluating a Proposed Credit Policy

Define:

P	= price per unit
v	= variable cost per unit
Q	= current quantity sold per period
Q'	= new quantity expected to be sold
R	= periodic required return (corresponds to the ACP)

The benefit of switching is the change in cash flow, i.e., (new cash flow – old cash flow):

$$(P - v) \times Q' - (P - v) \times Q = (P - v) \times (Q' - Q)$$

That is, the periodic benefit is the gross profit × change in quantity. The present value of switching is:

$$PV = [(P - v)(Q' - Q)]/R.$$

The cost of switching is the amount uncollected for the period + the additional variable costs of production:

$$Cost = PQ + v(Q' - Q)$$

Finally, the NPV of the switch is:

$$NPV = -[PQ + v(Q' - Q)] + (P - v)(Q' - Q)/R$$

1. *A break-even application*—what change in quantity would produce a $0 NPV?

$$Q' - Q = (PQ)/[(P - v)/R - v]$$

Lecture Tip, page 673: *The instructor should mention that the process for determining the NPV of a credit policy switch is no different from the process for determining the NPV of a capital asset replacement or switch. The analysis involves a comparison of the marginal costs with the marginal benefits to be realized from the switch. If a company liberalizes credit terms, the present value of the marginal profit is compared to the immediate investment in a higher receivables balance. If a company tightens credit, lower sales should be expected. The present value of the reduction in profit is compared to the cash realized from the lower amount invested in receivables.*

19.4 OPTIMAL CREDIT POLICY

In principle, an optimal credit policy is one under which incremental cash flows from sales are equal to incremental costs of carrying the increase in investment in accounts receivable.

A. The Total Credit Cost Curve

T19.7: The Costs of Granting Credit

Credit policy represents the trade-off between two kinds of costs:

Carrying costs:
-the required return on receivables
-the losses from bad debts
-the costs of managing credit and collections

Opportunity costs:
-potential profit from credit sales lost

19.5 CREDIT ANALYSIS

A. When Should Credit Be Granted?

1. *A One-Time Sale*
   Let π be the percentage of *new* customers who default
   $NPV = -v + (1 - \pi)P/(1 + R)$
   The firm risks $-v$ to gain P a period later.

2. *Repeat Business*
   $NPV = -v + (1 - \pi)(P - v)/R$

Lecture Tip, page 677: *The instructor might initiate this section with a discussion of the credit card offerings many banks provide for students. The instructor could mention that the default risk may be higher among college students but the marginal benefit, at 18% to 19% interest charges on unpaid balances, justifies this decision for the bank. However, the bank controls this risk with lower credit limits for riskier customer classes and providing the student with a credit card while in college allows the bank to establish student loyalty to their card. The instructor could also mention that when students graduate, secure favorable employment, and demonstrate the ability to manage debt, these lower credit limits are generally raised since the student is no longer evaluated as a higher credit risk.*

B. Credit Information

Some typical sources of credit information are:

1. Financial statements
2. Credit reports (i.e., Dun and Bradstreet report)
3. Banks
4. The customer's payment history

C. Credit Evaluation and Scoring

T19.8: The Five C's of Credit

The five C's of credit

1. *Character*—willingness to pay
2. *Capacity*—ability to pay out of cash flows
3. *Capital*—financial reserves
4. *Collateral*—pledged assets
5. *Conditions*—economic conditions in customer's area, line

Credit scoring—process of assigning a numerical rating to a customer to indicate their creditworthiness.

19.6 COLLECTION POLICY

A. Monitoring Receivables

Aging schedule—a breaking down of receivables accounts by their age.

Example:

Age of Account	Amount outstanding	% of receivables
0 - 30 days	$ 67,550	85.39%
31 - 60 days	10,480	13.25%
Over 60 days	1,075	1.36%

B. Collection Effort

Usual procedures for overdue accounts:

1. Send delinquency letter
2. Call customer
3. Employ collection agency
4. Sue

19.7 INVENTORY MANAGEMENT

A. The Financial Manager and Inventory Policy

B. Inventory Types

For a manufacturer, inventory is classified into one of three categories
-raw material, work-in-progress and finished goods.

Things to keep in mind:

1. Classification into category is a function of the nature of the firm's business.
2. Inventory types can be different in terms of their liquidity.
3. Demand for the first two categories of inventory is demand for finished goods.

C. Inventory Costs

Two basic types of costs associated with current assets in general and inventory in particular:
-carrying costs and shortage costs.

19.8 INVENTORY MANAGEMENT TECHNIQUES

A. The ABC Approach

T19.9: ABC Inventory Analysis (Fig. 19.3)

B. The Economic Order Quantity (EOQ) Model

Lecture Tip, page 686: *The EOQ model assumes that the firm's inventory is sold off at a steady rate until it hits zero. Firms with seasonal demand would experience a more difficult problem determining the optimal inventory level to maintain. In Section 19.6, "Collection Policy," the text states "Firms with seasonal sales will find the percentages on the aging schedule changing during the year." The instructor might ask the students to consider the impact that heavy seasonal demand would have on the EOQ model. If the* *heavy demand is to last for two months, the formula might be adjusted to assume annual sales based on this high level of demand. Total unit sales per year, the variable T in the (T/Q) component of total restocking cost, would increase, suggesting a larger Q to minimize restocking costs. However, the instructor could indicate that as Q increases, the (T/Q) component of restocking costs falls but the (Q/2) component of carrying costs would rise. The instructor could mention that we are finding a new optimal order quantity by trading off on these two costs. The instructor could also offer the students the basic intuition that if sales increase and no additional inventory is purchased, inventory turnover would increase and the students should remember that high levels of inventory turnover imply the danger of a stock-out. As a final note, when seasonal demand is low, T would be determined based on a monthly average of low sales. It should be emphasized that the EOQ model assumes a steady rate of sales throughout the year. If sales are not constant, an adjustment may have to be applied to the formula.*

T19.10: Costs of Holding Inventory (Fig. 19.4)

EOQ—the quantity which minimizes the total cost associated with inventory carrying costs and restocking costs.

Assumption: firm's inventory is *depleted* at a steady pace.

T19.11: Inventory Holdings for the Eyssell Corporation (Fig. 19.5)

Total carrying costs

= Average inventory × Carrying costs per unit

= (Q/2) × CC

Total restocking costs

= Fixed cost per order × Number of orders

= F × (T/Q)

Total costs

= Carrying costs + Restocking costs

= (Q/2) × CC + F × (T/Q)

$$EOQ = \sqrt{\frac{2T \times F}{CC}}$$

C. Extensions to the EOQ Model

While the EOQ tells the manager the optimal amount to reorder, the manager must also consider

1. *safety stocks*—the minimum level of inventory a firm must keep on hand.
2. *reorder points*—to allow for delivery time.

D. Managing Derived-Demand Inventories

1. Materials Requirements Planning
2. Just-in-Time Inventory

19.9 SUMMARY AND CONCLUSIONS

T19.12: Solution to Problem 19.13
T19.13: Solution to Problem 19.20
T19.14: Solution to Problem 19.22

APPENDIX 19A—MORE ON CREDIT POLICY ANALYSIS

A. Two Alternative Approaches

1. *The One-Shot Approach*

No switch cash flow: $(P - v)Q$
Switch cash flow: invest vQ' now, receive PQ' next period
Present value of switch net cash flow: $PQ'/(1 + R) - vQ'$

NPV = Switch net benefit − No switch cash flow = $[PQ'/(1 + R) - vQ'] - (P - v)Q$

If this is repeated every period, the firm gets the above NPV now and in every period, giving:

$$[PQ'/(1 + R) - vQ'] - (P - v)Q + \{[PQ'/(1 + R) - vQ'] - (P - v)Q\}/R$$

After some algebraic manipulation, this reduces to:

$$-[PQ + v(Q' - Q)] + (P - v)(Q' - Q)/R$$

the same NPV as shown before.

2. *The Accounts Receivable Approach*

Periodic benefit: $(P - v) \times (Q' - Q)$
Incremental investment in receivables: $PQ + v(Q' - Q)$
Carrying cost per period: $[PQ + v(Q' - Q)] \times R$
Net benefit per period: $(P - v) \times (Q' - Q) - \{[PQ + v(Q' - Q)] \times R\}$

NPV $= ((P - v) \times (Q' - Q) - \{[PQ + v(Q' - Q)] \times R\})/R$

It is easily seen that this reduces to:

$$-[PQ + v(Q' - Q)] + (P - v)(Q' - Q)/R,$$

the same NPV as shown before.

Example:

Suppose we had the following for Giffie International, which is considering a change from no credit to terms of net 20.

P = \$100
v = \$75
Q = 1,000
Q' = 1,050
R = 1.5% per 20 days

Using the original method:

$NPV = -[PQ + v(Q' - Q)] + (P - v)(Q' - Q)/R$
NPV = –[\$100 × 1,000 + \$75(1,050 – 1,000)] + (\$100 – \$75)(1,050 – 1,000)/.015
NPV = –\$100,000 + \$3,750 + \$1,250/.015 = –\$103,750 + \$83,333.33
= –\$20,416.67

Using the one-shot approach:

$NPV = [PQ'/(1+R) - vQ'] - (P - v)Q + \{[PQ'/(1+R) - vQ'] - (P - v)Q\}/R$
NPV = [(\$100 × 1,050)/1.015 – \$75 × 1,050] – (\$100 – \$75) × 1,000
+ {[(\$100 × 1,050)/1.015 – \$75 × 1,050] – (\$100 – \$75) × 1,000}/.015
NPV = [\$103,448.28 – \$78,750] – \$25,000 + {[\$103,448.28 – \$78,750]
– \$78,750 – \$25,000}/.015 = –301.72 – \$20,114.94
= –\$20,416.66

Using the accounts receivable approach:

$NPV = ((P - v) \times (Q' - Q) - \{[PQ + v(Q' - Q)] \times R\})/R$

$NPV = ((\$100 - \$75) \times (1{,}050 - 1{,}000) - \{[\$100 \times 1{,}000 + \$75(1{,}050 - 1{,}000)] \times .015\})/.015$

$= (\$1{,}250 - \{[\$100{,}000 + \$3{,}750] \times .015\})/.015 = (\$1{,}250 - \$1{,}556.25)/.015$

$= -\$20{,}416.66$

To break even, Giffie needs $(PQ)/[(P - v)/R - v] = 63$ additional units.

B. Discounts and Default Risk

Define:

π = percentage of credit sales that go uncollected
d = percentage discount allowed for cash customers
P' = credit price (no-discount price)
P = cash price = $P'(1 - d)$

Assume no change in Q, then:

Net incremental cash flow = $[(1 - \pi)P' - v] \times Q - (P - v) \times Q = P'Q \times (d - \pi)$

$$NPV = -PQ + P'Q \times (d - \pi)/R$$

A break-even application: $\pi = d - R \times (1 - d)$ is the break-even default rate.

CHAPTER 20
OPTIONS AND CORPORATE SECURITIES

TRANSPARENCIES

CHAPTER ORGANIZATION

T20.1: Chapter Outline

20.1 OPTIONS: THE BASICS
- Puts and Calls
- Stock Option Quotations
- Option Payoffs

20.2 FUNDAMENTALS OF OPTION VALUATION
- Value of a Call Option at Expiration
- The Upper and Lower Bounds on a Call Option's Value
- A Simple Model: Part I
- Four Factors Determining Option Values

ANNOTATED CHAPTER OUTLINE

20.1 OPTIONS: THE BASICS

An *option* is a contract giving its holder the right, but not the obligation, to buy or sell an asset at a fixed price anytime on or before a given date.

<u>A lexicon of option terminology:</u>

1. *Exercising the option*—using the option contract to buy (sell) the underlying asset.

2. *Strike or exercise price*—the fixed price feature of the option contract at which the asset may be bought (sold).

3. *Expiration date*—the last day on which the option may be exercised.

4. *American option*—can be exercised at any time up to the expiration date.

5. *European option*—can only be exercised on the expiration date.

Lecture Tip, page 711: *The instructor may find it beneficial to convey the meaning of an option by having the students consider a situation in which they place a downpayment on a car. The instructor could ask the students what action they might take if they are interested in buying a car for an agreed upon price of $5,000* (exercise price) *from a used car dealer. However, they would like a week (option's* expiration*) to decide whether or not they will purchase the car.*

The students should recognize that they would have to place a downpayment, assume $50 (option cost), with the dealer to hold the car. Over this weekly period, the student could shop around to find a lower price (market or stock price). If they could find an identical-type car at a lower price, they would call the dealer and simply state they are not interested in purchasing the car; in which case they would be out the $50 downpayment or cost of the option. However, if the student, after checking with a few dealers, would find that the lowest price any dealer would offer an identical-type car was $5,400, the value of the option to purchase at $5,000 would be $400 and the student would exercise the option to purchase from the original dealer at $5,000.

The instructor could introduce the time value of the option by asking the students if they would prefer the $50 downpayment to hold the car for one week or four weeks. Most should recognize that they would like a longer time to check with other dealers and decide.

The instructor could also ask the students to consider a car market in which prices are relatively flat (the student believes the price at alternative dealers would be either $4,900 or $5,100) versus a market in which car prices are very uncertain (the student believes the price at alternative dealers may be either $4,500 or $5,500). The students should recognize that if the price is on the high side, they would lose $100 in the flat car market but would lose $500 in the uncertain market and they should be more willing to place the downpayment on the car if the market is uncertain. Thus, the option would have a higher value in an uncertain market due to the much higher variability the ending market price could attain.

A. Puts and Calls

Call option—gives its holder the right, but not the obligation, to *buy* an asset at a fixed price during the option's life.

Put option—gives its holder the right, but not the obligation, to *sell* an asset at a fixed price during the option's life.

The party obligated to sell (buy) the asset at the strike price is said to have written an option. They receive a fee at the time they write the option.

B. Stock Option Quotations

CBOE (Chicago Board Options Exchange)—the largest organized stock options exchange. While stock options involve the shares of various companies, the firms themselves are not party to these contracts. Almost all options are the American type. (The American/European appellations have no geographic meaning. Most option contracts traded throughout Europe are of the American variety.)

T20.2: A Sample *Wall Street Journal* Option Quotation (Table 20.1)

An option is described as " Firm / Expiration month / Strike price / Type ."
For example, referring to Transparency T20.2, "IBM September 110 put."

<u>*More on option contracts:*</u>

r means the contract didn't trade that day; *s* indicates that no option is offered.

Contracts are for 100 shares, so a contract costs *price* × *100*.

Options expire on the third Friday of the expiration month.

Option prices under $3 trade in sixteenths, while those over $3 trade in eighths.

Lecture Tip, page 713: *The instructor may wish to add that the strike prices are standardized. The various exchanges that conduct option trading offer contracts in 2 1/2 and 5 dollar intervals. The investor may trade option contracts in small-priced stocks in terms of 2 1/2 dollar intervals (Example: 10, 12 1/2, 15). Higher-priced stocks trade in 5 dollar intervals (Example: 50, 55, 60).*

C. Option Payoffs

T20.3: Payoffs to a Call
T20.4: Payoffs to a Put

For calls, when the stock price is above the exercise price at expiration, the option is *in the money*. When the stock price is below the exercise price the option is *out of the money*. (The opposite is true of puts.)

Ignoring transaction costs, since no new money is raised or invested options are a *zero sum game*. That is, whatever one party to an options contract gains, the other party loses.

Lecture Tip, page 714: *Although the concept of a put and a call will initially seem clear to the students, students tend to have greater difficulty working with puts than calls. It may help the students' understanding by providing a very simplified example prior to presenting the option payoff text discussion. One could have the students consider the difference between a stock's price and the striking price (intrinsic value) for both a put and a call contract with an example showing the impact on the contracts' value given various stock price changes. The call's value equals (S – E) because the call's value increases as the stock price increases relative to an agreed-upon buying price (E). The put's value equals (E – S) since the put's value increases as the stock price falls relative to an agreed-upon selling price (E). Since we will simply throw the option away if we don't want to use it, the value of the option contract cannot be a negative number but will instead simply be worthless.*

Example: Consider a contract to buy or sell stock with a striking price of $30.

Strike Price(E)	***Stock Price(S)***	***Call Value (S – E)***	***Put Value (E – S)***
30	*24*	*0*	*6*
	27	*0*	*3*
	30	*0*	*0*
	33	*3*	*0*
	36	*6*	*0*

This example may help the students understand the opposite nature of puts and calls and that a call's value will fall, but a put's value will rise, as the stock price falls in value.

Lecture Tip, page 715: *The instructor may wish to mention that Example 20.1 (Put Payoffs) is an example of a protective put which provides insurance should the stock price fall heavily in value (answer to concept question 20.1b). Such insurance could save the cost of many bottles of aspirin (or, possibly, something providing much greater pain relief!) should the stock investor experience an event such as that which occurred on Black Monday '87.*

20.2 FUNDAMENTALS OF OPTION VALUATION

A. Value of a Call Option at Expiration

T20.5: Value of a Call Option at Expiration

Notation

S_1 = Stock price at expiration
S_0 = Stock price today
C_1 = Value of call option on the expiration date
C_0 = Price of call option today
E = Exercise price of option

If $S_1 \leq E$ then $C_1 = 0$ If $S_1 > E$ then $C_1 = S_1 - E$

B. The Upper and Lower Bounds on a Call Option's Value

T20.6: Value of a Call Option before Expiration

The Upper Bound: $C_0 \leq S_0$. A call option can never sell for more than the stock itself.

The Lower Bound: 0 or $S_0 - E$, whichever is larger. To prevent *arbitrage*, the value of a call must be greater than the stock price less the exercise price. Otherwise, buy the option, pay the exercise price, and get the stock for less than it sells for in the market.

Intrinsic value = 0 or $S_0 - E$, whichever is larger. What the option would be worth if it were about to expire.

C. A Simple Model: Part I

A lot can be learned about what influences an option's price by examining a couple of simple cases where call options and risk-free loans give the same payoffs as a straight stock investment.

Suppose there is a stock currently selling for $62 whose price will be either $70 or $90 in one period. Assume there is a call option on this stock with an exercise price of $65. Finally, let the one period risk-free interest rate be 10%.

1. The Basic Approach

Duplicating the payoff

1) Buy the stock. The stock will be worth either $70 or $90.

or

2) Buy the call and lend $65/(1.1) or $59.09 at 10%.

Stock value	Call value	Risk-free loan	Total payoff, call + loan
$70	$S_1 - E = \$5$	$65	$70
$90	$S_1 - E = \$25$	$65	$90

Whatever happens to the stock, the call + loan strategy has the same payoff as purchasing the stock. Since the stock can be purchased for $62, the current value of the call + loan must also be $62. Thus, $\$62 = \$59.09 + C_0 \rightarrow C_0 = \$2.91$ and $C_0 = S_0 - E/(1+R_f)$.

2. A More Complicated Case

Let the stock price be *anything* greater or equal to the exercise price in t periods. Again consider lending at the risk-free rate of 10% to receive $65 after t periods. The payoff to the call option + lending scheme is $\$65 + (S_1 - \$65)$, which is simply S_1. Since the stock and the (call + loan) have the same payoff, they must have the same price now. As long as the option finishes in the money its price is $C_0 = S_0 - E/(1+R_f)^t$.

D. Four Factors Determining Option Values

Using $C_0 = S_0 - E/(1+R_f)^t$:

Other things the same,
1. *The stock price*—the higher the stock price, the greater the price of a call.
2. *The exercise price*—the higher the exercise price, the smaller the price of a call.
3. *The time to expiration*—the longer the time to expiration, the greater the price of a call.
4. *The risk-free rate*—the larger the risk-free rate, the more the call is worth (The exercise price is a cash outflow whose present value declines as R_f increases).

20.3 VALUING A CALL OPTION

A. A Simple Model: Part II

When the stock price may be below the exercise price, loan the present value of the lowest stock price at the risk-free rate and buy enough calls to have the difference between the lowest and highest price.

Example:

Suppose a stock currently selling for $67 is expected to end up at either $60 or $80. There is a call option with an exercise price of $70 on the stock. The risk-free rate is 9%.

Duplicating the payoff

1) Loan $55.05 at the risk-free rate. The payoff is $60 at maturity at 9%.
2) At expiration, the call will be worth either $0 ($60 stock price) or $10 ($80 stock price). If worth $10, it will take 2 calls plus the loan to make the payoff $80.

Two calls plus a risk-free loan of $55.05 have the same payoff as a share of the stock, so

$$S_0 = 2 \times C_0 + \$60/(1 + .09) \Rightarrow C_0 = (\$67 - \$55.05)/2 = \$5.98$$

B. The Fifth Factor

Variance of return (σ^2)—the greater the variability in price (return), the more a call option is worth. Greater variability increases the likelihood of finishing in the money and the expected magnitude of the resulting payoff.

Example:

Suppose the stock in the example above is expected to end up at either $55 or $85 instead of $60 or $80. What happens to the price of the call?

Duplicating the payoff

1) Loan $50.46 at the risk-free rate. The payoff is $55 at maturity at 9%.
2) At expiration the call will be worth either $0 ($55 stock price) or $15 ($85 stock price). If worth $15, it will take 2 calls plus the loan to make the payoff $85.

Two calls plus a risk-free loan of $55.05 have the same payoff as a share of the stock, so

$$S_0 = 2 \times C_0 + \$55/(1 + .09) \rightarrow C_0 = (\$67 - \$50.46)/2 = \$8.27$$

Lecture Tip, page 724: *It may be beneficial to comment on the initial example of a car downpayment to offer the student additional intuition on why an option's value increases as the variance on the underlying asset increases. The students should recognize that they would be more willing to place a downpayment to hold a car if they felt the possible price range could be between $4,500 and $5,500 rather than between $4,900 and $5,100 on a $5,000 asking price for a car. The potential loss of $100 (should another dealer's price actually be $5,100) should not worry them but a loss of $500 (should the other dealer's price actually be $5,500) would encourage the purchaser to desire some insurance to hold the car. If the car shopper finds another dealer actually selling the car for the lower price, the shopper simply forfeits the downpayment, in which case, the value of the downpayment is lost.*

C. A Closer Look

Let ΔS equal the difference in the possible stock prices, and let ΔC be the difference in option values at expiration. Then the number of options needed to replicate the possible stock prices is $\Delta S/\Delta C$.

T20.7: Five Factors that Determine Option Values

20.4 EQUITY AS A CALL OPTION ON THE FIRM'S ASSETS

T20.8: Equity as a Call Option

-Viewing the common stock of a levered firm as a call option.

The underlying asset is the value of the firm (the value of its assets). The stockholders have a call on this value with an exercise price equal to the face value of the firm's debt. If the firm's assets are worth more than the debt, the option is in the money and stockholders "exercise" by paying off the debt. If, however, the face value of the debt is greater than the value of the firm's assets, the option expires unexercised (default and bankruptcy). The bondholders can be viewed as owning the firm's assets and having written a call against them.

A. Case I: The Debt is Risk-Free

The option will be in the money: Outlining the method

Suppose a firm with assets currently worth \$1,000 has a pure discount bond outstanding with a face value of \$1,000. Assume the firm's assets will be worth \$1,200 or \$1,400 in one period. Finally, the risk-free rate is 11%. What is the value of the firm's equity?

Duplicating the payoff

Since the option is sure to finish in the money, $C_0 = S_0 - E/(1+R_f)$ can be used to value the option. The value of the equity = C_0 = \$1,000 – \$1,000/(1.11) = \$99.10. Thus the debt must be worth \$1,000 – \$99.10 = \$900.90 (i.e., assets = liabilities + equity). This is confirmed by simply discounting the \$1,000 debt at 11%.

B. Case II: The Debt is Risky

-Suppose all the circumstances are the same as above except the firm's assets will be worth either \$900 or \$1,700 in one period. How much is the debt worth? The equity?

Duplicating the payoff

1) The present value of a $900 payoff at 11% is $810.81.
2) At expiration the call (equity) will either be worth $0 or $700. If $700, it will take $\Delta S/\Delta C$ = ($1,700 – $900)/($700 – $0) = 8/7 calls + the risk-free loan to make the payoff $1,700.

$$S_0 = \Delta S/\Delta C \times C_0 + \$810.81 \rightarrow \$1{,}000 = 8/7 \times C_0 + \$810.81 \rightarrow C_0 = \$165.54$$

Since the equity is one call, it is worth $165.54. The debt must be worth at total of $1,000 – $165.54 = $834.46 (which implies a discount rate or cost of debt of 19.84%).

Lecture Tip, page 727: *The instructor might ask why a company, operating under Chapter 11 bankruptcy protection, could have a positive market equity value since the company is generally not able to pay off its creditors, should the company be liquidated. The instructor could reference the option value imbedded in the firm's assets, yet controlled by management.*

One might provide a brief example:

Assets (M.V.) = $1,000	*Bonds (B.V.) = $1,500*
	Equity = ?

Assume the company is considering an investment in one of two projects:

1. Project A has an expected payoff of $1,000, but, because of its extremely high risk, has a NPV of only $50 .

2. Project B has an expected payoff of $400, but is considered a very secure investment, and has a NPV of $200.

Project B, with the higher NPV, would normally be preferred, but if they accept project B, its payoff, when combined with the current $1,000 value of assets, would fall short of the $1,500 necessary to pay off the bondholders. The only project which will possibly save the company is the lower NPV project, Project A, with the possible high payoff at the project's conclusion. If project A fails, the stockholder's allow the bondholders to take over the firm, which would have occurred with project B anyway, whether project B was successful or not.

The instructor could also use the Savings and Loan environment of the 1980s to provide examples of the risky investments the industry undertook due (at least in part) to their low or negative equity position.

20.5 WARRANTS

Warrant—security issued by firms that gives the holder the right, but not the obligation, to purchase common stock directly from the company at a fixed price for a given period of time.

Sweeteners or *equity kickers*—warrants issued in combination with privately placed loans or bonds, public issues of bonds, and new stock issues.

A. The Difference between Warrants and Call Options

Although similar to call options, warrants involve the firm issuing new stock and receiving cash.

B. Warrants and the Value of the Firm

Suppose Ms. Burton and Mr. Peterson put up $2,000 each and buy 125 barrels of crude oil at $32 a barrel. They incorporate, issue one share each to themselves and name the firm BP Incorporated.

1. The Effect of a Call Option

Suppose Mr. Peterson immediately writes a call giving Mr. Patel the right to buy the share at $2,400 any time in the next six months.

At the end of six months oil has gone to $40 a barrel, and the share is worth $2,500 (half of 125 barrels at $40). Mr. Patel exercises his call and pays Mr. Peterson $2,400 for the share.

The number of shares and their value is unaffected by the option transaction.

2. The Effect of a Warrant

Suppose that instead of Mr. Peterson selling a call, BP, Inc. had sold a warrant to Mr. Patel. The warrant has an exercise price of $2,400.

As before, oil goes to $40 a barrel. Mr. Patel exercises his warrant, pays $2,400 to BP, and receives one share.

The firm now has oil worth $5,000 plus the $2,400 in cash from Mr. Patel. With $7,400 in assets, each of the three shares is worth $2,466.67.

Mr. Patel has gained $66.67, while Ms. Burton and Mr. Peterson now have shares worth $33.33 less than what they would have been if no warrant was issued ($2,466.67 versus $2,500). Of course, Burton and Peterson got the proceeds from the sale of the warrant earlier.

3. Warrant Value and Stock Value

When in the money, outstanding warrants represent claims against the value of the firm that will be reflected in the market stock price. Thus, the stock price just before and just after the exercise of warrants will be the same.

4. Earnings Dilution

Exercise of warrants increases the number of shares outstanding, and EPS decreases.

Firms with significant amounts of warrants and convertibles outstanding report earnings on a *fully-diluted basis.*

20.6 CONVERTIBLE BONDS

Convertible bond—a bond that may be converted into a fixed number of shares of common stock on or before the maturity date.

A. Features of a Convertible Bond

Conversion ratio—the number of shares per $1,000 bond to be had at conversion.

Conversion price—the bond's (or preferred's) par value divided by the conversion ratio.

Conversion premium—difference between the conversion price and the current stock price divided by the current stock price.

Example:

Consider a convertible bond with a conversion price of $50 per share. The conversion ratio is 20. If the stock sells for $40 per share at issue, the conversion premium is ($50 – $40)/$40 = 25%.

B. Value of a Convertible Bond

1. *Straight bond value*—what the bond would sell for if it didn't have a conversion feature, i.e., the discounted coupons and face value at maturity.

2. *Conversion value*—what a convertible bond would be worth if it were converted right now.

T20.9: Minimum Value of a Convertible Bond

3. *Floor value for a convertible*—a convertible will not sell for less than the greater of the straight bond value or the conversion value.

T20.10: Value of a Convertible Bond

4. *Option value*—the convertible feature of a bond is in effect a call option on the stock. Holders in effect get a bond and a call, where the exercise price of the call is the bond. Unless the firm is forcing conversion or is in bankruptcy, the call option makes a convertible more valuable than a comparable straight bond.

20.7 REASONS FOR ISSUING WARRANTS AND CONVERTIBLES

Conventional wisdom on warrants and convertibles:

1. They make bonds "cheap"
2. They allow deferred common stock sales at relatively high prices

A. The Free Lunch Story

The firm does poorly:

The bonds carry a reduced rate compared to straight bonds. The warrants or convertibles are not exercised or converted. Free lunch.

The firm does well:

Because the conversion price is above the stock price at the time the bonds are issued, bondholders are buying the stock at "high" prices. Free lunch.

B. The Expensive Lunch Story

The firm does poorly:

Since the stock price falls, you can argue the firm should have sold "expensive" stock instead of bonds.

The firm does well:

The stock price rises and bondholders will exercise or convert at fixed prices. The firm in effect sells stock to them for less than it could get in the market.

C. A Reconciliation

The "best" course can only be seen in hindsight. If the firm does well, convertibles are better than common but worse than straight debt. On the other hand, if the firm does poorly, convertibles are better than straight debt but worse than common.

Some readers are not be completely satisfied with the hindsight argument. The key is that, in an efficient market, the choice of security is presumed to be a zero NPV proposition. That is, the potential value to the firm of issuing warrants or convertibles is reflected in bond prices. Thus, at the time of issue, unless the firm knows something the market doesn't, there is no net advantage to one or another security.

20.8 OTHER OPTIONS

A. The Call Provision on a Bond

Most corporate bonds are callable. The firm gets a call on its bonds, but since call options have value, the firm pays for this feature in the form of a lower bond price, other things the same.

B. Put Bonds

A combination of a straight bond and a put option. The holder can put the bond to the issuer at a fixed price for a given period.

C. The Green Shoe Provisions

In IPOs, underwriters sometimes get the right to purchase additional shares from the issuing firm at the offer price. Since new shares are issued, this is a type of warrant.

D. Insurance and Loan Guarantees

T20.11: Loan Guarantees

Insurance and loan guarantees can be viewed as combinations of the underlying asset + a put option. If the asset declines in value, the put holder exercises by putting the asset to the put writer.

20.9 SUMMARY AND CONCLUSIONS

T20.12: Solution to Problem 20.6
T20.13: Solution to Problem 20.13
T20.14: Solution to Problem 20.14
T20.15: Solution to Problem 20.16

APPENDIX 20A—THE BLACK-SCHOLES OPTION PRICING MODEL

$$C_0 = S_0 \times N(d_1) - E/(1+R_f)^t \times N(d_2)$$

where

$$d_1 = [\ln(S_0/E) + (R_f + \frac{1}{2} \times \sigma^2) \times t]/(\sigma \times \sqrt{t})$$

and

$$d_2 = d_1 - \sigma \times \sqrt{t}$$

In the model, $N(d_*)$ is the probability that a standardized, normally distributed, random variable is less than or equal to d_*.

CHAPTER 21
MERGERS AND ACQUISITIONS

TRANSPARENCIES

T21.1: Chapter Outline
T21.2: The Mechanics of Mergers and Acquisitions
T21.3: A Note on Takeovers
T21.4: Ten Largest Mergers, Acquisitions, and LBOs
T21.5: Reasons for Mergers and Acquisitions
T21.6: Acquisitions and EPS Growth
T21.7: Defensive Tactics
T21.8: Adoption of a Share Rights Plan (SRP) (Fig. 21.1)
T21.9: Evidence on Acquisitions
T21.10: Solution to Problem 21.6
T21.11: Solution to Problem 21.12

CHAPTER ORGANIZATION

T21.1: Chapter Outline

21.1 THE LEGAL FORMS OF ACQUISITIONS
- Merger or Consolidation
- Acquisition of Stock
- Acquisition of Assets
- Acquisition Classifications
- A Note on Takeovers

21.2 TAXES AND ACQUISITIONS
- Determinants of Tax Status
- Taxable versus Tax-Free Acquisition

21.3 ACCOUNTING FOR ACQUISITIONS
- The Purchase Method
- Pooling of Interests
- Which is Better: Purchase or Pooling of Interests?

21.4 GAINS FROM ACQUISITIONS

Synergy
Revenue Enhancement
Cost Reductions
Tax Gains
Changing Capital Requirements
Avoiding Mistakes
A Note on Inefficient Management

21.5 SOME FINANCIAL SIDE EFFECTS OF ACQUISITIONS

EPS Growth
Diversification

21.6 THE COST OF AN ACQUISITION

Case I: Cash Acquisition
Case II: Stock Acquisition
Cash versus Common Stock

21.7 DEFENSIVE TACTICS

The Corporate Charter
Repurchase/Standstill Agreements
Exclusionary Self-Tenders
Poison Pills and Share Rights Plans
Going Private and Leveraged Buyouts
Other Devices and Jargon of Corporate Takeovers

21.8 SOME EVIDENCE ON ACQUISITIONS

21.9 SUMMARY AND CONCLUSIONS

ANNOTATED CHAPTER OUTLINE

21.1 THE LEGAL FORMS OF ACQUISITIONS

Merger—loosely used to mean all combinations, but there are distinct types.

Bidder—the company making an offering to buy the stock or assets of another firm.

Target firm—the firm that is being sought.

Consideration—cash or securities offered in an acquisition or merger.

T21.2: The Mechanics of Mergers and Acquisitions

A. Merger or Consolidation

The difference between a merger and a consolidation is whether or not a new firm is created.

Merger—the complete absorption of one company by another (assets and liabilities). The bidder remains, the target ceases to exist.

Consolidation—a new firm is created. The joined firms cease their previous existence.

Advantages

Legally simple and relatively cheap.

Disadvantages

Must be approved by a majority vote of the shareholders of both firms, usually requiring the cooperation of both managements.

Lecture Tip, page 755: *The instructor may wish to mention the recent ruling by the Delaware Chancery Court concerning the merger between Time and Warner. (Refer to lecture tips provided in IM Section 1.4.) The court ruled that Time and Warner's Boards of Directors could pursue merger talks and avoid shareholder approval, even though Time's shareholders might prefer the immediate gains offered by rival Paramount's cash bid.*

B. Acquisition of Stock

Taking control by buying up the voting stock of another firm with cash, securities, or both.

Tender offer—offer by one firm or individual to buy shares in another firm from any shareholder. Such deals are often contingent on the bidder obtaining a minimum percentage of the shares, otherwise no go.

Some factors involved in choosing between a tender offer and a merger:

1. No shareholder vote is required for a tender offer. Shareholders either sell or don't.

2. Tender offer bypasses the board and management of target.

3. In an unfriendly combination, a tender offer may be the only way around an unwilling management.

4. In a tender offer, if the bidder ends up with less than 80% of the target's stock, it must pay taxes on any dividends paid by the target.

5. Complete absorption requires a merger. A tender offer is often the first step toward a formal merger.

Lecture Tip, page 756: *The instructor may wish to add that an acquiring firm's management will typically seek prior approval from the target firm's management. If the target management refuses to grant its approval of the takeover bid, the acquiring firm may appeal directly to the target firm's shareholders. This is referred to as a* hostile *takeover and, should the takeover prove successful, the hostile takeover typically results in a replacement of the non-cooperating target management team. In approximately 50 percent of takeovers, a negotiated agreement between acquiring and target management had been accomplished, resulting in a* friendly takeover.

C. Acquisition of Assets

In an acquisition of assets, one firm buys most or all of another's assets; liabilities aren't involved as in a merger. Transferring titles can make the process costly. Selling firm may remain in business.

D. Acquisition Classifications

1. *Horizontal acquisition*—firms in the same industry.

2. *Vertical acquisition*—firms at different steps in the production process.

3. *Conglomerate acquisition*—firms in unrelated industries.

Lecture Tip, page 756: *The instructor could mention some acquisitions during the 1980s and ask the class to consider how the acquisition would be classified. The instructor might provide an example of Phillip Morris (a tobacco producer) and their acquisition of Miller, General Foods, Kraft Foods, etc. Some students might argue that these product lines might relate to food retailing and the acquisitions would be horizontal acquisitions. A example of U.S. Steel's acquisition of Marathon Oil in the early 1980s would be an example of a conglomerate acquisition. A possible example of a vertical (although it may be argued this acquisition could be considered a horizontal acquisition) would be Texaco (with excess refining capacity) and its acquisition of Getty Oil, which owned a large amount of oil reserves. The dollar amounts of these acquisitions are provided at the end of subsection 21.2.*

E. A Note on Takeovers

T21.3: A Note on Takeovers

<u>Three means to gain control of a firm:</u>

1. *Acquisitions*—merger or consolidation, tender offer, acquisition of assets.

2. *Proxy contests*—gaining control by electing the board of directors using proxies.

3. *Going private*—shares are all purchased by a small group of investors (shares are not publicly traded after the purchase). *Leveraged buyouts (LBOs)*—going private with borrowed money.

T21.4: Ten Largest Mergers, Acquisitions, and LBOs

21.2 TAXES AND ACQUISITIONS

A. Determinants of Tax Status

Tax-free—acquisition must be for a business purpose, and there must be a continuity of equity interest. That is, stockholders in target firm must end up with an equity interest in the bidder or resulting firm.

Taxable—generally, if cash or a security other than stock is used, the acquisition is taxable.

B. Taxable versus Tax-Free Acquisition

Capital gains effect—if taxable, target's shareholders may end up paying capital gains taxes, driving up the cost of acquisition.

Write-up effect—if taxable, the target's assets may be revalued, i.e., written up, and depreciation increased. However, the Tax Reform Act of 1986 made the write up a taxable gain, making the process less attractive.

21.3 ACCOUNTING FOR ACQUISITIONS

Despite accounting differences, no cash flow effects from choice.

A. The Purchase Method

Target's assets are reported at fair market value on the bidder's books. The difference between the assets' market value and the acquisition price is *goodwill.*

Example:

Firm X borrows $10 million to acquire Firm Y, creating Firm XY.

Balance sheets (in millions) prior to the acquisition:

Firm X				Firm Y			
Working capital	$ 2	Equity	$20	Working capital	$ 1	Equity	$ 6
Fixed assets	18	Debt	0	Fixed assets	5	Debt	0
Total	$20	Total	$20	Total	$ 6	Total	$ 6

Firm Y's fixed assets have a fair market value of $8 million, total assets are $9 million.

Balance sheet after the acquisition:

Firm XY			
Working capital	$ 3	Equity	$20
Fixed assets	26	Debt	10
Goodwill	1		
Total	$30	Total	$30

B. Pooling of Interests

The balance sheets are added together, and the new firm is owned jointly by all the shareholders of the previously separate firms.

C. Which is Better: Purchase or Pooling of Interests?

The goodwill created by a purchase must be amortized. Similar to depreciation, it is a non-cash expense. Unlike depreciation, amortized goodwill is not tax-deductible. Thus, reported earnings (not cash flow) are lower than those under pooling. Also, the write-up of assets reduces ROA.

Lecture Tip, page 761: *The American Institute of Certified Public Accountants' Accounting Principles Board (APB) Opinion 16 offers guidelines on classifying a merger as a purchase or pooling. As an example, to be treated as a pooling of interest, the merger must meet certain tests such as a requirement that the stockholders of the acquired firm maintain an ownership position in the combined firms and only common stock can be issued by the acquiring firm. The instructor is advised to refer to APB Opinion 16 for more detailed information concerning the conditions for classifying an acquisition as a purchase or pooling.*

21.4 GAINS FROM ACQUISITIONS

T21.5: Reasons for Mergers and Acquisitions

A. Synergy

The difference between the value of the combined firms and the sum of the values of the individual firms is the incremental net gain, $\Delta V = V_{AB} - (V_A + V_B)$.

If the value of the whole exceeds the sum of the parts, $V_{AB} > V_A + V_B$, that is, if $\Delta V > 0$ it's called *synergy.*

Value of Firm B to Firm A = $V_B^* = \Delta V + V_B$. V_B^* will be greater than V_B if the acquisition produces positive incremental cash flows, ΔCF.

$$\Delta CF = \Delta EBIT + \Delta Depreciation - \Delta Taxes - \Delta Capital\ requirements$$
$$= \Delta Revenue - \Delta Costs - \Delta Taxes - \Delta Capital\ requirements$$

Lecture Tip, page 762: *The instructor may wish to provide a few examples of synergies that may be realized from merger. From an operational standpoint, the merger may result in better utilization of capacity that may not be available in the short run such as the Getty acquisition by Texaco discussed in a previous lecture tip. From a financial standpoint, the merger may provide economies of scale in flotation costs such as access to financial markets or, should the cash flows of the two firms be less than perfectly correlated, the probability and costs associated with bankruptcy may be lowered.*

B. Revenue Enhancement

1. *Marketing gains*—changes in advertising efforts, changes in the distribution network, changes in product mix.

2. *Strategic benefits (beachheads)*—acquisitions that allow a firm to enter a new industry which may become the platform for further expansion.

3. *Market power*—reduction in competition, increase in market share.

C. Cost Reductions

1. *Economies of scale*—per unit costs decline with increasing output.

2. *Economies of vertical integration*—coordinating closely related activities, technology transfers.

3. *Complementary resources* (*economies of scope*)—example: banks that allow insurance or stock brokerage services to be sold on premises.

D. Tax Gains

1. *Net operating losses*—a firm with losses and not paying taxes is attractive to a firm with significant tax liabilities.

   -Carry-back and carry-forward provisions reduce incentive to merge
   -IRS may disallow or restrict use of NOL (see Lecture Tip below)

2. *Unused debt capacity*—adding debt can provide important tax savings.

3. *Surplus funds*—firms with significant free cash flow can:

   -pay dividends
   -buy back shares
   -acquire shares or assets of another firm

Lecture Tip, page 765: *The IRS requires that the merger must have a justifiable business purposes for the NOL carry-over to be allowed. Additionally, if the acquisition involves cash payment to the target firm's shareholders, the acquisition is considered a taxable reorganization which results in a loss of NOLs. NOL carry-overs are allowed in tax-free reorganizations which involve an exchange of the acquiring firm's common stock for the acquired firm's common stock. Additionally, if the target firm operates as a separate subsidiary within the acquiring firm's organization, the IRS would allow the carry-over to shelter the subsidiary's future earnings but not the acquired firm's future earnings.*

E. Changing Capital Requirements

A firm that needs added capacity might acquire a firm with excess capacity rather than build new.

There may be advantages to raising capital given the economies of scale in issuing securities.

It may reduce the investment in working capital from more efficient handling of cash, inventory, and receivables.

F. Avoiding Mistakes

Do not ignore market values. Use as a starting point and ask, "What will change?"

Estimate only incremental cash flows. These are the basis for synergy.

Use the correct discount rate. The correct rate is that appropriate to the risk of incremental cash flows. Don't confuse the bidder's discount rate with the rate for incremental cash flows.

Be aware of transactions costs. These may be substantial, including fees to investment bankers and lawyers, and disclosure costs.

G. A Note on Inefficient Management

If management isn't doing its job, or others may simply do the job better, acquisitions are one way to replace management. Beyond the actual replacement of managers, the threat of takeover serves to discipline managers.

21.5 SOME FINANCIAL SIDE EFFECTS OF ACQUISITIONS

A. EPS Growth

T21.6: Acquisitions and EPS Growth

An acquisition may give the appearance of growth in EPS without actually changing cash flows. This happens when the bidder's stock sells for more than the target's, so that fewer shares are outstanding after the acquisition than before.

Example:

Pizza Shack wants to merge with Checkers Pizza. The merger won't create any additional value, so assuming the market isn't fooled, the new firm, Stop 'n Go Pizza, will be valued at the sum of the separate market values of the firms.

Stop 'n Go, valued at $1,875,000, is to have 125,000 shares outstanding at $15 each. 100,000 shares go to Pizza Shack stockholders and 25,000 shares go to Checkers Pizza stockholders.

Before and after merger financial positions

	Pizza Shack	Checkers Pizza	Stop 'n Go Pizza
Earnings per share	\$ 1.50	\$ 1.50	\$1.80
Price per share	15.00	7.50	15.00
Price-earnings ratio	10	5	8.33
Number of shares	100,000	50,000	125,000
Total earnings	\$ 150,000	\$ 75,000	\$ 225,000
Total value	\$1,500,000	\$ 375,000	\$1,875,000

B. Diversification

A firm's attempt at diversification does not create value because stockholders could buy the stock of both firms. Firms cannot reduce their systematic risk by merging. However, diversification may reduce the chances and costs of financial distress and thereby increase debt capacity.

21.6 THE COST OF AN ACQUISITION

The NPV of a merger is:

$$NPV = V_B^* - \text{Cost to Firm A of the acquisition}$$

where $V_B^* = \Delta V + V_B$.

Merger premium—amount paid above the stand-alone value.

Reconsider Pizza Shack's merger with Checkers Pizza. Suppose Shack acquires Checkers in a buyout. Shack has estimated the incremental value of the acquisition, ΔV, to be \$75,000. The value of Checkers to Shack is $V_C^* = \Delta V + V_C = \$75{,}000 + \$375{,}000 = \$450{,}000$. The Checker's stockholders are willing to sell for \$400,000. Thus the merger premium is \$25,000.

A. Case I: Cash Acquisition

Suppose Shack pays Checkers shareholders \$400,000 in cash.

$$NPV = V_C^* - \text{Cost to Shack of the acquisition} = \$450{,}000 - \$400{,}000 = \$50{,}000$$

The value of the combined firms becomes

$$V_S = V_S + (V_C^* - \text{Cost}) = \$1{,}500{,}000 + \$50{,}000 = \$1{,}550{,}000$$

With 100,000 shares outstanding, the price per share becomes \$15.50.

B. Case II: Stock Acquisition

Suppose that instead of cash, Shack gives Checkers stockholders Shack stock at $15 per share totaling $400,000. Checkers shareholders end up with 26,667 (rounded) shares. The new firm will have 126,667 shares outstanding, a value of $V_S + V_C + \Delta V = \$1{,}950{,}000$, and the price per share is $15.39.

The total consideration is 26,667 × $15.39 = $410,405.13. The extra $10,405.13 comes from allowing Checkers holders to participate in the $50,000 NPV on a proportional basis.

C. Cash versus Common Stock

1. *Sharing gains.* When cash is used, the target's shareholders can't gain beyond the purchase price. Of course, they can't fall below either.

2. *Taxes.* Cash transactions are generally taxable, exchanging stock is generally tax-free.

3. *Control.* Using stock may have implications for control of the merged firm.

Lecture Tip, page 772: *The instructor may wish to add that the logic in determining the NPV of an acquisition is identical to that used in establishing the NPV of a bid which was discussed in chapter 8. However, some financial theorists argue that the acquisition arena is effected by a "winner's curse." This argument essentially states that the winner of an acquisition contest is that firm which overestimates the true value of the target firm. If bidders' estimates are unbiased, with several bidders in the contest, the winner will be the firm with the highest estimate of target value and this bid will more than likely be excessive. For a more detailed discussion of the "winner's curse," see Nikhil Varaiya and Kenneth Ferris, "Overpaying in Corporate Takeovers: The Winner's Curse,"* Financial Analysts Journal, *1987, vol. 43, no. 3. Richard Roll, in "The Hubris Hypothesis of Corporate Takeovers" (*Journal of Business, *1986, vol. 59, no. 2 attributed the rationale for this behavior to hubris; i.e., the excessive arrogance or greed of management.*

21.7 DEFENSIVE TACTICS

T21.7: Defensive Tactics

Some ways target firms fend off bidders.

A. The Corporate Charter

Usually, 67% of shareholders must approve a merger. *Supermajority amendment* requires 80% or more to approve merger.

Also, staggered terms for board members can hinder takeovers or mergers.

B. Repurchase/Standstill Agreements

Getting the bidder to agree to back off (standstill), usually by buying the bidder's stock back at a substantial premium *(targeted repurchase)*, also called *greenmail.*

Case: Ashland Oil buys off Belzbergs of Canada in a targeted repurchase. Also, established employee stock ownership plan (ESOP) with 27% of outstanding shares, and had earlier adopted a supermajority provision.

C. Exclusionary Self-Tenders

The opposite of a targeted repurchase, a tender offer for stock while excluding targeted holders.

Case: Unocal made a tender offer for 29% of its shares at $26 a share *over* market price while excluding largest shareholder, Mesa Partners II (led by T. Boone Pickens).

This tactic is probably not legal.

D. Poison Pills and Share Rights Plans

T21.8: Adoption of a Share Rights Plan (SRP) (Fig. 21.1)

In a share rights plan, the firm distributes rights to purchase stock at a fixed price to existing shareholders. These can't be detached and sold or traded, can be bought back by the firm, and they can't be exercised until "triggered." Usually triggered when someone makes a tender offer.

Flip-over provision—the "poison" in the pill. Effectively, target firm's shareholders get to buy stock in the merged firm at half price.

E. Going Private and Leveraged Buyouts

Can prevent takeovers from management's point of view.

F. Other Devices and Jargon of Corporate Takeovers

1. *Golden parachutes*—compensation to top-level management in the event of a takeover. Supposed to make takeovers more attractive to managers.

2. *Poison puts*—forces the firm to buy stock back at a set price.

3. *Crown jewels*—a "scorched earth" strategy of threatening to sell major assets.

4. *White knights*—target of unfriendly takeover hopes to find friendly firm, white knight, to buy a large block of stock, often on favorable terms, to halt the takeover.

5. *Lockups*—an option granted to friendly party (white knight) giving the right to buy stock or major assets (*crown jewels*) at a fixed price in the event of an unfriendly takeover.

21.8 SOME EVIDENCE ON ACQUISITIONS

T21.9: Evidence on Acquisitions

Available evidence suggests target shareholders make significant gains. The gains are larger in tender offers than in mergers.

On the other hand, bidder shareholders earn comparatively little, breaking even on mergers, and making a couple of percent on tender offers.

21.9 SUMMARY AND CONCLUSIONS

T21.10: Solution to Problem 21.6
T21.11: Solution to Problem 21.12

CHAPTER 22
INTERNATIONAL CORPORATE FINANCE

TRANSPARENCIES

CHAPTER ORGANIZATION

T22.1: Chapter Outline

22.1 TERMINOLOGY

22.2 FOREIGN EXCHANGE MARKETS AND EXCHANGE RATES
- Exchange Rates
- Types of Transactions

22.3 PURCHASING POWER PARITY
- Absolute Purchasing Power Parity
- Relative Purchasing Power Parity

22.4 INTEREST RATE PARITY, UNBIASED FORWARD RATES, AND THE INTERNATIONAL FISHER EFFECT
- Covered Interest Arbitrage
- Interest Rate Parity (IRP)
- Forward Rates and Future Spot Rates
- Putting It All Together

ANNOTATED CHAPTER OUTLINE

22.1 TERMINOLOGY

T22.2: International Finance Terminology

American Depository Receipt (ADR)—security issued in the U.S. representing shares of a foreign stock and allowing that stock to be traded in the U.S.

Belgian dentist—stereotypical buyer of Eurobonds.

Cross-rate—implicit exchange rate between two currencies quoted in a third currency (usually the U.S. dollar).

European Currency Unit (ECU)—index of 10 European currencies intended to serve as a monetary unit for the European Monetary System.

Eurobond—bonds issued in many countries but denominated in a single currency.

Eurocurrency—money deposited outside the country whose currency is involved.

Eurodollars—U.S. dollars deposited in banks outside the U.S. banking system.

Foreign bonds—bonds issued in a single country, denominated in that country's currency, but not issued by a domestic firm. Nearly half are issued in Switzerland.

Gilts—British and Irish government securities.

LIBOR (London Interbank Offer Rate)—rate most international banks charge one another for overnight Eurodollar loans.

Swaps—agreements to exchange securities, currencies, or even commodities.

> ***Lecture Tip, page 788:*** *The instructor might emphasize that Eurodollars are, as the text states, "deposits of U.S. dollars in banks located outside the United States." However, the instructor should emphasize that Eurodollars are not actual U.S. currencies which are deposited in a bank but are rather bookkeeping entries on a bank's ledger. These deposits are loaned to the Eurobank's U.S. affiliate to meet liquidity needs, or the funds might be loaned to a corporation abroad that needs the loan denominated in U.S. dollars. Money does not normally leave the country of its origination; merely the ownership is transferred to another country.*
>
> *The instructor might add that a dollar-denominated Eurobond is free of exchange rate risk for a U.S. investor, regardless of where it is issued. A foreign bond would be subject to this risk if it is not issued in the U.S. The reason is that the Eurodollar bond would pay interest in U.S. dollars, but the foreign bond would pay interest in the currency of the country in which it was issued.*

22.2 FOREIGN EXCHANGE MARKETS AND EXCHANGE RATES

Foreign exchange market—market for exchanging different country's currencies.

T22.3: International Currency Symbols (Table 22.1)

A. Exchange Rates

T22.4: Exchange Rate Quotations (Table 22.2, 2 pages)

In practice, almost all trading of currencies is with prices quoted in U.S. dollars.

Direct or American quote—number of U.S. dollars to buy one unit of a foreign currency.

indirect or European exchange rate—amount of foreign currency per U.S. dollar.

<u>Example: Exchange Rate Quotations</u>

The quotations in T22.4 show that it takes .8449 U.S. dollars trade for one Canadian dollar, and conversely, 1.1835 Canadian dollars trade for one U.S. dollar. That is, $100 U.S. gets you $118.35 Canadian, and $100 Canadian fetches $84.49 American.

1. Cross-Rates and Triangle Arbitrage Implicit in exchange rate quotations is an exchange rate between non-U.S. currencies. For there to be no arbitrage opportunities, the exchange rate between two non-U.S. currencies must equal the cross-rate. That is, (Currency 1 indirect quote)/(Currency 2 indirect quote) should equal Currency 1 per unit Currency 2.

T22.5: Triangle Arbitrage

Example: Triangle Arbitrage

Suppose the indirect quote on the Japanese Yen (Currency 1) is 133.90 and the indirect quote on the South Korean Won (Currency 2) is 666.00. If the exchange rate is .1750 Yen per Won, does an arbitrage opportunity exist?

Yes. The no-arbitrage cross-rate is (133.90/666) = .20105 Yen per Won. So the Won is cheaper in Yen than in dollars. To make an arbitrage profit, first buy Yen with dollars, say ¥133900 for $1,000 U.S. Next, trade the Yen for 765,142.86 Won. Finally, trade the Won for $1,148.86 U.S. for a quick $148.86 profit.

In general:

If the exchange rate (Currency 1 per Currency 2) is less than the implied cross-rate (Currency 1 indirect quote)/(Currency 2 indirect quote), then buy Currency 1 with dollars, trade Currency 1 for Currency 2, trade Currency 2 for dollars.

If the exchange rate (Currency 1 per Currency 2) is above the implied cross-rate (Currency 1 indirect quote)/(Currency 2 indirect quote), then buy Currency 2 with dollars, trade Currency 2 for Currency 1, trade Currency 1 for dollars.

Lecture Tip, page 794: *The opportunity to exploit a triangle arbitrage may appear like an easy opportunity to make quick, riskless profit for the student. The instructor should mention that inequities among currency rates are slight and quickly driven back into equilibrium by professional traders. Even if a small investor was able to exploit any imbalance in currency rates, transaction costs would probably erase any profit realized from the triangle arbitrage.*

B. Types of Transactions

Spot trade—exchange of currencies based upon current quotes (*spot exchange rate*), for settlement within two days.

Forward trade—agreement for an exchange in the future at the *forward exchange rate.* If the direct quote forward exchange rate is higher than the spot rate, the currency is selling at a *premium*; if lower, at a *discount.*

22.3 PURCHASING POWER PARITY

A. Absolute Purchasing Power Parity (PPP)

Absolute PPP states that a commodity should sell for the same real price regardless of the currency used to purchase it.

Let S_0 be the spot exchange rate (indirect quote) between a currency and the U.S. dollar at time 0. Let P_F be the foreign price of a commodity, and P_{US} be the U.S. price. Absolute PPP states:

$$P_F = S_0 \times P_{US}$$

Because of product differences, barriers to trade, tariffs, and transportation costs, absolute PPP tends to hold only for traded commodities with low transfer costs.

<u>Example: Gold</u>

Gold is a commodity that is easily traded by receipt. If gold is selling for £195 in London, and the spot rate between pounds and dollars is .5940, what price is gold likely to sell for in New York? Rearranging $P_F = S_0 \times P_{US}$ gives $P_{US} = (P_F/S_0) =$ (£195/.5940) = \$328.28.

B. Relative Purchasing Power Parity

The *change* in the exchange rate is determined by the difference in the inflation rates between two countries.

$S_0 =$ Current indirect quote spot exchange rate

$E[S_t] =$ Expected exchange rate in t periods

$h_{US} =$ Inflation rate (expected) in the U.S.

$h_F =$ Foreign country inflation rate (expected)

In general, relative PPP states the expected exchange rate t periods hence is (approximately):

$$E[S_t] = S_0 \times [1 + (h_F - h_{US})]^t$$

1. <u>Currency Appreciation and Depreciation</u>—Statements such as "the dollar was stronger today" are made from the perspective of an indirect quote exchange rate. That is, a stronger dollar means more of a foreign currency is needed to buy one U.S. dollar and vice-versa for a "weaker" dollar.

Lecture Tip, page 798: *When asked, "Which is better; a stronger dollar or a weaker dollar?," most students answer a stronger one. While this makes imports relatively cheaper, it makes U.S. exports relatively more expensive. In general, consumers like a stronger dollar and producers (especially exporters) a weaker one.*

The U.S. government has spent considerable time and energy in recent times to make the dollar cheaper against the yen in an effort to reduce the U.S. trade deficit with Japan.

Lecture Tip, page 798: *The issue of relative PPP may be reinforced by having the students consider a product that sells in both England and the United States at identical relative prices; i.e., with a $1 to .5 pound relationship, the product would sell for $1 in the United States and .5 pounds in England. If the inflation rate is 4 percent per year in the U.S., the product would cost $1.04 in one year.*

However, if, in England, inflation is expected to average 10 percent per year, the product would cost .55 pounds in one year. The student should recognize that, if they received $1.04 aftertax from an investment, they would be able to purchase the product in the United States but, if the currency rate remained at $1 to .5 pounds, they would not be able to purchase the product in England one year later since converting $1.04 to pounds would yield .52 pounds, leaving the U.S. purchaser .03 pounds short of the required price of the product in England.

Thus, to maintain parity, the dollar should rise in value (purchase more than .5 pounds in the future) to maintain relative PPP. The instructor may wish to use this simplified example to introduce the issue of the International Fisher Effect in Section 22.4.

22.4 INTEREST RATE PARITY, UNBIASED FORWARD RATES, AND THE INTERNATIONAL FISHER EFFECT

F_t = Forward exchange rate for settlement at time t

R_{US} = U.S. nominal risk-free interest rate

R_F = Foreign country nominal risk-free interest rate

A. Covered Interest Arbitrage

A covered interest arbitrage exists when an arbitrage profit can be made by converting dollars into a foreign currency, investing at that country's interest rate, taking a forward contract to convert the foreign currency back into U.S. dollars for more than could earned than by directly investing at the U.S. nominal rate. The foreign investment yields a total of $S_0 \times (1+R_F)/F_1$ per dollar. If this is greater than the U.S. yield of $(1 + R_{US})$ per dollar, an arbitrage opportunity exists.

B. Interest Rate Parity (IRP)

To prevent covered interest arbitrage, $S_0 \times (1 + R_F)/F_1 = (1 + R_{US})$ must hold. Rearranging terms gives the *interest rate parity (IRP)* condition:

$$F_1/S_0 = (1 + R_F)/(1 + R_{US}).$$

Useful approximations:

$$(F_1 - S_0)/S_0 = R_F - R_{US}$$

and

$$F_t = S_0 \times [1 + (R_F - R_{US})]^t$$

Loosely, IRP says the difference in interest rates between two countries is just offset by the change in the relative value of the currencies.

Example:

Suppose the French Franc spot rate (indirect quote) is 6.3800. If $R_F = 6\%$ and $R_{US} = 8\%$, what F_1 will prevent covered interest rate arbitrage?

$$6.3800 \times [1 + (.06 - .08)] = \text{FF } 6.2524$$

C. Forward Rates and Future Spot Rates

Unbiased forward rates (UFR)—states the forward rate, F_t, is equal to the *expected* future spot rate, $E[S_t]$. That is, on average, forward rates neither consistently understate nor overstate the future spot rate.

$$F_t = E[S_t]$$

D. Putting It All Together

PPP:	$E[S_1] =$	$S_0 \times [1 + (h_F - h_{US})]$
IRP:	$F_1 =$	$S_0 \times [1 + (R_F - R_{US})]$
UFR:	$F_1 =$	$E[S_1]$

Uncovered interest parity (UIP)—combining UFR and IRP gives:

$E[S_1] = S_0 \times [1 + (R_F - R_{US})]$ and $E[S_t] = S_0 \times [1 + (R_F - R_{US})]^t$

The International Fisher Effect—combining PPP and UIP gives:

$$S_0 \times [1 + (h_F - h_{US})] = S_0 \times [1 + (R_F - R_{US})]$$

so that:

$h_F - h_{US} = R_F - R_{US}$

And finally:

$R_{US} - h_{US} = R_F - h_F$

The IFE says that *real* rates must be equal across countries.

22.5 INTERNATIONAL CAPITAL BUDGETING

A. Method 1: The Home Currency Approach

This method involves converting the foreign cash flows into dollars, then discount to find the NPV.

B. Method 2: The Foreign Currency Approach

In this approach, we determine the comparable foreign discount rate, find the NPV of foreign cash flows, and convert this NPV to dollars.

T22.6: International Capital Budgeting: An Example

Example:

Pizza Shack is considering opening a store in Mexico City, Mexico. The store would cost $1.5 million, or 3,646,500,000 pesos to open. Shack hopes to operate the store for 2 years and then sell it at the end of the second year to a local franchisee. The cash flows are expected to be 250,000,000 pesos the first year, and 5 billion pesos the second year. The current spot exchange rate for Mexican pesos is 2,431.00. The U.S. risk-free rate is 7% and the Mexican risk-free rate is 10%. The required return (U.S.) is 12%.

1. The home currency approach.

Using the uncovered interest parity relation $E[S_t] = S_0 \times [1 + (R_F - R_{US})]^t$, the projected exchange rates for the store are:

$$E[S_1] = 2{,}431 \times [1 + (.10 - .07)]^1 = 2{,}503.93$$
$$E[S_2] = 2{,}431 \times [1 + (.10 - .07)]^2 = 2{,}579.05$$

Year	Cash Flow (pesos)	Expected exchange rate	Cash Flow (dollars)
0	−3,646,500,000	2,431.00	−$1,500,000
1	250,000,000	2,503.93	99,843.05
2	5,000,000,000	2,579.05	1,938,698.36

$$\text{NPV} = -1{,}500{,}000 + 99{,}843.05/1.12 + 1{,}938{,}698.36/1.12^2 = \$134{,}664.04$$

2. The foreign currency approach.

Using the international Fisher effect, the difference in nominal rates, $R_F - R_{US}$, is equal to the difference in inflation rates, $h_F - h_{US}$. So a 3% inflation premium needs to be factored into the required U.S. return, giving [(1.12 × 1.03) − 1] = 15.36% considering inflation.

$$\begin{aligned}\text{NPV}_F &= -3{,}646{,}500{,}000 + 250{,}000{,}000/1.1536 + 5{,}000{,}000{,}000/1.1536^2 \\ &= 327{,}371{,}337.6 \text{ pesos}\end{aligned}$$

$$\text{NPV}_\$ = 327{,}371{,}337.6/2{,}431 = \$134{,}665.30$$

Note that the two approaches will produce *exactly* the same answers if the exact forms of the various parity equations are used.

C. Unremitted Cash Flows

Not all cash flows from foreign operations can be remitted to the parent.

Ways foreign subsidiaries remit funds to a parent:

1. Dividends
2. Management fees for central services
3. Royalties on trade names and patents

Blocked funds—funds that cannot be currently remitted.

Ethics Notes, page 807: *The following case may be used as a class example to expose the class to the ethical problems involving shell corporations which attempt to conduct business on the fringe of violating international law.*

In February 1989, the West German Chemical Industry Association suspended the membership of Imhausen Chemie, a major West German chemical manufacturer in response to the charge that Imhausen supplied Libya with the plant and technology to produce chemical weapons. In June 1990, the former Managing Director of Imhausen was convicted of tax evasion and violating West Germany's export control laws.

In November 1984, a shell corporation had been established in Hong Kong to conceal actual ownership of the chemical operations. In April 1987, a subsidiary of the shell corporation was established in Hamburg, West Germany for the sole purpose of acquiring materials from Imhausen; thus circumventing German export laws. An elaborate shipping network was established to fake end-user destinations and sell to Libya.

Reports later surfaced that Libya had constructed a chemical weapons factory. Imhausen did not deny the plant's existence but Imhausen, as well as the government of Libya, claimed that the plant was being used for the manufacture of medicinal drugs. International treaties forbade the use of chemical and biological weapons but did not restrict chemical weapons facility construction. The international community faced a further dilemma as aerial observation could not distinguish between a weapons plant and a pharmaceutical plant. Additionally, such plants could easily be switched to legitimate use in a few days.

While construction of the plant did not violate German or international law, the ease of conversion from legitimate use to weapons production raised questions regarding the technical knowledge transferred by Imhausen.

The instructor could question the class as to Imhausen's responsibility in the ultimate use of the plant, despite the fact that the development of the shell corporations was a positive net present value investment.

22.6 EXCHANGE RATE RISK

Risk arising from fluctuations in exchange rates.

A. Short-Run Exposure

A great deal of international business is conducted on terms that fix costs or prices while at the same time calling for payment or receipt of funds in the future. One way to offset the risk from changing exchange rates and fixed terms is to hedge with a forward exchange agreement.

Lecture Tip, page 807: *To stimulate interest in this area, the instructor might ask the students why U.S. auto producers would make a statement that the dollar was too strong and hurting their operations. One could use the example in 1985 when the dollar traded at approximately three German marks. If a U.S.-produced car costs $8,000 to produce and German competition dictated a selling price of $9,000, the U.S. auto producer would sell the car for 27,000 marks and make a profit of $1,000 (3,000 marks). This, of course, ignores excise taxes, transportation costs, etc. for simplicity.*

If the dollar fell to two marks (which it soon did after the 1985 meeting of international finance ministers), the 27,000 mark selling price would generate $13,500, resulting in a profit of $5,500. The student should recognize that a weak dollar generally benefits companies that conduct operations abroad and a volatile dollar can result in a great deal of exchange rate risk.

However, the instructor should also mention that a weak dollar results in higher cost products (inflation) in the United States since we now receive less foreign currency per dollar to purchase a foreign product. The foreign producer would eventually have to raise its price to compensate for the lower amount of its own currency it would receive per $1 of sales. The German producer would receive only two marks per $1 sales instead of three marks. If the product costs 2.5 marks to produce, the German producer could no longer sell the product at $1 in the United States and remain profitable.

B. Long-Run Exposure

Long-run changes in exchange rates can be partially offset by matching foreign assets and liabilities, and inflows and outflows.

C. Translation Exposure

U.S. based firms must translate foreign operations into dollars when calculating net income and EPS.

Problems:

1. What is the appropriate exchange rate to use for translating balance sheet accounts?

2. How should balance sheet accounting gains and losses from foreign currency translation be handled?

FASB 52 requires assets and liabilities be translated at prevailing exchange rates. Translation gains and losses are accumulated in a special equity account. Such gains and losses are not recognized in earnings until the underlying assets or liabilities are sold or liquidated.

D. Managing Exchange Rate Risk

For the large multinational, the net effect of fluctuating exchange rates depends on the firm's net exposure. This is probably best handled on a centralized basis to avoid duplication and conflicting actions.

22.7 POLITICAL RISK

Blocking funds and expropriation of property by foreign governments are among the routine political risks faced by multinationals. Worse, in many places acts of political terrorism are also of concern.

Blocking and expropriation can be hedged by making the operation dependent upon the parent firm, for example, for certain critical components or technical expertise.

22.8 SUMMARY AND CONCLUSIONS

T22.7: Solution to Problem 22.3
T22.8: Solution to Problem 22.10
T22.9: Solution to Problem 22.11

CHAPTER 23
LEASING

TRANSPARENCIES

T23.1: Chapter Outline
T23.2: Leasing versus Buying (Fig. 23.1)
T23.3: Leasing and the Balance Sheet (Table 23.1)
T23.4: Incremental Cash Flows for Tasha Co. from Leasing instead of Buying
T23.5: Solution to Problem 23.7
T23.6: Solution to Problem 23.8

CHAPTER ORGANIZATION

23.1: Chapter Outline

23.1 LEASES AND LEASE TYPES
- Leasing versus Buying
- Operating Leases
- Financial Leases

23.2 ACCOUNTING AND LEASING

23.3 TAXES, THE IRS, AND LEASES

23.4 THE CASH FLOWS FROM LEASING
- The Incremental Cash Flows
- A Note on Taxes

23.5 LEASE OR BUY?
- A Preliminary Analysis
- Three Potential Pitfalls
- NPV Analysis
- A Misconception

23.6 A LEASING PARADOX

23.7 REASONS FOR LEASING

Good Reasons for Leasing
Bad Reasons for Leasing
Other Reasons for Leasing

23.8 SUMMARY AND CONCLUSIONS

ANNOTATED CHAPTER OUTLINE

23.1 LEASES AND LEASE TYPES

Some basic terminology:

Lease—a contractual agreement between two parties: the lessee and the lessor.

Lessee—the party who has the right to use an asset and, in return, makes periodic payments to the asset's owner.

Lessor—the owner of the asset.

A. Leasing versus Buying

T23.2: Leasing versus Buying (Fig. 23.1)

The decision involves a comparison of the alternative financing methods employed to secure the use of the asset. In both cases the company ends up using the asset.

B. Operating Leases

Also called a *service lease*. Operating leases are often involved with the leasing of computers and automobiles.

-life of the lease contract is typically less than the asset's economic life; therefore, the total cost of the equipment is not recovered by the lessor over the contract's life.

-the lessor typically maintains the asset and assumes responsibility for paying taxes and insurance.

-lessee has a cancellation option prior to the contract's expiration date.

C. Financial Leases

Also called *capital leases.*

-payments are typically sufficient to cover the lessor's cost of purchasing the asset and provide the lessor a fair return (therefore, also termed a *fully amortized lease*).

-lessor is responsible for insurance, maintenance and taxes.

-generally, no cancellation clause without severe penalty.

The three financial lease types are:

1. *Tax-oriented leases*—the lessor is the owner for tax purposes.

2. *Leveraged leases*—lessor borrows a substantial portion of the purchase price on a nonrecourse basis.

3. *Sale and leaseback agreements*—lessee sells an asset to the lessor and leases it back from the lessor.

23.2 ACCOUNTING AND LEASING

T23.3: Leasing and the Balance Sheet (Table 23.1)

Statement of Financial Accounting Standards No. 13, "Accounting for Leases."

Financial leases—capitalized and reported on the balance sheet (a debit to the asset for the present value of the lease payments and a credit recognizing the financial obligation of the lease).

Operating leases—not disclosed on the balance sheet.

A lease is declared a capital lease if one or more of the following criteria is met:

1. Property ownership transferred to lessee by end of lease term.
2. Lessee can purchase asset below market value at lease's expiration.
3. Lease term is 75 percent of asset's economic life.
4. Present value of payments at least 90 percent of market value at inception.

Note: Often an arbitrary distinction between financial and operating leases. An advantage of operating lease classification is that balance sheet may appear stronger (such as a lower total debt to total asset ratio).

23.3 TAXES, THE IRS, AND LEASES

A valid lease from the *IRS's* perspective will meet these standards:

1. Lease term less than 80 percent of asset's economic life.

2. Contract should not have an option to buy at a price below fair market value when the lease contract expires.

3. Lease contract should not have a payment schedule which is initially very high and lower thereafter; it suggests that tax avoidance is the motive for the lease.

4. Lease payment plan should provide lessor a fair rate of return.

5. Renewal options must be reasonable, reflecting market value.

23.4 THE CASH FLOWS FROM LEASING

Lecture Tip, page 825: *Firm are confronted with a choice of financing a purchase via a lease agreement or acquiring property through a conventional loan. The analysis for the firm involves the unbundling of the lease agreement as a purchase and a finance contract. However, often firms bundle the asset as part of a lease and it is the only method available for property acquisition. The instructor may wish to mention that, as an example, large copiers and mainframe computers are often only available via lease agreements.*

A. The Incremental Cash Flows

T23.4: Incremental Cash Flows for Tasha Co. from Leasing instead of Buying

Three important cash flow differences between leasing and buying:

1. Lessee's lease payments are fully tax deductible. The aftertax lease payment is equal to the pretax payment × (1 – tax rate).
2. Lessee does not own and may not depreciate asset. Loss of depreciation tax shield occurs in the amount of Depr × tax rate.
3. Lessee does not have upfront cost of asset.

Lecture Tip, page 825: *The instructor may wish to provide an alternative example of a lease versus buy:*

Example:

A florist can purchase a delivery truck from her local GM dealer for \$25,000. The GM dealer will also lease the van for \$6,100 per year over five years. The van has an expected life of five years. If the florist wants to purchase the van she must borrow money from Boone National at a current rate of 10%. Which financing option is better?

The implied interest rate under the lease agreement is:

$$\$25{,}000 = \$6{,}100 \sum_{t=1}^{5} 1 / (1 + r)^t,$$

and solving for r yields 7%. This implies that the GM dealer is willing to loan money to the florist at 7% instead of the conventional 10% loan being offered by Boone National. Thus the decision would appear clear, lease the van.

Unfortunately, lease versus buy decisions are not quite this simple. The tax perspective is not straightforward; i.e., under leasing, the full lease payment is deductible for tax purposes but, under a purchase, the purchase price is only tax deductible through depreciation. The tax rules for depreciation thus impact the timing of the cash flows and therefore the evaluation of the lease versus buy decision. In addition, lease contracts are often bundled with other agreements such as maintenance, insurance, and operating expenses. Looking again at the florist's decision, the following incremental cash flows are the basis for the lease versus buy decision.

The florist has a 34% marginal tax rate and she uses the straight line depreciation method. Keeping the problem in its simplest form, the salvage value of the truck is zero at the end of the five years. To further simplify matters, the following table illustrates the incremental cash flows by subtracting the direct cash flows of the purchase option from the cash flows of the lease option.

Notes:

1. Lease Payment = \$6,100 at end of each year (cash outflow).
2. Tax benefit of lease = Tax rate × Lease payment = .34 × \$6,100 = \$2,074 (a reduction in the cash outflow).
3. If Buy, cost of truck = \$25,000 (cash outflow).
4. Lost depreciation tax shield = Depreciation × Tax rate = (\$25,000/5) × .34 = \$1,700. (lost benefit is a negative cash flow).

Incremental cash flows (lease − buy):

	Year 0	Year 1	Year 2	Year 3	Year 4	Year 5
Lease payment		−$6,100	−$6,100	−$6,100	−$6,100	−$6,100
Tax benefit		+$2,074	+$2,074	+$2,074	+$2,074	+$2,074
Aftertax payment		−$4,026	−$4,026	−$4,026	−$4,026	−$4,026
Cost	$25,000					
Depr. tax shield		−$1,700	−$1,700	−$1,700	−$1,700	−$1,700
Net cash flow	$25,000	−$5,726	−$5,726	−$5,726	−$5,726	−$5,726

What is the bank loan rate at which the buy option and lease option are the same?

$$\$25{,}000 = \$5{,}726 \sum_{t=1}^{5} 1 / (1 + r)^t$$

The bank would have to offer a 5% aftertax loan rate if the florist is to prefer the buy option. Note the pretax loan rate would therefore be 5% / (1 − .34) = 7.6%.

B. A Note on Taxes

Lease advantage is often a question of who can best utilize the tax shelters involved in the lease arrangement.

23.5 LEASE OR BUY?

A. A Preliminary Analysis

Leasing is advantageous if the implicit *aftertax* interest rate on the lease is less than the company's *aftertax* borrowing cost.

Lecture Tip, page 827: *The general rule for the leasing decision is that firms should discount riskless cash flows at the aftertax rate of interest. The leasing contract is generally not subject to uncertainty. However, there is not uniform agreement as to what constitutes guaranteed cash flows since the firm must generate sufficient cash flows to make the payments and receive the tax shields. However, it is important to note, as the example in the previous lecture tip demonstrates, that the cash flows analyzed are aftertax and therefore, the "r" or hurdle rate in the solution is also the aftertax rate.*

B. Three Potential Pitfalls

Potential pitfalls using the implicit rate on the lease:

1. Cash flows are not conventional since the first cash flow is positive. Therefore, the IRR represents the rate we pay, so the *lower* the IRR the better.
2. Advantage to leasing over borrowing—prefer the lower IRR. If we determine the advantage to borrowing over leasing, the cash flow signs would be reversed—prefer the higher IRR.
3. The implicit rate is based on the *net* cash flows of leasing instead of borrowing. A rate which is based only on the borrowing amount and the lease payments is not meaningful.

C. NPV Analysis

The *net advantage to leasing* can be determined by discounting the cash flows back at the lessee's aftertax borrowing rate.

23.6 A LEASING PARADOX

It is important to recognize that the cash flows to the lessee are exactly the opposite of the cash flows to the lessor. Thus, the lease arrangement is a zero-sum game. This situation presents a paradox which will be resolved in the following section:

> Since, in any leasing arrangement, one party must either lose or both parties break even, why would leasing take place?

23.7 REASONS FOR LEASING

A. Good Reasons for Leasing

1. Taxes may be reduced by leasing. A potential tax shield that cannot be used effectively by one firm can be transferred to another firm through a leasing arrangement. The firm in the higher tax bracket would want to act as the lessor and utilize the majority of the tax shields. *(The loser is the IRS).*

2. Leasing may reduce uncertainty regarding the asset's residual value which may result in a reduction of firm value.

3. Transaction costs may be lower for leasing than buying.

4. Leasing may require few restrictive covenants than borrowing.

5. Leasing may encumber fewer assets than secured borrowing.

Lecture Tip, page 832: *Many firms have different borrowing rates and therefore there is potential for the lease contract to be beneficial to both the lessor and lessee. For example, if a large firm (say an IBM or Xerox) has a very strong and stable earnings record, banks would be willing to lend at a lower rate. If the large firm desires to sell its large mainframe computer to the small company, it is in a better position to finance the loan than the small company. Thus, a lease contract is offered and the large company gets a sale. The small company gets a computer at a lower financing cost. This lease contract decision by the large firm (lessor) may also be considered a part of its credit policy in that it is designed to increase sales by offering favorable payment schedules.*

B. Bad Reasons for Leasing

1. By keeping leases off the books, the balance sheet and income statement may appear more favorable.

2. A firm may secure a lease arrangement when additional debt would violate a prior loan agreement.

3. Basing the lease decision on the interest rate implied by the lease payments and not on the incremental aftertax cash flows.

C. Other Reasons for Leasing

23.8 SUMMARY AND CONCLUSIONS

T23.5: Solution to Problem 23.7
T23.6: Solution to Problem 23.8

CHAPTER 24
RISK MANAGEMENT: AN INTRODUCTION TO FINANCIAL ENGINEERING

TRANSPARENCIES

CHAPTER ORGANIZATION

T24.1: Chapter Outline

24.1 HEDGING AND PRICE VOLATILITY
- Price Volatility: A Historical Perspective
- Interest Rate Volatility
- Exchange Rate Volatility
- Commodity Price Volatility
- The Impact of Financial Risk: The U.S. Savings and Loan Industry

24.2 MANAGING FINANCIAL RISK
- The Risk Profile
- Reducing Risk Exposure
- Hedging Short-Run Exposure
- Cash Flow Hedging: A Cautionary Note
- Hedging Long-Term Exposure

ANNOTATED CHAPTER OUTLINE

24.1 HEDGING AND PRICE VOLATILITY

Hedging—reducing a firm's risk to price or rate fluctuations.

Derivative security—financial asset that has a claim to another financial asset.

A. Price Volatility: A Historical Perspective

Both security prices and rates have experienced increasing volatility over the last 30 or 40 years.

B. Interest Rate Volatility

T24.2: Month-to-Month Changes in Five-Year Treasury Bond Rates (Fig. 24.4)

The abandonment of a stable interest rate environment by the Federal Reserve in 1979 has contributed to much higher volatility in interest rates over the 1980s.

C. Exchange Rate Volatility

The breakdown of the Bretton Woods or fixed exchange rate system has caused increased volatility in international exchange rates.

D. Commodity Price Volatility

E. The Impact of Financial Risk: The U.S. Savings and Loan Industry

Lecture Tip, page 844: *A discussion using the S&L industry's balance sheet structure may be appropriate to demonstrate the danger of an imbalance in the maturity structure of a financial institution's assets and liabilities.*

The instructor could reference the interest-rate environment in the mid- to late-1970s, when short-term interest rates on S&L CDs (S&L liabilities) were approximately 5 percent, and long-term home mortgage rates were approximately 8 percent (the return on an S&L's assets).

The instructor could have the students consider the impact of an S&L's issuing a $100,000, 30-year mortgage in the mid-1970s. Revenue from the assets would be about $8,000 (8% × $100,000), and this would be matched against the short-term interest expense of $5,000 (5% × $100,000). This would result in a $3,000 profit in a stable interest rate environment (ignoring administrative costs and the paydown of the principal). This profit would be maintained (again, ignoring any paydown of the mortgage principal) over the 30-year period as long as the short-term CDs could be turned over at 5 percent ever period.

One could present the March-April 1980 situation in which CD rates were approximately 18 percent. The instructor might ask the students to calculate the net profit for an S&L, instructing them to remember that the mortgage rate is fixed and the CD rate is the rate at which the liabilities must be rolled over. The students should recognize that, if C.D. rates held at 18 percent for the year, revenue on the mortgage would remain at $8,000 but interest expense on the CDs which support the mortgage would be $18,000 ($100,000 × 18%), resulting in a loss of $8,000 ($8,000 − $16,000).

However, the instructor might mention, as the text states, that there was a tremendous amount of interest rate volatility following 1979. In actuality, interest rates on 90-day CDs fell to approximately 10 percent by the first week of May 1980. Additionally, 30-year Treasury yields, which are a floor yield for comparable term mortgages, were approximately 14 percent during 1980 but fell to 8 percent by 1986.

The instructor might add that many institutions have now incorporated hedging strategies to partially immunize themselves from future uncertainty.

24.2 MANAGING FINANCIAL RISK

A. The Risk Profile

A plot showing how the value of the firm is affected by changes in prices or rates.

B. Reducing Risk Exposure

Although perfect hedging may be impossible, the normal goal is to reduce financial risk to bearable levels and thereby flatten out the risk profile.

Lecture Tip, page 845: *The instructor may wish to have the students consider the concept of a reduction in risk exposure by introducing a friendly wager they could make on a baseball game—say, the Minnesota Twins versus the Oakland Athletics. The wager could be as follows: for every run the Twins win by, the student would win $10 per run (A score of Minnesota 7, Oakland 2 would result in a profit of $50), but should the Twins lose, the student would also lose $10 per run differential. The payoff could easily be plotted on a risk profile.*

The instructor could then ask the students how they might reduce the risk of the bet, should they become nervous about the amount of the bet prior to the game. The instructor could add that there are many Oakland and Minnesota fans who would also like a similar wager. The students could hedge the wager by placing a similar wager on Oakland of, say, $6 per run. The combined wager could then be plotted on the risk profile, resulting in a net profit or loss of $4 per run differential, depending on the game's outcome.

The instructor could mention that if the students would have placed a $10 per run bet on Oakland to offset the $10 per run bet on Minnesota, they would have created a perfect hedge but, this perfect hedge would have resulted in zero profit.

T24.3: Risk Profile for a Wheat Grower (Fig. 24.7)
T24.4: Risk Profile for a Wheat Buyer (Fig. 24.8)

C. Hedging Short-Run Exposure

Often called *transactions exposure*—caused by the necessity of a firm entering into transactions in the near future at uncertain prices or rates.

D. Cash Flow Hedging: A Cautionary Note

Normally, hedging the risk of commodity price fluctuations or other product's price fluctuations essentially is a hedge for the firm's near-term cash flows.

E. Hedging Long-Term Exposure

Often called *economic exposure*—rooted in long-term economic fundamentals and more difficult to hedge on a permanent basis.

24.3 HEDGING WITH FORWARD CONTRACTS

A. Forward Contracts: The Basics

Forward contract—a legally binding contract between two parties (the *buyer*, who will take future delivery of the goods, and the *seller*, who will make future delivery) calling for the sale of an asset or product in the future (*the settlement date*) at a price agreed upon today (*the forward price*).

Lecture Tip, page 849: *In a forward contract, both parties are legally bound to execute at the agreed to price but no money changes hands today. Consider the example in which you desire to buy the book,* A Random Walk Down Wall Street *for $10, but the book is currently out of stock. The bookstore calls the publisher and orders the book, but the book will take approximately one month to be delivered. One month later, when the book arrives, the bookstore sends you a notice of the book's arrival and you then go to the bookstore and purchase the book for the $10 agreed-upon price. This is an example of a* forward contract. *The point to emphasize is that forward contracts are extremely common, but they often are not recognized as such.*

B. The Payoff Profile

T24.5: Payoff Profiles for a Forward Contract (Fig. 24.9)

A plot showing the gains and losses that will occur on a contract as the result of unexpected price changes.

C. Hedging with Forward Contracts

The basic concept in managing financial risk is that once we establish the firm's exposure to financial risk, we try to find a financial arrangement (such as a forward contract) with an offsetting payoff profile.

24.4 HEDGING WITH FUTURES CONTRACTS

Futures contract—identical to a forward contract except gains and losses are realized (*marked-to-market*) on a daily basis rather than only on the settlement date.

A. Trading in Futures

Typically, futures contracts are divided into two groups:
-commodity futures contracts
-financial futures contracts

B. Futures Exchanges

Lecture Tip, page 853: *It may be beneficial to demonstrate the issue of marking-to-market and open interest with a discussion of the May corn contract presented in Table 24.1 (Transparency T24.6).*

The instructor could have the students examine the May corn contract. The contract is standardized at 5,000 bushels and quoted in cents per bushel. The meaning of this contract is that a one-cent change in the contract price represents a $50 change in each outstanding contract ($.01 × 5,000 bushels)

The instructor could mention that an initial margin (cash deposit) is required by the brokerage account. Assume a $1,500 margin requirement for this transaction. The instructor could ask the class to compute a few calculations:

a) *The settle or close on the May corn was 253 and the change was –4 1/4. What was the previous day's close?*

Ans. *253 + 4 1/4 = 257 1/4.*

b) *If the student <u>bought</u> one May corn contract at the previous day's settle price, what is the day's profit or loss and what is the remaining amount in the student's margin account.*

Ans. *The corn contract would be worth $212.50 less (.0425 × 5,000 bu.). Since they purchased at a higher price than the current settlement price, this amount would be deducted from their margin account and they would start the next day with $1,287.50 in their account (and hope the price on May corn increases) .*

T24.6: Sample *Wall Street Journal* Futures Price Quotations (Table 24.1)

C. Hedging with Futures

Lecture Tip, page 855: *It may be beneficial to demonstrate a futures hedge and the potential payoffs for a soybean farmer who anticipates a harvest of 100,000 bushels in September. Costs to produce the soybeans are incurred long before the harvest, but the farmer is at risk should the price for soybeans fall by harvest time. To minimize this risk, the farmer could take a* ***short*** *position in the futures contract to offset the* ***long*** *position in the soybeans she will harvest.*

Futures contract terms:

-Size is 5,000 bushels
-September delivery at $4.50 per bushel.

The farmer can lock-in the delivery price of soybeans at $4.50 for her harvest by selling 20 soybean futures contracts on June 1st. Note that no cash changes hands today. The 20 contracts represents delivery of 100,000 bushels (5,000 per contract × 20 contracts).

Scenario:

Date	*Closing*	*Farmer*	*Net*
June 1st		*no money changes hands.*	
June 10th	*$4.60*	*pays $10,000*	*−$10,000 (100,000 × −$.10)*
June 15th	*$4.40*	*receives $20,000*	*+$10,000*
June 30th	*$4.20*	*receives $20,000*	*+$30,000*
July 20th	*$4.30*	*pays $10,000*	*+$20,000*
August 5th	*$4.40*	*pays $10,000*	*+$10,000*
August 16th	*$4.20*	*receives $20,000*	*+$30,000*
Sept 1st	*$4.20*	*delivers soybeans*	*receives $4.20 per bu + $30,000 profit on futures.*

Note: *Harvest* *Futures* *Futures Profit*
100,000 bu. × $4.50 = 100,000 bu. × $4.20 + $30,000.

If a bumper crop occurs and the farmer harvests 120,000 bushels, the farmer locked in the selling price of 100,000 bushels at $4.50 and would sell the remaining 20,000 bushels at $4.20 per bushel.

However, if a poor harvest occurs and the price of soybeans is, say $4.75, the farmer might only harvest 70,000 bushels. If we can assume the original contracts were forward contracts, the farmer must buy 30,000 bushels—6 contracts—at $4.75 to make delivery. The farmer would realize a net loss of 30,000 bu. × ($4.75 − $4.50) = $7,500 on this forward arrangement. With futures, the farmer would simply offset with a long futures position. The loss would be the same.

24.5 HEDGING WITH SWAP CONTRACTS

Swap contract—an agreement by two parties to exchange or swap specified cash flows at specified intervals in the future.

A. Currency Swaps

Two firms agree to exchange a specific amount of one currency for a specific amount of another at specific dates in the future.

Lecture Tip, page 856: *The following example illustrates that a currency swap is essentially a parallel loan.*

Example:

Two multinational companies with foreign projects need to obtain financing. Company A is based in England and has a U.S. project. Company B is based in the U.S. and has a British project.

1. Both firms want to avoid exchange rate fluctuations.

2. Both firms receive currency for investment at time zero and repay loan as funds are generated in the foreign project.

3. Both firms could have avoided exchange rate fluctuations if they could arrange loans in the country of the project.

-Funds generated in England for company B (U.S.) would be in £ and repayment would be in £.

4. Both firms may have been able to borrow cheaper in their home country.

The firms arrange parallel loans *for the initial investment and use the proceeds from the project to repay the loan.*

Cash flows: Assume, fixed exchange rate = \$2/£1, fixed interest rate = 10%, and a four-year loan. The matching cash flows are:

Co. A:	↓ £100,000	↓ \$20,000	↓ \$20,000	↓ \$20,000	↓ \$220,000
Co. B:	↑ \$200,000	↑ £10,000	↑ £10,000	↑ £10,000	↑ £110,000

Currency swaps are similar to parallel loans and are nothing more than a set of forward contracts.

Firm A would take a long position and accept delivery of \$200,000 for £100,000 (principal of loan). Firm A would take a series of short positions and deliver \$20,000 for £10,000 (interest payments). Firm A takes a short position and delivers \$200,000 for £100,000. Firm B takes the opposite side.

Result: The firms have (1) fixed the exchange rate for the entire loan period, and (2) fixed the interest rate for the entire loan period.

B. Interest Rate Swaps

C. Commodity Swaps

D. The Swap Dealer

A dealer who will take the opposite side of an agreement for a firm wishing to enter into a swap agreement.

E. Interest Rate Swaps: An Example

T24.7: Illustration of an Interest Rate Swap (Fig. 24.12)

24.6 HEDGING WITH OPTION CONTRACTS

Option contract—an agreement that gives the owner the right, but not the obligation, to buy or sell a specific asset at a specific price for a set period of time.

A. Option Terminology

Call option—a contract that gives the owner the right to buy an asset at a fixed price for a specified time.
Put option—a contract that gives the owner the right to sell an asset at a fixed price for a specified time.
Strike or exercise price—the fixed price agreed upon in the option contract.
Expiration date—the last date of the option contract.

B. Options versus Forwards

Forward contract—both parties are obligated to transact.
Option contract—contract owner has the right to transact.

C. Option Payoff Profiles

T24.8: Option Payoff Profiles (Fig. 24.14)

D. Option Hedging

T24.9: Hedging with Options (Fig. 24.15)

Buying a put option eliminates "downside risk."

E. Hedging Commodity Price Risk with Options

Futures options—a contract on an asset's current futures price.

Lecture Tip, page 862: *The instructor may wish to provide the class with an example of a farmer hedging with a futures option on wheat. A farmer, who wishes to avoid price movements against the crop (falling prices) will buy a put option on a futures contract. At a later date, if prices fall, the farmer exercises his option to enter into a futures contract. The farmer would receive a futures contract on the commodity and the cash difference between the strike price and the current commodity spot price. If the price of the commodity rises during the season, the farmer lets the option on the futures contract expire and simply sells his crop at the spot rate.*

F. Hedging Exchange Rate Risk with Options

G. Hedging Interest Rate Risk with Options

Interest rate cap—a call option on an interest rate.

Floor—a put option on an interest rate.

Collar—purchasing a cap and selling a floor.

24.7 SUMMARY AND CONCLUSIONS

T24.10: Solution to Problem 24.3
T24.11: Solution to Problem 24.11

PART II

END OF CHAPTER SOLUTIONS

CHAPTER 1
INTRODUCTION TO CORPORATE FINANCE

1. Such organizations frequently pursue social or political missions, so many different goals are conceivable. One goal that is often cited is revenue minimization; i.e., provide whatever goods and services are offered at the lowest possible cost to society. A better approach might be to observe that even a not-for-profit business has equity. Thus, one answer is that the appropriate goal is to maximize the value of the equity.

2. Presumably, the current stock value reflects the risk, timing, and magnitude of all future cash flows, both short-term *and* long-term. If this is correct, then the statement is false.

3. An argument can be made either way. At the one extreme, we could argue that in a market economy, all of these things are priced. There is thus an optimal level of, for example, ethical and/or illegal behavior, and the framework of stock valuation explicitly includes these. At the other extreme, we could argue that these are non-economic phenomena and are best handled through the political process. A classic (and highly relevant) thought question that illustrates this debate goes something like this: "A firm has estimated that the cost of improving the safety of one its products is $30 million. However, the firm believes that improving the safety of the product will only save $20 million in product liability claims. What should the firm do?"

4. The goal will be the same, but the best course of action toward that goal may be different because of differing social, political, and economic institutions.

5. We would expect agency problems to be less severe in other countries, primarily due to the relatively small percentage of individual ownership. Fewer individual owners should reduce the number of diverse opinions concerning corporate goals. The high percentage of institutional ownership might lead to a higher degree of agreement between owners and managers on decisions concerning risky projects. Finally, institutional owners should be able to implement more effective control mechanisms, based on their own corporation's experience.

CHAPTER 2
FINANCIAL STATEMENTS, TAXES, AND CASH FLOW

1. Income Statement

Sales	$500,000
COGS	200,000
Administrative expense	100,000
EBIT	$200,000
Interest paid	50,000
Taxable income	$150,000
Tax	51,000
Net income	$ 99,000

2. Dorff Company
Income Statement

Sales	$2,500
COGS	900
Depreciation	650
EBIT	$ 950
Interest paid	550
Taxable income	$ 400
Tax	136
Net income	$ 264

3. Operating cash flow = EBIT + Depr. − Taxes
= 950 + 650 − 136
= $1,464

4. Net income contains noncash deductions not included in operating cash flow. Operating cash flow could be positive with a negative income if, for example, the depreciation deduction were relatively large.

5. a.

Flying Lion Corp.
Income Statements for 19x2 and 19x3

	19x2	19x3
Sales	$1,000.00	$800.00
COGS	560.00	320.00
Depreciation	300.00	200.00
Operating expenses	75.00	56.00
EBIT	$ 65.00	$224.00
Tax	22.10	76.16
Net income	$ 2.90	$147.84

b.

Operating cash flow	=	EBIT + Depr. − Taxes		
For 19x2	=	65 + 300 − 22.10	=	$342.90
For 19x3	=	224 + 200 − 76.16	=	$347.84

c. The difference between accounting profit and cash flow lies with the noncash depreciation deduction.

6.

Senbet Discount Tire Company
Income Statement for 1991

Sales	$1,000,000
COGS	300,000
Selling expenses	200,000
Depreciation	100,000
EBIT	$ 400,000
Interest paid	100,000
Taxable income	$ 300,000
Taxes	102,000
Net income	$ 198,000

a. EBIT = $400,000

b. Net income = $198,000

c.

Operating cash flow	=	EBIT + Depr. − Taxes
	=	400,000 + 100,000 − 102,000
	=	$398,000

7. Liquidity refers to the speed and ease with which an asset can be converted to cash. The two dimensions represent the liquidity trade-off that exists with any asset—ease of conversion versus loss of value.

8.

Junior Corporation
Balance Sheet
For Period Ending December 31, 19xx

Assets		Liabilities and Equity	
Cash	$ 4,000	Accts. pay.	$ 6,000
Accts. rec.	8,000	Long-term debt	70,000
Total C/A	12,000	Total liabilities	76,000
Fixed assets	40,000	Common stock	20,000
Patents	82,000	Retained earnings	38,000
		Total owners' equity	58,000
Total assets	$134,000	Total liab. & own. equity	$134,000

9.

December 31, 1992

Long-term debt	$ 50,000,000
Common stock	110,000,000
Retained earnings	22,000,000
Total	$182,000,000

10. Tax bill = .15(50,000) + .25(75,000 – 50,000) + .34(100,000 – 75,000) + .39(140,000 – 100,000) = $37,850

Average tax rate = 37,850/140,000 = .2704 = 27.04%
Marginal tax rate = 39%

11. Tax bill = .15(50,000) + .25(75,000 – 50,000) + .34(100,000 – 75,000) + .39(335,000 – 100,000) + .34(640,000 – 335,000) = $217,600

Average tax rate = 217,600/640,000 = 34%
Marginal tax rate = 34%

12. Net capital spending = Ending fixed assets – Beginning fixed assets + Depreciation
= 60,000 – 50,000 + 17,000
= $27,000

13. Additions to net working capital = Ending NWC – Beginning NWC
= 140 – 175
= –$35

14. Depreciation = Beginning fixed assets + Investments – Ending fixed assets
= 147,000 + 65,000 – 133,000
= $79,000

15. The values shown on the balance sheet for the firm's assets are book values and, except for current assets, rarely correspond to the assets' market value. For a financial manager, market value is more relevant.

16.

RTE Corporation
Balance Sheet
December 31, 1991 and December 31, 1992

Assets	1991	1992	Liabilities	1991	1992
Current assets	$176	$208	Current liabilities	$ 98	$116
Fixed assets	770	881	Long-term debt	569	576
			Owners' equity	279	397
Total assets	$946	$1089	Total liabilities & OE	$946	$1089

RTE Corporation
Income Statement
For Period Ending December 31, 1992

Sales	$ 1,995
Costs	647
Depreciation	228
EBIT	$ 1,120
Interest paid	116
Taxable income	$ 1,004
Taxes	341
Net income	$ 663

a. Owners' equity for 1991 = 946 − 667 = $279
Owners' equity for 1992 = 1,089 − 692 = $397

b. NWC for 1991 = 176 − 98 = $78
NWC for 1992 = 208 − 116 = $92
Additions to NWC = 92 − 78 = $14

c. Net income for 1992 = $663
Operating cash flow = 1,120 + 228 − 341 = $1,007

d. Fixed assets sold = 500 + 770 − 881 − 228 = $161
Cash flow from assets = 1,007 − 339 − 14 = $654

e. Debt retired = 569 + 50 − 576 = $43
Cash flow to creditors = 116 − 576 + 569 = $109

17.

NearPerfect Company
Balance Sheet
December 31, 1991 and December 31, 1992

Assets	1991	1992	Liabilities	1991	1992
Current assets			Current liabilities		
Cash	$640	$735	Accounts pay.	$664	$659
Accounts rec.	912	967	Notes payable	122	103
Inventory	1,440	1,489	Total	$786	$762
Total	$2,992	$3,191	Long-term debt	2,349	2,666
Fixed assets	5,556	5,637	Owners' equity	5,413	5,400
Total assets	$8,548	$8,828	Total liabilities & OE	$8,548	$8,828

NearPerfect Company
Income Statement
For Periods Ending Dec. 31, 1991 and Dec. 31, 1992

	1991	1992
Sales	$1,145	$1,200
Cost of goods sold	450	537
Depreciation	128	128
Other expenses	110	98
EBIT	$ 457	$ 437
Interest	85	96
Taxable income	$ 372	$ 341
Taxes	126	116
Net income	$ 246	$ 225
Retained earnings	$ 146	$ 115
Dividends	100	110

18. a. Operating cash flow = 437 + 128 – 116 = $449
Net cap. spending = 5,637 – 5,556 + 128 = $209
Addition to NWC = (3,191 – 762) – (2,992 – 786) = $223
Cash flow from assets = 449 – 209 – 223 = $17

b. Cash flow to creditors = 96 – (2,666 – 2,349) = –$221

c. Cash flow to stockholders = 110 – (5,400 – 5,413 – 115) = $238

Note: $17 = $238 – 221, so the cash flow identity holds

CHAPTER 3
WORKING WITH FINANCIAL STATEMENTS

1. a. If inventory is purchased with cash then there is no change in the current ratio. If inventory is purchased on credit then there is a decrease in the current ratio (assuming that it exceeds 1.0).

b. Reducing accounts payable with cash increases the current ratio (assuming that it exceeds 1.0).

c. Reducing short-term debt with cash increases the current ratio (assuming that it exceeds 1.0).

d. As long-term debt approaches maturity both the principal payment and the interest obligations become current liabilities. Thus, if the debt is paid with cash, then the current ratio will increase (assuming that it exceeds 1.0).

e. A reduction in accounts receivable from a cash payment causes no change in the current ratio.

f. If inventory items are sold for cash at book value, then there is no change in the current ratio; it will increase if the inventory is sold for an amount in excess of book.

2. The firm has increased inventory relative to other current assets; therefore, liquidity has decreased.

3. Debt/equity ratio = .4/.6 = .667
Equity multiplier = 1/.6 = 1 + .667 = 1.667

4. ROA = .05(2) = 10%
ROE = .05(2)(2) = 20%

5. Quick ratio = ($90,000 – 12,000)/$30,000 = 2.6

6. Akella Co. spent $130 + 80 = $210 on fixed assets. This is a use of cash.

7. Montana Dental Floss Corporation
Common-Size and Common-Base-Year Balance Sheets
December 31, 1991 and December 31, 1992

Assets	Common Size 1991	Common Size 1992	Common Base 1992
Current assets			
Cash	2.22%	2.20%	1.05
Accounts receivable	5.16%	5.99%	1.23
Inventory	12.59%	11.95%	1.00
Total	19.97%	20.14%	1.07
Fixed assets	80.03%	79.86%	1.06
Total assets	100.00%	100.00%	1.06
Liab. and OE			
Current liabilities			
Accounts payable	13.31%	12.76%	1.01
Notes payable	11.44%	11.84%	1.09
Total	24.75%	24.60%	1.05
Long-term debt	10.14%	6.17%	0.64
Owners' equity			
Com. stk. & surplus	13.48%	12.75%	1.00
Retained earnings	51.63%	56.48%	1.16
Total	65.11%	69.23%	1.12
Total liab. and OE	100.00%	100.00%	1.06

Long-term debt ratio = $4,356/($4,356 + 48,852) = .08

8. The largest use of cash was in fixed assets. The largest source of cash is from retained earnings.

9. a. Current ratio for 1991 = $13,330/$16,518 = .81
Current ratio for 1991 = $14,212/$17,358 = .82

b. Quick ratio for 1991 = ($13,330 – 8,402)/$16,518 = .30
Quick ratio for 1992 = ($14,212 – 8,430)/$17,358 = .33

c. NWC/TA for 1991 = ($13,330 – 16,518)/$66,738 = –.048
NWC/TA for 1992 = ($14,212 – 17,358)/$70,566 = –.045

d. Total debt ratio for 1991 = ($66,738 – 43,456)/$66,738 = .35
Total debt ratio for 1992 = ($70,566 – 48,852)/$70,566 = .31
Debt/equity ratio for 1991 = ($66,738 – 43,456)/$43,456 = .54
Debt/equity ratio for 1992 = ($70,566 – 48,852)/$48,852 = .44
Equity multiplier for 1991 = 1 + .54 = 1.54
Equity multiplier for 1992 = 1 + .44 = 1.44

e. Long-term debt ratio for 1991 = $6,764/($6,764 + 43,456) = .135
Long-term debt ratio for 1992 = $4,356/($4,356 + 48,852) = .08

10. Receivables turnover = \$24,890/\$4,388 = 5.67 times
Days' sales in receivables = 365/5.67 = 64.35 days
The average collection period is the same thing as the days' sales in receivables, so the average collection period is 64.35 days.

11. Inventory turnover = \$74,882/\$10,980 = 6.82 times
Days' sales in inventory = 365/6.82 = 53.52 days

12. Receivables turnover = \$5,885/\$880 = 6.69 times
Average collection period = 365/6.69 = 54.58 days
Payables turnover = \$4,021/\$642 = 6.26 times
Payables period = 365/6.26 = 58.28 days
It takes PVI an average of 54.58 days to collect on credit sales and an average of 58.28 days to pay its creditors.

13. 60 = 365/Inventory turnover
Inventory turnover = 6.08 times
6.08 = COGS/5,000
COGS = \$30,417

14. ROA = \$3,299/\$120,655 = .0273 = 2.73%

15. A decrease in inventory is a source of cash; this caused cash to increase by \$100.
A decrease in accounts payable is a use of cash; this caused cash to decrease by \$200.
A decrease in notes payable is a use of cash; this caused cash to decrease by \$300.
An increase in accounts receivable is a use of cash; this caused cash to decrease by \$500.
Change in cash = \$100 − 200 − 300 − 500 = −\$900, so cash decreased by \$900.

16. Taxable income = \$1,200/(1 − .34) = \$1,818
EBIT = \$1,818 + 4,000 = \$5,818
TIE = \$5,818/\$4,000 = 1.45 times

17. 1 = (Total assets − 5)/5
Total assets = \$10 million
.1 = Net income/10
Net income = \$1 million
ROE = 1/5 = .2 = 20%
Equity multiplier = 1 + 1 = 2 times

18. PM = 346,262/8,021,042 = 4.317%
As long as both sales and net income are expressed in the same currency, the calculation is straightforward:

NI = PM × Sales = (.04317)(55,701,681) = \$2,404,597

19. Short-term Solvency Ratios

Current ratio for 1991 = ($200 + 650 + 1,045)/($500 + 543 + 214) = 1.51 times
Current ratio for 1992 = ($503 + 688 + 700)/($530 + 460 + 183) = 1.61 times
Quick ratio for 1991 = ($200 + 650)/$1,257 = .68 times
Quick ratio for 1992 = ($503 + 688)/$1,173 = 1.02 times
Cash ratio for 1991 = $200/$1,257 = .16 times
Cash ratio for 1992 = $503/$1,173 = .43 times

Asset Management Ratios

Total asset turnover = $1,400/$3,580 = .39 times
Inventory turnover (using ending figure) = $700/$700 = 1 time
Inventory turnover (using average) = $700/$872.5 = .80 times
Receivables turnover (using ending figure) = $1,400/$688 = 2.03 times
Receivables turnover (using average) = $1,400/$669 = 2.09 times

Long-term Solvency Ratios

Debt ratio for 1991 = ($3,385 − 190 − 400 − 441)/$3,385 = .70
Debt ratio for 1992 = ($3,580 − 240 − 480 − 503)/$3,580 = .66
Debt/equity ratio for 1991 = $2,354/$1,031 = 2.28
Debt/equity ratio for 1992 = $2,357/$1,223 = 1.93
Equity multiplier for 1991 = 2.28 + 1 = 3.28
Equity multiplier for 1992 = 1.93 + 1 = 2.93
TIE ratio = 500/150 = 3.33 times
Cash coverage ratio = ($500 + 200)/$150 = 4.67 times

Profitability Ratios

Profit margin = $231/$1,400 = .165 = 16.5%
ROA = $231/$3,580 = .0645 = 6.45%
ROE = $231/$1,223 = .1889 = 18.89%

20. Du Pont identity: ROE = PM(TAT)(EM) = .165(.39)(2.93) = .1885 = 18.85%

21.

Stowe Enterprises
Statement of Cash Flows
For Period Ending December 31, 1992

Cash, beginning of the year	$200
Operating activities	
Net income	$231
Plus:	
Depreciation	200
Increase in accounts payable	30
Decrease in inventory	345
Less:	
Increase in accounts receivable	− 38
Decrease in other current liabilities	− 31
Net cash from operating activities	$737
Investment activities	
Fixed asset acquisition	−$399
Net cash from investment activities	−$399
Financing activities	
Decrease in notes payable	−$ 83
Dividends paid	− 169
Increase in long-term debt	87
Increase in common stock	50
Increase in capital surplus	80
Net cash from financing activities	−$ 35
Net increase in cash	$303
Cash, end of year	$503

22. Average daily operating costs = $700/$365 = $1.92
Interval measure = $1,891/$1.92 = 984.9 days
Stowe could operate for 985 days or approximately 2.7 years

23. EPS = $231/60 = $3.85
P/E = $40/$3.85 = 10.39 times
Book value per share = $1,223/60 = $20.38
Market-to-book ratio = $40/$20.38 = 1.96 times

24. ($500 − Equity)/Equity = 1
Equity = $250
.2 = Net income/$250
Net income = $50

25. .05 = Net income/1,000; Net income = $50
.2 = $50/Equity; Equity = $250
.5 = Long-term debt/(Long-term debt + $250)
Long-term debt = $250
Total assets = $200 + 250 + 250 = $700
2 = Current assets/$200; Current assets = $400
Fixed assets = $700 − 400 = $300

26. 10 = 365/Receivables turnover
Receivables turnover = 36.5 times
36.5 = Sales/$4,000
Sales = $146,000
Profit margin = $14,000/$146,000 = .0959 = 9.59%
Total asset turnover = $146,000/$100,000 = 1.46 times
.4 = ($100,000 − Equity)/Equity
Equity = $71,429
ROE = $14,000/$71,429 = .196 = 19.6%

27. Profit margin (store) = $1.42/$114 = .0125 = 1.25%
Profit margin (child) = $.25/$10 = .025 = 2.5%
Total asset turnover = $114/$8 = 14.25 times
ROA = $1.42/$8 = .1775 = 17.75%
ROE = $1.42/($8 − 3) = .284 = 28.4%

The store does have a profit margin equal to half of the child's profit. However, relatively narrow profit margins are characteristic of grocery stores. Turnover, on the other hand, is quite high. As a result, in this case, the store's return on assets is 17.75%, and its return on equity is 28.4%. Thus, the claim is not necessarily inaccurate, but it is arguably misleading.

CHAPTER 4
LONG-TERM FINANCIAL PLANNING AND GROWTH

1. Pro forma income statement / Pro forma balance sheet

Pro forma income statement			Pro forma balance sheet		
Sales	$1,250	Assets	$625	Debt	$312.50
Costs	1,125			Equity	312.50
Net income	$ 125	Total	$625	Total	$625.00

Net income is $125, but equity only increased by $62.50; therefore, a dividend of $62.50 must have been paid. Dividends paid is the plug variable.

2. Pro forma income statement / Pro forma balance sheet

Pro forma income statement			Pro forma balance sheet		
Sales	$1,250	Assets	$625	Debt	$250.00
Costs	1,125			Equity	312.50
Net income	$ 125	Total	$625	Total	$562.50

Dividends $62.50
Ret. earnings 62.50

EFN = $625 − 562.50 = $62.50

3. Pro forma income statement / Pro forma balance sheet

Pro forma income statement			Pro forma balance sheet		
Sales	$550	Assets	$1,430	Debt	$ 800
Costs	220			Equity	830
Net income	$330	Total	$1,430	Total	$1,630

EFN = $1,430 − 1,630 = −$200. No external financing is needed. There is a surplus of cash, so either debt can be retired or dividends can be paid after all.

4. Pro forma income statement / Pro forma balance sheet

Pro forma income statement			Pro forma balance sheet		
Sales	$920.00	Assets	$2,760	Debt	$1,500.00
Costs	230.00			Equity	1,140.35
EBIT	$690.00	Total	$2,760	Total	$2,640.35
Taxes (8.33%)	57.50				
Net income	$632.50				

Dividends $392.15
Ret. earnings 240.35

EFN = $2,760 − 2,640.35 = $119.65

5.

Pro forma income statements		Pro forma balance sheet			
Sales	$640.00	C/A	$ 512	C/L	$ 256.00
Costs	563.20	F/A	1,024	LTD	200.00
Taxes	38.40			Equity	811.52
Net income	$ 38.40	Total	$1,536	Total	$1,267.52

Dividends	$26.88
Ret. earnings	11.52

EFN = $1,536 − 1,267.52 = $268.48

6. ROE = 90/500 = .18
b = 1 − .2 = .8
g = [.18(.8)]/[1 − .18(.8)]
g = .1682 = 16.82%

7. Growth may conflict with wealth maximization if negative NPV investments are undertaken merely to increase the size of the firm.

8. ROE = 50/1,230 = .04065
b = 1 − .3 = .7
g^* = .04065(.7)/[1 − .04065(.7)] = .0293 = 2.93%
Maximum increase in sales = 490(.0293) = $14.35

9.

Pro forma income statement	
Sales	$4,400
Costs	3,300
Taxable income	$1,100
Taxes (34%)	374
Net income	$ 726
Dividends	$ 121
Retained earnings	605

10.

Gerald Corporation
Balance Sheet

Assets	($)	(%)	Liabilities & OE	($)	(%)
Current assets			Current liabilities		
Cash	500	12.5	Accounts payable	2,000	50.0
Accounts rec.	1,000	25.0	Notes payable	1,000	n/a
Inventory	1,000	25.0	Total	3,000	n/a
Total	2,500	62.5	Long-term debt	1,000	n/a
			Owners' equity		
Fixed assets			Common stk & APIC	500	n/a
Plant & equip.	3,000	75.0	Retained earnings	1,000	n/a
			Total	1,500	n/a
Total assets	5,500	137.5	Total liab. & equity	5,500	n/a

11. Gerald Corporation
Pro Forma Balance Sheet

Assets		Liabilities & OE	
Current assets		Current liabilities	
Cash	$ 550	Accounts payable	$2,200
Accounts rec.	1,100	Notes payable	1,000
Inventory	1,100	Total	$3,200
Total	$2,750	Long-term debt	1,000
		Owners' equity	
Fixed assets		Common stk & APIC	500
Plant & equip.	3,300	Retained earnings	1,605
		Total	$2,105
Total assets	$6,050	Total liab. & equity	$6,305

EFN = $6,050 – 6,305 = –$255

12. Gerald Corporation
Pro Forma Balance Sheet

Assets		Liabilities & OE	
Current assets		Current liabilities	
Cash	$ 550	Accounts payable	$2,200
Accounts rec.	1,100	Notes payable	1,000
Inventory	1,100	Total	$3,200
Total	$2,750	Long-term debt	745
		Owners' equity	
Fixed assets		Common stk & APIC	500
Plant & equip.	3,300	Retained earnings	1,605
		Total	$2,105
Total assets	$6,050	Total liab. & equity	$6,050

ROE = 726/2,105 = .3449 = 34.49%

13.
1. Profit margin. As the profit margin increases, the firm's sustainable growth rate increases.
2. Dividend payout. As the dividend payout increases, the firm's sustainable growth rate decreases.
3. Debt/equity ratio. As the debt/equity ratio increases, the firm's sustainable growth rate increases.
4. Total asset turnover. As the total asset turnover increases, the firm's sustainable growth rate increases.

If these are fixed and no new equity will be issued, then there is only one growth rate which is possible, and that is the sustainable growth rate.

14. Financial planning models tend to rely on accounting numbers instead of the financial concepts of risk, timing, and size of cash flows.

15. EFN = $-(.05)(\$2{,}000)(.5) + [\$5000 - (.05)(\$2{,}000)(.5)](.1) = \$445$

16.

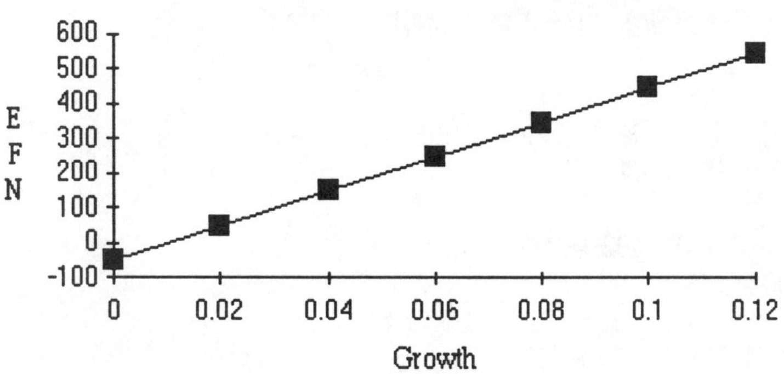

EFN = $-50 + 4{,}950g$
$0 = -50 + 4{,}950g$
$g = .0101 = 1.01\%$

If growth is 0, then there is a \$50 surplus in funds that could be used to retire debt or pay a larger dividend.

17. ROE = $.05(\$2{,}000/\$5{,}000)(1 + 1) = .04$
$g^* = .04(.5)/[1 - (.04)(.5)] = .0204 = 2.04\%$

18. $b = 1 - .4 = .6$
$g^* = .2(.6)/[1 - .2(.6)] = .1364 = 13.64\%$

19. One plus is that it is easy to implement. A big minus is that the relationships between factors are assumed to be static, at least within each scenario. It is probably true that sales, costs, and asset needs are closely associated over the long run, but, in the short run, they need not be.

20. Retained earnings = $\$1{,}000 - 300 = \$700$
$b = \$700/1{,}000 = .7$
ROE = $.04(1/2)(1+.5) = .03 = 3\%$
$g^* = .03(.7)/[1 - .03(.7)] = .0215 = 2.15\%$

21. $b = 1 - .6 = .4$
ROE = $.05(1)(1 + .5) = .075$
$g^* = .075(.4)/[1 - .075(.4)] = .0309 = 3.09\%$

22. D/E = $.5/.5 = 1$
ROE = $.1(.6)(1 + 1) = .12$
$g^* = .12(.8)/[1 - .12(.8)] = .1062 = 10.62\%$

23. $.05 = .4(1.5)(.5)p/[1 - .4(1.5)(.5)p]$
$p = .1587 = 15.87\%$

24. $.1 = .8(.1)(.5)(1 + D/E)/[1 - .8(.1)(.5)(1 + D/E)]$
$D/E = 1.27$

25. $.04 = 1.5(.2)(.08)(1{,}500/A)/[1 - 1.5(.2)(.08)(1{,}500/A)]$
$A = \$936$

26. $g^* = .04(2)(2)(.4)/[1 - .04(2)(2)(.4)] = .0684 = 6.84\%$
$ROA = .04(2) = .08 = 8\%$

27. $ROE = \$200/\$10{,}000 = .02 = 2\%$
$b = \$150/\$200 = .75$
$g^* = .02(.75)/[1 - .02(.75)] = .0152 = 1.52\%$
$TA = \$15{,}000(1.0152) = \$15{,}228$
$D/E = .5$
$3 \times D = \$15{,}228$
$D = \$5{,}076$
Additional borrowing = \$5,076 − \$5,000 = \$76
$p = \$200/\$4{,}000 = .05$
$0 = -.05(\$4{,}000)(.75) + [\$15{,}000 - .05(\$4{,}000)(.75)]g$
$g = .0101 = 1.01\%$

28. $.08 = .04(.5)(1.25)b/[1 - .04(.5)(1.25)R]$
$b = 2.96$
This is 296% retention; therefore, the growth rate is not consistent with the other constraints.

29. Show that $EFN = -PM(S)b + [A - PM(S)b]g$

EFN = Increase in Assets − Addition to retained earnings
Increase in assets = $A \times g$
Addition to retained earnings = $(NI \times b)(1 + g)$
$NI = PM(S)$

Putting this all together, we have

$$\begin{aligned} EFN &= A(g) - PM(S)b(1 + g) \\ &= A(g) - PM(S)b - [PM(S)b]g \\ &= -PM(S)b + [A - PM(S)b]g \end{aligned}$$

30. Internal growth rate:

$$EFN = 0 = -PM(S)b + [A - PM(S)b]g$$
$$g = (PM(S)b)/[A - PM(S)b]$$

Since ROA = NI/A = PM(S)b/A, divide the top and bottom of the right side by A, giving

$$g = [(PM(S)b)/A]/([A - PM(S)b]/A)$$
$$= ROA(b)/[1 - ROA(b)]$$

Sustainable growth rate:

To maintain a constant D/E ratio with no external equity, EFN must equal the addition to retained earnings multiplied by the D/E ratio:

$$EFN = (D/E)[PM(S)b(1 + g)] = A(g) - PM(S)b(1 + g)$$

Solving for g and then dividing the top and bottom by A:

$$g = PM(S)b(1 + D/E)/[A - PM(S)b(1 + D/E)]$$
$$= ROA(1 + D/E)b/[1 - ROA(1 + D/E)b]$$
$$= ROE(b)/[1 - ROE(b)]$$

Appendix

A.1 A simple model might look like this:

DOTSA LOT COMPANY
INCOME STATEMENT

Sales (S)	Input by user
Costs (C)	.8(S)
Taxable income (TI)	S – C
Taxes (T)	.34(TI)
Net income (NI)	TI – T
Addition to retained earnings (ARE)	NI – Div
Dividends (Div)	(2/3)(NI)

BALANCE SHEET

Current assets (CA)	TA – FA	Total debt (D)	TA – E
Net fixed assets (FA)	.6(TA)	Owners' equity (E)	550 + ARE
Total assets (TA)	2(S)	Total liabilities (L)	TA

To use the model, assume a 10% projected growth rate:

INCOME STATEMENT

Sales (S)	$550.00
Costs (C)	440.00
Taxable income (TI)	$110.00
Taxes (T)	37.40
Net income (NI)	$ 72.60
Addition to retained earnings (ARE)	$24.20
Dividends (Div)	48.40

BALANCE SHEET

Current assets (CA)	$ 440.00	Total debt (D)	$ 525.80
Net fixed assets (FA)	660.00	Owners' equity (E)	574.20
Total assets (TA)	$1,100.00	Total liabilities (L)	$1,100.00

A.2 The only change occurs on the right-hand side of the balance sheet:

Total debt (D)	450
Owners' equity (E)	TA – 450

In this case, a stock repurchase may implicitly occur.

A.3 The right-hand side of the balance sheet in Table 4A.2 can be modified by letting a_8 be the total debt ratio (D/TA):

Total debt (D)	a_8(TA)
Owners' equity (E)	TA – D

Once again, a stock repurchase may implicitly occur.

A.4 Let ΔD be the new borrowing, and let ΔS be the change in sales. Also, let $S_1 = S + \Delta S$ be the projected sales level. In this case, we have:

$$\begin{aligned}\Delta D &= \Delta TA - \Delta E = a_7(\Delta S) - ARE \\ &= a_7(\Delta S) - [S_1 - a_1S_1 - a_2FA - a_3(D + \Delta D)](1 - a_4)(1 - a_5) \\ &= a_7(\Delta S) - (S_1 - a_1S_1 - a_2FA - a_3D)(1 - a_4)(1 - a_5) + \Delta Da_3(1 - a_4)(1 - a_5)\end{aligned}$$

Therefore,

$$\Delta D = [a_7(\Delta S) - (S_1 - a_1S_1 - a_2FA - a_3D)(1 - a_4)(1 - a_5)]/[1 - a_3(1 - a_4)(1 - a_5)]$$

The numerator in this expression is just EFN calculated with debt held at its original level. In the denominator, $a_3(1 - a_4)$ is the after-tax interest rate, and $(1 - a_5)$ is the retention rate. For each new dollar borrowed, the product $a_3(1 - a_4)(1 - a_5)$ is the reduction in the addition to retained earnings that arises from the added interest expense. The denominator thus "grosses up" the numerator by the amount needed to cover the extra interest expense.

CHAPTER 5
FIRST PRINCIPLES OF VALUATION: THE TIME VALUE OF MONEY

1. a. $PV = 498/(1.13)^7 = \$211.68$
b. $PV = 1{,}033/(1.06)^{13} = \$484.31$
c. $PV = 14{,}784/(1.04)^{23} = \$5{,}998.26$
d. $PV = 898{,}156/(1.31)^4 = \$304{,}976.65$

2. a. $FV = 123(1.13)^{13} = \$602.46$
b. $FV = 4{,}555(1.08)^8 = \$8{,}430.99$
c. $FV = 74{,}484(1.1)^5 = \$119{,}957.23$
d. $FV = 167{,}332(1.01)^9 = \$183{,}008.54$

3. $20{,}000 = 10{,}000(1 + r)^{12}$
$r = 5.95\%$

4. 8%: $PV = 100/(1.08) + 200/(1.08)^2 + 700/(1.08)^3 = \$819.74$
12%: $PV = 100/(1.12) + 200/(1.12)^2 + 700/(1.12)^3 = \$746.97$

5. $EAR = (1.025)^4 - 1 = 10.38\%$
$FV = 5{,}000(1.1038)^{12} = \$16{,}357.45$

6. Monthly rate = .09/12 = .75%
2 years: $FV = 700(1.0075)^{24} = \$837.49$
2.5 years: $FV = 700(1.0075)^{30} = \$875.89$

7. $EAR = (1.04)^4 - 1 = 16.99\%$
Option 1: $PV = 40{,}000/(1.1699) + 40{,}000/(1.1699)^2 = \$63{,}419.78$
Option 2: $PV = 30{,}000 + 20{,}000/(1.1699) + 20{,}000/(1.1699)^2 = \$61{,}709.89$
Assuming that salary will be received at the end of each year, you should choose the $40,000 a year. You reach the same conclusion if you assume that one-fourth of your salary is received each quarter. The first option has a PV = $67,327.44, and the second option has a PV = $63,663.72 under this assumption.

8. a. $EAR = (1.02)^2 - 1 = 4.04\%$
b. $EAR = (1.015)^4 - 1 = 6.14\%$
c. $EAR = (1.00049315)^{365} - 1 = 19.72\%$
d. $EAR = e^{.22} - 1 = 24.61\%$

9. a. $1.06 = [1 + (APR/2)]^2$
APR = 5.91%
b. $1.08 = [1 + (APR/4)]^4$
APR = 7.77%
c. $1.12 = [1 + (APR/365)]^{365}$
APR = 11.33%
d. $1.14 = e^{APR}$
APR = 13.10%

10. First National: EAR = $(1.025)^4 - 1$ = 10.38%
First Federal: EAR = $(1.0525)^2 - 1$ = 10.78%
As a borrower, you would prefer First National.

11. A: PV = 100 × PVIFA(3,10%) = \$248.69
B: PV = 80 × PVIFA(4,10%) = \$253.59
At a 10% discount rate, investment B has a higher present value.
A: PV = 100 × PVIFA(3,25%) = \$195.20
B: PV = 80 × PVIFA(4,25%) = \$188.93
At a 25% discount rate, investment A has a higher present value.

12. Double: $2 = 1(1.12)^t$
t = 6.12 periods
Triple: $3 = 1(1.12)^t$
t = 9.69 periods

13. PV = $55{,}000e^{-3(.08)}$ = \$43,264.53

14. FV = 500 million$(1.04)^8$ = 684,284,525 people
$1{,}000{,}000{,}000 = 500{,}000{,}000(1.04)^t$
t = 17.67 years

15. $2{,}500 = 1{,}000(1 + r)^{10}$
r = 9.60%

16. A: $9{,}400 = 5{,}000(1 + r)^8$
r = 8.21%
B: $11{,}300 = 5{,}000(1 + r)^{12}$
r = 7.03%
Investment A has a higher return.

17. a. $350 = 100(1.12)^t$
t = 11.05 years
b. $251 = 123(1.10)^t$
t = 7.48 years
c. $8{,}523 = 4{,}100(1.05)^t$
t = 15 years
d. $26{,}783 = 10{,}543(1.06)^t$
t = 16 years

18. APR = .20(12) = 240%
EAR = $(1.2)^{12} - 1$ = 791.61%

19. t=10: PV = 500 × PVIFA(10,10%) = $3,072.28
t=30: PV = 500 × PVIFA(30,10%) = $4,713.46
t=50: PV = 500 × PVIFA(50,10%) = $4,957.41
t=∞: PV = 500/.1 = $5,000

20. Payment = 100,000/PVIFA(6,12%) = $24,322.57

21. a. 305 = $100(1 + r)^5$
r = 24.99%
b. 218 = $123(1 + r)^6$
r = 10.01%
c. 8,523 = $4{,}100(1 + r)^7$
r = 11.02%
d. 21,215 = $10{,}543(1 + r)^{12}$
r = 6.00%

22. Payment = 100,000/PVIFA(10,12%) = $17,698.42
No, the company cannot afford the computer system.

23. There is an inverse relationship between the value of an annuity and the level of the interest rate. The value of the annuity would drop if the interest rate suddenly increased.
5%: PV = 100 × PVIFA(10,5%) = $772.17
10%: PV = 100 × PVIFA(10,10%) = $614.46
15%: PV = 100 × PVIFA(10,15%) = $501.88

24. Monthly rate = .14/12 = 1.17%
Payment = 12,000/PVIFA(60,1.17%) = $279.22
EAR = $(1.011666667)^{12} - 1$ = 14.93%

25. Loan amount = .8(400,000) = $320,000
320,000 = 3000 × PVIFA(240,monthly rate)
Monthly rate = .7985%
APR = .7985(12) = 9.58%
EAR = $(1.007985)^{12} - 1$ = 10.01%

26. 5,000 = 112 × PVIFA(t,.8%)
t = 55.45 months (4.62 years)

27. 8 years: FV = 2,000 × FVIFA(8,11%) = $23,718.87
10 years: FV = 2,000 × FVIFA(8,11%)$(1.11)^2$ = $29,224.02

28. FV = 2,000 × FVIFA(10,11%)(1.11) = $37,122.86

29. $5 = 4(1 + \text{daily rate})^6$
daily rate = 3.789%
$\text{EAR} = (1.03789)^{365} - 1 = 78{,}588{,}434.9\%$

30. $1{,}050{,}000 = 850{,}000(1.14)^t$
$t = 1.61$ years

31. Semiannual: $\text{EAR} = (1.08)^2 = 16.64\%$
Monthly: $\text{EAR} = (1.01333)^{12} = 17.23\%$

32. Semiannual: $1.14 = (1 + r)^2$
$r = 6.77\%$
Quarterly: $1.14 = (1 + r)^4$
$r = 3.33\%$
Monthly: $1.14 = (1 + r)^{12}$
$r = 1.10\%$

33. $PV = 1{,}000{,}0000/(1.06)^{24} = \$246{,}978.55$

34. $PV = 70{,}000/(1.1)^2 = \$57{,}851.24$
No, the firm did not make a profit.
$60{,}000 = 70{,}000/(1 + r)^2$
$r = 8.01\%$

35. a. 0%: Alt. 1: $PV = 10{,}000/(1.0)^1 = \$10{,}000$
Alt. 2: $PV = 20{,}000/(1.0)^5 = \$20{,}000$
Choose Alternative 2.
b. 10%: Alt. 1: $PV = 10{,}000/(1.1)^1 = \$9{,}090.91$
Alt. 2: $PV = 20{,}000/(1.1)^5 = \$12{,}418.43$
Choose Alternative 2.
c. 20%: Alt. 1: $PV = 10{,}000/(1.2)^1 = \$8{,}333.33$
Alt. 2: $PV = 20{,}000/(1.2)^5 = \$8{,}037.55$
Choose Alternative 1.

36. a. $PV = 1{,}000 + 1{,}000/.1 = \$11{,}000$
b. $PV = [500/.1]/(1.1) = \$4{,}545.45$
c. $PV = [2{,}420/.1]/(1.1)^2 = \$20{,}000$

37. $PV = [2{,}000 \times \text{PVIFA}(20{,}8\%)]/(1.08)^2 = \$16{,}834.96$

38. Value at $t = 7$: $[100/.08]/(1.08)^4 = \$918.79$

39. Alternative 1: After-tax cash flow = $160{,}000(1 - .28) = \$115{,}200$
$PV = 115{,}200 + 115{,}200 \times \text{PVIFA}(30{,}10\%) = \$1{,}201{,}180.55$
Alternative 2: After-tax cash flow = $1{,}750{,}000(1 - .28) = \$1{,}260{,}000$
$PV = \$1{,}260{,}000$
You should choose alternative 2.

40. PV = [300 × PVIFA(10,10%)]/$(1.15)^5$ = $916.48

41. 10,000 = 8,500(1 + r)
r = 17.65%
You are actually paying 17.65%, not 15%.

42. Amount received = PV = 100,000(1 − .14) = $86,000
100,000 = 86,000(1 + r)
r = 16.28%

43. 110 = 98(1 + r)
r = 12.24%

44. 1.16 = .97(1 + r)
r = 19.59%
58 = 48.5(1 + r)
r = 19.59%
The effective interest rate is 19.59%, and it is not affected by the amount borrowed.

45. $1,000 = 39 × PVIFA(36, monthly rate)
Monthly rate = 1.96%
APR = 1.96(12) = 23.56%
EAR = $(1.0196)^{12}$ − 1 = 26.27%
This is called add-on interest because interest is added to principal before payments are calculated.

46. 10,000 = 1,000 × PVIFA(12, monthly rate)
Monthly rate = 2.92%
APR = 2.92(12) = 35.07%
EAR = $(1.0292)^{12}$ − 1 = 41.30%
35.07% is the rate that would legally have to be quoted.

47. PV at age 65 = 10,000 × PVIFA(10,8%) = $67,100.82
a. 67,100.82 = PMT × FVIFA(30,8%)
PMT = $592.33
b. PV = 67,100.82/$(1.08)^{29}$ = $7,201.76

48. PV on July 1, 1984 (thousands) = 875 + 650/1.09 + 800/$(1.09)^2$ + 1,000/$(1.09)^3$ + 1,000/$(1.09)^4$ + 300/$(1.09)^5$ + [240 × PVIFA(17,9%)]/$(1.09)^5$ + [125 × PVIFA(10,9%)]/$(1.09)^{22}$ = $5,273.40503

PV on Jan. 1, 1984 (thousands) = 5,273.40503/1.044 = $5,051.15424
5,051.15424 = PMT × PVIFA(5,9%)
PMT (thousands) = $1,298.61365

49. FV at year 6 = 730 × FVIFA(3,6%)$(1.06)^3$ + 855 × FVIFA(3,6%) = $5,489.93
FV at year 65 = 5,489.93$(1.07)^{59}$ = $297,310.25
No, the policy is not worth buying.

50. 1,000 × FVIFA(6,r) = 3,000 × PVIFA(4,r)
r = 14.521%

51. Effective two year rate = $(1 + .16)^2 - 1$ =.3456
a. PV = [100/.3456](1.16) = $335.65
b. PV = 100/.3456 = $289.35

52. a. Difference = 6,000 × PVIFA(5,6%)(1.06) – 6,000 × PVIFA(5,6%) = $1,516.45
b. Value of annuity due = (value of ordinary annuity) × (1 + r).

Appendix

A.1

Year	Beg. Bal.	Tot. Pay.	Int. Paid	Prin. Paid	End. Bal.
1	$6,000.00	$2,671.55	$ 960.00	$1,711.55	$4,288.45
2	4,288.45	2,671.55	686.15	1,985.40	2,303.05
3	2,303.05	2,671.55	368.49	2,303.06	0.00
			$2,014.64		

A.2

Year	Beg. Bal.	Tot. Pay.	Int. Paid	Prin. Paid	End. Bal.
1	$6,000.00	$2,960.00	$ 960.00	$2,000.00	$4,000.00
2	4,000.00	2,640.00	640.00	2,000.00	2,000.00
3	2,000.00	2,320.00	320.00	2,000.00	0.00
			$1,920.00		

A.3

100,000	= PMT × PVIFA(120,1%)
PMT	= $1,434.71
Balloon	= 1,434.71 × PVIFA(120 − 36,1%)
	= $81,274.07

CHAPTER 6
VALUING STOCKS AND BONDS

1. Price = 100 × PVIFA(8,14%) + 1,000/$(1.14)^8$ = \$814.45

2. Price = 50 × PVIFA(16,7%) + 1,000/$(1.07)^{16}$ = \$811.07
It's different from the value in Problem 1 for two reasons. First, the \$50 semiannual coupon is more valuable than the \$100 annual coupon. However, this advantage is more than offset by the fact that the 7% semiannual yield results in an effective annual yield greater than 14%.

3. Price = [.11(1,000)/2] × PVIFA(30,6%) + 1,000/$(1.06)^{30}$ = \$931.18

4. CY = 110/931.18 = 11.81%

5.
a. Yield to maturity on bond A = 12%.
b. Price = 30 × PVIFA(10,6%) + 1,000/$(1.06)^{10}$ = \$779.20
c. Price = 30 × PVIFA(10,4%) + 1,000/$(1.04)^{10}$ = \$918.89

6.
a. It is an inverse relationship.
b. The longer the time to maturity, the greater the change in bond values for a given change in interest rates, all else equal.
c. The lower the coupon rate, the greater the change in bond values for a given change in interest rates, all else equal.

7.
a. With a YTM of 12%, the bond will sell at par.
b. With a YTM of 10%, the bond will sell at a premium.
c. With a YTM of 14%, the bond will sell at a discount.

8. Bond B would have the larger price change because it has a longer maturity.
Bond A: Price = 90 × PVIFA(4,11%) + 1,000/$(1.11)^4$ = \$937.95
Bond B: Price = 90 × PVIFA(8,11%) + 1,000/$(1.11)^8$ = \$897.08

9. 900 = 30 × PVIFA(20,r%) + 1,000/$(1 + r)^{20}$
r = 3.718%
YTM = 7.435%
So, the coupon rate should be 7.435%.

10. Price = 160/$(1.25)^4$ + 160/$(1.25)^5$ + 1,640/$(1.25)^6$ = \$547.88

11. Current yield = 100/850 = 11.76%
\$850 = 100 × PVIFA(12,r%) + 1,000/$(1 + r)^{12}$
r = 12.475%
Therefore, yield to maturity = 12.475%, assuming annual coupons.

12. $\$945 = C \times PVIFA(8,12\%) + 1{,}000/(1.12)^8$
$C = \$108.93$
Coupon rate = 108.93/1,000 = 10.89%

13. $P_0 = [1.1(1.08)]/(.14 - .08) = \$19.80$
$P_4 = 19.80(1.08)^4 = \$26.94$

14. $P_0 = 1.52/(.2 - .12) = \$19.00$

15. Dividend yield = 1.1(1.08)/19.80 = 6%
Capital gains yield = 8% (equal to the growth rate of the dividend)

16. a. $50 = 2(1.1)/(r - .1)$
$r = 14.4\%$
b. Dividend yield = 2(1.1)/50 = 4.4%

17. $50 = 2/(r - .1)$
$r = 14\%$

18. $P_4 = 5(1.16)^4(1.05)/(.18 - .05) = \$73.12$
$P_0 = 5(1.16)/(1.18) + 5(1.16)^2/(1.18)^2 + 5(1.16)^3/(1.18)^3 + [5(1.16)^4 + 73.12]/(1.18)^4$
$= \$56.88$

19. $P_0 = [4/(.25 - .12)]/(1.25)^3 = \$15.75$

20. a. $V = 2/.2 = \$10$
b. $V = 2(1.05)/(.2 - .05) = \$14$

21. $60 = 4(1 + g)/(.12 - g)$
$g = 5\%$

22. $82 = D_1/(.14 - .06)$
$D_1 = \$6.56$

23. $P_3 = 1.15(1.18)^2(1.15)(1.06)/(.12 - .06) = \$32.53$
$P_0 = 1.15(1.18)/(1.12) + 1.15(1.18)^2/(1.12)^2 + [(1.15)^2(1.18)^2 + 32.53]/(1.12)^3$
$= \$26.95$

24. $P_0 = 5(1 - .1)/(.14 + .1) = \$18.75$

25. $12 = [2.5/(r - .06)]/(1 + r)^4$
$r = 17.08\%$

26. $D_1 = 8.5(1.25) = \$10.625$; $D_2 = 10.625(1.2) = \$12.75$;
$D_3 = 12.75(1.15) = \$14.6625$; $D_4 = 14.6625(1.1) = \$16.12875$
$P_4 = 16.12875(1.05)/(.16 - .05) = \$153.95625$
$P_0 = 10.625/1.16 + 12.75/(1.16)^2 + 14.6625/(1.16)^3 + (16.12875 + 153.95625)/(1.16)^4$
$= \$121.96$

27. $\$120 = 10.625/(1 + r) + 12.75/(1 + r)^2 + 14.6625/(1 + r)^3 + 16.12875/(1 + r)^4$
$+ [16.12875(1.05)/(r - .05)]/(1 + r)^4$

$r = 16.17\%$

28. $P_0 = 2(1 - .1)/(.2 + .1) = \$6$

29. $V = [1.2M/(.16 + .04)] - 5M = \$1$ million

30. a. $P_3 = 7(1.08)/(.15 - .08) = \$108$
$P_0 = 5/(1.15) + 6/(1.15)^2 + (7 + 108)/(1.15)^3 = \$84.50$

b. $P_1 = 6/(1.15) + (7 + 108)/(1.15)^2 = \$92.17$
$P_2 = (7 + 108)/1.15 = \$100$
$P_3 = \$108$

c.

Year	Dividend Yield		Capital Gains Yield	
1	5/84.5	= 5.92%	(92.17 – 84.5)/84.5	= 9.08%
2	6/92.17	= 6.51%	(100 – 92.17)/92.17	= 8.50%
3	7/100	= 7.00%	(108 – 100)/100	= 8.00%
4	7(1.08)/108	= 7.00%	(116.64 – 108)/108	= 8.00%

The sum of the dividend yield and the capital gains yield is always equal to 15%, the required return.

CHAPTER 7
NET PRESENT VALUE AND OTHER INVESTMENT CRITERIA

1. a. Payback period = 1000/200 = 5 years
   b. Payback period = 1500/200 = 7.5 years
   c. Payback period does not exist.

2. a. Payback period A: 100 − 52 = 48; 48/63 = .76
      Payback = 1.76 years
      Payback period B: 100 − 41 − 55 = 4; 4/110 = .04
      Payback = 2.04 years
   b. Investment A would be accepted.
   c. It is not necessarily the best because payback ignores cash flows that occur after the cutoff period, resulting in a bias for short-term projects.

3. Investment A: NPV = $-100 + 52/1.05 + 63/(1.05)^2 + 77/(1.05)^3$ = \$73.18
   Investment B: NPV = $-100 + 41/1.05 + 55/(1.05)^2 + 110/(1.05)^3$ = \$83.96
   Investment B is the better investment.

4. $100 = 72/(1 + IRR) + 57.6/(1 + IRR)^2$
   IRR = 20%

5. a. Payback period = 600/100 = 6 years
   b. 600 = 100 × PVIFA(t,5%)
      t = 7.31 years = Discounted payback period
   c. 100/.2 = 500 < 600, so no discounted payback period exists when the discount rate is 20%.
   d. The payback period is not affected by the different discount rates. The discounted payback period is affected by the different discount rates.

6. No, the discounted payback will always be greater than the regular payback for any discount rate greater than zero (assuming conventional cashflows).

7. The NPV is positive because the present value of the cashflows from the project is greater than the initial cost of the project.

8. a. Payback < Discounted payback < Life of project
   b. Benefit/cost ratio > 1
   c. IRR > Required rate of return

9. $1{,}200 = 1{,}100/(1 + IRR) + 242/(1 + IRR)^2$
   IRR = 10%

10. $0 = (80 - 70)/(1 + IRR) + (90 - 102)/(1 + IRR)^2$
IRR = 20%
Prefer Project A if the required return is greater than 20%.

11. A: $100 = 100/(1 + IRR) + 200/(1 + IRR)^2 - 100/(1 + IRR)^3$
IRR = 80.19% or −55.50%
B: $100 = 100/(1 + IRR)^2 + 200/(1 + IRR)^3$
IRR = 52.14%

12. a. Project A: $400 = 241/(1 + IRR) + 293/(1 + IRR)^2$
IRR = 20.86%
Project B: $200 = 131/(1 + IRR) + 172/(1 + IRR)^2$
IRR = 31.10%

b. If the required rate of return is less than the cross-over rate.

c. $200 = 100/(1 + IRR) + 121/(1 + IRR)^2$
IRR = 10% = cross-over rate. Mr. Femus will be indifferent between the two projects at this discount rate.

13. A: $200 = 200/(1 + IRR) + 800/(1 + IRR)^2 - 800/(1 + IRR)^3$
IRR = 0% or 100%
B: $150 = 50/(1 + IRR) + 100/(1 + IRR)^2 + 100/(1 + IRR)^3$
IRR = 27.08%

14. Average NI = [2,133 + 2,455 + 3,241 + 3,566]/4 = $2,848.75
AAR = 2,848.75/5,000 = 56.98%

15.

Year	0	1	2	3	4
Gross BV	$160	$160	$160	$160	$160
Less acc depr	0	40	80	120	160
Net BV	$160	$120	80	40	0
Sales		$74.00	$67.00	$91.00	$90.00
Costs		50.00	43.00	45.00	49.00
Depr		40.00	40.00	40.00	40.00
Taxes		− 5.44	− 5.44	2.04	0.34
Net income		−$10.56	−$10.56	$3.96	$0.66

Average NI = [−10.56 − 10.56 + 3.96 + .66]/4 = −$4.125
AAR = −4.125/80 = −5.16%

On average, this project earns a negative accounting return.

16. r=0: NPV = 1,459 + 2,012 + 2,234 + 1,005 − 5,346 = $1,364
r=∞: NPV = −$5,346

$5{,}346 = 1{,}459/(1 + IRR) + 2{,}012/(1 + IRR)^2 + 2{,}234/(1 + IRR)^3 + 1{,}005/(1 + IRR)^4$
IRR = 10.07%

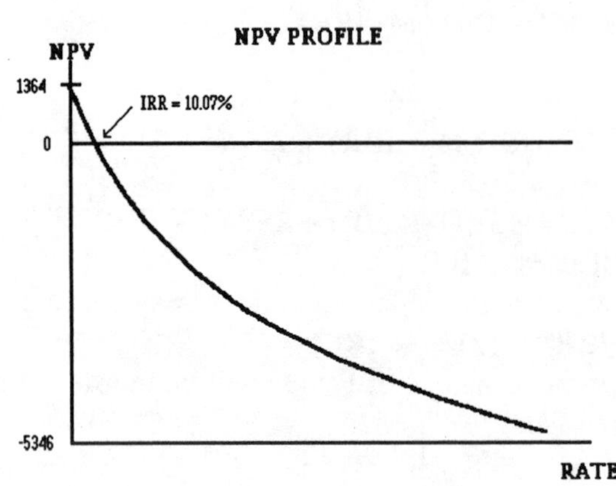

17.

Year	Cash Flow Undiscounted	Cash Flow Discounted	Accumulated Cash Flow Undiscounted	Accumulated Cash Flow Discounted
1	$50.00	$44.64	$50.00	$44.64
2	40.00	31.89	90.00	76.53
3	60.00	42.71	150.00	119.24

a. Payback period = 3 years
Payback period = 2.17 years
The cashflows occur evenly throughout the year.

b. Discounted payback = 3 years

c. $NPV = -100 + 50/1.14 + 40/(1.14)^2 + 60/(1.14)^3 = \$15.14$

18. a. A: $NPV = -100 + 44/1.15 + 56/(1.15)^2 + 65/(1.15)^3 = \$23.34$
$100 = 44/(1 + IRR) + 56/(1 + IRR)^2 + 65/(1 + IRR)^3$
IRR = 27.71%

B: $NPV = -100 + 69/1.15 + 51/(1.15)^2 + 32/(1.15)^3 = \$19.60$
$100 = 69/(1 + IRR) + 51/(1 + IRR)^2 + 32/(1 + IRR)^3$
IRR = 28.23%

Both projects are acceptable.

b. C: $NPV = -200 + 113/1.15 + 107/(1.15)^2 + 97/(1.15)^3 = \$42.94$
It is the sum of the NPVs of A and B.
Yes, we could have added the NPV's of the two projects.

c. C: $200 = 113/(1 + IRR) + 107/(1 + IRR)^2 + 97/(1 + IRR)^3$
IRR = 27.94%
It is a complicated weighted average of the IRRs; there is no obvious way in general of calculating it.

19. a. A: Payback period = 2 years

B: Payback period = 100/60 = 1.67 years

Project B has the shorter payback period.

b. Investment A is preferred when the required return < 22.5%.

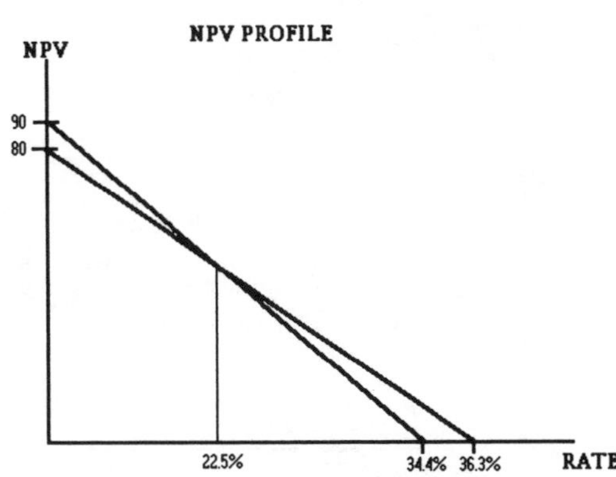

c. A: $100 = 40/(1 + IRR) + 60/(1 + IRR)^2 + 90/(1 + IRR)^3$

IRR = 34.4%

B: $100 = 60 \times \text{PVIFA}(3,\text{IRR})$

IRR = 36.3%

d. $0 = -20/(1 + IRR) + 30/(1 + IRR)^3$

IRR = 22.5%

e. You would prefer Investment A if the required return were 8%.

20. a. A: 600 + 40 − 95 − 203 − 245 = 97; 97/290 = .33

Payback period = 4.33 years

B: 800 + 60 − 175 − 210 − 270 = 205; 205/375 =.55

Payback period = 4.55 years

b. A: PV cash flows $= -40/1.2 + 95/(1.2)^2 + 203/(1.2)^3 + 245/(1.2)^4 + 290/(1.2)^5 + 1{,}240/(1.2)^6$

= \$800.09

PI = 800.09/600 = 1.33

B: PV cash flows $= -60/1.2 + 175/(1.2)^2 + 210/(1.2)^3 + 270/(1.2)^4 + 375/(1.2)^5 + 1{,}510/(1.2)^6$

= \$979.66

PI = 979.66/800 = 1.22

Since the profitability indices are greater than one, both projects have a positive net present value.

c. They don't always rank projects the same way. PI does not take into consideration the total value a project adds.

A: NPV = 800.09 − 600 = \$200.09

B: NPV = 979.66 − 800 = \$179.66

Project A is the better project.

21. The NPV for A will be greater than the NPV for B for discount rates between 0% and 20%. A crossover rate does not exist in the relevant range.

22. a. $100 = 50 \times \text{PVIFA}(3,\text{IRR})$
IRR = 23.38%

b. $\text{NPV} = 100 - 50/1.3 - 50/(1.3)^2 - 50/(1.3)^3 = \$9.19$
Yes, we should take the project.

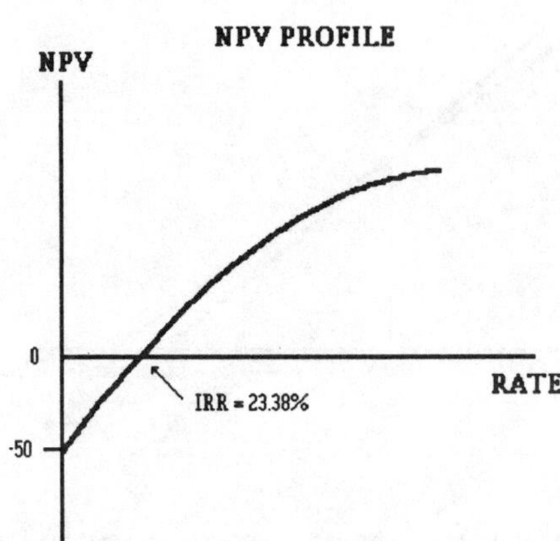

c. We should take this investment whenever our required return is greater than 23.38%. Since we receive money today and make payments in the future, the higher the discount rate, the less future outflows are worth.

23. Payback period = 1/IRR; the IRR for long-lived investments with relatively constant cash flows is approximately equal to the reciprocal of the payback period.

24. NPV index = PI – 1

25. The worst case is when all \$1,200 is recovered in year 5.
$\text{NPV} = 1{,}200/(1.2)^5 - 1{,}200 = -\$717.75$

26. The maximum number of IRR's is 4, and there are 4 in this case. The project should be accepted when $25\% \le r \le 33.33\%$ or $42.85\% \le r \le 66.67\%$.

CHAPTER 8
MAKING CAPITAL INVESTMENT DECISIONS

1.

Sales	$125,000
Variable costs	62,500
Fixed costs	20,000
Depreciation	15,000
EBIT	$ 27,500
Taxes	9,350
Net income	$ 18,150

2.

Sales	$144,600
Costs	84,780
Depreciation	15,000
EBIT	$ 44,820
Taxes	17,480
Net income	$ 27,340

Operating cash flow = (144,600 – 84,780)(1 – .39) + .39(15,000) = $42,340
Depreciation tax shield = .39(15,000) = $5,850

3.

Sales	$11,996.00
Costs	8,443.00
Depreciation	3,210.00
EBIT	$ 343.00
Taxes	116.62
Net income	$ 226.38

a. OCF = EBIT + D – Taxes = 343 + 3,210 – 116.62 = $3,436.38
b. OCF = $(S - C)(1 - T_c) + T_c D$ = (11,996 – 8,443)(1 – .34) + .34(3,210) = $3,436.38
c. OCF = NI + D = 226.38 + 3,210 = $3,436.38
d. OCF = S – C – Taxes = 11,996 – 8,443 – 116.62 = $3,436.38

4.

Beginning Book	Depreciation	Ending Book
$168,000.00	$24,007.20	$143,992.80
143,992.80	41,143.20	102,849.60
102,849.60	29,383.20	73,466.40
73,466.40	20,983.20	52,483.20
52,483.20	15,002.40	37,480.80
37,480.80	15,002.40	22,478.40
22,478.40	15,002.40	7,476.00
7,476.00	7,476.00	0.00

5.

Beginning Book	Depreciation	Ending Book
$80,000	$16,000	$64,000
64,000	25,600	38,400
38,400	15,360	23,040

At the end of year 3 the asset is sold for $16,000, a loss of 23,040 – 16,000 = $7,040. Therefore, a tax credit of .34(7,040) = $2,393.60 is received. After-tax proceeds are 16,000 + 2,393.60 = $18,393.60.

6. Cash flow year 0 = –$140,000
Cash flow years 1 through 5 = 50,000(1 – .34) + [140,000/5](.34) = $42,520
NPV = –140,000 + 42,520 × PVIFA(5,10%) = $21,184.25

7. Cash flow year 0 = –10,000 – 140,000 = –$150,000
Cash flow years 1 through 4 = 50,000(1 – .34) + [140,000/5](.34) = $42,520
Cash flow year 5 = 42,520 + 10,000 + 20,000(1 – .34) = $65,720
NPV = –150,000 + 42,520 × PVIFA(4,10%) + $65{,}720/(1.1)^5$ = $25,589.63

8. Cash flow Year 0 = –10,000 – 140,000 = –$150,000

Year	1	2	3	4	5
EBIT	$3,338	–$12,216	$29,252	$39,626	$50,000
Depreciation	46,662	62,216	20,748	10,374	0
Taxes	1,135	–4,153	9,946	13,473	17,000
OCF	48,865	54,153	40,054	36,527	33,000
Add. NWC					–10,000
Salvage					13,200
CF frm assets	$48,865	$54,153	$40,054	$36,527	$56,200

NPV = $29,114.65
The NPV is larger because the ACRS depreciation deductions are larger early on.

9. Neither one is correct. What should be considered in the analysis is the opportunity cost of using the land, at the very least what the land could be sold for today.

10. Cash flow year 0 = –40,000 – 150,000 = –$190,000
Cash flow years 1 through 4 = (300,000 – 200,000 – 30,000)(1 – .34) + 30,000(.34)
= $56,400
Cash flow year 5 = 56,400 + 40,000 = $96,400
NPV = $24,400.51
Since the NPV is positive, it is probably a good project.

11. 500 – 60 = $440

12.

Sales	$15,778	inflow
Costs	10,554	outflow
Accts. rec.	190	inflow
Inventory	267	outflow
Accts. pay.	504	inflow
Net CF	$5,651	inflow

13. Cash flow year 0 = 220,000 – 900,000 = –$680,000
Cash flow years 1 through 4 = 500,000(1 – .34) + [900,000/5](.34) = $391,200
Cash flow year 5 = 391,200 – 220,000 + 330,000(1 – .34) = $389,000
IRR = 49.91%

14. Jazzmaster: NPV = –45,000 – 5,000 × PVIFA(3,12%) = –$57,009.16
EAC = –57,009.16/PVIFA(3,12%) = –$23,735.70
Discomaster: NPV = –65,000 – 4,000 × PVIFA(5,12%) = –$79,419.10
EAC = –79,419.10/PVIFA(5,12%) = –$22,031.63
We prefer the Discomaster because it has a lower equivalent annual cost.

15. Jazzmaster: Cash flow year 0 = –$45,000
Cash flow years 1 and 2 = –5,000(1 – .34) + .34(15,000) = $1,800
Cash flow year 3 = 1,800 + 10,000(1 – .34) = $8,400
NPV = –$35,978.95
EAC = –35,978.95/PVIFA(3,12%) = –$14,979.80
Discomaster: Cash flow year 0 = –$65,000
Cash flow years 1 through 4 = –4,000(1 – .34) + .34(13,000) = $1,780
Cash flow year 5 = 1,780 + 6,600 = $8,380
NPV = –$54,838.48
EAC = –54,838.48/PVIFA(5,12%) = –$15,212.73
Now we prefer the Jazzmaster because it has a lower equivalent annual cost.

16. Cash flow year 0 = –60,000 – 250,000 = –\$310,000
310,000 = OCF × PVIFA(3,16%) + 175,250/(1.16)^3
OCF = \$88,038.50
Net income = 88,038.50 – 50,000 = \$38,038.50
Sales = 38,109.81/.61 + 50,000 + 700,000 = \$812,358.20
Bid price = 812,358.20/20 =\$40,617.91

17. No replacement: NPV method 1 = –\$949.74
NPV method 2 = –\$1,053.59
We prefer method 1 because it has a higher NPV.
Replacement: EAC method 1 = –\$381.90
EAC method 2 = –\$332.38
We prefer method 2 because it has a lower equivalent annual cost.

18. Method 1: Cash flow year 0 = –\$900
Cash flow years 1 and 2 = –20(1 – .34) + .34(300) = \$88.80
Cash flow year 3 = 88.80 + 120(1 – .34) = \$168
EAC = –\$249.18
Method 2: Cash flow year 0 = –\$800
Cash flow years 1 through 3 = –80(1 – .34) + .34(200) = \$15.20
Cash flow year 4 = 15.20 + 160(1 – .34) = \$120.80
EAC = –\$214.42
Method 2 is the preferred method because it has the lower equivalent annual cost.

19. Cash flow year 0 = –585,000 – 6,500,000 = –\$7,085,000

Year	1	2	3	4	5
Sales	\$5,035,000	\$6,175,000	\$7,220,000	\$8,170,000	\$4,370,000
VC	3,180,000	3,900,000	4,560,000	5,160,000	2,760,000
FC	25,000	25,000	25,000	25,000	25,000
Depr.	928,850	1,591,850	1,136,850	811,850	580,450
EBIT	\$ 901,150	\$ 658,150	\$1,498,150	\$2,173,150	\$1,004,550
Taxes	306,391	223,771	509,371	738,871	341,547
Net income	\$ 594,759	\$ 434,379	\$ 988,779	\$1,434,279	\$ 663,003
OCF	\$1,523,609	\$2,026,229	\$2,125,629	\$2,246,129	\$1,243,453
Add. NWC	925,500	342,000	313,500	285,000	–2,451,000
Net cap. sp.					–1,780,051
CF from assets	\$ 598,109	\$1,684,229	\$1,812,129	\$1,961,129	\$5,474,504

NPV = –\$1,222,445.71

20. New computer:

Cash flow year 0 = −$35,000
Cash flow in years 1 through 4 = 5,000(1 − .34) + .34(7,000) = $5,680
Cash flow in year 5 = 5,680 + 5,000(1 − .34) = $8,980
NPV = −$11,419.29
EAC = −$3,012.38

Old computer:

Cash flow year 0 = −$18,120
Cash flow year 1 = $3,400
Cash flow year 2 = $10,760
NPV = −$6,136.53
EAC = −$3,535.81

Change in after-tax cash flow

Year	Change
0	−16,880
1	2,280
2	−5,080
3,4	5,680
5	8,980

NPV = −$5,282.76 (which is simply the difference in the NPV's)

a. If we just look at replacing the computer without worrying about what will happen in two years, the NPV is −$5,282.76, and we should not buy the new system.

b. If the computer systems will always be replaced at the end of their lives, we should buy the new system because it has a lower equivalent annual cost.

21.

Year	Depreciation	Tax Shield	PV Tax Shield
1	$19,798.02	$6,731.32	$6,119.38
2	26,397.36	8,975.10	7,417.44
3	8,803.08	2,993.05	2,248.72
4	4,401.54	1,496.52	1,022.14

Total present value of depreciation tax shield = $16,807.68.

a. 59,400 − 16,807.68 = PMT × PVIFA(5,10%)
PMT = $11,235.74
Cost savings = 11,235.74/.66 = $17,023.86

b. 59,400 − 16,807.68 = PMT × PVIFA(5,10%) + 7,260/$(1.1)^5$
PMT = $10,046.58
Cost savings = 10,046.58/.66 = $15,222.09

22.

Cash flow year 0	= −40,000,000 − 2,400,000 − 8,000,000 − 1,400,000(1 − .34)
	= −$51,324,000
Cash flow years 1 - 7	= [(10,000)(9,615 − 7,400) − 12,000,000](1 − .34) + 5,000,000(.34)
	= $8,399,000
Cash flow year 8	= 8,399,000 + 8,000,000 + 2,400,000 + 6,000,000(1 − .34)
	= $22,759,000
NPV	= $183,091.12

The net present value is positive, so they should produce the robots.

CHAPTER 9
PROJECT ANALYSIS AND EVALUATION

1. a. VC = 2.60 + 1.15 =$3.75

b. TC = 3.75(280,000) + 320,000 = $1,370,000

c. Cash break-even = 320,000/(5.30 – 3.75) = 206,452 units
Yes, since 280,00 units are sold, and the firm only needs to sell 206,452 units. Therefore, it more than breaks even on a cash basis.
Accounting break-even = (320,000 + 13,000)/(5.30 – 3.75) = 290,323 units

2. a. Cash break-even = 100/(2 – 1) = 100 units
Accounting break-even = (100 + 200)/(2 – 1) = 300 units
The difference in the two is due to non-cash items.

b. Cash break-even = 14,000/(25 – 14) = 1,273 units
Accounting break-even = (14,000 + 75,000)/(25 – 14) = 8,091 units

c. Cash break-even = 40,000,000/(20,000 – 15,000) = 8,000 units
Accounting break-even = (40,000,000 + 25,130,000)/(20,000 – 15,000) = 13,026 units

3. a. Accounting break-even = (25,000 + 10,000)/(5.95 – 2.63) = 10,542 units
DOL = 1 + 25,000/10,000 = 3.5

b. OCF = [15,000(5.95 – 2.63) – 25,000](1 – .34) + 10,000(.34) = $19,768
NPV = –70,000 + 19,768 × PVIFA(7,10%) = $26,238.90
NPV best case = –70,000 + 27,985 × PVIFA(7,10%) = $66,242.70
NPV worst case = –70,000 + 11,551 × PVIFA(7,10%) = –$13,764.89

c. Best Case: OCF = [17,250(6.25 – 2.50) – 23,750](1 – .34) + 10,000(.34)
= $30,407.37
NPV = $78,036
Worst Case: OCF = [12,750(5.65 – 2.76) – 26,250](1 – .34) + 10,000(.34)
= $10,402.77
NPV = –$19,355

4. %Δ in OCF = 4 × 20% = 80%
The new level of operating leverage is lower since FC/OCF is smaller.

5. OCF (Q = 10,000) = 50,000/(4 – 1) = $16,667
OCF (Q = 12,000) = 16,667(1.8) = $30,000
DOL = 1 + 50,000/30,000 = 2.667

6. TC = 40,000(2.3 + 24) + 360,000 = $1,412,000
Average costs = 1,412,000/40,000 = $35.30
MC = 2.3 + 24 = $26.30
Minimum acceptable total revenue = 1,000(26.30) = $26,300

7. It is true that if average revenue is less than average cost, the firm is losing money. This much of the statement is therefore correct. At the margin, however, accepting a project with a marginal revenue in excess of its marginal cost clearly acts to increase operating cash flow.

8. At accounting break-even, net income = 0, taxes = 0, and EBIT = 0.

OCF = EBIT + D − taxes
= 0 + D − 0
DOL = 1 + FC/OCF = 1 + FC/D

9.

a.	Accounting basis:	OCF = D Payback period = life of project Return = 0
b.	Financial basis:	Discounted payback period = life of project Return = required rate of return
c.	Cash basis:	Return is −100%.

10. FC = 15(12,000) − 130,000 = $50,000

11. 0 = (48 − v)12,000 − 80,000 − 130,000
v = $30.50

12. DOL = 1 + 50,000/125,000 = 1.4
Δ in OCF = 1.4(⅓)(125,000) = $58,333
DOL = 1 + 50,000/183,333 = 1.27

13. Forecasting risk is the risk that a poor decision is made because of errors in projected cash flows. The danger is greatest with a new product because the cash flows are probably harder to predict.

14. The option to expand reflects our ability to increase cash flows from a project if we find our initial estimates were too pessimistic. The option to abandon reflects our ability to reallocate assets if we find our initial estimates were too optimistic. Since the option to expand can increase cash flows and the option to abandon can reduce losses, failing to consider these two options will generally lead to an underestimate of a project's NPV.

15.

2,500 units:	OCF	= 4,500(1.5)	= $6,750
1,500 units:	OCF	= 4,500(.5)	= $2,250

16.

2,500 units:	DOL = 1 + 4,500/6,750 = 1.67
1,500 units:	DOL = 1 + 4,500/2,250 = 3

17. a.

	Base	Upper	Lower	Best	Worst
Q	80	88	72	88	72
P	$35,000	35,000	35,000	35,000	35,000
V	$21,900	24,090	19,710	19,710	24,090
FC	$500,000	550,000	450,000	450,000	550,000
OCF	$468,780	377,753	536,681	698,143	262,543

NPV (base) = –945,000 + 468,780 × PVIFA(3,20%) = $42,476
NPV (best) = –945,000 + 698,143 × PVIFA(3,20%) = $525,625
NPV (worst) = –945,000 + 262,543 × PVIFA(3,20%) = –$391,958

b. NPV (FC = 450,000) = $111,990
NPV (FC = 550,000) = –$27,038
NPV decreases by $1.39 for each dollar increase in fixed costs.

c. Cash break-even = 500,000/(35,000 – 21,900) = 38 units

d. Accounting break-even = (500,000 + 315,000)/(35,000 – 21,900) = 62 units
DOL = 1 + 500,000/315,000 = 2.59
For each 1% increase in unit sales, OCF will increase by 2.59%.

18. Accounting break-even is unaffected (taxes are zero at that point).
Cash break-even is lower (assuming a tax credit).
Financial break-even will be higher (because of taxes paid).

19. a. NPV = –55,000 + 10,000 × PVIFA(10,20%) = –$13,075

b. 40,000 = (20 × Q) × PVIFA(9,20%)
Q = 496 units
Should abandon if Q ≤ 496 units.

c. The $40,000 is the market value of the project. If you continue the project, you forego the $40,000 that could have been used for something else.

20. a. Success: PV = 750(20) × PVIFA(9,20%) = $60,464.50
Failure: PV = $40,000
Expected value in year 1 = (60,464.50 + 40,000)/2 + 10,000 = $60,232.25
NPV = –55,000 + 60,232.25/1.2 = –$4,806.46

b. Failure: PV if can't abandon = $20,154.83
Gain from option to abandon = 40,000 – 20,154.83 = $19,845.17
V (option) = (19,845.17)(.5)/1.2 = $8,268.82

21. a. Success: PV = 1,500(20) × PVIFA(9,20%) = $120,929
Failure: PV = $40,000
Expected value in year 1 = (120,929 + 40,000)/2 + 10,000 = $90,464.50
NPV = –55,000 + 90,464.50/1.2 = $20,387.08

b. Expand: PV if can't expand = $60,464.50
Gain from option to expand = 120,929 – 60,464.50 = $60,464.50
V (option) = (60,464.50)(.5)/1.2 = $25,193.54

22. a.

$$
\begin{aligned}
OCF &= EBIT + D - \text{taxes} \\
&= [(P - v)Q - FC - D] + D - \text{taxes} \\
&= [(P - v)Q - FC - D] + D - [(P - v)Q - FC - D]t \\
&= [(P - v)Q - FC](1 - t) + Dt
\end{aligned}
$$

$$
\begin{aligned}
(P-v)Q - FC &= (OCF - Dt)/(1 - t) \\
Q &= [FC + (OCF - Dt)/(1 - t)]/(P - v)
\end{aligned}
$$

b.

Accounting break-even= {5,000,000 + [700,000 − 700,000(.34)]/(1 − .34)}/20,000
= 60 units

Cash break-even = 7 units

Financial break-even = 96 units

c. Since at the accounting break-even, OCF = D,

$$
\begin{aligned}
Q &= [FC + (OCF - t \times D)/(1 - t)]/(P - v) \\
&= [FC + (OCF - t \times OCF)/(1 - t)]/(P - v) \\
&= [FC + OCF \times (1 - t)/(1 - t)]/(P - v) \\
&= (FC + OCF)/(P - v),
\end{aligned}
$$

which is not affected by the tax rate.

23.

$$
\begin{aligned}
DOL &= (P - v)(1 - t)Q/OCF \\
&= [OCF + FC(1 - t) - t \times D]/OCF \\
&= 1 + [FC(1 - t) - t \times D]/OCF
\end{aligned}
$$

The tax rate has an inverse effect on DOL.

24. Accounting break-even = 7,222 units

Cash break-even = 3,013 units

The cash break-even is smaller since OCF = 0 here and $[t/(1 - t)]D$ is subtracted from FC.

DOL (at accounting break-even) = 1.716

CHAPTER 10
SOME LESSONS FROM CAPITAL MARKET HISTORY

1. % Return = (31 + 2.40 – 42)/42 = –20.48%

2. Dividend yield = 2.40/42 = 5.71%
Capital gain yield = (31 – 42)/42 = –26.19%

3. % Return = (60 + 2.40 – 42)/42 = 48.57%
Dividend yield = 2.40/42 = 5.71%
Capital gain yield = (60 – 42)/42 = 42.86%

4. Approximate real rate = .09 – .05 = .04 = 4%
Exact real rate = (1.09)/(1.05) – 1 = .0381 = 3.81%

5. R = .03 + .12 + .03(.12) = .1536 = 15.36%

6. Expected inflation rate = (1.2)/(1.12) – 1 = .0714 = 7.14%

7. a. From Figure 10.10: R = 12.1%
b. From Figure 10.10: h = 3.2%
r = (1.121)/(1.032) – 1 = .0862 = 8.62%

8. Long-term government bonds: r = (1.049)/(1.032) – 1 = .0165 = 1.65%
Long-term corporate bonds: r = (1.055)/(1.032) – 1 = .0223 = 2.23%

9. Pr(R < –3.8 or R > 13.2) = $^1/_3$, but we are only interested in one tail, therefore, Pr(R < –4) ≈ $^1/_6$
95%: 4.9 – 2(8.5) to 4.9 + 2(8.5) = –12.1% to 21.9%
99%: 4.9 – 3(8.5) to 4.9 + 3(8.5) = –20.6% to 30.4%

10. A negative real rate implies that the inflation rate exceeds the nominal rate. Certainly this has happened in the past, but it is unlikely that securities would be priced before the fact with a negative real rate. A negative inflation rate implies that the real rate exceeds the nominal rate. This is unlikely to occur, but it is not impossible.

11. σ = 35.4%; 2σ = 70.8%; 3σ = 106.2%
The mean is 17.1%. Money will double between two and three standard deviations above the mean, so the probability is between 0.5% and 2.5%, implying an event once every 40 to 200 years. More precisely, money will double at about 2.34 standard deviations above the mean: z = (100 – 17.1)/35.4 = 2.34. Assuming normality, this will occur about 1% of time, or about once every 100 years.

12. It is impossible to lose more than 100% of your investment. Thus, return distributions are truncated at −100%.

13. $\bar{R}_x = (.15 + .04 - .09 + .08 + .09)/5 = .054 = 5.4\%$

$\sigma_x = \{[(.15 - .054)^2 + (.04 - .054)^2 + (-.09 - .054)^2 + (.08 - .054)^2 + (.09 - .054)^2]/(5 - 1)\}^{.5}$

$= .0896 = 8.96\%$

$\bar{R}_y = (.18 - .03 - .1 + .12 + .05)/5 = .044 = 4.4\%$

$\sigma_y = \{[(.18 - .044)^2 + (-.03 - .044)^2 + (-.1 - .044)^2 + (.12 - .044)^2 + (.05 - .044)^2]/(5 - 1)\}^{.5}$

$= .1124 = 11.24\%$

14. a.

Year		Risk Premium
1980	32.4 − 11.2	= 21.2%
1981	−4.9 − 14.7	= −19.6%
1982	21.4 − 10.5	= 10.9%
1983	22.5 − 8.8	= 13.7%
1984	6.3 − 9.9	= −3.6%
1985	32.2 − 7.7	= 24.5%
1986	18.5 − 6.2	= 12.3%

b. $\bar{R}_{CS} = (32.4 - 4.9 + 21.4 + 22.5 + 6.3 + 32.2 + 18.5)/7 = 18.34\%$

$\bar{R}_{TB} = (11.2 + 14.7 + 10.5 + 8.8 + 9.9 + 7.7 + 6.2)/7 = 9.86\%$

Avg. risk premium = (21.2 − 19.6 + 10.9 + 13.7 − 3.6 + 24.5 + 12.3)/7 = 8.49%

c. $\sigma_{CS} = \{[(32.4 - 18.34)^2 + (-4.9 - 18.34)^2 + (21.4 - 18.34)^2 + (22.5 - 18.34)^2 + (6.3 - 18.34)^2 + (32.2 - 18.34)^2 + (18.5 - 18.34)^2]/(7 - 1)\}^{.5}$

$= 13.55\%$

$\sigma_{TB} = \{[(11.2 - 9.86)^2 + (14.7 - 9.86)^2 + (10.5 - 9.86)^2 + (8.8 - 9.86)^2 + (9.9 - 9.86)^2 + (7.7 - 9.86)^2 + (6.2 - 9.86)^2]/(7 - 1)\}^{.5}$

$= 2.73\%$

$\sigma_{RP} = \{[(21.2 - 8.49)^2 + (-19.6 - 8.49)^2 + (10.9 - 8.49)^2 + (13.7 - 8.49)^2 + (-3.6 - 8.49)^2 + (24.5 - 8.49)^2 + (12.3 - 8.49)^2]/(7 - 1)\}^{.5}$

$= 15.28\%$

d. The risk premium can be negative, but such a relationship is unlikely to persist for any length of time.

15. They were highest in the early eighties. This was during a period of high inflation and is consistent with the Fisher effect.

16. Yes, historical price information is public information.

17. The market is weak form inefficient.

18. Ignoring trading costs, on average, such investors merely earn what the market offers; the trades all have zero NPV. If trading costs exist, then these investors lose by the amount of the costs.

19. On average, the only return that is earned is the required return.

20. Unlike gambling, the stock market is a positive sum game; everybody can win. Also, speculators provide liquidity to markets and thus help promote efficiency.

21. Let:

h = inflation rate
R_S = nominal rate on some security
R_T = nominal rate on T–bills
r_S = real rate on some security
r_T = real rate on T–bills

so:

$R_S - R_T$ = nominal risk premium, RP_N
$[(1 + r_S)(1 + h) - 1] - [(1 + r_T)(1 + h) - 1] = RP_N$
$(1 + r_S) - (1 + r_T) = RP_N/(1 + h)$
$r_S - r_T = RP_N/(1 + h) = RP_R$ = real risk premium

CHAPTER 11
RETURN, RISK, AND THE SECURITY MARKET LINE

1. $E(R) = .5(.12) + .5(.18) = 15\%$

2. $E(R) = .2(.12) + .8(.18) = 16.8\%$

3. Total value = 20(50) + 30(20) = $1600
Weight of security 1 = 1000/1600 = 62.5%
Weight of security 2 = 600/1600 = 37.5%

4. No to both questions.

5. A: $E(R_A) = .2(.1) + .4(.24) + .4(.44) = 29.2\%$
$\sigma_A = [.2(.1 - .292)^2 + .4(.24 - .292)^2 + .4(.44 - .292)^2]^{½} = 13.12\%$
B: $E(R_B) = .2(.55) + .4(.2) + .4(.1) = 23\%$
$\sigma_B = [.2(.55 - .23)^2 + .4(.2 - .23)^2 + .4(.1 - .23)^2]^{½} = 16.61\%$

6. False. The variance of individual assets is a measure of total risk. The return of a well-diversified portfolio is a function of systematic risk only.

7. a. $E(R_A) = .4(.1) + .6(.08) = 8.8\%$
$\sigma_A = [.4(.1 - .088)^2 + .6(.08 - .088)^2]^{½} = .98\%$
$E(R_B) = .4(.15) + .6(.04) = 8.4\%$
$\sigma_B = [.4(.15 - .084)^2 + .6(.04 - .084)^2]^{½} = 5.39\%$
$E(R_C) = .4(.2) + .6(0) = 8\%$
$\sigma_C = [.4(.2 - .08)^2 + .6(0 - .08)^2]^{½} = 9.80\%$
b. $E(R_p) = (1/3)(.088) + (1/3)(.084) + (1/3)(.08) = 8.4\%$

8. a. $E(R_A) = .1(.25) + .2(.1) + .5(.15) + .2(-.12) = 9.6\%$
$E(R_B) = .1(.18) + .2(.2) + .5(.04) + .2(0) = 7.8\%$
b. $\sigma_A = [.1(.25 - .096)^2 + .2(.1 - .096)^2 + .5(.15 - .096)^2 + .2(-.12 - .096)^2]^{½}$
$= 11.47\%$
$\sigma_B = [.1(.18 - .078)^2 + .2(.2 - .078)^2 + .5(.04 - .078)^2 + .2(0 - .078)^2]^{½}$
$= 7.72\%$
c. $E(R_p) = .2(.096) + .8(.078) = 8.16\%$
d. $E(R_p) = .6(.096) + .4(.078) = 8.88\%$
$\sigma_P^2 = .1(.222 - .0888)^2 + .2(.14 - .0888)^2 + .5(.106 - .0888)^2 + .2(-.072 - .0888)^2$
$= .0077$

9. Yes, the standard deviation can be less, but the β cannot be less than the smallest β in the portfolio.

10. Some of the risk in holding any asset is unique to the asset in question. By investing in a variety of assets, this unique risk is eliminated at little cost. On the other hand, there are some risks that affect all investments and cannot be costlessly avoided. In other words, systematic risk can be controlled, but only by a costly reduction in expected returns.

11. It depends on what expectations were. If the market had "priced" securities for 4% growth, then there would be no change. If, for example, the market had expected zero growth, then the prices would, in all likelihood, increase.

12. This is merely another way of saying that there are few true "surprises" in the marketplace. In this respect, the statement rings true.

13.
a. systematic
b. unsystematic
c. both—probably mostly systematic
d. unsystematic
e. unsystematic
f. systematic

14.
a. $x_A = 5{,}000/20{,}000 = .25$
$x_B = 5{,}000/20{,}000 = .25$
$x_C = 6{,}000/20{,}000 = .30$
$x_D = 4{,}000/20{,}000 = .20$
b. $E(R_p) = .25(.09) + .25(.1) + .3(.11) + .2(.12) = 10.45\%$
c. $\beta_p = .25(.8) + .25(1) + .3(1.2) + .2(1.4) = 1.09$

15.
a. $E(R_p) = .5(.09) + .5(.12) = 10.5\%$
b. $.5 = x(0) + (1 - x)(.7)$
$x = .286$
So, 28.6% invested in the risk-free asset and 71.4% invested in the stock.
c. $.1 = .09x + .12(1 - x)$
$x = .667$
$\beta_p = .333(.7) = .233$
d. $1.5 = 0(1 - x) + .7x$
$x = 214\%$
214% invested in the stock and −114% invested in the risk-free asset. This represents borrowing at the risk-free rate.

16.

Percentage of A	$E(R_p)$	β_p
0%	8.0%	0.00
25%	10.5%	0.35
50%	13.0%	0.70
75%	15.5%	1.05
100%	18.0%	1.40
125%	20.5%	1.75
150%	23.0%	2.10

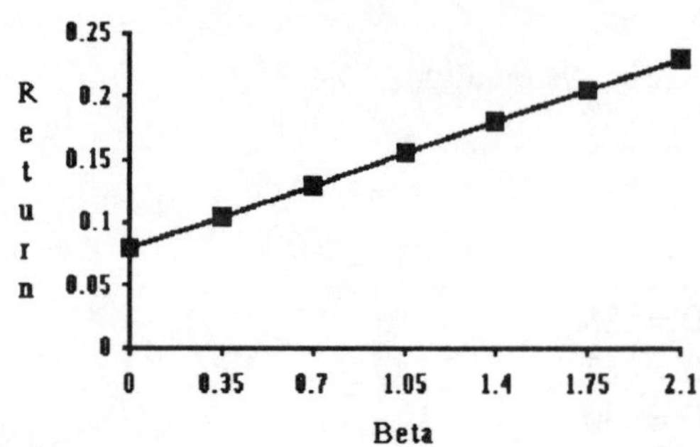

The slope of the above line is (.105 − .08)/.35 = .0714.

17. a. R_p = .5(.121) + .5(.055) = .088 = 8.8%
b. R_p = .5(.171) + .5(.037) = .104 = 10.4%

18. a. E(R) = .08 + .6(.14 − .08) = .116 = 11.6%
b. .2 = .08 + β(.14 − .08)
β = 2

19. (.1 − .06)/.8 > (.08 − .06)/.6; therefore, the stocks are *not* priced correctly.
(.1 − R_f)/.8 = (.08 − R_f)/.6
R_f = .02 = 2%

20. (.12 − .08)/.8 = .05 = 5%

21. a. .14 = R_f + 1.8(.1 − R_f)
R_f = 5%
b. (.14 − .05)/1.8 = .05

22. $[E(R_a) - R_f]/\beta_a = [E(R_b) - R_f]/\beta_b$
$RP_a/\beta_a = RP_b/\beta_b$
$\beta_b/\beta_a = RP_b/RP_a$

23. Note that a portfolio with equal weights of Smith Co. and MBI Co. has a beta of 1. Thus, the expected return on the market is .5(.19) + .5(.15) = .17 = 17%.

$.19 = R_f + 1.25(.17 - R_f)$

$R_f = 9\%$

24. Yes. It is possible, in theory, to construct a zero beta portfolio of risky assets whose return would be equal to the risk-free rate. It is also possible to have a negative beta. The expected return would bé less than the risk-free rate. A negative beta asset would carry a negative risk premium because of its value as a diversification instrument.

CHAPTER 12
LONG-TERM FINANCING: AN INTRODUCTION

1. Common stock = 1,500(1) = $1,500
Total = 1500 + 50,000 + 100,000 = $151,500

2.

Common stock	
(2500 shares, $1 par)	2,500
Capital surplus	99,000
Retained earnings	100,000
Total	$201,500

Market/book ratio = 50/80.6 = .62

3. The stock is called treasury stock.

Common stock (2,500 shares outstanding,	
100 of which are treasury stock, $1 par)	2,500
Capital surplus	99,000
Retained earnings	100,000
less: Treasury stock	5,000
Total	$196,500

4. a. Straight votes needed: .5(1,000,000) + 1 = 500,001
b. Cumulative votes needed: .2(1,000,000) + 1 = 200,001

5. Corporate bond yields are generally higher. Corporations have a tax break on preferred stock dividends so they are willing to accept a lower pretax yield. Other corporations are the big investors in preferred stock.

6. a. Main Differences:
1. Debt carries no ownership interest.
2. Interest paid on debt is tax deductible.
3. Unpaid debt is a liability.

b. To gain tax benefits of debt and bankruptcy benefits of equity.

c. 1. Preferred holders receive a stated dividend.
2. In case of liquidation, preferred holders get a stated amount.
3. Preferred stock carries credit ratings.
4. Preferred is sometimes convertible into common stock.
5. Preferred is sometimes callable.
6. Preferred may have a sinking fund.
7. Preferred may have an adjustable dividend.

7. A good guess would be:
.8(5,000,000) = $4,000,000 (80% internal funds)
.2(5,000,000) = $1,000,000 (20% external funds—more likely debt than equity)

8. The two most basic options are liquidation or reorganization, though creative alternatives may exist.

9. $PV_{alive} = 8/.2 = \$40$ million
Since the PV_{alive} is less than the $50 million liquidation value, the firm should be liquidated. It is worth more "dead than alive."

10.

Year	Beginning Value	Ending Value	Implicit Interest	Straight-line Interest
1	$621	$683	$62	$75.80
2	683	751	68	75.80
3	751	826	75	75.80
4	826	909	83	75.80
5	909	1000	91	75.80
			$1379	$379.00

Greater tax deductions can be taken earlier with the straight-line depreciation.

11.
a. Increases coupon—investors require a higher return for the risk of the bond being called before maturity.
b. Decreases coupon—investors require a lower return because they have an option to convert.
c. Decreases coupon—investors require a lower return because they have the option of forcing the company to buy back the bond early.
d. Probably decreases the coupon, but it depends on what the coupon is tied to.

Appendix

A.1 NPV = [(.20 − .16)/.16](1,000) − 200 = \$50 (refund)

A.2 $0 = [(.2 - C_n)/C_n](1,000) - 200$

$C_n = 16.67\%$

A.3 a. Expected price in 1 year = .5(120/.1) + .5(120/.15) = \$1,000

$P_0 = (120 + 1,000)/1.12 = \$1,000$

b. Expected price in 1 year = .5(150/.1) + .5(150/.15) = \$1,250

$P_0 = (150 + 1,250)/1.12 = \$1,250$

A.4 a. $1,000 = [C + .5(C/.15) + .5(1,060)]/1.12$

$C = \$136.15$

b. $P_0 = [136.15 + .5(136.15/.15 + 136.15/.1)]/1.12 = \$1,134.62$

Cost of call = 1,134.62 − 1,000 = \$134.62

A.5 NPV = [(.08 − .06)/.06](20,000,000) − 4,600,000 = \$2,066,667 (refund)

Note: \$4,600,000 includes the premium

A.6 $NPV = [(.08 - C_n)/C_n](20,000,000) - 4,600,000$

$C_n = 6.5\%$

A.7 PV of savings from refunding = 400,000 × PVIFA(20,6%) = \$4,587,968

NPV of refunding = 4,587,968 − 4,600,000 = −\$12,032

A.8 NPV of refunding operation = {(.20 − .16)(.66)/[.16(.66)]}(1,000) − 200(.66) = \$118.

The net effect of taxes on the NPV of refunding is to make it more attractive by making the call premium tax deductible. The difference between the NPV here and in A.1 is simply the \$68 tax saving from deducting the call premium.

CHAPTER 13
ISSUING SECURITIES TO THE PUBLIC

1. The evidence suggests that the costs associated with non-underwritten rights offerings are substantially less than those of cash offers.

2. a. V_R = (25 – 20)/(10 + 1) = \$.45
   b. V_{XR} = [10(25) + 20]/11 = \$24.55
   c. V_{New} = 110,000(24.55) = 2.7 million
   d. A rights offering costs less, protects the proportionate interests of existing shareholders, and protects against underpricing.

3. a. [400,000 + 40(5,000)]/15,000 = \$40; no change
   b. [400,000 + 20(5,000)]/15,000 = \$33.33
   c. [400,000 + 10(5,000)]/15,000 = \$30

4. He could have done worse since his access to the oversubscribed and, presumably, underpriced issues was restricted while the bulk of his funds were allocated to stocks from the undersubscribed (overpriced?) issues.

5. a. The price will probably go up because IPO's are generally underpriced. This is especially true for smaller issues such as this one.
   b. It is probably safe to assume that they are having trouble moving the issue, and it is likely that the issue is not substantially underpriced.

6. IPO's are not always underpriced. Your ability to make money is directly related to your ability to purchase only the IPO's that are underpriced.

7. a. 45 = [50(N) + 25]/(N + 1)
   N = 4; so 4 rights are needed to buy 1 share
   b. 5,000,000/25 = 200,000 shares to be sold
   c. 4(200,000) = 800,000 shares outstanding before the offering

8. a. (i) # shares = 10M + 60M/40 = 11.5M shares outstanding
   (ii) Original P/E = 40/2 = 20 times
   New EPS = 22M/11.5M = \$1.91
   (iii) Price = 1.91(20) = \$38.26
   (iv) BVS = (600M + 60M)/11.5M = \$57.39
   (v) M/B = 38.26/57.39 = .667
   (vi) Accounting dilution has occurred and the project has an NPV of [(440 – 400) – (660 – 600)] = –\$20M
   b. For the price to remain unchanged with a constant P/E ratio, EPS must remain unchanged.
   NI = 2(11.5) = \$23M

9. a. NI = 50,000(.05) + 10,000 = \$12,500
EPS = 12,500/2,000 = \$6.25
b. Price = 5(6.25) = \$31.25
c. BVS = 250,000/2,000 = \$125
d. NPV = [31.25(2,000) − 50,000] − 50,000 = −\$37,500

10. a. EPS needs to remain unchanged, so NI = 10(2,000) = \$20,000
20,000 = 50,000(ROE on investment) + 10,000
ROE on investment = 20%
b. NPV = [50(2,000) − 50,000] − 50,000 = \$0
c. Yes because BVS falls from 200,000/1,000 = \$200 to 250,000/2,000 = \$125

11. Amount raised = 15(5,000,000) = \$75,000,000
Flotation costs = 120,000 + 80,000 + (22 − 15)(5,000,000) = \$35,200,000
(Direct costs = \$15,200,000; Indirect costs = \$20,000,000)
% Flotation costs = 35,200,000/75,000,000 = 46.93%

12. a. If you receive 100 of each, then profit = (100)(1) − (100)(.5) = \$50
b. Expected profit = 50(1) − 100(.5) = \$0
c. This is the winner's curse.

13. a. Max = \$25, Min = anything > \$0
b. 50,000,000/15 = 3,333,333 shares
22,000,000/3,333,333 = 6.6 rights
c. V_{XR} = [25(6.6) + 15]/7.6 = \$23.68
V_R = 25 − 23.68 = \$1.32
d. After: 100(23.68) + 100(1.32) = \$2,500
Before: 100(25) = \$2,500

14. # shares sold = $40M/P_S$
rights to buy 1 share = $10M(P_S)/40M = .25P_S$
$20 = [40(.25P_S) + P_S]/(.25P_S + 1)$
$P_S = \$3.33$

15. Value of right $= P_{RO} - P_X$
$= P_{RO} - [P_{RO}(N) + P_S]/(N + 1)$
$= [(N + 1)P_{RO} - P_{RO}(N) - P_S]/(N + 1)$
$= (P_{RO} - P_S)/(N + 1)$

CHAPTER 14
COST OF CAPITAL

1. a. $R_E = 4(1.08)/60 + .08 = 15.2\%$
b. $R_E = .075 + .8(.086) = 14.38\%$
If we average these, then GDI's cost of equity is approximately 14.79%

2. a) $R_D = 5.696\%$ (the bond's yield to maturity, assuming annual coupons)
b) $R_D = 5.696(1 - .34) = 3.759\%$
c) The after-tax rate is more relevant because that is the actual cost to the company.

3. WACC = .45 (.09)(.66) + .55 (.18) = 12.573%

4. a) unadjusted WACC = .24(1/1.4) + .14(.4/1.4) = 21.14%
b) WACC = .24(1/1.4) + .14(.4/1.4)(1 − .39) = 19.58%
c) The WACC in part b is more relevant because we are concerned with after-tax costs.

5. $R_E = .06 + 1.4(0.085) = 17.9\%$
WACC = (2/3)(17.9) + (1/3)(12)(.66) = 14.573%

6. .14 = (E/V)(.2) + (D/V)(.09)(.66)
E/V = .573; D/V = .427; D/E = 74.5%

7. a. This only considers the dividend yield component of the required return.
b. This is the current yield only, not the promised yield to maturity. It is based on the book value of the liability, and it ignores taxes.
c. Equity is inherently more risky than debt (except, perhaps, in the unusual case where a firm's assets have a negative beta). For this reason, the cost of equity always exceeds the cost of debt.

8. a. $E_{Book} = 3.2 \times 10 = \$32M$
$D_{Book} = 25 + 14 = \$39M$
$V_{Book} = 32M + 39M = \$71M$
E/V = 32/71 = .45
D/V = 39/71 = .55
b. $E_{MV} = 3.2 \times 46 = \$147.2M$
$D_{MV} = 25(.96) + 14(.9) = \$36.6M$
$V_{MV} = 147.2M + 36.6M = \$183.8M$
E/V = 147.2/183.8 = .8
D/V = 36.6/183.8 = .2
c. Market value is more relevant.

9. $R_{Sup} = .12 + .75\,(.08) = 18\%$
Both should proceed. The appropriate discount rate does not depend on which company is investing; it depends on the risk of the project. Since Superior is in the business, it is closer to a pure play. Therefore, its cost of capital should be used. With an 18% cost of capital, the project has an NPV of $1 million regardless of who takes it.

10. a. Projects C and D
b. Projects A and C using the appropriate return; projects C and D using the firm's cost of capital
c. A would be incorrectly rejected. It should be accepted because the market requires a return of 11.5%, and the expected return is 12%
D would be incorrectly accepted. It should be rejected because the market requires a return of 19.2%, and the expected return is 19%

11. a. $.16 = (1/1.5)(.22) + (.5/1.5)(R_D)(1 - .39)$
$R_D = 6.56\%$
b. $.16 = (1/1.5)(R_E) + (.5/1.5)(.11)(1 - .39)$
$R_E = 20.65\%$

12. a. $WACC = .35(.2) + .55(.12)(1 - .34) + .1(.1) = 12.36\%$
b. Since interest is tax deductible and dividends are not, we must look at the after-tax cost of debt, which is $.12(1 - .34) = 7.92\%$. Therefore, on an after-tax basis, debt is cheaper than preferred.

13. $E = 4(80) = \$320M$
$D = 15(.86) = \$12.9M$
$V = 320 + 12.9 = \$332.9M$
$R_E = .08 + 1.4(.08) = .192 = 19.2\%$
$WACC = (320/332.9)(.192) + (12.9/332.9)(.09)(.66) = 18.69\%$

14. $R_P = 7.6/80 = 9.5\%$

15. $WACC = (1/6)(.2) + (5/6)(.12) = 13.33\%$
$PV_{savings} = 6M/(.1333 - .04) = \$64{,}285{,}714.52$
The project should be undertaken if the initial investment is less than $64,285,715.

16. a. He should look at the overall flotation costs, not just the debt costs.
b. $f_A = .6(.12) + .4(.03) = 8.4\%$
c. $600{,}000/(1 - .084) = \$655{,}021.83$

17. $WACC = (20/29)(.19) + (9/29)(.12)(1 - .34) = 15.56\%$

18. a. $f_A = .12(1/1.4) + .04(.4/1.4) = .0971$
Actual cost $= 15M/(1 - .0971) = \$16{,}613{,}924.05$
b. $WACC = (1/1.4)(.2) + (.4/1.4)(.1)(1 - .34) = .1617$
$PV_{CF} = 3M/.1617 = \$18{,}551{,}236.75$
c. $NPV = 18{,}551{,}236.75 - 16{,}613{,}924.05 = \$1{,}937{,}312.70 > 0$
Since NPV > 0, the project should be accepted.

19. The reasoning is that limiting the interest deduction increases the effective cost of a takeover, so such legislation would act to reduce takeover activity.

20. a. Yes, they should take the project. Using debt is fine, but if they use debt now, they will have to use equity later to keep their target capital structure, so they should use the weighted average flotation cost.

b. WACC = .20(1/3) + .10(2/3)(.66) = 11.067%
f_A = .15(1/3) + .01(2/3) = .0567
Actual cost = 20M/(1 – .0567) = \$21,201,413
PV = 8M/.11067 = \$72,289,157
NPV = 72,289,157 – 21,201,413 = \$51,087,744

21. a. i: WACC = .10(.25)(.66) + .08(.25)(.66) + .15(.5) = 10.47%
ii: WACC = .10(.1)(.66) + .08(.25)(.66) +.15(.65) = 11.73%
iii: WACC = (1/4)(.1)(.66) + (1/4)(.08)(.66) + (1/2)(.15) = 10.47%
Notice that, in this particular case, the target weights and the book weights are identical in percentage terms. This is not what would usually happen.

b. They should use market value weights.

22. WACC = (.10)(1/4)(.66) + WACC(1/4)(.66) + (.15)(1/2) = 10.96%

CHAPTER 15
FINANCIAL LEVERAGE AND CAPITAL STRUCTURE POLICY

1.

	Earnings	1,200	1,000	600
a.	EPS	12	10	6
	Δ	20%		–40%
b.	EPS	15	11	3
	Δ	36%		–73%

The variance in earnings per share increases when debt is added.

2.
a. Plan I: NI = 1,000; EPS = 1,000/200 = \$5
Plan II: NI = 1,000 – .12(5,000) = 400; EPS = 400/100 = \$4
Plan I results in a higher EPS.
b. Plan I: NI = 2,000; EPS = 2,000/200 = \$10
Plan II: NI = 2,000 – 600 = 1,400; EPS = 1,400/100 = \$14
Plan II results in a higher EPS.
c. EBIT/200 = (EBIT – 600)/100
EBIT = \$1,200

3. P = 5,000/100 = \$50; the price per share is \$50 under both plans.

4.
a. CF to Ms. Lyndi = (400/100)(10) = \$40
b. V = 100(120) = \$12,000
D = .4(12,000) = \$4,800
Shares outstanding = 100 – 4,800/120 = 60 shares
NI = 400 – .08(4,800) = \$16
EPS = 16/60 = \$.267
CF to Ms. Lyndi = .267(10) = \$2.67
c. Sell 4 shares and lend the proceeds.
Earnings for 6 shares = \$1.60
Interest = 4(120)(.08) = \$38.40
Total CF = 1.60 + 38.40 = \$40
d. The capital structure is irrelevant because the shareholders can create their own leverage position which will give them the payoff they desire.

5.
a. Return = 12%
b. Sell all T.S. Max shares for \$1 million, borrow \$1 million and invest \$2 million in A.B. Min.
c. 12%; cost of equity and the required return are the same
d. WACC = 10% for both firms. This illustrates MM Proposition II.

6. a.

	Plan I	Plan II	Equity
EBIT	2,000	2,000	2,000
Interest	400	250	0
Income	1,600	1,750	2,000
Shares out	1,000	1,150	1,400
EPS	1.60	1.52	1.43

The all-equity plan has the lowest EPS and Plan I has the highest EPS.

b. Plan I: EBIT/1,400 = (EBIT − 400)/1,000
EBIT = $1,400
Plan II: EBIT/1,400 = (EBIT − 250)/1,150
EBIT = $1,400
One is *not* higher than the other because of MM Proposition I.

c. (EBIT − 400)/1,000 = (EBIT − 250)/1,150
EBIT = $1,400

d. (a)

	Plan I	Plan II	Equity
EBIT	2,000	2,000	2,000
Interest	400	250	0
Income	960	1,050	1,200
Shares out	1,000	1,150	1,400
EPS	.96	.91	.86

Plan I has the highest EPS and the all equity plan has the lowest EPS.

(b) Plan I: EBIT(.6)/1,400 = [EBIT − 400](.6)/1,000
EBIT = $1,400
Plan II: EBIT(.6)/1,400 = [EBIT − 250](.6)/1,150
EBIT = $1,400

(c) [EBIT − 400](.6)/1,000 = [EBIT − 250](.6)/1,150
EBIT = $1,400

The break-even EPS does not change because the addition of taxes reduces the income of all three plans by the same percentage, therefore, they do not change relative to one another.

7. Plan I: Price = 8,000/(1,400 − 1,000) = $20
Plan II: Price = 5,000/(1,400 − 1,150) = $20
This shows that in a world without taxes, the stockholder does not care about the capital structure of the firm. This is MM Proposition I in a world without taxes.

8. Business risk is the equity risk arising from the nature of the the firm's operating activity, and is directly related to the systematic risk of the firm's assets. Financial risk is equity risk that is due entirely to the firm's chosen capital structure. As financial leverage, or the use of debt financing, increases, so does financial risk.

If firm A and B have the same financial structure, and all other factors are the same, A's higher business risk will result in a higher cost of equity capital. If B has a higher degree of financial risk, B's cost of equity could be the same as, or even higher than, A's.

9. a. $R_E = .2 + (.2 - .09)(.5) = 25.5\%$
b. $R_E = .2 + (.2 - .09)(1) = 31\%$
c. WACC = .5(.31) + .5(.09) = 20%

10. a. $.12 = 1(R_E) + 0(.09)(1 - .34)$

$R_E = 12\%$

b. $R_E = .12 + (.12 - .09)(1/3)(.66) = 12.66\%$

c. $R_E = .12 + (.12 - .09)(.66) = 13.98\%$

d. b: $WACC = .75(.1266) + .25(.09)(.66) = 10.98\%$

c: $WACC = .50(.1398) + .50(.09)(.66) = 9.96\%$

11. $V_U = 1{,}000(.66)/.14 = \$4{,}714.29$

$V_L = 4{,}714.29 + .34(2{,}000) = \$5{,}394.29$

12. $EBIT/.1 = \$5$ million

$EBIT = \$500{,}000$

13. $EBIT(1 - .2)/.1 = \$5$ million

$EBIT = \$625{,}000$

14. a. $V_U = 6{,}000(.6)/.12 = \$30{,}000$

b. $V_L = 30{,}000 + .4(20{,}000) = \$38{,}000$

$E = 38{,}000 - 20{,}000 = \$18{,}000$

15. $R_E = .12 + (.12 - .08)(20/18)(1 - .4) = 14.67\%$

$WACC = .1467(18/38) + .08(20/38)(.6) = 9.48\%$

The more debt the firm uses, the lower its WACC.

16. No, it doesn't follow. While it is true that the equity and debt costs are rising, the key thing to remember is that the cost of debt is still less than the cost of equity. Since we are using more and more debt, the WACC does not necessarily rise.

17. $V_U = 5{,}000(1 - .34)/.18 = \$18{,}333.33$

$V_L = 18{,}333 + 18{,}333(.34) = \$24{,}567$

18. $R_E = R_U + (R_U - R_D)(D/E)(1 - T_c)$

$WACC = (E/V)R_E + (D/V)R_D(1 - T_c)$

Substitute for R_E in the WACC equation and collect terms:

$WACC = R_U[1 - T_c(D/V)]$

19. $R_E = (EBIT - R_D D)(1 - T_c)/E$
$= R_U V_U/E - R_D(1 - T_c)(D/E)$
$= R_U(V_L - DT_c)/E - R_D(1 - T_c)(D/E)$
$= R_U(E + D - DT_c)/E - R_D(1 - T_c)(D/E)$
$= R_U + (R_U - R_D)(D/E)(1 - T_c)$

20. M&M Proposition II, with $R_D = R_f$ (default can't occur):

$$R_E = R_A + (R_A - R_f)(D/E)$$

CAPM:

$$R_E = \beta_E(R_M - R_f) + R_f$$
$$R_A = \beta_A(R_M - R_f) + R_f$$

Substituting for R_E and R_A in Proposition II:

$$\beta_E(R_M - R_f) + R_f = \beta_A(R_M - R_f) + R_f + [(\beta_A(R_M - R_f) + R_f) - R_f](D/E)$$

Simplifying,

$$\beta_E(R_M - R_f) = \beta_A(R_M - R_f) + [\beta_A(R_M - R_f)](D/E)$$
$$\beta_E(R_M - R_f) = \beta_A(1 + D/E)(R_M - R_f)$$
$$\beta_E = \beta_A(1 + D/E)$$

CHAPTER 16
DIVIDENDS AND DIVIDEND POLICY

1.

a.	Common stock ($1 par)	55
	Capital surplus	745
	Retained earnings	4,750
	Total	$5,550
b.	Common stock ($.1 par)	50
	Capital surplus	500
	Retained earnings	5,000
	Total	$5,550

2. It would not be irrational to find low-dividend, high-growth stocks. The university should be indifferent between receiving dividends or capital gains since it does not pay taxes on either one (ignoring possible restrictions on invasion of principal, etc.). It would be irrational, however, to hold municipal bonds. Since it does not pay taxes on interest received, it does not need the tax break with the muni's. Therefore, it should prefer to hold the higher yielding, taxable bonds.

3. Thursday, June 29, is the ex-dividend day. Remember not to count July 4 because it is a holiday, and the exchanges are closed. The shareholder who buys the stock will receive the dividend as long as she does not sell it again before June 29.

4. Price today = 1,000/100 = $10
Price tomorrow = 10 – .5 = $9.50
Value of equity = 100(9.50) = $950

5. 50/[1,000/100] = 5 shares of stock purchased
Value of equity = 95(10) = $950
Price per share = 950/95 = $10
If a cash dividend is distributed, each share receives $.50 in cash plus the new price of $9.50. Therefore, a repurchase is effectively the same as a cash dividend.

6. After-tax dividend = 2(1 – .28) = $1.44
Ex-dividend price = 20 – 1.44 = $18.56

7. New shares outstanding = 500(1.2) = 600 shares
Ex-dividend price = 950/600 = $1.58

8. After-tax dividend yield for Piker = .08(1 – .28) = .0576
1.0576/1.15 = .91965
(1.15 – .91965)/.91965 = 25.05% pretax yield for Piker

9. $P_0 = .35/1.18 + 15/(1.18)^2 = \$11.07$
$P_1 = 15/(1.18) = \$12.71$
.35(100) + 12.71(S) = 15(100 – S)
S = 52.87, so sell 52.87 shares in 1 year

10. .35(100) − 12.71(S) = 20
S = 1.18 shares, so buy 1.18 shares in 1 year
Dividend in 2 years = 101.18(15) = $1,517.70

11. a. 10 million/.5 = $20 million; increase borrowing by $10 million

b. RE = .5(12 million) = $6 million
Dividends = 10 − 6 = $4 million
DPS = 4/1 = $4 per share

c. Borrowing = $6 million
RE = $6 million

d. Dividends = $10 million or $10 per share
No new borrowing

12. No, because the money could be better invested in stocks that pay dividends in cash that will benefit the fundholders.

13. The change in price is due to the change in dividends, not to the change in dividend <u>policy</u>. Dividend policy can still be irrelevant without a contradiction.

14. The stock price dropped because of an expected drop in future dividends. Since the stock price is the present value of all future dividends payments, if the expected future dividend payments decrease, then the stock price will decline.

15.

Common stock ($1 par) = 1,000,000 + .05(1,000,000) =	1,050,000
Excess over par = 2,000,000 + 50,000(6 − 1) =	2,250,000
Retained earnings = 5,000,000 − 50,000 − 250,000 =	4,700,000
Total common equity	$8,000,000

16. The equity accounts will be unchanged except the par value will now be 1/4 = $.25
Total dividends this year = .2(1,000,000)(4) = $800,000
Dividends last year = 800,000/1.05 = $761,904.76
Dividend per share last year = 761,904.76/1,000,000 = $.76

17. The plan will probably have little effect on shareholder wealth. The shareholders can reinvest on their own, and the shareholders must pay the taxes on the dividends either way. However, the shareholders who take the option may benefit at the expense of the ones who don't (because of the discount). Also, as a result of the plan, the firm will be able to raise equity by paying a 10% flotation cost (the discount), but this is a fairly typical flotation cost.

18. If these firms just went public, they probably did so because they were growing and needed the additional capital. Growth firms typically pay very small cash dividends, if they pay a dividend at all. This is because they have numerous projects, and they therefore reinvest the earnings in the firm instead of paying cash dividends.

19. a. First, it probably is not a good time to raise dividends if earnings are not good, and it is not certain that the higher dividend can be maintained. It would be worse to raise the dividend and then to later cut it back again. Second, if the firm can invest the money profitably, then it should do so. That is the basis for positive net present value projects.

b. On theoretical grounds, there is nothing inherently wrong with "borrowing to pay dividends," but most practitioners would probably feel that this is not the soundest financial policy. For example, it may have adverse capital structure consequences. In any case, once again, if the firm needs the money to fund profitable investments, it should probably not raise the dividend.

c. Neither one, really. Its dividend policy should probably be based on its long-range capital needs.

d. The company should not be too worried about the little old lady in Iowa. If she wishes higher dividends, she can sell her stock in Clark and buy stock in a company that pays a higher dividend, or she can sell off portions of Clark stock as needed to achieve the cash flow she desires.

20. Capital outlays were (100 – 60) × 2 = $80
New borrowing = $40

21. a. Payout ratio = .5/1.4 = .357 = 35.7%

b. (1.4 – .5)(5 million) + 14 million = $18.5 million
D/E = 14/4.5 = 3.1

22. a. Maximum capital spending = 600,000(2) = $1,200,000

b. No, they will not pay a dividend because the planned investment is greater than the maximum investment without an additional equity issue.

c. No, they do not maintain a constant dividend payout because, with the strict residual policy, the dividend will depend on the investment opportunities and earnings. As these two things vary, the dividend payout will also vary.

23. a. Cash dividend: DPS = 1,000/20 = $50 per share
New stock price = 100 – 50 = $50 per share
Wealth per share = 50 + 50 = $100

Stock repurchase: 1,000/100 = 10 shares will be repurchased
Share price before repurchase = share price after repurchase = $100
Wealth per share = $100

Therefore, neither a cash dividend nor a stock repurchase will affect the stockholders' wealth.

b. Div.: EPS = $5; P/E = 50/5 = 10
Rep.: EPS = 5(20)/10 = $10; P/E = 10

c. A share repurchase would seem to be the preferred course of action. Only those shareholders who wish to sell will do so, and, as a result, no one is forced to pay taxes.

24. The chief drawback to a strict dividend policy is the variability in dividend payments. This is a problem because investors tend to want a somewhat predictable cash flow. Also, if there is information content to dividend announcements, then the firm may be inadvertently telling the market that it is expecting a downturn when it cuts a dividend, when, in reality, its prospects are very good. In a compromise policy, the firm maintains a relatively constant dividend. It increases dividends only when it expects earnings to remain higher so it can continue to pay the higher dividend, and it lowers the dividend only if it absolutely has to.

CHAPTER 17
SHORT-TERM FINANCE AND PLANNING

1. Cash = 400 + 1,500 + 600 − 1,250 − 1,000 = $250
   Current Assets = 1,250 + 250 = $1,500

2. a. Use - The cash balance decreased by $210 to pay off creditors.
   b. Use - The cash balance decreased by $90 to pay the dividend.
   c. Source - The cash balance increased by $430 assuming that the inventory was sold for cash or the accounts receivables were collected.
   d. Source - The cash balance increased by $800 from receipts from the loan.
   e. Use - The cash balance decreased by $600 to pay for fixed assets.

3.

a.	D	b.	D	c.	N
d.	I	e.	N	f.	N
g.	I	h.	I	i.	D
j.	I	k.	N	l.	N
m.	D	n.	D	o.	D

4.

a.	I	b.	I	c.	N
d.	D	e.	N	f.	D

5. Carrying costs will decrease because they are not holding goods in inventory. Shortage costs will probably increase depending on how close the suppliers are and how well they can estimate need. The operating cycle will decrease because the inventory period is decreased.

6.

	Cash	Oper.		Cash	Oper.		Cash	Oper.
a.	D	N	b.	D	D	c.	I	N
d.	D	D	e.	I	I	f.	D	D

7.

Inventory turnover	= 13,776/[.5(2,567 + 2,331)]	= 5.625 times
Inventory period	= 365/5.625	= 64.89 days
Receivables turnover	= 23,750/[.5(1,108 + 1,426)]	= 18.745 times
Receivables period	= 365/18.745	= 19.47 days
Operating cycle	= 64.89 + 19.47	= 84.36 days
Payables turnover	= 13,776/[.5(4,927 + 5,300)]	= 2.694 times
Payables period	= 365/2.694	= 135.48 days
Cash cycle	= 84.36 days − 135.48 days	= −51.13 days

This firm is receiving the cash 51.13 days before it pays its bills.

8. The 60-day collection period implies that all of the beginning receivables are collected and one-third of that quarter's sales are collected.

	Q1	Q2	Q3	Q4
Beg. receivables	$100.00	$80.00	$106.67	$133.33
Sales	120.00	160.00	200.00	140.00
Cash collections	140.00	133.33	173.33	180.00
End. receivables	$80.00	$106.67	$133.33	$93.33

The 30-day collection period implies that all of the beginning receivables are collected and two-thirds of that quarter's sales are collected.

	Q1	Q2	Q3	Q4
Beg. receivables	$100.00	$40.00	$53.33	$66.67
Sales	120.00	160.00	200.00	140.00
Cash collections	180.00	146.67	186.67	160.00
End. receivables	$40.00	$53.33	$66.67	$46.67

9. a. Q1: .6(330) = $198
Q2: .6(263) = $157.80
Q3: .6(290) = $174
Q4: .6(345)(1.2) = $248.40
Payables period = 0 days

b. Q1: .6(345) = $207
Q2: .6(330) = $198
Q3: .6(263) = $157.80
Q4: .6(290) = $174

c. Q1: .6/3[2(345) + 330] = $204
Q2: .6/3[2(330) + 263] = $184.60
Q3: .6/3[2(263) + 290] = $163.20
Q4: .6/3[2(290) + 414] = $198.8

10. Payments equal 1/2 of payables for the current period and the next.

	Q1	Q2	Q3	Q4
Payment of accts	$480.00	$464.00	$352.00	$388.00
Wages, taxes, expenses	50.00	70.00	46.00	42.00
Interest & dividends	50.00	50.00	50.00	50.00
Total	$580.00	$584.00	$448.00	$480.00

11. a. Borrow $100 million for one year
Interest = $100M(1.03)^4 - 100M$ = $12,550,881
Usable Funds = 100M(.95) = $95 million
EAR = 12,550,881/95,000,000 = 13.21%

b. Amount borrowed = 50/.95 = $52,631,579
Interest = $52,631,579(1.03)^2 - 52,631,579$ = $3,205,263
Note: If interest is paid quarterly,
Interest = 52,631,579(.03)(2) = $3,157,895

12. Number of periods per year = 365/60 = 6.08
EAR = $(1 + .04/.96)^{6.08} - 1$ = 28.19%

13. Since the cash cycle = operating cycle − accounts payable period, it is not possible for the cash cycle to be longer than the operating cycle if the accounts payable period is positive. (It is unlikely to be negative since that implies that the firm pays its bills before they are incurred.)

14. a. Cash collected is 2/3 of sales plus beginning receivables. Cash paid to suppliers is equal to 1/3 of the previous quarter's orders plus 2/3 of the current quarter's orders.

Sample calculation for net cash inflow—first quarter:

$\$108 + (2/3)(340) - .6[1/3(340) + 2/3(443)] - .2(340) - 40 = -\$18.53$

RANDY'S CANDY
Cash Balance
(in $millions)

	Q1	Q2	Q3	Q4
Beg. cash balance	$35.00	$16.47	−$21.67	−$169.73
Net cash inflow	−18.53	−38.13	−148.07	126.53
End cash balance	16.47	−21.67	−169.73	−43.20
Min. cash balance	25.00	25.00	25.00	25.00
Cum. surplus (deficit)	−8.53	−46.67	−194.73	−68.20

b.

RANDY'S CANDY
Short-term Financial Plan
(in $millions)

	Q1	Q2	Q3	Q4
Beg. cash balance	$35.00	$16.47	−$21.67	−$169.73
Net cash inflow	−18.53	−38.13	−148.07	126.53
New short-term debt	8.53	38.39	149.47	0.00
Int. on ST debt	0.00	−0.26	−1.41	−5.89
ST debt repaid	0.00	0.00	0.00	−120.64
End cash balance	25.00	25.00	25.00	25.00
Min. cash balance	25.00	25.00	25.00	25.00
Cum. surplus (deficit)	0.00	0.00	0.00	0.00
Beg. ST debt	$0.00	$8.53	$46.92	$196.40
Change in ST debt	8.53	38.39	149.47	−120.64
End. ST debt	8.53	46.92	196.40	75.76

Total interest paid = $7.56 million

15. a. Cleveland Compressor (CC) finances its current assets with a combination of short-term and long-term borrowing, whereas Pnew York Pneumatic (PYP) finances its current assets with short-term borrowing only (very little cash).

b. CC has a higher investment on an absolute basis, and PYP has a higher investment on a relative basis. The relative basis is more important for determining working capital policy because the absolute basis does not consider the size of the firm and how that should affect policy.

c. PYP is more likely to incur carrying costs because it has a lower inventory turnover. For the same reason, CC is more likely to incur shortage costs, but since its inventory turnover is 1.22, its chances of being short may not be that great either.

16. a. December sales = 30,000/.7 = $42,857

b. January = 6000 + .4(42,857) + .3(90,000) = $50,143
February = .3(42,857) + .4(90,000) + .3(100,000) = $78,857
March = .3(90,000) + .4(100,000) + .3(120,000) = $103,000

17.

	April	May	June
Beg. cash balance	$200,000	226,000	$282,000
Cash receipts	152,000	134,000	152,000
Total cash avail.	$352,000	$360,000	$434,000
Cash disbursements			
Purchases	65,000	68,000	64,000
Wages, taxes, exp.	8,000	7,000	8,400
Interest	3,000	3,000	3,000
Equip. purchases	50,000	0	4,000
Total	126,000	78,000	79,400
Ending cash balance	$226,000	$282,000	$354,600

18. a. Usable funds = $.97 for every $1 borrowed
Annual interest = $1.04^4 - 1$ = $.1699 on every $1 borrowed
EAR = .1699/.97 = .175 = 17.5%
This assumes that the interest is actually paid at year end, rather than every quarter.

b. Usable funds = .97(40 million) = $38.8 million
Interest = $40M(1.04)^4 - 40M$ = $6.794 million
Up-front fee = .002(500M) = $1 million
Net borrowing = $38.8 – 1 = $37.8
EAR = $6.794/37.8 = 17.97%

CHAPTER 18
CASH AND LIQUIDITY MANAGEMENT

1. Net disbursement float is more desirable because the bank thinks the firm has more money than it actually does, and the firm is therefore receiving interest on funds it has already spent.

2. The firm has a net disbursement float of $.4 million. If this is an ongoing situation, the firm may be tempted to write checks for more than it actually has in its account.

3. Average daily float = 4(35,000)/30 = $4,666.67 (assuming a 30 day month)

4.

a.	Disbursement float	= 5(12,000)	= $60,000
	Collection float	= 3(15,000)	= $45,000
	Net float	= 60,000 – 45,000	= $15,000
b.	Collection float	= 4(15,000)	= $60,000
	Net float	= 60,000 – 60,000	= $0

5.
a. Total float = 4(5,000) + 8(2,000) = $36,000
b. Average daily float = 36,000/30 = $1,200
c. Average daily receipts = 7,000/30 = $233.33
Weighted average delay = 4(5,000/7,000) + 8(2,000/7,000) = 5.14 days

6.
a. Float = 4(5,000) = $20,000
b. Total opportunity cost = $20,000
c. Daily opportunity cost = (20,000/30)(.0002) = $.13

7.
a. Average daily float = [2,000(30)(2) + 8,000(60)(4)]/30 = $68,000
On average, there is $68,000 that is uncollected and not available.
b. Weighted average delay = 60,000(2)/540,000 + 480,000(4)/540,000 = 3.78 days
3.78(18,000) = $68,000
c. $68,000
d. 68,000(.0002109) = $14.35
e. 18,000(2) = $36,000

8. Average daily collections = 10(25,000) = $250,000
PV = 250,000(3) = $750,000
Daily interest earned = 750,000(.0002) = $150
The firm would save $150 a day. So if the bank would charge less than $150 per day, the firm should take the lockbox.

9.
a. PV = 100(1,000)(3) = $300,000
b. NPV = 300,000 – .75(100)/.0003 = $50,000
c. 300,000(.0003) – .75(100) = $15 per day
3(1,000)(.0003) – .75 = $.15 per check

10. PV = 200(10,000)(3) = \$6,000,000
No annual fee: NPV = 6,000,000 − .5(200)/.0002 = \$5,495,352
The lockbox should be adopted.
Annual fee: NPV = 6,000,000 − .5(200)/.0002 − 50,000/.075 = \$4,828,685
The lockbox should still be adopted.

11. N(4,500)(2)(.00016) − 15,000/365 − .25N = 0
N = 35 (to the nearest whole customer)

12.
a. Reduction = 100,000(3) = \$300,000
b. Return = 300,000(.0003) = \$93.16 per day (12% per year)
c. 300,000 − charge/.0095 = 0
charge = \$2,847

13. Interest = .0004(200,000)(3)(52/2) = \$6,240 (ignoring compounding)

14. The NPV is \$4 million − (\$600,000 − \$500,000) = \$3.9 million, so the system should be implemented. If the interest rate is 7%, then the annual savings is \$3.9 million × .07 = \$273,000 per year.

Appendix

A.1 a. D - this will increase the holding cost which will cause a decrease in the target cash balance.

b. I - this will increase the trading cost which will cause an increase in the target cash balance.

c. D - this will decrease the amount of cash that the firm has to hold in a non-interest bearing account, so they will move it to the interest bearing money markets.

d. D - if it is cheaper to borrow, then it will not be as costly if the firm runs short of cash because they can borrow at cheaper rates.

e. I - if the credit rating declines, then the firm will not be able to borrow as easily, consequently they will need to hold more cash.

f. D - this depends somewhat on what the fees apply to, but if direct fees are established, then the compensating balance may be lowered, thus lowering the target cash balance. If, on the other hand, fees are charged on the number of transactions, then the firm may wish to hold a higher cash balance so they are not transferring money into the account as often.

A.2 $C^* = [2(2{,}250)(5)/.09]^{½} = \$500$
The initial balance should be \$500, and whenever the balance drops to \$0, another \$500 should be transferred in.

A.3 Holding cost = 100(.08) = \$8
Trading cost = 10,000(4)/[100(2)] = \$200
Total cost = 200 + 8 = \$208
$(C^*/2)(.08) = 10{,}000(4)/C^*$
$C^* = \$1{,}000$
They should increase their average daily balance to 1,000/2 = \$500, in this way they will minimize cost. Total cost = 500(.08) + 10,000(4)/1,000 = \$80.

A.4 a. Opportunity cost = 1,000(.16)/2 = \$80
Trading cost = 5,000(100)/1,000 = \$500
It keeps too little in cash because the trading cost is greater than the opportunity cost.

b. $C^* = [2(5{,}000)(100)/.16]^{½} = \$2{,}500$

A.5 T = 345,000(12) = \$4,140,000
$C^* = [2(4{,}140{,}000)(500)/.07]^{½} = \$243{,}193$
Invest 800,000 – 243,193 = \$556,807
4,140,000/243,193 = 17; sell 17 times a year

A.6 The lower limit is the minimum balance allowed in the account, and the upper limit is the maximum balance allowed in the account. When the account balance drops to the lower limit, then 30,000 – 10,000 = \$20,00 in marketable securities will be sold, and the proceeds deposited in the account. This moves the account balance to the target amount. When the account balance rises to the upper limit, 100,000 – 30,000 = \$70,000 of marketable securities will be purchased with cash from the account. This moves the account balance to the target amount.

A.7 $C^* = 1{,}000 + [(3/4)(100)(90)^2/.0002]^{1/3} = \$2{,}448$
$U^* = 3(2{,}448) - 2(1{,}000) = \$5{,}344$
When the balance in the cash account drops to \$1,000, \$1,448 of marketable securities will be sold, and the proceeds will be deposited in the account. On the other hand, when the cash account balance rises to \$5,344, \$2,896 of marketable securities will be purchased with cash.

A.8 As variance increases, the upper limit and the spread will increase, while the lower limit remains unchanged. The lower limit does not change because it is an exogenous variable set by management. As the variance increases, however, the amount of uncertainty increases. When this happens, the target cash balance and therefore the upper limit and the spread will need to be higher. If variance drops to zero, then the lower limit, the target balance, and the upper limit will all be the same.

A.9 $C^* = 20{,}000 + [(3/4)(600)(1{,}440{,}000)/.0002]^{(1/3)} = \$34{,}538$
$U^* = 3(34{,}538) - 2(20{,}000) = \$63{,}614$

A.10 $\$707 = [2(10{,}000)(2)/R]^{1/2}$
$R = 8\%$

CHAPTER 19
CREDIT AND INVENTORY MANAGEMENT

1.
1. Terms of sale
2. Credit analysis
3. Collection policy

2.
1. The credit period
2. The cash discount and the discount period
3. The type of credit instrument

3.
a. 120 days; 100(20) = $2,000
b. 2%; 30 days; $2,000(.98) = $1,960
c. $2,000 − 1,960 = $40; 120 − 30 = 90 days

4.
1. Perishability and collateral value
2. Consumer demand
3. Cost, profitability, and standardization
4. Credit risk
5. The size of the account
6. Competition
7. Customer type

If the credit period exceeds a customer's operating cycle, then we are financing receivables and other aspects of the customer's business that go beyond the purchase of our merchandise.

5.
a. B - since firm A's merchandise is perishable and firm B's is not, firm B will probably have a longer credit period
b. B - firm A is likely to sell for cash only (unless the product really works). If it does work, then they might grant longer credit periods to entice buyers
c. A - landlords have significantly greatly collateral, and that collateral is not mobile.
d. A - rugs are fairly standardized and they are transportable. Carpets are custom fit, and they are not particularly transportable.
e. A - since firm A's customers turn over their inventory less frequently, they have a longer inventory period and thus likely will be granted a longer credit period

6.
a. Time draft—a commercial draft that does not require immediate payment
b. Promissory note—an IOU that the customer signs
c. Sight draft—a commercial draft payable immediately
d. Trade acceptance—the buyer accepts the commercial draft and promises to pay in the future
e. Banker's acceptance—a bank guarantees payment of a commercial draft at a future date

7. Trade credit is usually granted on open account. The invoice is the instrument of credit.

8. Costs of credit: cost of debt, probability of nonpayment, and cash discount
Costs of no credit: lost sales
Sum of costs = carrying costs

9.

1. Character - determines if a customer is willing to pay his debts
2. Capacity - determines if a customer is able to pay debts out of operating cash flow
3. Capital - determines the customer's financial reserves in case of a problem with operating cash flow
4. Collateral - assets that can be liquidated to pay off the loan in case of default
5. Conditions - customer's ability to weather an economic downturn and whether a downturn is likely

10. Receivables turnover = 365/60 = 6.083 times
Average receivables = \$45 million/6.083 = \$7,397,260

11.
a. ACP = .6(10) + .4(60) = 30 days
b. Average balance = 200(\$1,400) = \$280,000

12. Average accounts receivables = 3 months sales = \$600,000(3) = \$1,800,000

13. .02/.98 = .0204
EAR = $(1.0204)^{(365/20)} - 1 = 44.6\%$
a. the effective rate would increase (74.3%)
b. the effective rate would decrease (15.89%)
c. the effective rate would increase (63.5%)

14. Receivables turnover = 365/50 = 7.3 times
Annual credit sales = 7.3(\$3M) = \$21.9 million

15. The three main categories of inventory are:

Raw material: the initial input(s) to the firm's production process
Work-in-progress: partially completed products
Finished goods: products ready for sale

From the firm's perspective, the demand for finished goods is independent from the demand for the other types of inventory. The demand for raw material and work-in-progress is derived from, or dependent on, the firm's needs for these inventory types in order to achieve the desired levels of finished goods.

16. a. NPV $= -2 + (1 - .1)3/1.025 = \$.63$ per unit; Fill the order

b. $0 = -2 + (1 - \pi)3/1.025$

$\pi = .3167 = 31.67\%$

c. NPV $= -2 + (1 - .1)(3 - 2)/.025 = \$34$ per unit; Fill the order

$0 = -2 + (1 - \pi)(3 - 2)/.025$

$\pi = .95 = 95\%$

d. It is assumed that if a person has paid her bills in the past, then they will pay their bills in the future. This implies that if someone doesn't default when credit is first granted, then they will be a good customer far into the future, and the possible gains from the future business outweigh the possible losses from granting credit the first time.

17. JIT systems reduce inventory amounts. Assuming no adverse effects on sales, inventory turnover will increase. Since assets will decrease, total asset turnover will also increase. Recalling the Du Pont equation, an increase in total asset turnover has a positive effect on ROE.

18. Total credit sales = \$85,000(55) = \$4,675,000
ACP = .4(15) + .6(40) = 30 days
Receivables turnover = 365/30 = 12.167 times
Average receivables = \$4,675,000/12.167 = \$384,247
If they increase the cash discount, then more people will pay sooner, thus lowering the average collection period. If the average collection period falls, the receivables turnover will increase which will lead to a decrease in average receivables.

19. ACP = 45 + 45 = 90 days
Receivables turnover = 365/90 = 4.06 times
Receivables = 5,000,000/4.06 = \$1,232,877

20. \$840(345) + \$690(390 − 345) = \$320,850
(\$840 − 690)(390 − 345) = \$6,750
NPV = −\$320,850 − \$320,850/1.01 + \$6,750/(1.01)(.01) = \$29,794
The firm will have to bear the cost of sales for 2 months before they receive any revenue from credit sales, which is why the initial cost is for two months. Receivables will grow over the two month credit period, and then will remain about stable with payments and new sales off-setting one another.

21. Carrying costs should be equal to order costs. The firm needs to carry more inventory.

22. Carrying costs = \$20(6,000) = \$120,000
Order costs = \$52(2,000) = \$104,000
The firm's policy is not optimal, since the costs are not equal. The firm should increase order size and reduce the number of orders.

23. Carrying costs = \$10(50) = \$500
Restocking costs = 52(\$1,200) = \$62,400
EOQ = $[2(5{,}200)(1{,}200)/10]^{1/2}$ = 1,117.14 pots per order
Order 4.65 times per year

24. CF(old) = (\$10 − \$6)(40,000) = \$160,000
CF(new) = (\$12 − \$7)(40,000) = \$200,000
Incremental CF = \$200,000 − 160,000 = \$40,000
NPV = −10(40,000) − 40,000 + 40,000/.01 = \$3,560,000; Switch

25. a. CF(old) = (\$20 − \$12)(2,000) = \$16,000
CF(new) = (\$22 − \$12)(2,150) = \$21,500
Incremental CF = \$21,500 − 16,000 = \$5,500
NPV = −20(2,000) − 12(2,150 − 2,000) + 5,500/.02 = \$233,200

b. Accounts receivable approach:
Carrying cost = [\$20(2,000) + \$12(150)](.02) = \$836
NPV = (5,500 − 836)/.02 = \$233,200

c. One-shot approach:
Present value of \$22(2,150) to be received next month
= 47,300/1.02 = \$46,373
Net benefit = 46,373 − 12(2,150) = \$20,573
NPV for 1 month = 20,573 − 16,000 = \$4,573
NPV = 4,573 + 4,573/.02 = \$233,200

26. Carrying costs = (Q/2)(CC)
Restocking costs = F(T/Q)
(Q/2)(CC) = F(T/Q)
Q(CC) = 2F(T/Q)
Q^2(CC) = 2F(T)
Q^2 = 2F(T)/CC
Q = $[2T(F)/CC]^{1/2}$
Q = EOQ

Appendix

A.1 CF(old) = 1,000(15,000) = \$15 million
CF(new) = (1 − .05)(1,000)(16,000) = \$15.2 million
Incremental CF = 15.2M − 15M = \$.2 million
NPV = −15 million + 200,000/.02 = −\$5 million

A.2
a. 2.5/10, net 30
b. 10,000(78) = \$780,000 (at a maximum)
c. Because the quantity sold does not change, variable cost is the same under either plan.
d. No, because $d - \pi = 2.5 - 3 = -.5$, the NPV will be negative. The breakeven credit price is $P(1 + r)/(1 - \pi)$ = \$81.22, which implies that the breakeven discount is 3.22/81.22 =3.96%. NPV = −15 million + 200,000/.02 = −\$5 million

A.3
a. NPV = −3,000 + (1 − .2)(7,000)/(1.04) = \$2,385
Yes, they should fill the order.
b. $0 = -3{,}000 + (1 - \pi)(7{,}000)/1.04$
$\pi = 55.4\%$
c. Effectively the cash discount = 100/1,400 = 7.14% Since the discount rate is less than the default rate, credit should not be granted. The firm would be better off taking the \$1,300 up front than taking an 80% chance of making \$1,400.

A.4
a. Cash discount = 1 − 25/27 = 7.41%;
Probability of default = 1 − .9 = .1 = 10%
Credit should not be granted because the discount is less than the probability of default, thus the NPV is negative.

b. Due to the increase in volume and variable price, the firm incurs an additional cost of \$7,800 = 1(3,000) + 16(300). Thus:

$$0 = -25(3{,}000) - 7{,}800 + \{[(1 - .1)P' - 16](3{,}300) - (25 - 15)(3{,}000)\}/[(1.01)^3 - 1]$$
$$P' = \$28.72$$

c. $$NPV = -25(3{,}000) - 7{,}800 - .25(3{,}300) + (27 - 16)(2{,}970)/[(1.01)^3 - 1]$$
$$= \$994{,}557$$
Yes, credit should be extended.

A.5
$$CF(old) = (P - v)Q$$
$$CF(new) = (P - v)(1 - \alpha)Q' + [(1 - \pi)P' - v]\alpha Q'$$
$$\text{Incremental CF} = (P - v)(1 - \alpha)Q' + [(1 - \pi)P' - v]\alpha Q' - (P - v)Q$$
$$= (P - v)(Q' - Q) + [(1 - \pi)P' - P]\alpha Q'$$
$$NPV = (P - v)(Q' - Q) - \alpha PQ' + \{ (P - v)(Q' - Q) + [(1 - \pi)P' - P]\alpha Q' \}/R$$

CHAPTER 20
OPTIONS AND CORPORATE SECURITIES

1. A call option confers the right, without the obligation, to buy an asset at a given price on or before a given date. A put option confers the right, without the obligation, to sell an asset at a given price on or before a given date. You would buy a call option if you expect the price of the asset to increase. You would buy a put option if you expect the price of the asset to decrease. A call option has unlimited potential profit, while a put option has limited potential profit.

2.
a. Buyer of call pays for right to buy asset
b. Buyer of put pays for right to sell asset
c. Seller of call receives cash for obligation to sell asset
d. Seller of put receives cash for obligation to buy asset

3. There is an arbitrage opportunity. You can buy a call option for \$15, exercise it for \$60, and then sell the stock for \$80. You will have made a profit of \$5.

4. The intrinsic value of a call is S – E or 0, whichever is greater. It is what the option is worth if it is about to expire, and it is the lower bound for the value of the option anytime before expiration.

5. The value of a put option at maturity is the greater of E – S or 0. Before maturity, the put must sell for at least this amount, so this represents the intrinsic value of the put.

6.
a. The call options are in the money. The intrinsic value, IV = 50 – 40 = \$10

b. June call should sell for at least \$10:

Arbitrage:	Buy call	(8)
	Exercise	(40)
	Sell share	50
	Profit	\$2

c. The June call can't sell for more than the July call, so the most it can sell for is something less than \$11.50.

7.
a. 50(100)(2.875) = \$14,375
b. 50(100)(100 – 90) = \$50,000
c. (90 – 16)(10)(100) = \$74,000 (net profit)
(90 – 75)(10)(100) = \$15,000 (option value)
d. (16 – 15)(10)(100) = \$1,000
16(10)(100) = \$16,000
e. 16 = (90 – P)
P = \$74

8. False; the value of a call option depends on the total variance of the value of the underlying asset.

9. The call option will sell for more since it has higher potential profit.

10. The prices of both the call and the put option should increase. When the risk increases, the value of the option when it finishes out of the money doesn't change but the value of the option will be greater when it finishes in the money.

11.
a. $C_0 = 28 - 20/1.08 = \$9.48$
b. $C_0 = 28 - 10/1.08 = \$18.74$
c. $P_0 = \$0$; there is no chance that the put will finish in the money.

12. The value of a call option will increase, and the value of a put option will decrease (assuming it's an American put).

13.
a. $C_0 = 65 - 55/1.07 = \$13.60$
b. $C_0 = (15/20)(65 - 60/1.07) = \$6.69$

14. $C_0 = 1{,}000/100 = \$10$
$S_0 = 10(20/15) + 20/1.1 = \$31.52$

15.
a. $E = 800 - 500/1.08 = \$337.04$
b. $D = 800 - 337.04 = \$462.96$
The interest rate on the debt is 8%.
c. The value of the equity will increase. The debt requires a higher return, therefore the present value of the debt is less while the value of the firm does not change.

16.
a. $E = (800/1{,}000)(1{,}200 - 800/1.06) = \$356.23$
$D = 1{,}200 - 356.23 = \$843.77$
b. $E = (1{,}000/1{,}500)(1{,}200 - 500/1.06) = \$485.53$. The stockholders will prefer such a move since their potential gain increases while their potential loss remains unchanged.

17.
a. $C_0 = \text{MAX}[50 - 55/1.08, 0] = \$0$. The option is not worth anything.
b. Relative to the possible prices, the current stock price is too low; the minimum possible return is 10% which exceeds the risk-free rate.

18. $CR = 1{,}000/180 = 5.56$
$CV = 60 \times 5.56 = \$333.60$

19.
a. $CV = (1{,}000/50)(52) = \$1{,}040$
$SB = 90 \times \text{PVIFA}(10,10\%) + 1{,}000/(1.1)^{10} = \$938.55$
The bond should sell for at least \$1,040.
b. The option embedded in the bond adds the extra value.

20.
a. $SB = 60 \times \text{PVIFA}(30,7\%) + 1{,}000/(1.07)^{30} = \$875.91$
b. $CV = 10(50.12) = \$501.20$
$CP = (100 - 50.12)/50.12 = 99.52\%$

21. a. CR = 50
CP = 1,000/50 = $20
Conversion premium = (20 − 16)/16 = 25%

b. SB = 40 × PVIFA(16,6%) + $1{,}000/(1.06)^{16}$ = $797.88
CV = 16(50) = $800

c. S = $797.88/50 = $15.96

d. There are actually two option values to consider with a convertible bond. The conversion option value, defined as market less floor value, and the speculative option value, defined as floor less SB value. When the conversion value is less than the SB value, the speculative option value is zero.
Conversion option value = 840 − 800 = $40
Speculative option value = 800 − 797.88 = $2.12
Total option value = 40 + 2.12 = $42.12

22. B, with A you could buy the bond for $900, immediately convert it to stock, sell the stock for $1,000 and make an easy profit of $100.

23. W_0 = {1,000 − [80 × PVIFA(10,11%) + $1{,}000/(1.11)^{10}$]}/20 = $8.83

24. $8.83/4 = $2.21 ≤ S (the warrant can't be worth more than the stock)
$1,000/80 = $12.5 ≥ S (the conversion value of the bond can't exceed $1,000)

25. a. P_0 = [(700,000 − 200,000) + 80(10)(100)]/[5,000 + 10(100)] = $96.67
W_0 = 10(96.67) − 10(80) = $166.67

b.

BEFORE

Assets		Liabilities and Equity	
Assets	$700,000	Debt	$200,000
		Equity	483,333
		Warrants	16,667
	$700,000		$700,000

AFTER

Assets		Liabilities and Equity	
Assets	$700,000	Debt	$200,000
Cash	80,000	Equity	580,000
	$780,000		$780,000

c. Effective exercise price = $66.67

26. Straight bond price = 60 × PVIFA(30,8%) + $1{,}000/(1.08)^{30}$ = $774.84
Conversion value = 50.12(1,000/100) = $501.20

$501.20(1.1)^n$ = $1,300
n = 10 years; the bond will be called in 10 years, thereby forcing conversion.

Given these cash flows,

Bond value = 60 × PVIFA(10,11%) + $1{,}300/(1.11)^{10}$ = $811.19

Appendix

A.1 a. $d_1 = \{\ln(50/60) + [.08 + .5(.2)](.5)\}/[.2(.5)]^{½} = -.292$
$N(d_1) = .3821$
$d_2 = -.292 - [.2(.5)]^{½} = -.608$
$N(d_2) = .2743$
$C_0 = 50(.3821) - [60/(1.08)^{.5}](.2743) = \$3.27$

b. $d_1 = 1.409$; $N(d_1) = .9192$
$d_2 = .935$; $N(d_2) = .8264$
$C_0 = 25(.9192) - [15/(1.06)^{.75}](.8264) = \$11.12$

c. $d_1 = -.095$; $N(d_1) = .4602$
$d_2 = -.542$; $N(d_2) = .2946$
$C_0 = 50(.4602) - [60/(1.08)^{.5}](.2946) = \$6.00$

d. $S = 0$, which implies that $C_0 = 0$

e. $T = \infty$, which implies that $C_0 = S = \$90$

f. $E = 0$, which implies that $C_0 = S = \$50$

A.2 $d_1 = \{\ln(1,200/1,000) + [.06 + .5(.3)](1)\}/[.3(1)]^{½} = .7163$
$N(d_1) = .7642$
$d_2 = .7163 - .3^{½} = .1686$
$N(d_2) = .5675$
$E = 1,200(.7642) - [1,000/(1.06)](.5675) = \$381.66$
$D = 1,200 - 381.66 = \$818.34$

A.3 a. Project A: $d_1 = \{\ln(1,300/1,000) + [.06 + .5(.4)]\}/(.4)^{½} = .8259$
$N(d_1) = .7956$
$d_2 = .8259 - .4^{½} = .1935$
$N(d_2) = .5793$
$E_A = 1,300(.7956) - [1,000/1.06](.5793) = \$487.77$
$D_A = 1,300 - 487.77 = \$812.23$

Project B: $d_1 = \{\ln(1,350/1,000) + [.06 + .5(.25)]\}/(.25)^{½} = .9702$
$N(d_1) = .834$
$d_2 = .9702 - .25^{½} = .4702$
$N(d_2) = .6809$
$E_B = 1,350(.834) - [1,000/1.06](.6809) = \$483.54$
$D_B = 1,350 - 483.54 = \$866.46$

b. Stockholders prefer Project A. The value of the option to default is more than the additional $50 net present value.

c. Yes, then Project B would be the better project because, in this case, it is total firm value that matters (this assumes that each investor owns the same percentage of the stock and the bonds)

d. Stockholders may have an incentive to take on more risky, less profitable projects if the firm is financed with some debt.

CHAPTER 21
MERGERS AND ACQUISITIONS

1. 10 million – 8 million = \$2 million

2.
a. V_B^* = 100 + 40 = \$140
NPV = 140 – 6(20) = \$20
b. P = (500 + 20)/50 = \$10.40
c. Premium = 6(20) – 5(20) = \$20
d. V_{AB} = 500 + 100 + 40 = \$640
P = 640/60 = \$10.67
Cost = 10(10.66) = \$106.67
NPV = 140 – 106.67 = \$33.33
e. P = \$10.67
f. B receives benefit of merger, not just A.

3.

	Advantages	Disadvantages
Taxable:	Write-up	Capital gains tax
Tax-free:	No capital gains tax	No write-up

The basic determinant of tax status is whether or not the old stockholders will continue to participate in the new company. An LBO is usually taxable because the acquiring group pays off the current stockholders, usually in cash.

4. Purchase: assets must be recorded at market value and goodwill is created to account for the difference between market value and book value.
Pooling: combine the balance sheets, no goodwill is created.
Cash flows are not directly affected by the choice of accounting method.
EPS will probably be lower under purchase accounting because the reported income is generally lower due to the amortization of goodwill.

5. Stock value: 40(40) = \$1,600
A gives up 1,600/160 = 10 shares
a. EPS = 1,000/110 = \$9.09
b. P = 20(9.09) = \$181.82
c. Assuming the merger has a zero NPV, the share price will remain at \$160, and the new P/E = \$160/9.09 = 17.6 times.
If the pre-merger value of B is the total value of the merger to A (a negative NPV), then the new share price would be 17,200/110 =\$156.36, and P/E falls to 17.2.

6. Purchase:

	Assets		L & OE
From A	$ 11,000		
From B	10,000		
Goodwill	2,500	Equity	$ 23,500
	$ 23,500		$ 23,500

Pooling:

Assets	$ 16,000	Equity	$ 16,000

7.

CA	300	CL	200
FA	1,500	LT/D	300
		E	1,300
	$ 1,800		$ 1,800

8. MV of FA = 900

Goodwill = 1,200 − 900 − 200 = 100

CA	300	CL	60
F/A	1,800	LT/D	1,400
GW	100	E	740
	$ 2,200		$ 2,200

9. A scale economy exists when the average cost declines with the quantity of output. A merger in this particular case might make sense because Eastern and Western may need less total capital investment to handle the peak power needs, thereby reducing average generation costs.

10.

Current assets	480	Current liabilities	280
Other assets	140	Long-term debt	100
Net fixed assets	580	Equity	820
Total	$1,200	Total	$1,200

11.

Current assets	480	Current liabilities	200
Other assets	140	Long-term debt	400
Net fixed assets	620	Equity	700
Goodwill	60		
Total	$1,300	Total	$1,300

12. After-tax cash flow = $1.6 million

Gain = 1.6/.07 = $22.857 million

$V_B^* = 20 + 22.857$ = $42.857 million

a. Cash: = $25 million

Equity: V_{AB} = $77.857 million

Cost = .35(77.857) = $27.25 million

b. NPV_{Cash} = 42.857 − 25 = $17.857 million

NPV_{Stock} = 42.857 − 27.25 = $15.607 million

c. Choose cash

13. a. $EPS_A = 225/100 = \$2.25$
$EPS_C = 100/50 = \$2.00$
$EPS_{AC} = 325/130 = \$2.50$
b. Probably none

14. a. $P_P = 12(3) = \$36$ (current)
$R_E = 1.8(1.05)/36 + .05 = .1025 = 10.25\%$
$P_P = 1.8(1.07)/(.1025 - .07) = \$59.26$
Value $= 59.26(250{,}000) = \$14{,}815{,}385$
b. Gain $= 14{,}815{,}385 - 36(250{,}000) = \$5{,}815{,}385$
c. $NPV_C = 14{,}815{,}385 - 40(250{,}000) = \$4{,}815{,}385$
d. $P_F = (15{,}000{,}000 + 14{,}815{,}385)/(1{,}000{,}000 + 600{,}000) = \$18.63$
$NPV_S = 14{,}815{,}835 - 18.63(600{,}000) = \$3{,}637{,}385$
e. Yes, and cash should be used.
f. Value $= \$11{,}223{,}529$
Gain $= \$2{,}223{,}529$
$NPV_C = \$1{,}223{,}529$
$NPV_S = \$1{,}389{,}706$
Yes, and stock should be used.

15. Show NPV $= \Delta V - (\text{Cost} - V_B)$
Since $V_B^* = \Delta V + V_B$,
NPV $= V_B^* - \text{Cost}$
$= \Delta V + V_B - \text{Cost}$
$= \Delta V - (\text{Cost} - V_B)$

CHAPTER 22
INTERNATIONAL CORPORATE FINANCE

1.
a. 100(3061.01) = Ps306,101
b. .03267 cents
c. 1,000,000(.0003267) = $326.67
d. Italian lira
e. Singapore dollar
f. $1 = FF 5.4305; $1 = BF 32.83
BF1 = FF.1654 cross rate
g. The most: Kuwaiti Dinou = $3.4358
The least: Mexican Peso = $.00009634
h. Soviet Union; the currency is controlled.

2.
a. £100, since £100 = $179.95.
b. £100, since £100 = $179.95 > $62.68 = DM 100
c. DM1 = £.348
£ = DM 2.87

3.
a. ¥128.13 per $; the yen is selling at a discount because it's less expensive in the forward market ($.007805 vs. $.007843).
b. $.6945 per SF; the dollar is selling at a premium because it's more expensive in the forward market (SF 1.4398 vs. SF 1.4280).
c. The value of the dollar will rise relative to the yen, since the dollar is worth more in the future than it is today. The same is true for the dollar relative to the Swiss franc.

4.
a. U.S. dollar is worth more
b. 1.5(1/1.2) = $1.25
tariffs, differences in local tastes, transportation costs, etc.
c. Discount, since the Canadian dollar is less expensive in the future than it is today.
d. US $
e. $R_{CAN} > R_{US}$

5.
a. Premium
b. No, need more FF to buy $1
c. Inflation in France > Inflation in US
$R_{FR} > R_{US}$

6.
a. $1 = Can $1.25 = FF5
Can $1 = FF4
b. Yes, there is an arbitrage. Buy Can $ with U.S. $, then buy FF with Can $, and then buy U.S. $ with FF. You will make $.125 for every U.S.$ used.

7. The exchange rate will increase. This relies on purchasing power parity.

8. a. Weaker
b. Japan's is higher
c. Nominal rates will be higher in Japan. The relative real rates will be the same.

9. A Samurai is most accurately described by choice c.

10. $R_{US} = 1\%$; $R_{UK} = .75\%$
$S_0 = .5$; $F_1 = .49$
$\$5M(1.01)^3 = \$5.1515$ million
£2.5M$(1.0075)^3/.49 = \$5.2177$ million
Invest in UK.

11. Pay 50,000(2,000) = 100,000,000 pesetas in 90 days
Sell for 25(50,000) = \$1,250,000
Goes up by 10%: 100.47(1.1) = 110.517
1,250,000 − 100,000,000/110.517 = \$345,161.83
Goes down by 10%: 100.47(.9) = 90.423
1,250,000 − 100,000,000/90.423 = \$144,086.68
Break-even: 1,250,000 = 100,000,000/x
x = 80 Pesetas

12. Purchasing power parity: $2.5 = 3(1 + \text{diff. in infl.})^4$
US expected inflation exceeds Germany's expected inflation by 4.456%

13. $S_0 = 1.1$; $R_{US} = 8\%$ (= 4% per 180 days, ignoring compounding)
$F_1 = 1.15$; $R_C = 9\%$ (= 4.5% per 180 days, ignoring compounding)
a. Yes, there is; the forward premium is too large. Borrow Can \$1 for 180 days at 9%, convert to U.S. dollars, invest at 8%, forward contract to convert back. Profit per \$ per 180 days is:
Can \$1 × (1/1.1) × 1.04 × 1.15 − Can \$1 × 1.045 = Can \$.04
b. $F_1 = 1.1\ (1 + .045 - .04) = 1.1055$

14. $S_0 = 6$; $R_{US} = 9\%$, $F_1 = 6.02$
a. Weaker
b. Inflation difference over 90 days is

$$h_{FR} - h_{US} = .00333$$
$$\text{or } (1.003333)^4 - 1 = 1.34\% \text{ annually}$$

15. In one year: $E[S_1] = 200(1 + (.24 - .12)) = 224$
In two years: $E[S_2] = 200(1 + (.24 - .12))^2 = 250.88$
Relative PPP is the principle.

16. a. False, more yen will be needed to buy \$1
b. False, the forward exchange rates would already reflect the projected deterioration in the value of the franc.
c. True, others are only correct on average. You would be correct all the time.

17. Interest rate parity is the most likely to hold because of arbitrage opportunities. Relative purchasing power parity is the least likely to hold because of transportation costs, tariffs, and other barriers.

18. a. Implicitly, it is assumed that interest rates won't change, but the exchange rate is projected to decline.

b. $E[S_t] = 2[1 + (.04 - .06)]^t = 2(.98)^t$

t	DM	$E[S_t]$	US $
0	−9M	2.000	−4,500,000
1	4M	1.960	2,040,816
2	4M	1.921	2,082,466
3	4M	1.882	2,124,965

NPV = \$494,794

c. $R_{DM} = 1.12(.98) - 1 = 9.76\%$
NPV = DM 989,588 = \$494,794
or, using the approximation
$R_{DM} = 1.12 - .02 = 10\%$
NPV = DM 947,408 = \$473,704

19. a. $(1 + R_{US})/(1 + h_{US}) = (1 + R_{FC})/(1 + h_{FC})$

b. $E[S_1] = S_0(1 + R_{FC})/(1 + R_{US})$

c. $E[S_1] = S_0(1 + h_{FC})/(1 + h_{US})$

d. Home Currency Approach:
$E[S_t] = 5(1.07/1.05)^t = 5(1.019)^t$
$NPV = -4 + [9/5(1.019)]/1.1 + [9/5(1.019)^2]/(1.1)^2 + [9/5(1.019)^3]/(1.1)^3 = \$.32$

Foreign Currency Approach:
$R_{FC} = 1.10 \times (1.07/1.05) = 1.121$
$NPV = -20 + 9/1.121 + 9/(1.121)^2 + 9/(1.121)^3 =$ FF1.58 million
$NPV_{\$} = 1.58/5 = \$.32$

CHAPTER 23
LEASING

1. a. Leasing is a form of secured borrowing. It reduces a firm's cost of capital only if it is cheaper than other forms of secured borrowing. The reduction of uncertainty is not particularly relevant; what matters is the NAL.

b. The statement is not always true. For example, a lease often requires an advance lease payment or security deposit and may be implicitly secured by other assets of the firm.

c. Leasing would probably not disappear, since it does reduce the uncertainty about salvage value and the transactions costs of transferring ownership. However, the use of leasing would be greatly reduced.

2. A lease must be disclosed on the balance sheet if one of the following criteria is met:

1. The lease transfers ownership of the asset by the end of the lease. In this case, the firm essentially owns the asset and will have access to its residual value.
2. The lessee can purchase the asset at a price below fair market value (bargain purchase option) when the lease ends. The firm essentially owns the asset, and will have access to most of its residual value.
3. The lease term is 75% or more of the estimated economic life of the asset. The firm basically has access to the majority of the benefits of the asset, without any responsibility for the consequences of its disposal.
4. The present value of the lease payments is 90% or more of the fair market value of the asset at the start of the lease. The firm is essentially purchasing the asset on an installment basis.

3. The lease must meet the following IRS standards for the lease payments to be tax deductible:

1. The lease term must be less than 80% of the economic life of the asset. If the term is longer, the lease is considered to be a conditional sale.
2. The lease should not contain a bargain purchase option. This option would imply an equity interest in the asset.
3. The lease payment schedule should not provide for very high payments early and very low payments late in the life of the lease. This would indicate that the lease is being used simply to avoid taxes.
4. Renewal options should be reasonable and based on the fair market value of the asset at renewal time. This indicates that the lease is for legitimate business purposes, not tax avoidance.

4. As the term implies, off-balance sheet financing involves financing arrangements that are not required to be reported on the firm's balance. Such activities only appear in the footnotes. Operating leases (those that do not meet the criteria in problem 2) provide off-balance sheet financing. For accounting purposes, total assets will be lower and some financial ratios may be artificially high. Financial analysts are generally not fooled by such activities. There are no economic consequences, since the cashflows of the firm are not affected.

5. The lessee may not be able to take advantage of the depreciation tax shield and may be able to obtain favorable lease arrangements for "passing on" the tax shield benefits. The lessee may need the cash flow from the sale to meet immediate needs, but will be able to meet the lease obligations in the future.

6. Since the relevant cash flows are all after-tax, the after-tax discount rate is appropriate.

The following information applies to Problems 7 through 12:

Cost of machine = \$540,000
Straight-line depreciation tax shield = (\$540,000/4)(.34) = \$45,900 per year for 4 years
Salvage value = \$0
After-tax (AT) lease payment = 160,000(1 – .34) = \$105,600
After-tax cost of capital = .08(1 – .34) = .0528

7. Lessee's incremental cash flows (in thousands) from leasing instead of buying:

	Year 0	Year 1	Year 2	Year 3	Year 4
AT lease payment		–105.6	–105.6	–105.6	–105.6
Lost depr. tax shield		– 45.9	– 45.9	– 45.9	– 45.9
Machine cost	540				
Total cash flow	540	–151.5	–151.5	–151.5	–151.5

NAL = 540,000 – 151,500{[1 – $(1/1.0528)^4$]/.0528]} = \$6,264

NAL is greater than zero, so the asset should be leased.

8. The cash flows to the lessor would be the same as those in problem 7, with the signs reversed.
NAL to lessor = –\$6,264

9. NAL = 0 = 540,000 – CF{[1 – $(1/1.0528)^4$]/.0528}
CF = \$153,278 (the after-tax cash flow)
CF = Depr. tax shield + Pmt(1 – .34)
153,278 = 45,900 + Pmt(1 – .34)
Pmt = (153,278 – 45,900)/(1 – .34)
Pmt = \$162,694

10. If the lessee expects to pay no taxes, then:
After-tax lease payment = \$160,000
Depreciation tax shield = \$0
Cost of capital = .08
NAL = 540,000 – 160,000{[1 – $(1/1.08)^4$]/.08}
NAL = \$10,059

11. If the lessee expects to pay no taxes, then for the lessee:
NAL = 0 = 540,000 – Pmt$\{[1 - (1/1.08)^4]/.08\}$
Pmt = \$163,037
For the lessor, NAL = \$0 if Pmt = \$162,694 (from problem 9)
Therefore, the lease will have a positive NAL for both when the payment is between \$162,694 and \$163,037.

12. With 3 year ACRS depreciation schedule (.3333, .4444, .1482, .0741), the depreciation tax shield must be adjusted.

Sample calculation for Year 1 tax shield:

.3333(540,000)(.34) = \$61,194

Lessee's incremental cash flows (in thousands) from leasing instead of buying:

	Year 0	Year 1	Year 2	Year 3	Year 4
AT lease payment		–105.6	–105.6	–105.6	–105.6
Lost depr. tax shield		– 61.2	– 81.6	– 27.2	– 13.6
Machine cost	540				
Total cash flow	540	–166.8	–187.2	–132.8	–119.2

NAL = $540{,}000 - 166{,}794/(1.0528) - 187{,}192/(1.0528)^2 - 132{,}810/(1.0528)^3 - 119{,}205/(1.0528)^4$
NAL = \$1,840

The machine should still be leased.

13. After-tax lease payment = 6,961(1 – .34) = \$4,594
Depreciation tax shield = (24,000/3)(.34) = \$2,720 per year
After-tax cost of capital = .1(1 – .34) = .066

Lessee's incremental cash flows from leasing instead of buying:

	Year 0	Year 1	Year 2	Year 3
AT lease payment	–4,594	–4,594	–4,594	–4,594
Lost depr. tax shield		–2,720	–2,720	–2,720
Machine cost	24,000			
Total cash flow	19,406	–7,314	-7,314	–7,314

NAL = 19,406 – 7,314$\{[1 - (1/1.066)^3]/.066\}$
NAL = \$71

The Year 0 cash flow is the net benefit today of the lease, or the savings from not buying less the advance lease payment. The opportunity cost of the lease is reduced, but so is NAL.

14. After-tax lease payment = 9,000(1 − .34) = $5,940
Depreciation tax shield = (24,000/3)(.34) = $2,720 per year
After-tax cost of capital = .1(1 − .34) = .066
After-tax salvage value = 2,000(1 − .34) = $1,320

Lessee's incremental cash flows from leasing instead of buying:

	Year 0	Year 1	Year 2	Year 3
AT lease payment		−5,940	−5,940	−5,940
Lost depr. tax shield		−2,720	−2,720	−2,720
Machine cost	24,000			
Lost AT salvage				−1,320
Total cash flow	24,000	−8,660	−8,660	−9,980

$$NAL = 24{,}000 - 8{,}660[1 - (1/1.066)^2/.066] - 9{,}980/(1.066)^3$$
$$NAL = \$16.6$$

Notice that the after-tax salvage value is a lost inflow, or a negative flow due to leasing. Still, leasing has a positive NAL. Also, the residual value is discounted at the after-tax cost of debt (this is common in practice). However, it's not really a debtlike cash flow, so a higher rate might be appropriate.

15. Loan Payment:
$24{,}000 = Pmt\{[1 - (1/1.1)^3]/.1\}$
Pmt = $9,650.76
After-tax payment = Payment − Interest tax shield =
Year 1: 9,650.76 − [24,000(.1)(.34)] = $8,834.76
Year 2: 9,650.76 − [16,749.24(.1)(.34)] = $9,081.29
Year 3: 9,650.76 − [8,773.40(.1)(.34)] = $9,352.46

Lessee's incremental cash flows from leasing instead of buying:

	Year 0	Year 1	Year 2	Year 3
AT lease pmt		−5,940	−5,940	−5,940
Lost depr. tax shield		−2,720	−2,720	−2,720
AT loan pmt		8,835	9,081	9,352
Total cash flow		175	421	692

$$NAL = 0 + 175/(1.066) + 421/(1.066)^2 + 692/(1.066)^3$$
$$NAL = \$1{,}106$$

The NAL is the same because the present value of the after-tax loan payments, discounted at the after-tax cost of capital, equals $24,000.

CHAPTER 24
RISK MANAGEMENT

1. Since the firm is selling futures, it wants to be able to deliver the lumber, therefore it is lier. The value of the firm moves with the price of lumber. By selling futures, the firm is re its exposure to a decline in lumber prices.

2. Buying call options gives the firm the right to purchase pork bellies, so it must be a us value of the firm moves in the opposite direction of pork belly prices.

3. If you had bought the December 1992 cocoa futures contract, you agreed to pay $1,076 p If the actual price at expiration turned out to be $1,000 per ton, you would lose $76 per to contract is for 10 tons, so you would lose a total of $760.

4. If you had bought the September 100 put options, you paid 2.70 cents per pound of cop the right to sell copper at $1.00 per pound. If the price at expiration was $0.80 per pour would have a gain of (1.00 – .80)(25,000) = $5,000 per contract. Your net gain would be – .027(25,000) = $4,325 per contract.

5. Forward contracts are usually designed by the parties involved for their specific needs a rarely sold in the secondary market. All gains and losses are realized at settlement time. F contracts are standardized, and each party realizes gains and losses on a daily basis marking-to-market). This process reduces default risk, and is probably the main reas organized trading of futures is much more common.

6. The firm could buy put options on bonds or buy call options on interest rates. Either strate reduce the firm's exposure to rising interest rates.

7. The firm should sell oil futures to reduce its exposure to declining oil prices. The fir probably not be able to achieve a completely flat risk profile, since it will be difficult to match the quantity of oil it will sell with the contracts. Second, the firm may not prod exact grade of oil specified in the futures contract.

8. The firm is directly exposed to natural gas price fluctations, since it is a user of gas. Th of the firm moves in the opposite direction of gas prices. The firm is indirectly expose price fluctuations. If oil becomes less expensive relative to gas, the competition will hav costs and be at an advantage in the market.

9. The utility can lock in a price of $20.29 per barrel with the November 1992 futures contrac contract is for 1,000 barrels, so the firm should buy 20 contracts. There is no initial cos strategy, but the firm may be exposed to costs over the life of the contract because of mark market.

10. Buying the call options would allow the firm to hedge against increases in cotton prices without being obligated to exercise the option if the price of cotton declines. However, buying options involves an initial cost, the premium for the option. The futures strategy would require no initial investment, but would lock the firm to one price for cotton.

11. The call options give the manager the right to purchase oil at $20 per barrel. The manager will exercise the calls if the price rises above $20. Selling the put options obligates the manager to buy oil at $20 per barrel. The owner of the puts will exercise when the price falls below $20. The payoffs are:

Oil price:	10	15	20	25	30
Call value:	0	0	0	5	10
Put value:	−10	− 5	0	0	0
Total value:	−10	− 5	0	5	10

The payoff profile is identical to that of a forward (futures) contract with a $20 strike price.

12. A put option on a bond gives the owner the right to sell the bond at the option's striking price. If interest rates increase, bond prices decrease. If the price falls enough, the put will be exercised. A call option on interest rates gives the owner the right to "cap" his or her interest rate and will also be exercised if rates increase. Both securities protect the owner from rising interest rates, so they are conceptually the same.

13. Transactions exposure is the short-term exposure due to uncertain prices in the future. Economic exposure is the long-term exposure due to changes in overall economic conditions. There are a variety of instruments available to hedge transaction exposure, but very few long-term hedging instruments. It is much more difficult to hedge against economic exposure, since fundamental changes in the business generally must be made to offset long-run changes in the economic environment.

14.
a. Buy futures or futures calls on oil and natural gas.
b. Buy futures or futures calls on sugar and cocoa.
c. Buy futures or futures calls on oil and gasoline.
d. Buy futures or futures calls on silver or other chemicals involved in manufacturing film.

If any of the firms have a large international exposure, they can buy forwards or futures calls on currencies and exchange rates.

15. The firm would sell the futures contract since it is a contract for 12.5 million yen. The exporter will be paid in yen and will need to convert the yen to dollars.

16. The firm will borrow at a fixed rate and then swap the fixed payments for floating rate payments. The swap dealer will make the fixed payments and will receive the floating rate payments from the firm.

17. A swap contract is an agreement to exchange assets at several intervals in the future. A forward is a contract to exchange assets at one time in the future. Therefore, the swap contract is essentially a series of forward contracts with differing maturities. The firm faces the risk that the dealer will not meet the cash flow obligations of the contract, say by not making timely payments. The dealer faces the same risk, but can hedge that risk more easily by entering an offsetting swap with another party.

18. The financial engineer can replicate the payoffs of owning a put option by selling a forward contract and buying a call. For example, suppose the forward contract has a settlement price of $100 and the exercise price of the call is also $100. The payoffs below show that the position is the same as owning a put with an exercise price of $100.

Price of coal:	90	95	100	105	110
Forward value:	10	5	0	−5	−10
Call value:	0	0	0	5	10
Total value:	10	5	0	0	0
Put value:	10	5	0	0	0

The payoffs for the combined position are exactly the same as those of owning a put. This means that, in general, the relationship between puts, calls, and forwards must be such that the cost of the two strategies will be the same, or an arbitrage opportunity (a "money machine") will exist. In general, given any two of these instruments, the third can synthesized.

PART III

SELECTED TRANSPARENCY MASTERS

Taxes (T2.4)

Key issues:

- What are corporate versus personal tax rates?
- Average versus marginal tax rates.

A. The brackets

Corporate rates		Personal rates	
$0 - 50	15%	$0 - 20.35	15%
50 - 75	25%	20.35 - 49.3	28%
75 - 100	34%	49.3+	31%
100 - 335	39%		
335+	____%		

B. Example: Corporate taxable income is $180,000:

Tax = .15($50) + .25($25) + .34($25) + .39($80) = $53.45

Average tax rate = $53.45/$180 = 29.6944%

Marginal tax rate = ? (39%)

C. Example: Corporate taxable income is $580,000:

Tax = .15($50) + .25($25) + .34($25) + .39($235) + .34($245)

= $197.2

Average tax rate = $197.2/$580 = 34%

Marginal tax rate = ? (34%)

Cash Flow Example (T2.6)

Balance Sheet

	Beg	End		Beg	End
Cash	$100	$150	A/P	$100	$150
A/R	200	250	N/P	200	200
Inv	300	300	C/L	300	350
C/A	$600	$700	LTD	$400	$420
NFA	400	500	C/S	50	60
			R/E	250	370
				$300	$430
Total	$1000	$1200	Total	$1000	$1200

Income Statement

Sales	$2000
Costs	1400
Depreciation	100
EBIT	500
Interest	100
Taxes	200
Net income	$200

Addition to R/E	$120
Dividends	80

Cash Flow Example (T2.6 concluded)

A. Cash flow from assets

1. Operating cash flow = EBIT + Dep - Taxes
   = \$500 + 100 - 200
   = \$400

2. Addition to NWC (NWC spending) = END NWC - BEG NWC
   = \$350 - \$300
   = \$50

3. Capital spending = END NFA + Dep - BEG NFA
   = \$500 + 100 - 400
   = \$200

4. Cash flow from assets = OCF - NWC sp. - Cap. sp.
   = \$400 - 50 - 200 = \$150

B. Cash flow to B/H and S/H

1. Cash flow to B/H = Int. paid - NET NEW DEBT
   = \$100 - \$20
   = \$80

2. Cash flow to S/H = Div. paid - NET NEW EQUIT
   = \$80 - \$10
   = \$70

Check: \$150 from assets = \$80 to B/H + \$70 to S/H ✓

The Du Pont Identity (T3.11)

1. Return on equity (ROE) can be decomposed as follows:

ROE = Net income/Total equity
= Net income/Total equity × Total assets/Total assets
= Net income/Total assets × Total assets/Total equity

= ROA × *Equity multiplier*

Check: 6.86% × 1.56 = 10.7% ✓

2. Return on assets (ROA) can be decomposed as follows:

ROA = Net income/Total assets × Sales/Sales
= Net income/Sales × Sales/Total assets

= Prof. Mar. × Tot. Asset T/O

Check: 17.8% × .385 = 6.86% ✓

3. Putting it all together gives the Du Pont identity:

ROE = ROA × Equity multiplier

= *Profit margin* × *Total asset turnover* × *Equity mult.*

Check: 17.8% × .385 × 1.56 = 10.7% ✓

4. Profitability (or the lack thereof!) thus has three parts:

- Operating efficiency
- Asset use efficiency
- Financial leverage

Example: A Simple Financial Planning Model (T4.3)

Recent Financial Statments

Income statement		Balance sheet			
Sales	$100	Assets	$50	Debt	$20
Costs	90			Equity	30
Net	$ 10	Total	$50	Total	$50

Assume that:

1. sales are projected to rise by 25%
2. the debt/equity ratio stays at 2/3
3. costs and assets grow at the same rate as sales

Pro Forma Financial Statements

Income statement		Balance sheet			
Sales	$125	Assets	$62.5	Debt	25
Costs	112.5			Equity	37.5
Net	$12.5	Total	$62.5	Total	$62.5

What's the plug? (the dividend)

Suppose that:

1. half of net income is paid out in dividends
2. new equity sales are not feasible.

Something will have to give; these assumptions are not consistent. In fact, given these assumptions, the maximum possible growth rate is 20%. Why? Stay tuned.

The Percentage of Sales Approach (T4.4)

Income Statement
(projected growth = 30%)

	Original	*Pro forma*	
Sales	$2000	$2600	(+30%)
Costs	1700	2210	(= 85% of sales)
Taxable	300	390	
Taxes (34%)	102	132.6	
Net income	198	257.4	
Dividends	66	85.8	(= 1/3 of net)
Retained	132	171.6	(= 2/3 of net)

Preliminary Balance Sheet

	Orig.	% of sales		Orig.	% of sales
Cash	$100	5%	A/P	$ 60	3%
A/R	120	6%	N/P	140	7%
Inv	140	7%	Total	200	10
Total	$360	18%	LTD	$200	n/a
NFA	640	32%	C/S	10	n/a
			R/E	590	n/a
				$600	n/a
Total	$1000	50%	Total	$1000	n/a

Note that the ratio of total assets to sales is $1000/$2000 = 0.50. This ratio is the cap. intensity *ratio*. It is the reciprocal of tot. asset t/o.

The Percentage of Sales Approach, Continued (T4.5)
Pro forma statements

	Proj.	(+/-)		Proj.	(+/-)
Cash	$130	$30	A/P	$78	$18
A/R	156	36	N/P	140	-
Inv	182	42	Total	$218	$18
Total	$468	$108	LTD	200	-
NFA	832	192	C/S	10	-
			R/E	761.6	171.6
				$771.6	$171.6
Total	$1300	$300	Total	$1189.6	$189.6

Financing needs are $300, but internally generated sources are only $189.60. The difference is *external financing needed*:

EFN = $300 - 189.60 = $110.40

One possible financing strategy:

1. Borrow short-term first
2. If needed, borrow long-term next
3. Sell equity as a last resort

Constraints:

1. Current ratio must not fall below 2.0.
2. Total debt ratio must not rise above 0.40.

The Percentage of Sales Approach, Continued (T4.6)
A financing plan

Determine maximum borrowings:

1. • $468/CL = 2.0 implies maximum CL = $234
   • Maximum short-term borrowing = $234 - $218 = $16

2. • .40 × $1300 = $520 = maximum debt
   • $520 - 234 = $286 = maximum long-term debt
   • Maximum long-term borrowing = $286 - 200 = $86

3. • Total new borrowings = $16 + 86 = $102
   • Shortage = $110.4 - 102 = $8.4

A possible plan:

New short-term debt	= $ 8.0
New long-term debt	= 43.0
New equity	= 59.4
	$110.4

Completed *Pro Forma* Balance Sheet

	Proj.	(+/-)		Proj.	(+/-)
Cash	$130	$ 30	A/P	$ 78	$ 18
A/R	156	36	N/P	148	8
Inv	182	42	Total	$226	$ 26
Total	$468	$108	LTD	243	43
NFA	832	192	C/S	69.4	59.4
			R/E	761.6	171.6
				$831	$231
Total	$1300	$300	Total	$1300	$300

The Percentage of Sales Approach, Concluded (T4.7)
An alternative scenario

So far, 100% capacity has been assumed. Suppose that, instead, current capacity use is 80%.

1. At 80% capacity:

   - \$2000 = .80 × full capacity sales
   - \$2000/.80 = \$2500 = full capacity sales

2. At full capacity, fixed assets to sales will be:

   - \$640/\$2500 = 25.60%

3. So, NFA will need to be just:

   - 25.60% × \$2600 = \$665.6, not \$832
   - \$832 - \$665.60 = \$166.4 *less* than originally projected

4. In this case, original EFN is substantially overstated:

   - New EFN = \$110.40 - \$166.40 = -\$56, a surplus

Moral of the story: Assumptions matter. Don't blindly apply approach.

Growth and External Financing Needed (T4.8)

Key issue:

- **What is the relationship between sales growth and financing needs?**

Recent Financial Statements

Income statement		Balance sheet			
Sales	$100	Assets	$50	Debt	$20
Costs	90			Equity	30
Net	$ 10	Total	$50	Total	$50

Assume that:

1. costs and assets grow at the same rate as sales
2. 60% of net income is paid out in dividends
3. no external financing is available (debt or equity)

Q. What is the *maximum* growth rate achievable?

A. The maximum growth rate is given by

$$\textit{Internal growth rate (IGR)} = \frac{ROA \times b}{1 - ROA \times b}$$

- ROA = $10/50 = 20%
- b = 1 - .60 = .40

- IGR = (20% × .40)/[1 - (20% × .40)]
  = .08/.92 = 8.7% (= 8.695656 . . . %)

Internal Growth Rate (T4.10)

Assume sales do grow at 8.7 percent:

Pro Forma **Financial Statements**

Income statement			Balance sheet			
Sales	$108.70	Assets	$54.35	Debt	$20.00
Costs	97.83			Equity	34.35
Net	$ 10.87	Total	$54.35	Total	$54.35
Dividends	$6.52				
Add to R/E	4.35				

Now assume:

1. no external *equity* financing is available
2. the current debt/equity ratio is optimal

Q. What is the *maximum* growth rate achievable now?

A. The maximum growth rate is given by

$$\textit{Sustainable growth rate (SGR)} = \frac{ROE \times b}{1 - ROE \times b}$$

- ROE = $10 / 30 = 1/3 (= 33.333 . . . %)
- b = $1 - .60 = .40

- SGR = (1/3 × .40)/[1 - (1/3 × .40)]
  = 15.385% (= 15.38462 . . . %)

Sustainable Growth Rate (T4.11)

Assume sales do grow at 15.385 percent:

Pro Forma Financial Statements

Income statement			Balance sheet			
Sales	$115.38	Assets	$57.69	Debt	$ 20
Costs	103.85			Equity	34.61
Net	$ 11.53	Total	$57.69	Total	$ 54.61
Dividends	$6.92			EFN	$ 3.08
Add to R/E	4.61				

If we borrow the $3.08, the debt/equity ratio will be:

$23.08 / 34.61 = 2/3

So, everything checks out.

Thus, sustainable growth depends on four factors:

1. ***profitability*** **(operating efficiency)**
2. ***asset management efficiency*** **(capital intensity)**
3. ***financial policy*** **(capital structure)**
4. dividend policy

Key result: Given fixed values for these 4 variables, the SGR is the <u>only</u> g.

Future Value for a Lump Sum (T5.2)

Notice that

1. \$110 = \$100 × (1 + .10)
2. \$121 = \$110 × (1 + .10) = \$100 × 1.1 × 1.1 = \$100 × 1.1^2
3. \$133.10 = \$121 × (1 + .10) = \$100 × 1.1 × 1.1 × 1.1
   = \$100 × 1.1^3

In general, the future value, FV_t, of \$1 invested today at r% for t periods is

$$FV_t = \$1 \times (1 + r)^t$$

The expression $(1 + r)^t$ is called the *future value factor.*

Q. Deposit \$5000 today in an account paying 12%. How much will you have in 6 years? How much is simple interest? How much is compound interest?

A. Multiply the \$5000 by the future value factor:

$\$5000 \times (1 + r)^t$ = \$5000 × 1.12^6
= \$5000 × 1.9738227
= \$9869.1135

At 12%, the simple interest is .12 × \$5000 = \$600 per year. After 6 years, this is 6 × \$600 = \$3600; the compound interest is thus \$4869.11 - \$3600 = \$1269.11

Present Value for a Lump Sum (T5.5)

Q. Suppose you need \$20,000 in three years to pay tuition at MU. If you can earn 8% on your money, how much do you need today?

A. Here we know the future value is \$20,000, the rate (8%), and the number of periods (3). What is the unknown present amount (called the *present value*)? From before:

$FV_t = (1 + r)^t$
\$20,000 = PV × 1.08³

Rearranging:

PV = \$20,000/(1.08)³
= \$15,876.65

In general, the present value, PV, of a \$1 to be received in t periods when the rate is r is

$$PV = \frac{\$1}{(1 + r)^t}$$

Basic Vocabulary:

1. The expression $1/(1 + r)^t$ is called the *present value factor* or, more often, discount factor
2. The r is usually called the discount rate
3. The approach is often called DCF valuation

The Basic Present Value Equation (T5.7)

Notice that FV_t = PV × $(1+r)^t$

Rearranging, we get that, in general, the relationship between present value, PV, future value, FV_t, the discount rate, r, and the length of time t is:

$$PV = \frac{FV_t}{(1 + r)^t}$$

This is the *basic present value equation.* It has four components, and, given any three, we can solve for the fourth.

Q. Deposit \$5000 today in an account paying r. If we will get \$10,000 in 10 years, what *rate of return* are we being offered?

A. The PV is \$5000. The FV is \$10,000. The time, t, is 10 years. From the basic PV equation:

$$PV = FV_t/(1 + r)^t$$
$$\$5000 = \$10{,}000/(1 + r)^{10}$$

Three ways to find r:

1. Hit relevant buttons on financial calculator.
2. Solve equation for r:

$$(1 + r)^{10} = 2$$
$$(1 + r) = 2^{1/10} = 1.0717735$$
$$r \approx 7.2\%.$$

3. Know the rule of 72.

An Example: A Penny Saved (T5.8)

Benjamin Franklin died on April 17, 1790. In his will, he gave 1,000 pounds sterling to Massachusetts and the city of Boston. He gave a like amount to Pennsylvania and the city of Philadelphia. The money was paid to Franklin when he held political office, but he believed that politicians should not be paid for their service (!).

Franklin originally specified that the money should be paid out 100 years after his death and used to train young people. Later, however, after some legal wrangling, it was agreed that the money would be paid out 200 years after Franklin's death in 1990. By that time, the Pennsylvania bequest had grown to about \$2 million; the Massachusetts bequest had grown to \$4.5 million. The money was used to fund the Franklin Institutes in Boston and Philadelphia.

Q. Assuming that 1,000 pounds sterling was equivalent to 1,000 dollars, what rate did the two states earn (the dollar didn't become the official U.S. currency until 1792)?

A. For Pennsylvania, the future value is \$ 2 M and the present value is \$1000. There are 200 years involved, so we need to solve for r in the following:

$$\$1000 = \$2M/(1 + r)^{200}$$

$$(1 + r)^{200} = 2000$$

Solving for r, the Pennsylvania money grew at about 3.87% per year. The Massachusetts money did better; check that the rate of return in this case was 4.3%. Small differences can add up!

The Basic Present Value Equation—Revisited (T5.9)

Q. Deposit $5000 today in an account paying 10%. If we will need $10,000, how long will we have to wait.?

A. The PV is $5000. The FV is $10,000. The rate is 10%. From the basic PV equation:

$$PV = FV_t / ((1 + r)^t$$

$$\$5000 = \$10,000/(1.10)^t$$

Three ways to find t:

1. Hit relevant buttons on financial calculator.

2. Solve equation for t:

   $(1.10)^t = 2$

   $\log(1.10)^t = \log(2)$

   $t = \log(2)/\log(1.10) \approx .693/.0953$

   $= 7.27$ years

3. Know the rule of 72.

Present Value for Annuities—A Short Cut (T5.12 continued)

Q. Suppose you need $20,000 each year for the next three years to pay tuition. Important: you need the first $20,000 in exactly one year. If you can earn 8% on your money, how much do you need today?

A. Here we know the periodic cash flows are $20,000 each. Using the most basic approach:

PV = $20,000/1.08 + $20,000/1.08² + $20,000/1.08³
= $18,518.52 + $17,146.78 + $15,876.65
= $51,541.94

Using the shortcut:

PV = $20,000 × {1 − 1/1.08³}/.08
= $20,000 × 2.577097
= $51,541.94

In the previous example, we had $1000 per year for 5 years at 6% per year.

PV = $1000 × {1 − 1/1.06⁵}/.06
= $1000 × {1 - .74726}/.06
= $1000 × 4.212362
= $4212.364

Suppose the cash flow was $1000 per year *forever.* This is called a *perpetuity* (or *consol*). In this case, the PV is easy to calculate:

PV = C/r = $1000/.06 = $16.666.66 . . .

Notice that, as with the basic PV equation, there are only four pieces here, PV, C, r, and t. Given any three, we can find the fourth.

Finding C:

Q. You want to buy a Mazda Miata to go cruising. It costs \$17,000. With a 10% down payment, the bank will loan you the rest at 12% per year (1% per month) for 60 months. What will your payment be?

A. You will borrow .90 × \$17,000 = \$15,300. This is the amount today, so it's the PV. The rate is 1%, and there are 60 periods:

$$\$15{,}300 = C \times \{1 - \frac{1}{1.01^{60}}\}/.01$$
$$= C \times \{1 - .55045\}/.01$$
$$= C \times 44.955$$

$$C = \$15{,}300/44.955$$
$$C = \$340.34$$

Q. Suppose you owe \$2000 on a VISA card, and the interest rate is 2% per month. If you make the minimum monthly payments of \$50, how long will it take you to pay it off?

A. A *long* time:

$$\$2000 = \$50 \times \{1 - \frac{1}{1.02^t})\}/.02$$
$$.80 = 1 - 1/1.02^t$$
$$1.02^t = 5.0$$
$$t = 81.27 \text{ } \textit{months}\text{, or about } 6.8 \text{ years}$$

Finding the Discount Rate (T5.12 concluded)

Q. Suppose you are offered an investment that will pay you \$8000 per year for the next 12 years for \$50,000. Is this a good deal?

A. Depends on the return:

\$ 50,000 = \$ 8,000 $\times$ {1 - 1/(1 + r)^{12})/r

Good news: can't be solved algebraically
Bad news: solve it with trial and error (or get a financial calculator)

Try r = 10%:

PV = \$8000 $\times$ {1 - 1/(1.10)^{12})/.10 = \$ 54,510 (nice guess)

Is 10% too high or too low?

Try r = 12%:

PV = \$8000 $\times$ {1 - 1/(1.12)^{12})/.12 = \$ 49,555 (a little high)

From here it's "plug and chug," check that 11.8% is close.

Future Value for Annuities—A Short Cut (T5.14)

Q. Suppose you deposit \$2,000 each year for the next three years into an account that pays 8%. How much will you have in three years? Important: you make the first deposit in exactly one year.

A. Here we know the periodic cash flows are \$2,000 each. Using the most basic approach:

$$\begin{aligned} FV &= \$2{,}000 \times 1.08^{2} + \$2{,}000 \times 1.08^{1} + \$2{,}000 \\ &= \$2332.80 + \$2{,}160 + \$2{,}000 \\ &= \$6{,}492.80 \end{aligned}$$

Using the shortcut:

$$\begin{aligned} FV &= \$2{,}000 \times (1.08^{3} - 1)/.08 \\ &= \$2{,}000 \times 3.2464 \\ &= \$6{,}492.80 \end{aligned}$$

In a previous example, we had \$2,000 per year for 5 years at 10% per year.

$$\begin{aligned} FV &= \$2000 \times (1.10^{5} - 1)/.10 \\ &= \$1000 \times (1.61051 - 1)/.10 \\ &= \$1000 \times 6.1051 \\ &= \$12{,}210.20 \end{aligned}$$

With annuity future values there are still only four pieces, FV, r, t, and C. Given any three of these you can find the fourth. The procedures are the same as those for annuity PV's.

What about perpetuity future values?

EARs and APRs (T5.15 continued)

If a rate is quoted at 16%, compounded semiannually, then the actual rate is 8% per six months. Is 8% per six months the same as 16% per year?

NO. If you invest \$1000 for one year at 16%, then you'll have \$1160 at the end of the year. If you invest at 8% per period for two periods, you'll have

$$\begin{aligned} FV &= \$1000 \times (1.08)^2 \\ &= \$1000 \times 1.1664 \\ &= \$1166.40, \end{aligned}$$

or \$6.40 more. Why? What rate per year is the same as 8% per six months?

The *Effective Annual Rate (EAR)* is 16.64%. The "16% compounded semiannually" is the quoted or stated rate, not the effective rate.

By law, in consumer lending, the rate that must be quoted on a loan agreement is equal to the rate per period multiplied by the number of periods. This rate is called the Annual Perc. Rate (APR).

A bank charges 1% per month on car loans. What is the APR? What is the EAR?

The APR is 1% × 12 = 12%. The EAR is:

EAR = 1.01^{12} - 1 = 1.126825 - 1 = 12.6825%

e APR is thus a quoted rate, not an effective rate!

In general, if we let q be the quoted rate and m be the number of periods, then the general relationship between the quoted rate and the effective rate is:

$$1 + EAR = \left(1 + \frac{q}{m}\right)^m$$

Q. If a VISA card quotes a rate of 18% APR, what is the EAR?

A. Assuming that the billing period is monthly (which it usually is), then the APR is the quoted rate, and the number of periods is 12. The EAR is thus

$$1 + EAR = (1 + .18/12)^{12}$$
$$= 1.015^{12}$$
$$= 1.1956$$
$$EAR = 19.56\ \%$$

Q. Suppose a bank wants to offer a savings account that has quarterly compounding and an EAR of 7%. What rate must it quote?

A. Here we have to find the unknown quoted rate:

$$1.07 = (1 + q/4)^4$$
$$1.07^{.25} = 1 + q/4$$
$$1.018245 = 1 + q/4$$
$$q = 6.8234\%$$

How to Lie, Cheat, and Steal with Interest Rates (T5.17)

RIPOV RETAILING
Going out for business sale!
note sleazy ad!
$1000 instant credit!
12% simple interest!
Three years to pay!
Low, low monthly payments!

Your payment is calculated as:

1. Borrow $1000 today at 12% per year for three years, you will owe $\$1000 \times 1.12^3 = \$1404.93$.

2. To make it easy on you, make 36 low, low payments of $1404.93/36 = $39.03.

3. Is this a 12% loan? HAH!

$$\$1{,}000 = \$39.03 \times (1 - 1/(1 + r)^{36})/r$$

$$r = 1.96\% \textit{ per month}$$

$$\text{APR} = 12 \times 1.96\% = 23.52\%$$
$$\text{EAR} = 1.0196^{12} - 1 = 26.23\% \text{ (!)}$$

A Mortgage Application (T5A.3)

You want to buy a house for \$140,000. The bank will loan you 80% of the purchase price. The mortgage terms are "30 years, monthly payments, 9% APR, 2 points, 10 year balloon."

Q. What will your payments be? What will the balloon payment be? What is the EAR on the mortgage?

A. You will borrow .80 × \$140,000 = \$112,000. The interest rate is 9%/12 = .75% per month. There are 360 payments, so your payment is

$$\$112{,}000 = C \times (1 - 1/1.0075^{360})/.0075$$
$$= C \times 124.2819$$
$$C = \$901.18 \text{ per month}$$

If you pay two "points," you will actually only get .98 × \$112,000 = \$109,760 The monthly interest rate is thus

$$\$109{,}760 = \$901.18 \times (1 - 1/(1 + r)^{360})/r$$

$$r = .769\,\%\text{ per month}$$

APR = 9.227
EAR = 9.628

After 10 years, you owe 240 payments of \$901.18 each. The balloon payment is the PV of these payments:

$$\text{Balloon} = \$901.18 \times (1 - 1/1.0075^{240})/.0075$$
$$= \$100{,}161.31$$

Bond Features (T6.2)

When a corporation (or government) wants to borrow money, it often sells a *bond*. An investor gives the corporation some money for the bond. The corporation promises to give the investor:

1. Regular *coupon* payments every period until the bond matures.

2. The *face value* of the bond when it matures.

If a bond has five years to maturity, an $80 annual coupon, and a $1000 face value, its cash flows would look like this:

Time	0	1	2	3	4	5
Coupons		$80	$80	$80	$80	$80
Face value						$1000
						$1080

How much is the bond worth? It depends on current interest rates. If the going rate on bonds like this one is 10%, then this bond is worth $924.18. Why? Stay tuned.

Bond Rates and Yields (T6.3)

Suppose a bond currently sells for \$932.90. It pays an annual coupon of \$70, and it matures in 10 years. It has a face value of \$1000. What are its coupon rate, current yield, and yield to maturity (YTM)?

1. **The *coupon rate* (or just "coupon") is the annual dollar coupon expressed as a percentage of the face value:**

   Coupon rate = \$70/\$1000 = 7%

2. **The *current yield* is the annual coupon divided by the price:**

   Current yield = \$70/932.90 = 7.5%

3. **The *yield to maturity* (or just "yield") is the rate that makes the price of the bond just equal to the present value of its future cash flows. It is the unknown r in:**

   $\$932.9 = \$70 \times (1 - 1/(1 + r)^{10})/r + \$1000/(1 + r)^{10}$

   The only way to find the yield is trial and error:

   a. Try 10%: $\$70 \times (1 - 1/(1.10)^{10})/.10 + \$1000/(1.10)^{10} = \$816$

   b. Try 9%: $\$70 \times (1 - 1/(1.09)^{10})/.09 + \$1000/(1.09)^{10} = \$872$

   c. Try 8%: $\$70 \times (1 - 1/(1.08)^{10})/.08 + \$1000/(1.08)^{10} = \$933$

   ($\therefore$) The yield to maturity is 8%

More on Dividend Growth (T6.15)

---

1. **Constant growth example:**

   Suppose a stock has just paid a $5 per share dividend. The dividend is projected to grow at 5% per year indefinitely. If the required return is 9%, then the price today is

   $P_0 = D_1/(r - g)$
   $= \$5 \times (\underline{1.05})/(\underline{.09} - \underline{.05})$
   $= \$5.25/.04$
   $= \$131.25$ per share

   What will the price be in a year? It will rise by 5%:

   $P_t = D_{t+1}/(r - g)$
   $P_1 = D_{\underline{2}}/(r - g) = (\$\underline{5.25} \times 1.05)/(.09 - .05) = \$137.8125$

2. **The required return:**

   Suppose a stock has just paid a $5 per share dividend. The dividend is projected to grow at 5% per year indefinitely. If the stock sells today for $65 5/8, what is the required return?

   $P_0 = D_1/(r - g)$
   $(r - g) = D_1/P_0$
   $r = D_1/P_0 + g$
   $= \$5.25/\$65.625 + .05$
   = dividend yield ($\underline{8\%}$) + capital gain yield ($\underline{5\%}$)
   = 13%

More on Dividend Growth (T6.15 concluded)

Suppose a stock has just paid a $5 per share dividend. The dividend is projected to grow at 10% for the next two years, the 8% for one year, and then 6% indefinitely. The required return is 12%. What is the stock value?

Time	Dividend	
0	$5.00	
1	$5.5	(10% growth)
2	$6.05	(10% growth)
3	$6.534	(8% growth)
4	$6.926	(6% growth)

At time 3, the value of the stock will be:

$P_3 = D_4/(r - g) = \$6.926/(.12 - .06) = \$115.434.$

The value today of the stock is thus:

$P_0 = D_1/(1 + r) + D_2/(1 + r)^2 + D_3/(1 + r)^3 + P_3/(1 + r)^3$

$= \$5.5/1.12 + \$6.05/1.12^2 + \$6.534/1.12^3 + \$115.434/1.12^3$

$= \$96.55$

Multiple Rate of Return (T7.9)

The cash flows are

Year	Cash flow
0	-$ 252
1	1431
2	-3035
3	2850
4	-1000

What's the IRR?

at 25.00%: NPV = $0

at 33.33%: NPV = $0

at 42.86%: NPV = $0

at 66.67%: NPV = $0

Two questions:

1. What's going on here?

2. How many IRRs can there be?

Capital Budgeting Case: *Pro Formas* (T8.3)

Background info:

1. Sales of 10,000 units/year @$5/unit. Life of 3 years.
2. Variable cost/unit is $3. Fixed costs are $5000/year.
3. Fixed assets are $21,000. Depreciation is $7000/year. No salvage value.
4. Net working capital is $10,000. Req. return is 20%.

Pro Forma Financial Statements

Projected Income Statements

Sales	$50,000
Var. costs	30,000
	$20,000
Fixed costs	5,000
Depreciation	7,000
"EBIT"	$8,000
Taxes (34%)	2,720
Net income	$5,280

Projected Balance Sheets

	0	1	2	3
NWC	$10,000	$10,000	$10,000	$10,000
NFA	21,000	14,000	7,000	0
Total	$31,000	$24,000	$17,000	$10,000

Capital Budgeting: The DCF Valuation (T8.4)

A. Project operating cash flows:

EBIT	$8,000
Depreciation	+7,000
Taxes	-2,720
OCF	$12,280

B. Project total cash flows:

	0	1	2	3
OCF		$12,280	$12,280	$12,280
NWC Sp.	-10,000			+10,000
Cap. Sp.	-21,000			
Total	-31,000	$12,280	$12,280	$22,280

C. Valuation:

NPV= -$31,000 + $12,280/1.20^1 + $12,280/1.20^2 + $22,280/1.20^3
= $655

IRR = 21%

PBP= 2.3 years

AAR= $5280/{(31,000 + 24,000 + 17,000 + 10,000)/4} = 25.76%

A Closer Look: NWC Spending (T8.5)

1. Fixed asset spending is zero.
2. Net working capital spending is $200:

	0	1	Change	S/U
A/R	$100	$200	+100	U
INV	100	150	+50	U
-A/P	100	50	-50	U
NWC	$100	$300		

(∴) NWC Spending = $200

3. Operating cash flow is $100:

Sales	$300
Costs	200
Depreciation	0
EBIT	$100
Tax	0
Net	$100

(∴) OCF = $100

(∴) Cash flow = OCF - NWC spending - FA spending
= –$100

What *really* happened?

Cash sales = $300 - 100 = $200 (collections)
Cash costs = $200 + 50 + 50 = $300 (disbursements)

Cash flow = $200 - 300 = –$100 (cash in – cash out)

MACRS Depreciation: An Example (T8.7)

A. The deductions on a $30,000, 5-year property:

Year	(%)	($)
1	20%	$6,000
2	32%	9,600
3	19.20%	5,760
4	11.52%	3,456
5	11.52%	3,456
6	5.76%	1,728
	100%	$30,000

B. Salvage values, book values, and taxes

Year	Book	Salvage	Tax	
0	$30,000			
1	24,000			
2	14,400	20,000	1904	(= 5600 × .34)
3	8,640			
4	5,184	2,000	-1083	(= -3184 × .34)
5	1,728			
6	0			

C. Land and real estate

D. Recapture versus capital gains

Sample Problems (T8.13)

Background:

1. NWC investment = $40; cost = $60; 3 year life
2. Sales = $100; costs = 50; straight line depreciation to $0
3. Salvage = $10; tax rate = 34%; Payback = ?

- The aftertax salvage is $10 - ($10 - 0) × .34 = $6.6
- OCF = (100 - 50 - 20) + 20 - (100 - 50 - 20) × .34 = $39.8

The cash flows are thus:

	0	1	2	3
OCF		$39.8	$39.8	$39.8
Add. NWC	-40			40
Cap. Sp.	-60			6.6
	-100	$39.8	$39.8	$86.4

NPV = $28.76 (@12%)

PBP = 2.24 years

Sample Problems (T8.13 concluded)

Background:

1. No NWC; cost = \$200,000; 3 year MACRS
2. Cost saving = \$70,000/year; 4 year life; salvage is \$50,000
3. Tax rate = 39%; r = 10%; find NPV

Depreciation:

Year	(%)	(\$)
1	33.33%	\$66,660
2	44.44%	88,880
3	14.82%	29,640
4	7.41%	14,820
	100%	\$200,000

The aftertax salvage is \$50,000 - (\$50,000 - 0) × .39 = \$30,500

The cash flows are thus:

	0	1	2	3	4
AT saving		\$42,700.0	\$42,700.0	\$42,700.0	\$42,700.0
Tax shield		25,997.4	34,663.2	11,559.6	5,779.8
"OCF"		\$68,697.4	\$77,363.2	\$54,259.6	\$48,479.8
Cap. Sp.	-200,000				30,500
	-200,000	\$68,697.4	\$77,363.2	\$54,259.6	\$78,978.8

NPV = \$21,099.02 (IRR = 14.77%)

Evaluating Cost Cutting Proposals (T8.15)

In thousands of dollars:

Cost = \$900
Depreciation = \$180
Life = 5 years
Salvage = \$330
Savings = \$500/year, pretax
Add. to NWC = –\$220 (note the minus sign)

1. *Aftertax* cost saving: \$500 × (1 – .34) = \$330 /year.

2. Depreciation *tax shield*: \$180 × .34 = \$61.2 /year.

3. *Aftertax* salvage value: \$330 - (\$330 - 0) × .34 = \$217.8

4. The cash flows are thus:

	0	1	2	3	4	5
AT saving		\$330.0	\$330.0	\$330.0	\$330.0	\$330.0
Tax shield		61.2	61.2	61.2	61.2	61.2
"OCF"		391.2	391.2	\$391.2	\$391.2	\$391.2
NWC Sp.	220					-220
Cap. Sp.	-900					217.8
	-680	\$391.2	\$391.2	\$391.2	\$391.2	389

The IRR is about 50%, so it looks good!

Setting the Bid Price (T8.16 continued)

ckground (in $000):

Bid calls for 20 units/year; 3 years
Costs are $25/unit hardware; $10 unit other; $35 total
Cap. spending of $250; depreciation = $250/5 = $50/year
Salvage in 3 years is half of cost, $125.
NWC investment of $60,000
r = 16%; tax rate = 39%

The aftertax salvage is $125 - ($125 - 100) × .39 = $115.25

cash flows are:

	0	1	2	3
CF		$OCF	$OCF	$OCF
dd. to NWC	-$60			60
ap. Sp.	-250			+115.25
	-$310	$OCF	$OCF	$OCF + 175.25

d OCF such that NPV is zero at 16%:

$+\$310{,}000 - 175{,}250/1.16^3 = OCF \times (1 - 1/1.16^3)/.16$

$\$197{,}724.74 = OCF \times 2.2459$

OCF = $ 88,038.5 /year

Setting the Bid Price (T8.16 continued)

If OCF is to be $88,038.50/year, what price do we have to bid?

OCF	= Net income + depreciation
$88,038.50	= Net income + $ 50,000
Net income	= 38,038.50

Sales	?
Costs	700,000.00
Depreciation	50,000.00
EBIT	$ 62,338
Tax	24,319.70
Net income	$38,038.50

Sales = $62,358.20 + 50,000 + 700,000 = $812,358.20/year

The bid price should be $812,358.20/ 20 = $40,618 /unit

The Unequal Lives Problem (T8.17 concluded)

This problem comes up when we have *both* of the following:

1. Mutually exclusive investments
2. The investment will be *repeated*--it's not a "one-shot" deal

	Jazz	Disco
Cost	= \$45	= \$65
Life	= 3 yrs.	= 5 years
Op. Cost	= \$5/yr.	= \$4/yr.
r	= 12%	

PV(costs) for Jazz: $\$45 + \$5 \times (1 - 1/1.12^3)/.12 = \$\underline{57.01}$

PV(costs) for Disco: $\$65 + \$4 \times (1 - 1/1.12^5)/.12 = \$\underline{79.42}$

For each investment, find the *equivalent annual cost (EAC)*; i.e., the cash amount paid every year that has the same PV.

EAC for Jazz: $\$\underline{57.01} = \text{EAC} \times (1 - 1/1.12^3)/.12$

EAC $= \$\underline{23.74}$

EAC for Disco: $\$79.42 = \text{EAC} \times (1 - 1/1.12^5)/.12$

EAC $= \$\underline{22.03}$ ✓

More on Break-Even Analysis (T9.10)

Background:

1. Price = $ 5/unit; variable costs = $3/unit.
2. Fixed costs are $10,000/year
3. Initial cost is $20,000; life is 5 years; .depreciation is $4,000/year, no salvage.
4. Ignore taxes; r = 20%

In general, if taxes are ignored:

Q = (Fixed costs + OCF) / (Price - variable cost)

A. Accounting break-even

= (Fixed costs + depreciation)/(Price - variable cost)
= ($10,000 + $4,000)/($5 - $3) = 7000 units

IRR = 0; NPV < 0 (= -$8,038)

B. Cash break-even

Q = (Fixed costs + $0)/(Price - variable cost)
= $10,000/($5 - $3) = 5,000 units

IRR = -100%; NPV = -20,000

B. Financial break-even

Q = (Fixed costs + $6,688)/(Price - variable cost)
= $16,688/($5 - $3) = 8,344 units

IRR = 20%; NPV = $0

Inflation and Returns (T10.2)

Key issues:

- What is the difference between a real and a nominal return?
- How can we convert from one to the other?

Background:

We have $1000, and Diet Coke costs $2.00/six pack. We can buy 500 six packs. Suppose the rate of inflation is 5%, so that the price rises to $2.10 in one year. We invest the $1000, and it grows to $1100 in one year. What's our return in dollars? In six packs?

A. *Dollars*. Our return is

($1100 - $1000)/$1000 = $100/$1000 = 10%.

(∴) The percentage increase in the amount of green stuff is 10%; our return is 10%.

B. *Six packs*. We can buy $1100/$2.10 = 523.81 six packs, so our return is

(523.81 - 500)/500 = 23.81/500 = 4.76%

(∴) The percentage increase in the amount of brown stuff is 4.76%; our return is 4.76%.

Average Returns and Volatility (T10.11)

Key issues:

- How are average returns measured?
- How is volatility measured?

Average returns:

Your portfolio has had returns of 10%, –7%, 28%, and -11% over the last four years.

Your *average annual return* is simply:

[.10 + (-.07) + .28 + (-.11)]/4 = 5 % per year

Return volatility:

The usual measure of volatility is the *standard deviation*, which is the square root of the variance:

Year	Actual return	Average return	Return deviation	Squared deviation
1	.10	.05	.05	.0025
2	-.07	.05	-.12	.0144
3	.28	.05	.23	.0529
4	-.11	.05	-.16	.0256
Total	.20		.00	.0954

The variance, σ^2 or Var(R) = .0954/(3) = .0318

The standard deviation, σ or SD(R) = $\sqrt{.0318}$ = .1783 or 17.83%

Using Capital Market History (T10.14)

Key issues:

- What is a risk premium?
- What is the reward for bearing risk?

Risk premiums:

The risk premium is the difference between a risky investment's return and a riskless return:

Investment	Average return	Standard deviation	Risk premium
Common stocks	12.1%	20.8%	8.4 %
Small stocks	17.1%	35.4%	13.4%
Long-term T-bonds	4.9%	8.5%	1.2%
Short-term T-bills	3.7%	3.4%	0.0%

Using market history:

- Suppose the current T-bill rate is 5%. An investment has "average" risk relative to a typical share of stock. It offers a 10% return. Is this a good investment?

- Suppose an investment is similar to buying small company equities. If the T-bill rate is 5%, what return would you demand?

The Capital Asset Pricing Model (T11.16)

Key issues:

- What is the CAPM?
- What are the components of an expected return?

The market as a whole has a beta of 1. It plots on the SML, so:

$$E(R_M) - R_f = \frac{E(R_i) - R_f}{\beta_i}$$

Rearranging, the Capital Asset Pricing Model is

$$E(R_i) = R_f + [E(R_M) - R_f] \times \beta_i$$

The expected return on a risky asset thus depends on:

1. *Pure time value of money.*

2. *Reward for bearing systematic risk*

3. *Amount of systematic risk*

Example: The historic risk premium has been about 8.5%. The risk-free rate is currently about 5%. GTE has a beta of about .85. What return should you expect from GTE?

$E(R_{GTE})$ = 5% + 8.5 × .85
= 12.225%

Common Stock (T12.6)

Common stock and other shareholders' equity	
Common stock, \$1 par value, authorized 100,000,000 shares in 1990; issued 54,234,665	\$ 54,235
Capital in excess of par value	88,554
Retained earnings	973,493
	\$1,116,282
Less 2,559,333 shares of treasury stock	31,224
	\$1,085,058

- Par vs. nonpar
- Authorized vs. issued
- Capital surplus
- Retained earnings

Shareholder Rights

- Corporate democracy: cumulative vs. straight voting

  Example: There are a total of 1000 shares, and 3 directors are up. How many shares do you need to win a seat with straight voting? Cumulative voting?

- Proxy voting and proxy fights
- Dividends
- Classes of stock

Effect of a Stock Sale (T12.7)

Before:

Common stock and other shareholders' equity	
Common stock, $1 par value	$10,000
Capital surplus	90,000
Retained earnings	800,000
Total	$900,000

After: sell 100 share at $40 per share:

Common stock and other shareholders' equity	
Common stock, $1 par value	$10,100
Capital surplus	93,900
Retained earnings	800,000
Total	$904,000

Rights Offerings: Basics (T13.12)

Key issues:

- How does a rights offering work?
- What is the value of a right?

Mechanics of a rights offering:

1. Early steps same as cash offer (SEC approval, etc.)
2. You are notified that you can buy 1 new share at a special "subscription" price for every N that you currently own (or: you have 1 right for every share you own, and it takes N rights to buy 1 new share--same thing).
3. You can (1) buy the stock, (2) sell your rights, or (3) do nothing.

Subscription price and the number of rights:

Suppose a firm with 200,000 shares out wants to raise $1 million. Current price is $40 per share. The subscription price, the number of new shares that have to be sold and the number of rights needed to buy 1 share are related like this:

Subscription price	Number of new shares	Number of rights to buy 1 share
$25	40,000	5
$20	50,000	4
$10	100,000	2
$5	200,000	1

Rights Offerings: Value of a Right (T13.13)

Effect on share price (subscription price = $20):

1. Firm sets "holder of record" day. Beginning 4 days before, the stock sells "ex rights." Before that it sells "rights-on, cum rights, or with rights" at $40.

2. After rights offering, 250 K shares are out. Total value is old $8 million plus new $1 million = $9 million.

3. New ex rights stock price is $9 million/250,000 =$36

Value of a right:

The stock sells for $40 "rights-on," vs. $36 "ex rights," so the value of right is $4. Consider acquiring 5 shares:

1. Buy 4 shares "with rights" at $40. Exercise your rights and buy new share at $20. Total for 5 shares is $180 or $36 /share.

2. Buy 4 × 5 = 20 rights for $80 and buy 5 shares @$20. Total cost of 5 shares is $180 or $36/share.

3. Buy 5 @ $36, total cost is $180.

Dividend Growth Approach (T14.3)

Implementing the approach

1. Need the current price and annual dividend from financial press (Ch. 6). Suppose these are \$50 and \$5 respectively.

2. Need an estimate of the *future* growth rate in dividends:

   a. Analyst forecasts
   b. Historical
   c. Other

3. Suppose g is estimated at 9%, then, using the approach,

$R_E = D_1 / P_0 + g$

$= \$5 \times (\underline{1.09})/\$50 + .09$

$= \underline{19.90}\ \%$

Advantages of the approach

1. Easy to do/widely recognized

Disadvantages

1. Only strictly applicable to steady dividend payers.

2. Sensitive to *g* estimates

3. No direct adjustment for risk

SML Approach (T14.5)

Implementing the approach

1. Need the risk-free rate from financial press--usually the Treasury bill rate, say 6%.

2. Need *estimates* of market risk premium and security beta.

   a. Risk premium historical--8.5% (Ch. 10)
   b. Beta--historical
      (1) Investment services
      (2) Estimate from historical data

3. Suppose the beta is 1.40, then, using the approach:

$$R_E = R_f + \beta_E \times (R_M - R_f)$$

$$= 0.06 + 1.40 \times .085$$

$$= 17.9\%$$

Advantages of the approach

1. Widely applicable

2. Explicit risk adjustment

Disadvantages

1. Need estimates of β_E and market risk premium.

Costs of Debt and Preferred (T14.6)

Cost of debt

1. Cost of debt, R_D, is the interest rate on new borrowing.

2. Cost of debt is *observable*:

   a. Yield on currently outstanding debt.
   b. Yields on newly-issued similarly-rated bonds.

3. Historic debt cost is irrelevant.

   Example: We sold a 20-year, 12% bond 10 years ago at par. It is currently priced at 86. What is our cost of debt?

   The *yield to maturity* (Ch. 6) is 14.8 %, so this is what we use as the cost of debt, not 12%.

Cost of preferred

1. Preferred stock is a perpetuity, so the cost is

   $R_P = D/P_0$

2. Notice that cost is simply the dividend yield.

   Example: We sold an $8 preferred issue 10 years ago. It sells for $120/share today.

   The dividend yield *today* is $ 8 /$ 120 = 6.67%, so this what we use as the cost of preferred.

The Weighted Average Cost of Capital (T14.7)

Capital structure weights

1. Let: E = the *market* value of the equity.
   D = the *market* value of the debt.

   Then: V = E + D
   1 = E/V + D/V = 100%

2. Thus, the firm's capital structure weights are E/V and D/V.

3. The *unadjusted weighted average cost of capital* is then

   $$\text{WACC (unadjusted)} = (E/V) \times R_E + (D/V) \times R_D,$$

   a simple weighted average of the equity and debt costs.

The weighted average cost of capital (adjusted)

1. Interest payments on debt are tax-deductible, so the *aftertax* cost of debt is the pretax cost multiplied by (1 - corporate tax rate).

   Aftertax cost of debt = $R_D \times$ (1 − T_c)

2. The weighted average cost of capital that we actually use is thus

   $$\text{WACC} = (E/V) \times R_E + (D/V) \times R_D \times (1 - T_C)$$

Breakeven EBIT: A Quick Note (T15.4)

Ignoring taxes:

A. With no debt:

$$EPS = EBIT/500{,}000$$

B. With \$2,500,000 in debt at 10%:

$$EPS = (EBIT - \$\underline{250{,}000})/250{,}000$$

C. These are equal when:

$$EPS_{BE} = EBIT_{BE}/\underline{500{,}000} = (EBIT_{BE} - \$250{,}000)/250{,}000$$

D. With a little algebra:

$$EBIT_{BE} = \$500{,}000$$

So $EPS_{BE} = \$\underline{\ 1\ }$/share

The interest tax shield and firm value

For simplicity: (1) perpetual cash flows
(2) no depreciation
(3) no fixed asset or NWC spending

A firm is consider going from zero debt to $400 at 10%:

	Firm U (unleveraged)	Firm L (leveraged)
EBIT	$200	$200
Interest	0	$40
Tax (40%)	$80	$64
Net income	$120	$96
Cash flow from assets	$120	$ 136

- Tax saving = $16 = .40 × $40 = $T_C \times R_D \times D$

MM Proposition I (with taxes)

- PV(tax saving) = $16/ .10 = $ 160
  $= (T_C \times R_D \times D)/R_D = T_C \times D$

$$V_L = V_U + T_C \times D$$

Debt, Taxes, and the WACC (T15.11)

Taxes and firm value: an example

- EBIT = \$100
- T_C = 30%
- R_U = 12.5%

Q. Suppose debt goes from \$0 to \$100 at 10%, what happens to equity value, E?

V_U = \$100 × (1 − .30)/.125 = \$560

V_L = \$560 + .30 × \$ 100 = \$590, so E = \$ 490 .

WACC and the cost of equity (MM Proposition II with taxes)

With taxes:

$$R_E = R_U + (R_U - R_D) \times (D/E) \times (1 - T_C)$$

R_E = .125 + (.125 - .10) × (100 / 490) × (1 - .30)

= 12.86%

WACC = (490 / 590) × .1286 + (100/590) × .10 × (1 - .30)

= 11.86%

(∴) The WACC decreases as more debt financing is used. Optimal capital structure is all debt!

Accounting Treatment of Splits and Stock Dividends (T16.2 concluded)

A. Before:

Common ($1 par; 1 milion shares)	$1M
Add. paid in capital	9M
Retained earnings	100M
Total equity	$110M
Market price per share	$50

B. "Small" stock dividend (10%)

- 100,000 new shares at $50 each = $5M, so

Common ($1 par; 1.1 milion shares)	$1.1M
Add. paid in capital	13.9M
Retained earnings	95M
Total equity	$110M
Market price per share	$50

C. A 4-for-1 stock split

D. A "large" stock dividend (300%)

Does Dividend Policy Matter? (T16.4)

idend policy versus cash dividends

illustration of dividend irrelevance

Original dividends

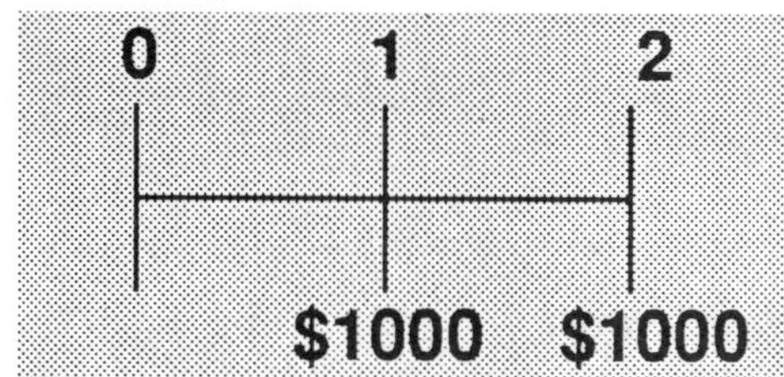

$_E$ = 20%: P_0 (total) = \$1000/1.2 + \$1000/1.2^2 = \$1527.78

New dividend plan

0	1	2
	\$1000	\$1000
	+200	-240
	\$1200	\$760

P_0 (total) = \$1200/1.2 + \$760/1.2^2 = \$1527.78

An illustration of "homemade" dividends

- Original dividends if you own 10% of the stock

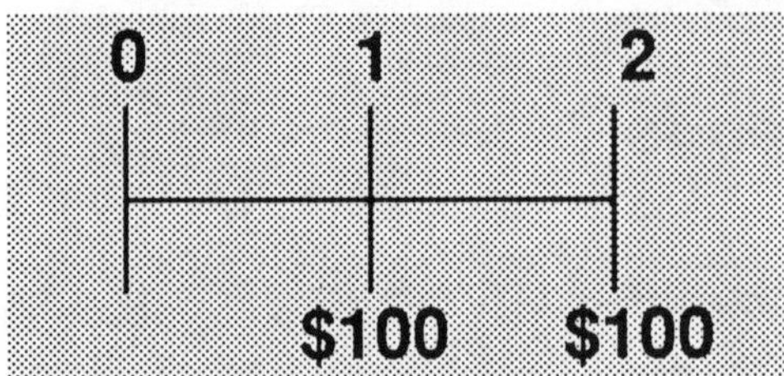

- Dividends under new plan

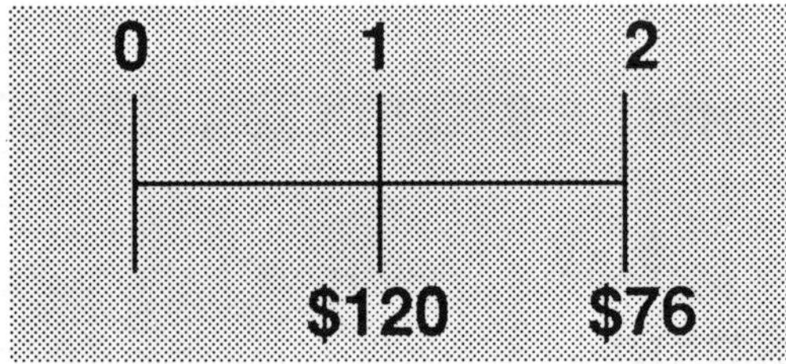

- Undo the new plan

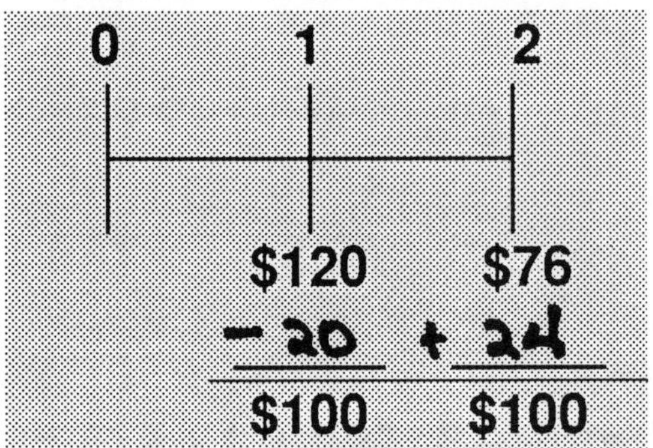

- ADRs (DRIPs)

Establishing a Dividend Policy (T16.7)

A residual policy

- Net income (projected) = \$200M
- D/E (target) = 2/3 (E/V = 60 %; D/V = 40 %)
- Capital budget (planned) = \$260
- Maximum capital spending with no outside equity:

  $.60 \times X = \$200M \Rightarrow X = \$333\ 1/3\ M$

- (∴) A dividend will be paid
- New equity needed = .60 × \$260 = \$156 M
  New debt needed = .40 × \$260 = \$104 M
- Dividend = \$200 M - \$156 = \$ 44 M

Dividend stability

- Constant payout
- Constant dividend

Return, Risk, and Equilibrium (T11.15)

Key issues:

- What is the relationship between risk and return?
- What does security market equilibrium look like?

The fundamental conclusion is that the ratio of risk premium to beta is the same for every asset. In other words, the reward-to-risk ratio is *constant* and equal to

$$\textit{Reward/risk ratio} = \frac{E(R_i) - R_f}{\beta_i}$$

Example:

Asset A has an expected return of 12% and a beta of 1.40. Asset B has an expected return of 8% and a beta of 0.80. Are these assets valued correctly relative to each other if the risk-free rate is 5%?

a. For A, (.12 - .05)/1.40 = .05

b. For B, (.08 - .05)/0.80 = .0375

What would the risk-free rate have to be for these assets to be correctly valued?

$(.12 - R_f)/1.40 = (.08 - R_f)/0.80$

R_f = 2 2/3 %